GRANBURY'S
TEXAS BRIGADE

CONFLICTING WORLDS
New Dimensions of the American Civil War

T. Michael Parrish, Series Editor

GRANBURY'S
TEXAS BRIGADE

DIEHARD WESTERN CONFEDERATES

JOHN R. LUNDBERG

LOUISIANA STATE UNIVERSITY PRESS ✦ BATON ROUGE

Published with the assistance of the V. Ray Cardozier Fund

Published by Louisiana State University Press
Copyright © 2012 by Louisiana State University Press
All rights reserved
Manufactured in the United States of America
First printing

Designer: Barbara Neely Bourgoyne
Typefaces: Chaparral Pro and Belizio
Printer: McNaughton & Gunn, Inc.
Binder: Acme Bookbinding, Inc.

Library of Congress Cataloging-in-Publication Data

Lundberg, John R.
  Granbury's Texas Brigade : diehard western confederates / John R. Lundberg.
      p. cm. — (Conflicting worlds : new dimensions of the American Civil War)
  Includes bibliographical references and index.
  ISBN 978-0-8071-4347-6 (cloth : alk. paper) — ISBN 978-0-8071-4348-3 (pdf) — ISBN 978-0-
8071-4349-0 (epub) — ISBN 978-0-8071-4350-6 (mobi)
  1. Confederate States of America. Army. Granbury's Texas Brigade. 2. Texas—History—
Civil War, 1861–1865—Regimental histories. 3. United States—History—Civil War, 1861–
1865—Regimental histories. 4. United States—History—Civil War, 1861–1865—Campaigns.
5. Granbury, Hiram Bronson, 1831–1864. I. Title.
  E580.5.G73L86 2012
  973.7'464—dc23
                                                                            2011034846

For my parents, Hank and Cindy Lundberg, and my wife, Jessica,

without whom none of this would have been possible

CONTENTS

Photographs follow page 138.

MAPS

ACKNOWLEDGMENTS

It would have been impossible to complete an endeavor of this magnitude without a great deal of support. When I first began working on this project eight years ago, I was a young historian who thought I knew much more than I actually did. I owe a great debt of gratitude to my mentor, Steven Woodworth of Texas Christian University, for his guidance about studying, writing, and publishing Civil War history and for his ability to gently knock me down a peg or two when my ego started to get in the way. Steve has been with me from the conception of this project to its completion. I also wish to acknowledge other historians in the field who helped me conceive this book. To Gregg Cantrell, Mark Gilderhus, and Richard Lowe, I truly owe a debt I cannot repay. Many thanks to Charles Grear of Prairie View A&M University, who not only agreed to make the maps for this book, but has always been a good friend and has given me valuable feedback on this project. I also want to thank Danny Sessums of the Museum of Southern History in Houston, who generously made available his research on Granbury's Brigade and encouraged me in publishing this work.

In addition, I am grateful to the staffs of various libraries and archives who are unfortunately too numerous to name here. In particular, Donaly Brice at the Texas State Archives and Library Commission and Peggy Fox of the Harold B. Simpson Confederate Research Center stand out as individuals who offered extensive help and support. I also want to thank George

Forgie of the University of Texas at Austin, who taught me how to become a historian, and Norman Brown, also of the University of Texas, who befriended me and always had useful advice for me.

I would also like to express my gratitude to T. Michael Parrish, of Baylor University, who showed interest in this work before it was finished and helped me greatly in preparing the final manuscript, and Rand Dotson of LSU Press, who has proved immensely helpful in the publishing process. Without them this book would never have come to fruition.

Finally, I would like to thank my parents, Hank and Cindy Lundberg, who always believed in me and provided the love and support necessary to become the person I am, and my wife, Jessica, who had to live with me while I conceived, researched, and wrote this work. Without her love and understanding, I never would have finished what I started.

GRANBURY'S
TEXAS BRIGADE

INTRODUCTION

Granbury's Texas Brigade contributed immeasurably to the Confederate war effort in the West. Although the brigade suffered high rates of desertion, the men who remained became the diehard Confederates of the West. The question that has divided Civil War historians since the end of the war is why. Why did Confederate soldiers stay with the cause as long as they did, and why in particular did Confederate soldiers in the western theater, deprived of battlefield victories and effective army leadership, fight for so long? Another important question is, What role did the common Confederate soldiers play in the larger Confederate war effort? A study of Granbury's Texas Brigade, as perhaps the premier brigade in the premier division in the Confederate Army of Tennessee, can provide some answers to these questions.

The role the common soldiers played in the Confederate war effort has been analyzed by various historians, especially since the 1980s. There are two distinct schools of thought. Some historians have contended that a lack of Confederate nationalism and devotion to the cause among the South's soldiers doomed the Confederacy from the outset. Most notable among the studies arguing this point of view is *Why the South Lost the Civil War*, by Richard E. Beringer, Herman Hattaway, Archer Jones, and William Still. These authors maintain that class divisions, the idea of a "rich man's war and a poor man's fight," spiritual doubts about God being on their side, political dissent, and guilt over slavery doomed the efforts of the common Confederate soldiers, who deserted in increasing numbers toward the end of the war. Another work in this school of thought is Mark A. Weitz's *More Damning Than Slaughter: Desertion in the Confederate Army*. Weitz argues that Confederate soldiers deserted in large numbers throughout the war, dooming the Confederacy and causing more harm than battlefield slaughter. Other authors, such as David Williams in his *Rich Man's War: Class, Caste, and Confederate Defeat in the Lower Chattahoochee Valley*, maintain that class conflict helped cause the failure of the Confederate war effort.[1]

Despite these studies, the more convincing school of thought is that common soldiers in the Confederate ranks upheld the Confederacy much longer than it otherwise would have lasted. The most prominent in these arguments is Gary Gallagher's *The Confederate War*. In this work, Gallagher maintains that Robert E. Lee and his Army of Northern Virginia achieved battlefield victories early and often enough to encourage a vibrant Confederate nationalism among soldiers in the field and civilians on the home front until nearly the end of the war. Ancillary to these claims, Gallagher argues that historians should focus on Confederates' determination to wage bloody war for four long years in the face of overwhelming odds. Another study that bolsters Gallagher's argument is Jason Phillips's *Diehard Rebels: The Confederate Culture of Invincibility*, in which Phillips argues that Confederates maintained their devotion to the cause even long after the Civil War had ended. Steven E. Woodworth, in his work *While God Is Marching On: The Religious World of Civil War Soldiers*, demonstrates that without a doubt Confederates believed God remained on their side because of the institutionalization of the idea of slavery as a positive good into Southern churches and religious life. James McPherson, in his *For Cause and Comrades* and *What They Fought For*, also maintains that Confederates believed strongly in their cause and fought not only for slavery, but also for their homes and the Southern way of life, which centered on slavery.[2]

A study of Granbury's Texas Brigade strongly supports the argument of Gallagher and others that Confederate soldiers extended the life of the Confederate cause much longer than it would have otherwise lasted. Although desertion became endemic in many of the dismounted cavalry regiments of Granbury's Brigade, desertion is not an absolute concept. Contrary to the claims of Weitz and others, desertion did not indicate a lack of nationalism; rather, it often indicated a desire to fight for the Confederacy closer to home. Most of the "deserters" from the regiments of Granbury's Texas Brigade rejoined other home guard units in Texas, and many of the survivors from Arkansas Post even formed their own regiment, the 17th Texas Dismounted (Consolidated) Cavalry. This regiment fought and suffered heavy casualties at the battles of Mansfield and Pleasant Hill in 1864. Paradoxically, desertion helped shape the history of Granbury's Brigade. Desertion served to winnow the ranks, especially of the dismounted cavalry regiments, and left a hard core of devoted men who were willing to fight east of the Mississippi. These men formed the backbone of what became Granbury's Brigade.

Previous histories of Granbury's Brigade have lacked such historical context. Three previous studies of the brigade have appeared. The first is the journal and diary of Captain Samuel T. Foster, edited by Norman Brown and published by the University of Texas Press in 1980. Although not a history of the brigade per se, Brown's footnotes are substantial enough to be considered a rough history of the unit, especially the 24th Texas Dismounted Cavalry, of which Foster was a member. Because of the inherent gaps in any unit history centered on one primary source, Brown's account leaves much to be desired as a full history of Granbury's Brigade. The second work is an actual history of the brigade, titled *This Band of Heroes: Granbury's Texas Brigade, C.S.A.*, by James McCaffrey, which appeared through Texas A&M Press in 1984. Covering the entire history of the brigade in 130 pages, McCaffrey's work is really a sketch, or outline, of the brigade's history. It lacks an overarching thesis, socioeconomic context, and a bottom-up approach to Granbury's men, but it does have an extensive bibliography. The third history of Granbury's Brigade is the doctoral dissertation of Danny Sessums, titled "A Force to Be Reckoned With: Granbury's Texas Brigade, C.S.A." Sessums's work contains some valuable information but lacks organization and clarity. Clearly a new, detailed, concise, relevant history of this important fighting unit is needed.[3]

Granbury's Texas Brigade served as the shock troops, the diehard Confederates of the Confederate Army of Tennessee, for roughly a year, from its formation in November 1863 to November 1864, but the story of how these regiments developed from 1861 to 1863 is just as important to understanding the unit. Because Granbury's Texas Brigade as a unit did not coalesce in its final form until after the Battle of Chickamauga in late 1863, much of the history of these men centers on the history of the individual regiments that later comprised the brigade, and so it is necessary to spend the first part of this study discussing these histories.

Cavalry units converted into infantry, or "dismounted cavalry regiments," comprised about half of the brigade. In addition, the brigade contained three infantry regiments, making a total of eight original regiments consolidated into five: the 6th & 15th Texas (infantry and dismounted cavalry), the 7th Texas (infantry), the 10th Texas (infantry), the 17th & 18th Texas (dismounted cavalry), and the 24th & 25th Texas (dismounted cavalry).

The demographics of Granbury's Texas Brigade point toward an important trend when determining which soldiers would stay with their regiments and which would desert to fight closer to home. The fact that the men of the dismounted cavalry regiments averaged six years older than the average Civil War soldier and hence tended to be married with children and property led to high desertion rates after the dismounting of their regiments in 1862 and the subsequent surrender at Arkansas Post in January 1863. In fact, in several of these dismounted cavalry regiments 60 percent of the men deserted at some point during the war.

The three infantry regiments that later became part of Granbury's Brigade had much lower desertion rates and tended to be younger than their counterparts in the dismounted cavalry regiments. Nevertheless, their time in prison winnowed the ranks just as effectively as desertion because many took the oath of allegiance to the United States and many more perished in Camps Butler, Douglas, and Chase. The men remaining from these experiences of desertion and prison became the diehard Confederates of the Army of Tennessee. The time in prison also gave all the Texans something in common—a bitter anger born of suffering that made them fight harder to prove their mettle.

The history of the brigade can be broken down into four distinct phases. Phase one began in 1861 with the formation of the various regiments and ended with the capture of the 7th Texas at Fort Donelson and of the other regiments at Arkansas Post. The experiences in this first phase served to shrink the ranks of the brigade into the hard core of veterans that later emerged as Granbury's Brigade. The second phase extended from the bloodletting of the 7th Texas at the Battle of Raymond, Mississippi, on May 12, 1863, to the intense combat all the regiments experienced at Chickamauga in September of that year. The third phase in the history of the brigade began during the siege of Chattanooga, when the Confederate high command united the 7th Texas with the other regiments into a single brigade under Brigadier General James Smith. In their first true engagement as a brigade, at Tunnel Hill on November 25, what became Granbury's Brigade hit its stride as Smith went down wounded and Granbury took command of the brigade for the first time. In the aftermath of this battle Patrick Cleburne first referred to the Texans as a "band of heroes." All through the Atlanta campaign Granbury's men made a name for themselves—at Pickett's Mill, Bald Hill, the Battle of Atlanta, and Jonesboro—as one of the finest combat units in the army. Finally, at Franklin on November 30, 1864, the brigade reached its zenith, suffering 60 percent casualties as well as the deaths of Cleburne and Granbury. After Franklin, the fourth and final phase of the history of the brigade began as the unit rapidly declined due to a lack of leadership and greatly reduced numbers. They fought only one major battle after Franklin—at Nashville—but their behavior in the last days of the war clearly shows the decline of the effectiveness of the brigade. This last phase ended in the surrender of the Army of Tennessee at Greensboro, North Carolina, on April 28, 1865.

Although the esprit and nationalism of soldiers in Robert E. Lee's Army of Northern Virginia have been extensively documented and explained in works such as J. Tracy Power's *Lee's Miserables* and Gary Gallagher's *The Confederate War,* the motivation of Confederate soldiers who fought in the western theater is harder to understand and fewer historians have documented and explained it. Perhaps the best book on this subject is Larry Daniels's *Soldiering in the Army of Tennessee.* Daniels argues that the history of the Army of Tennessee can only be understood from the ground up, from the perspective of the common soldiers, because a study of the army from the top down only leaves the reader wondering how it stayed together and remained an effective fighting force as long as it did. The soldiers had very few battlefield victories to sustain them, and incompetence, at best, prevailed in the higher echelons of the army. Although Richard McMurry in his work *Two Great Rebel Armies* points toward the distinctiveness that characterized the Army of Tennessee, Daniels explores the army in detail through the use of thousands of letters and diaries from the Confederates in the ranks. Daniels argues that morale and esprit developed from the ground up, rather than from the top down as in Lee's army. Although the men in the ranks did not enjoy battlefield victories from the perspective of historians, from their localized perspective they frequently won victories, and these boosted their morale. Furthermore, they enjoyed stellar leadership at the regimental, brigade, and division levels that helped offset the lack of leadership at the corps and army levels. The men of the Army of Tennessee did not fight for Jefferson Davis or Braxton Bragg; they fought for men such as Hiram Granbury and Patrick Cleburne. Daniels also maintains that the men of the Army of Tennessee formed strong bonds in the ranks, so that they considered their comrades and lower echelon commanders their family, encouraging them to fight harder for each other. Finally, according to Daniels, religion played an important role in the morale of these western Confederates. The religious revivals that swept the army camps during lulls in the fighting and campaigning gave the men a renewed sense of purpose and a pervasive feeling that God was on their side.[4]

Granbury's Texas Brigade fits perfectly into this paradigm of the western Confederate. Granbury's Texans remained loyal to the cause because of their localized perspective. They experienced battlefield triumphs at almost every turn, such as at Tunnel Hill, Pickett's Mill, and Atlanta, even as the rest of the army often let them down. The leadership Granbury's men enjoyed became just as important. Commanders like Hiram Granbury, James Deshler, and Patrick Cleburne all inspired confidence and devotion in their men, to the point that they would follow them anywhere they led. The Texans took pride in becoming members of Cleburne's Division, widely recognized by historians as the crack division in the Army of Tennessee, and responded by becoming the best brigade in that division. It is no coincidence that after the Battle of Franklin, in which both Granbury and Cleburne perished, Granbury's Texas Brigade largely lost its effectiveness as a fighting unit. Religion also played a factor in the motivation of Granbury's Texans, especially following the camp revivals that took place in the spring of 1864.

Granbury's Texans appear to have mirrored the behavior of Texas Confederates as a whole. As Charles Grear points out in his study "Texans to the Front," Texans initially joined the Confederate army for the same reasons as most other Confederates: to seek adventure, defend slavery and the slaveholding society, and gain glory. Despite this initial enthusiasm, Texans did desert more heavily than the men of other states late in the war, primarily for one reason: they wanted to fight for the Confederacy closer to home. These Texans deserted due to their fear of being cut off from home by Union control of the Mississippi River. When Texas faced no danger, desertions in Texas regiments east of the Mississippi stayed low; when the men perceived a danger to their homes, they deserted in large numbers.[5]

This study argues that, in adjusting Grear's argument to Granbury's Texas Brigade, the psychological blows that caused the most desertions occurred earlier: for the cavalrymen, when Confederate authorities dismounted the various cavalry regiments, taking their horses away; and for the infantry, when they faced surrender at Fort Donelson and Arkansas Post in 1862 and early 1863. By far the largest number of desertions that occurred in the ranks of the dismounted cavalry regiments came at the time Confederate authorities dismounted them, indicating that the dismounting struck just as severe a psychological blow as the severing of the Mississippi River later in the war. For the infantry, the most desertions occurred directly before the surrender of their respective garrisons, or in a prisoner-of-war camp. Because of these desertions relatively early in the war, Granbury's Texans actually suffered few desertions after the closing of the Mississippi.

Granbury's Texas Brigade bears remarkable similarities to other western Confederate units, and other Texas units, but what makes the history of the brigade valuable to a greater understanding of the Confederate war effort in the West remains the unique shared experiences of dismounting and prison camp. It appears that in addition to the motivations experienced by other western Confederates, this shared history gave the men of Granbury's Texas Brigade an edge, a hunger for victory unrivaled in most other western brigades. This shared history, coupled with their localized perspectives, stellar leadership, and superior field officers, made them into perhaps the most distinguished brigade in the most distinguished division in the Army of Tennessee, and has earned them the sobriquet of Diehard Western Confederates.

CHAPTER ONE

OFF TO WAR

As the various regiments that became Granbury's Brigade came together and headed for the front, their very organization and demographics demonstrated the early strength of Confederate nationalism. In recent years, several studies have outlined the Confederate nationalism inherent in Texans in the early months of the Civil War. In his study "Victory Is Our Only Road to Peace," Andrew Lang demonstrates that Confederate nationalism on the Texas home front peaked in 1861 but stayed strong throughout the war. This nationalism impelled many of the men in the regiments that became Granbury's Brigade to join in the first place. Lang also points out that Texas occupied a unique position among the Confederate states because of its history of nationalism during the Republic of Texas era. Lang argues that Texans took this identity from the Republic era and easily reshaped it into loyalty to the South and the Confederacy. The accounts of many of the men of Granbury's Brigade early in the war bear out this thesis. In addition, some historians have attempted to portray the Confederate war effort as a "rich man's war and a poor man's fight," but authors such as Richard Lowe, in his *Walker's Texas Division, C.S.A.*, demonstrate beyond a shadow of a doubt that all classes of Texans joined to defend the Confederacy. The demographics of Granbury's Brigade also bear this out.[1]

Stark differences existed in the demographics and loyalty between the infantry and cavalry regiments that later became Granbury's Brigade. The infantry regiments tended to contain younger, more unattached men, often from more affluent families, increasing their idealism and propensity toward loyal service to their original regiments. Meanwhile, the cavalry regiments tended to contain older, married men, who were often reluctant to fight dismounted or, even more serious, to fight far from their families or from the boundaries of Texas. The fact that many of the cavalrymen signed up ahead of the enactment of the Confederate Conscription Act of 1862 indicates that they were more than willing to serve their country, but perhaps held back because they wanted to serve close to home, rather than being forwarded to Virginia or Tennessee. The demographics of the various regiments and the chronology in which they came into Confederate service laid the groundwork for their later contributions to the Confederate cause.

Within the Civil War armies, the company was the basic unit of a regiment. Each company, ideally consisting of about a hundred men, formed gradually as volunteers congregated at a common mustering point, usually the nearest county seat. Prominent local citizens generally provided the impetus for forming these companies. In the case of Granbury's Brigade, lawyers, judges, and planters comprised this group—in short, the wealthier and more educated individuals of the community. From the mustering points the leaders loosely organized these companies and shuttled them to camps of instruction, where the regiments began to take shape. Ten companies formed a regiment, organized by a prominent citizen armed with a commission from the governor or the Confederate government. The government then eventually ordered these regiments to the front, where generals organized them into brigades of three to five regiments.

Leading citizens organized all the regiments of Granbury's Brigade before the passage of the Confederate Conscription Act in April 1862. Because of this, the state considered them volunteer regiments. Infantry provided the core of armies based on the Napoleonic model. Texan leaders soon found it extremely difficult, though, to persuade men to volunteer as foot soldiers. In 1863, British observer Lieutenant Colonel Arthur Fremantle noted, after watching a cavalry regiment in Galveston, "At the outbreak of the war it was found very difficult to raise infantry in Texas, as no Texan walks a yard if he can help it. Many mounted regiments were therefore organized, and afterwards dismounted."[2] While trying to raise a company of infantry in 1862, Oran Roberts of Hopkins County noted, "If it was cavalry I could succeed better as Texans dislike to walk." James H. Jones of the same regiment wrote, "We have some good material for the service yet in our country—men of position and good moral characters—who are willing to go as infantry. We will have some prejudices to remove against walking."[3] Because infantry formed the backbone of nineteenth-century armies, the Confederate government sought to raise foot soldiers in any manner possible, and their zeal in this endeavor ultimately led to problems among the Texas cavalrymen when the authorities dismounted these regiments. The transformation of cavalry to infantry led to a great deal of dissatisfaction that dealt a mortal wound to any loyalty these men felt to their original regiments. They still wanted to serve the Confederacy, but closer to home and on their own terms.

For the most part, each company of Granbury's Brigade hailed from a single county. This shared locality often provided a name for the company. For example, the "Travis Rifles" of Travis County became Company G, 6th Texas Infantry. In this company, of those whose residency could be verified, 71 percent of the members came from Travis County. The other 29 percent hailed from Hays, Burnet, Bastrop, or Williamson counties, all contiguous with Travis. Only one member of the company came from a county not contiguous with Travis County.[4] The companies in the other regiments of Granbury's Brigade had similar patterns of residency.

Early indications of Confederate nationalism abounded in Texas during the early months of the war. Robert Collins, a clerk in a dry goods store in Decatur, Texas, wrote that in February 1862 "the idea of the Yankees heading for Texas soil to despoil our fair homes, insult our women and eat up the substance of the people was just a little more than we proposed to submit to." Wise County, which Decatur served as seat, had only about two hundred voters, and according to Collins all those who were not teachers or clerks occupied themselves as "cowboys." George Sweet commissioned George Pickett to raise a company for his regiment then assembling near McKinney, north of Dallas. Collins wrote that once Pickett received his commission he "then commenced the rushing to and fro getting things in shape to enlist, go to the wars and get honor, glory and some immortality. The day was set Saturday for the enrolling of names and organization of the company, and in they came on their little fingertail, frosty-necked, calico Spanish ponies, all clamorous to get into the cavalry service." He continued, "After the organization of our company until the order to march

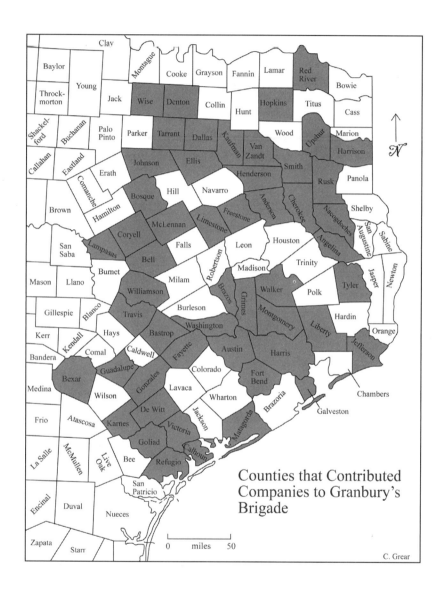

Counties that Contributed
Companies to Granbury's
Brigade

C. Grear

was received all hands were busy getting things in shape to take the field, and the people either from pure patriotism, or fear of the consequences of resistance, opened their doors to the boys."

Members of Pickett's new company fashioned themselves the "Wise Yankee Catchers." Collins reported that patriotic sentiment predominated, and all the women of the town went about their business humming "Dixie" or "The Bonnie Blue Flag." The Texans armed themselves with whatever firearms they could get. Most had shotguns, double-barreled and single-barreled, used for hunting in the days before the war. Around the first of March, Pickett, whom the company had elected captain, received orders to report his company immediately to Dallas.[5]

The presentation of a flag by the ladies of the town and accompanying patriotic fanfare became a common feature of these companies that enlisted in the early days of the war. Private Jim Turner of the Travis Rifles recounted the experience of his company in Austin:

> During the forenoon of Saturday, November 2, 1861 the company assembled at the armory and loaded our baggage and tents into the wagons. . . . We were then marched up Congress Avenue to the corner of Ninth Street where the company was presented by the ladies with a beautiful silk flag, the Stars and Bars of the Confederacy, in the presence of a large crowd of people. Patriotic speeches of presentation and acceptance were made, and after giving three hearty cheers, the company marched down the street amidst cheers and waving of handkerchiefs by the people who thronged the sidewalks. At noon we crossed the Colorado River at the ferry which was then near the foot of Colorado Street, just above the old Glasscock Mill, and proceeded on our way to the war.[6]

Turner's description certainly did not stand alone. Most if not all companies had a flag presentation of some sort. Later the regiments put away these individual company flags in favor of one regimental flag.

These volunteers soon took part in another ritual, the election of company and regimental officers. At an early hour on April 19, 1861, the "'neigh of the war horse' and the assembling of the Cavalry" disturbed the quiet of Marshall, wrote William Heartsill. The best men from Harrison, Panola, and Marion counties assembled in the Marshall town square. The new cavalrymen possessed everything necessary for service except weapons, which they expected to get from the arsenal at Austin. Heartsill recounted, "At 3 o'clock we proceeded to the organization of the company; which was consummated as follows; tickets had been previously prepared with the names of aspirants, and in some instances unauthorized; but as all are willing to serve in any capacity that their friends may desire; consequently there was a full ticket, and considerable stir among the friends of the respective candidates. The ballots were deposited in a ballot box, and while the officers of the election were counting out the vote—the Company was called together in the Courthouse, and the oath administered by Judge Frazer." The soldiers elected Samuel J. Richardson captain of the company, which styled itself the "W. P. Lane Rangers," after William P. Lane, a prominent citizen of Marshall.[7] After their organization the Rangers served as an independent company of cavalry until captured at the Arkansas Post. Thereafter most of the company served in Granbury's Brigade as dismounted cavalry.

The demographics of these various companies reveal something of the type of men who served in Granbury's Brigade. Eight companies will serve as a representative sample, one from each regiment in the brigade. These particular eight had diverse geographic origins within Texas and give a good cross-sample of differences based on locality. In some companies heads of households in their twenties and thirties predominated, while in others dependents between the ages of fourteen and nineteen comprised almost the whole command.

Taking the results from the several companies together, a picture emerges of an average member of Granbury's Brigade in 1860. The average soldier tended to be twenty-five years old, six years older than the average Civil War soldier, and a little less likely (69 percent) than the average Texan to be a farmer. A relatively high percentage (38 percent) had married before the war, with most of the married men claiming children as dependents. Roughly 35 percent of the brigade hailed from the Upper South, 45 percent came from the Lower South, while about one in five men came from the North or Europe. About 37 percent of the brigade reported net assets on the 1860 census, with a holding of about $3,518 apiece.[8] (See Appendix 1.)

The average member of Granbury's Brigade owned only a little over half the total wealth of the average Texas head of household in 1860, but proved almost exactly as wealthy as the average member of Walker's Texas Division.[9] As for age, Granbury's men were comparable, if not a bit younger, than Walker's or the members of the 13th Texas Cavalry, which mustered at about the same time. In terms of occupations, the percentage of Granbury's men who were farmers coincided almost exactly with the percentage of farmers in Texas as a whole, while the states of origin for the men of Granbury's Brigade also coincided almost exactly with Texas as a whole. This clearly backs up assertions of authors such as Richard Lowe, who claim that members of all economic classes in Texas signed up in proportional numbers to defend their new country. This runs directly contrary to any claims of class conflict, or of a "rich man's war and a poor man's fight."

After the raising and organizing of the companies, the governor ordered them to come together at a designated camp of instruction for their regiment. The 6th Texas Infantry was one of the first regiments to organize. On June 12, 1861, Adjutant and Inspector General of the Confederacy Samuel Cooper ordered Brigadier General Earl Van Dorn, commander of the Confederacy's Department of Texas, to raise twenty companies of infantry for Confederate service. Van Dorn instructed the volunteers to organize themselves, elect their own officers, and report to two camps of instruction designated by the governor. Less than three weeks later Confederate Secretary of War Leroy Pope Walker instructed Governor Edward Clark to establish three camps of instruction. Meanwhile Colonel Henry McCulloch had replaced Van Dorn as Confederate commander of the Department of Texas. McCulloch suggested to Clark that he select Victoria as one of the sites. Clark agreed, and designated Millican, Texas, as the second camp of instruction.[10]

In September 1861, Major Alexander Haskell chose Nunner's Mott, four miles north of Victoria as the specific site for the first camp of instruction. The location was central and punctuated by large oak trees, but some complained that insects infested the site and made it an unhealthy environment. Nevertheless, Nunner's Mott became the staging area for what would become the 6th Texas Infantry. The volunteers named the encampment Camp Henry E. McCulloch in honor of the commander of the Department of Texas.[11]

The Lavaca Guards, a company from Calhoun County, became the first men to arrive at Nunner's Mott. Alexander Hamilton Phillips Jr., a Port Lavaca attorney, led the company. On September 27, 1861, Confederate officials mustered Phillips and his men into service as Company A. Three days later the Lone Star Rifles from Victoria County, led by James Rupley, arrived and became Company B. Rupley had previously served in the Mexican War and proved one of the more experienced company commanders in the newly forming regiment. The third group of men, under Captain

Alonzo Bass, hailed from Gonzales County. They took the oath of allegiance to the Confederacy on October 3, 1861, and became Company C. The next day Dr. A. E. Pearson oversaw the mustering in of his Matagorda Coast Guards as Company D.[12]

The next three companies moved a little slower in arriving at Camp Mc-Culloch. On October 30 a company from Guadalupe County arrived under the command of Seguin lawyer John P. White, and officials mustered the group in as Company E. Four days later Captain Henry E. Bradford's company from Bell County, the "Bell County Invincibles," mustered in as Company F. On November 12, 1861, Captain Rhoads Fisher, Austin attorney and son of Texas pioneer Samuel Fisher, arrived at the head of his Travis Rifles, who became Company G.[13]

In contrast to its treatment of most of the other volunteer regiments that flocked to the colors in 1861, the Confederate Congress authorized President Jefferson Davis to appoint the field officers of the 6th Texas. For colonel of the new regiment, Davis selected Robert R. Garland. Garland had served a captain in the 7th U.S. Infantry Regiment before the war. Prior to secession Garland found himself stationed at Fort Fillmore, New Mexico. He hailed from Virginia and considered his loyalty to the Old Dominion more important than his loyalty to the United States. When Garland resigned from the U.S. Army, Davis appointed him to an equal rank in the Confederate Army as inspector general to the Department of Texas. When Davis chose him to command the 6th Texas, he elevated Garland to colonel, effective December 12, 1861, and instructed him to proceed to Nunner's Mott. Davis chose Thomas S. Anderson, a former Texas secretary of state and practicing attorney in Austin, as the regiment's lieutenant colonel. Davis selected Alexander Haskell, the man who had selected Nunner's Mott, as major, and Samuel J. Garland, nephew of Colonel Garland, as adjutant. The next month Walker reassigned Haskell and promoted Captain Alexander Phillips to lieutenant colonel in his stead.[14] (See Appendix 2, "The 6th Texas Infantry.")

The steady stream of volunteers for infantry service began to dry up by the end of 1861. Things became so critical that in February 1862 Governor Francis Lubbock made an impassioned plea to the citizens of Texas to volunteer for Confederate service. The impetus from this appeal allowed Garland to fill out his regiment with the last three companies. On March 27, 1862, a company-sized group of volunteers from Calhoun and Lavaca counties arrived at Camp McCulloch under George P. Finley, and Garland swore them in as Company H. Four days later a group of volunteers under Samuel McCallister arrived from Bexar County calling themselves the "Alamo Rifles," and Garland designated them Company K. Finally, Garland received a company from DeWitt County under Captain C. P. Nanuheim. It became Company I on April 11, 1862.[15]

Even though the 6th Texas had a full contingent of recruits, the weapons and clothing of most of the companies proved far from satisfactory. The Lavaca Guards arrived in full uniform, attired in linen jeans with a narrow red stripe, blue flannel frock coats trimmed with red braid, and blue caps with leather visors and the silver letters "LG" stitched on the crown of the cap. The Travis Rifles were the other best-dressed company at Nunner's Mott. The women of the capital city had provided the Austinites with salt-and-pepper gray uniforms trimmed in green that created "quite a war-like appearance," according to Jim Turner. The men of the other eight companies arrived primarily dressed in whatever clothing they brought from home. The state government eventually solved the problem of clothing when the legislature homogeneously outfitted the troops in butternut (or light brown) uniforms sewn from cloth made at the State Penitentiary in Huntsville.[16]

The weapons that the Texans brought with them varied even more than their uniforms. Most individuals carried their weapons from home, usually shotguns or old flintlock rifles that lacked any uniformity whatsoever. Company A arrived armed with percussion rifles, while Company B came with Minié rifles purchased by the county officials at Brownsville and loaned to the company. Other counties, such as Matagorda and Guadalupe, loaned the heads of the companies from those localities money to purchase weapons for their companies. Rhoads Fisher armed his Travis Rifles with flintlocks converted to percussions by an Austin gunsmith. Before they departed from Camp McCulloch, the state government provided the Rifles with new Springfield percussion muskets. Later in the year several other companies in the regiment acquired Enfield rifles, making them some of the best-armed Confederates in the Trans-Mississippi.[17]

The drill that transformed the raw volunteer into a seasoned soldier commanded the first order of business in camp. Garland assigned each company in the regiment a location in the camp where its men erected tents and commenced drilling from one of the standard drill manuals of the day, such as *Hardee's Rifle and Light Infantry Tactics.* Its author, William J. Hardee, would one day become their corps commander in the Army of Tennessee. In the morning the companies worked on the company-level drilling in their camps, and in the afternoon they focused on battalion drills under the watchful eye of Colonel Garland. Because of Garland's experience in the U.S. Army, the 6th Texas became one of the better drilled and disciplined regiments in Texas. William J. Oliphant of the Travis Rifles wrote that Garland was "a perfect martinet and a very fine drill officer," adding that the colonel "kept us hard at work drilling until he converted the regiment into a regular machine which would move on the drill ground with clock-like precision."[18]

Soon after the drilling began, several distractions punctuated the monotony of camp life. In December 1861 Confederate officials ordered four companies of the regiment, A, B, D, and G, to Matagorda Island under Colonel Garland. Captain Daniel Shea, who commanded an artillery battery at Saluria, had sighted a Federal vessel and called on Garland for reinforcements. Taking the four companies with him, Garland went to survey the situation. He ordered Lieutenant Colonel Anderson to take the men and proceed to Indianola, where they arrived about midnight. Garland dispatched Captain Rupley and his Company B to Saluria to guard the ferry across the main bayou. The feared attack never materialized, but the four companies of the 6th Texas under Anderson greatly enjoyed their time at Indianola, where they feasted on the abundant seafood. The detachment remained for nine days before returning to Camp McCulloch.[19]

In February 1862 Garland dispatched companies A and D under Major Phillips to Fort Esparanza near Saluria as a second threat of Union incursion developed. Again, the threat never materialized, and the two companies returned to Nunner's Mott.[20] Aside from these small distractions Garland's regiment remained at Camp McCulloch through the beginning of March 1862, training and preparing for war.

About the same time that the first four companies of the 6th Texas began to drill on the prairie near Victoria, another regiment began to assemble near Marshall, Texas. In late January 1861 the Texas Secession Convention had met at Austin to discuss the possibility of seceding from the Union. John Gregg, a lawyer from Fairfield, served as one of the delegates. An Alabama by birth, Gregg had immigrated to Texas in 1854. The Texas Secession Convention chose the Alabama native as one of the representatives to the newly forming Confederate States of America at Montgomery, Alabama. Gregg traveled to Montgomery, where he obtained permission from newly appointed Secretary of War Leroy Pope Walker to raise a regiment of infantry for Confederate service. Gregg communicated his intentions to personal friends in Texas, including Jeremiah Clough of Marshall, who began to assemble the regiment in Gregg's absence. In September 1861 Gregg returned to Texas and began to gather ten companies of volunteers to Marshall. In the first few days of October Gregg mustered the companies into Confederate service for a period of three years or the duration of the war.[21] (See Appendix 2, "The 7th Texas Infantry.")

Gregg organized his regiment and rushed it to the front with amazing speed. With only six companies ready at Marshall, Gregg received a dispatch from Secretary of War Walker, dated October 4, directing him to report with whatever companies he had available to General Albert Sidney Johnston at Memphis. Gregg started out immediately with his six companies. Two days later the seventh company started out, and five days after that the eighth and ninth companies began their journey.[22]

The first six companies started out from Marshall on October 10 and marched overland to Monroe, Louisiana. Thence they took the railroad to Vicksburg, Mississippi, before traveling by steamboat north to Memphis. There Gregg informed the garrison commandant of the presence of his companies despite their limited arms. At Memphis Gregg received instructions from Assistant Adjutant General W. W. Mackall to move immediately to Clarksville, Tennessee, northwest of Nashville. Gregg inquired as to whether or not he should take the men then available at Memphis or wait for the entire regiment. Mackall replied that he should proceed at once to Hopkinsville, Kentucky (about twenty-five miles north of Clarksville), in support of General Lloyd Tilghman. With these instructions Gregg and his Texans set out via railroad and steamboat. According to Gregg his men remained three whole nights in open cars and steamboats. Once they reached Clarksville incessant rain kept the entire regiment in wet clothes for several days.[23]

The exposure and fatigue of their rapid journey induced sickness in many of the Texans. On November 7 Gregg sent a dispatch to Mackall stating, "Except for a number of sick men on the road our nine companies are all here. The number is 749. Five of our number died on the way. From exposure to cold and wet on our journey we have more coughs and colds than I ever saw among the same number of men."[24]

Along with illness, other impediments hampered the Texans in Kentucky. Like that of the 6th Texas, the weaponry of the 7th Texas left much to be desired. In his dispatch to Mackall on November 7, Gregg enumerated in detail the pitiful armament of his nine companies. Captain Khleber Van Zandt's Company D had thirteen double-barreled shotguns and sixteen rifles in good order. The men also had nine double-barreled shotguns and twenty-five rifles in disrepair. Hiram Granbury's Waco Guards had no firearms that they brought with them. W. B. Hill's company had nineteen double-barreled shotguns and eight rifles in good order. The company also had fourteen double-barreled shotguns and twenty rifles in disrepair. William Smith's Company F possessed sixty-nine muskets but no other equipment. Apparently, the state of Louisiana had loaned these muskets to the state of Texas. Jack Davis's Company E had thirteen rifles in good order and three in disrepair. It also had fourteen double-barreled shotguns in good order and two that needed work. R. S. Camp's men had one musket, twenty-seven double-barreled shotguns, and eleven rifles, all in good order. Camp's men also had thirty-one firearms that had been left behind at Clarksville. E. T. Broughton's Company C possessed thirty-one muskets from Louisiana similar to those of Smith's men. William L. Moody's men could muster three muskets, thirteen double-barreled shotguns, and twenty-six rifles, along with twelve other firearms left at Clarksville. Finally, John W. Brown's company found itself equipped with thirty-two rifles, twelve double-barreled shotguns, three Mississippi rifles, and two German-made Jaeger rifles. All of the weapons left behind at Clarksville were unfit for immediate use.[25] It would take a lot of work before the 7th Texas became well-enough armed to go into battle.

Despite these shortcomings, Gregg went ahead with organizing the regiment two days later, on November 9. The election of officers was the first order of business. The men elected John Gregg colonel of the regiment, Jeremiah Clough lieutenant colonel, and Hiram Granbury of the Waco Guards major. Colonel Gregg then appointed his staff from adjutant to sergeant major, after which the companies officially elected their officers and drew lots for their alphabetic designation within the regiment.[26] With the final organization the Texans made camp at Hopkinsville to wait out the winter. It would be a long winter indeed.

Another regiment of Texas infantry began to take shape in late 1861 and early 1862 under the guidance of a prominent Wacoan, Allison Nelson. Born in Fulton County, Georgia, Nelson had an active pre–Civil War career. After enlisting in the Georgia militia during the Mexican War, he went on to fili-buster in Cuba and served as an officer in General Francisco López's army in the early 1850s. When he returned to the United States, Nelson, an ad-vocate of the expansion of slavery, took an active part in the struggle over "Bleeding Kansas" in 1854. The next year he returned to Atlanta, Georgia, and entered politics. The voters elected him mayor of Atlanta and after only a short time in that office he opted to go west, to the Texas frontier.[27]

Nelson settled in Bosque County, northwest of Waco, serving for a brief time as the state of Texas's Indian agent. Joining the Texas Rangers, he took part in Lawrence S. "Sul" Ross's excursions against Indians on the Texas frontier. Nelson entered the legal profession and soon found it nec-essary to move his offices to Waco due to the size of his practice. Wacoans elected him to the Texas House of Representatives, and he took an active part in the secession of the state in 1861.[28]

Always more interested in military affairs than in politics, Nelson applied to General Paul Hebert, then commander of the Military District of Texas, for permission to raise a regiment of infantry for coastal defense. Nelson instructed the various volunteer companies to rendezvous at Galveston as soon as possible.[29] Thus began the nucleus of the 10th Texas Infantry.

In October Nelson organized his regiment. He began by enrolling eight volunteer companies of infantry, which he designated Companies A–H. Then, in late October, Nelson completed his organization by electing of-ficers. The men elected Robert B. Young, a Georgia native and stock raiser from Bosque County, major, and Roger Q. Mills, a Corsicana politician, lieu-tenant colonel, while they chose Allison Nelson as colonel. On January 16, 1862, the Stockton Cavalry under Captain James Formwalt arrived from Johnson County, and Nelson designated the men Company I. Twelve days later a company from Bosque and Coryell counties under Captain Byron Bassell arrived, and Nelson designated them Company K, giving the 10th Texas Infantry its full complement of ten companies.[30] (See Appendix 2, "The Tenth Texas Infantry.")

While the original eight companies waited for the last two to arrive, military life commenced uneventfully on the Texas coast. Colonel Nelson stationed his new regiment at Virginia Point, located on the mainland side of the West Bay in Galveston County at the west end of the old Galves-ton Causeway. In 1857 residents had built a bridge from Virginia Point to Galveston Island, and in 1861 locals had fortified the point due to the blockade.[31] Everything continued quietly at the point until November 10, when the U.S.S. *Santee* appeared off the coast and fired a few shells in the direction of the Texas volunteers. Private Benjamin M. Seaton of the Laba die Rifles reported that the men of the 10th Texas received news of the war from the East "almost every day" and could follow operations in Virginia.

The day after the *Santee* appeared, Seaton reported that his company officers placed him on regimental guard duty for the first time. He didn't seem to mind it much then, but by December 1 he reported that guard duty had become "vary hard for one that is not used to it and confining." While on guard duty a few days later he scribbled in his diary that there was "some excitement in camp about a fleet of Yankeys coming to take Galveston and we are expecting a battle to be fought her this month."

Though the threat never materialized, martial discipline did, and the volunteers began to take the rough shape of soldiers. Seaton reported that they drilled six to eight hours a day. "We think," Seaton wrote, "that it is very hard to do to be commanded by a set of white men to have the command of another one but never the less it is so."[32]

As the drill and the normality of being commanded by another white man took hold, so did sickness. Private Elijah Hull of the Stockton Cavalry wrote to his parents that he had contracted a severe cold that settled in his breast and back. He wrote that more bad colds had developed in camp than he had ever seen before. Many of them could not get to sleep until ten or eleven at night because of the heaviness of the air. "This is the lowest place that ever was," he concluded. Hull reported that some time would pass before he could return to guard duty. In December Private Seaton also took sick, and could not resume duty until January 25, 1862.[33] The sickness in the low-lying area along the Texas coast claimed many men before they ever saw battle.

Shortages and hardships also plagued the new soldiers. The new volunteers had received neither arms nor clothing as of late November 1861. Clothes proved particularly short for Private Isaiah Harlan, also of the Laba die Rifles. He wrote that someone stole his clothing on the way to Virginia Point, leaving him ill-clad. Though the commissary proved tardy in providing them with clothes, they did issue the men large tents apparently capable of holding up to half a dozen men. In the midst of these hardships, Confederate officials issued rations of fresh bread, beef, and bacon, with occasional coffee. After the U.S.S. *Santee* appeared, the amount of drilling increased. "We drill more than we did," wrote Harlan, "a great deal more than we did." This increased drilling did nothing to endear the enlisted men to their officers, whom they already disliked due to the strict discipline and lack of supplies.[34]

In mid-February 1862 another scare gripped the city of Galveston. At that time six to eight blockading vessels lay off the coast, and Benjamin Seaton reported that the local officials busied themselves transferring everything they could to Houston post-haste. Apparently the increased number of vessels spooked the city authorities, who anticipated an invasion of the island. Again the invasion never materialized, and the volunteers of the 10th Texas spent the remainder of February and the majority of March doing guard duty along the Texas coast.[35]

In November 1861, as Allison Nelson organized his regiment, another prominent Texan, Middleton T. Johnson, received authority from the Confederate Department of War to raise a brigade of cavalry for twelve months' service. Johnson sent out a call for volunteers, and community leaders raised fifty companies of cavalry in response. These fifty companies eventually became the 14th, 15th, 16th, 17th, and 18th Regiments of Texas Cavalry. George H. Sweet of San Antonio guided one of the first regiments to take shape, the 15th Texas Cavalry.[36]

Sweet, a San Antonio politician before the war, proceeded to Dallas in late 1861 armed with his commission from Johnson to raise a regiment of cavalry. Johnson gave Sweet to believe that the state intended his regiment for service in the Indian Territory, now Oklahoma, and Sweet chose Dallas as his rendezvous point. From Dallas he sent out a call for volunteers. As his headquarters Sweet chose the fairgrounds southeast of Dallas, known as Fair Park. He instructed his volunteers to provide their own horses, weapons, and equipment for service as "ranging companies." Most of the companies for the new regiment arrived at the fair grounds in December, though some did not arrive until early 1862.[37] (See Appendix 2, "The 15th Texas Cavalry.")

In early January 1862 the new regiment elected officers. The men selected George Sweet as colonel, William Masten of Company C to be lieutenant colonel, and George Pickett of the Wise Yankee Catchers for major. Before Sweet could complete the organization of his new regiment an outbreak of measles forced him to relocate the regiment to McKinney, north of Dallas. As the 15th Texas began to take shape the regiment relocated again, this time north to Camp McKnight near Clarksville. At Clarksville on April 1, 1862, Sweet officially mustered the 15th Texas Cavalry into Confederate service.[38]

Life at Camp McKnight continued uneventfully for the Texan recruits amid the adoring fanfare of the local citizenry. Rain often interrupted the routine, but when it stopped raining military drill ruled the day. Robert Collins reported that the officers varied the drill, with some company and some regimental maneuvers. In addition to this drilling, the soldiers received a dose of religion from the Reverend J. W. P. McKinzie, who preached patriotism in addition to Christianity. In early April the ladies of Clarksville ventured out the fifteen miles to Camp McKnight to present Company G with a flag. Miss Ida De Morse led the delegation and addressed the company before the presentation of the silk flag. Captain A. Faulkner, commander of the company, replied, thanking the women for the banner.[39] This melding of Christianity with the Confederate cause served to turn it into a holy one for these soldiers, who consistently saw God as being on their side.

While the 15th Texas lay encamped at Clarksville the other regiments of Johnson's Brigade began to arrive. When six regiments had arrived they held a review of the men, "And when these six regiments, six thousand in all, were strung out in line of battle on the prairie, it just appeared," Robert Collins recalled, "that we had men enough to whip the United States, with Canada and Mexico thrown in for good count, and we were really uneasy for fear the rebels would clean up the Yankees before we got a taste of the war. Us boys were all puffed up as to our numbers, and it was no uncommon thing to hear some of them in camps giving such commands as 'Attention, World! By nations right wheel into line m-a-r-c-h!'" Collins observed, "At the beginning of the war young Texas in the saddle was regarded as a whole set put together in thirds, one-third man and bell spurs, one-third gun, pistol and knife, and one-third pony."[40]

The 17th Texas Cavalry under Colonel George F. Moore was one of the regiments that marched into Camp McKnight in March 1862. Moore, a prominent resident of Nacogdoches, decided to put out a call for volunteers for a regiment to serve in Johnson's Brigade. From north and east Texas ten companies responded to the call. The regiment rendezvoused at Jamestown in March and elected its field officers. The men elected Moore colonel, Sterling Hendricks of Company C as lieutenant colonel, and John McClarty of Company F major. Soon after their organization Colonel

Moore put his troopers on the road to Camp McKnight.[41] (See Appendix 2, "The 17th Texas Cavalry.")

Later in March Nicholas H. Darnell led yet another regiment, the 18th Texas, into Camp McKnight. Darnell had moved to Texas in the 1830s, where citizens elected him to the Texas House of Representatives. By 1842 he had risen to the post of Speaker of the House and in 1858 moved to Dallas while continuing to occupy his House seat. Darnell became a fire-eater in the sectional crisis of the 1850s and stressed to his constituents the inability of the federal government to defend the frontier against Indian attacks. He also stressed the expediency of using military force to leave the Union.[42] After Texas seceded, Darnell put out a call for volunteers, specifically a cavalry regiment, to rendezvous at Fair Park southeast of Dallas, the same place that George Sweet had assembled his regiment. In his call for volunteers, Darnell assumed that state officials would assign his regiment to frontier service. He passed on this impression to those commissioned to raise and organize the individual companies, but interestingly enough only a handful of the companies came from areas affected by Indian depredations. Darnell soon detached an eleventh company under Captain Wade Witt, never to rejoin the regiment. The men confirmed Darnell as colonel in the regimental elections, chose John T. Coit of Company E lieutenant colonel, and picked Charles C. Morgan major.[43] (See Appendix 2, "The 18th Texas Cavalry.")

Only one company of Darnell's new regiment arrived at the rendezvous in any sort of uniforms. The Morgan Rangers caused quite a stir when they arrived at Fair Park dressed in "yellow-grey tunic and pantaloon made of penitentiary 'jeans' with two rows of brass buttons down the front coat and a stripe down . . . the pantaloons." The men had these uniforms made from cloth acquired from the Lone Star Mill, and they presented a more warlike appearance than many of the other volunteers in the regiment.[44] Soon after the 18th Texas completed its organization it too headed for Camp McKnight near Clarksville. As Middleton Johnson reviewed and trained his men at Camp McKnight, he had no way of knowing that his brigade would soon be split up and ordered north.

In late 1861 a series of events occurred that resulted in the organization of the last two regiments to see service in Granbury's Brigade. George Washington Carter, a Methodist minister and president of Soule University in Chappell Hill, Texas, went to Richmond to obtain permission from the Confederate government to raise and outfit a regiment of cavalry. Confederate Secretary of War George Randolph agreed, and Carter apparently decided to arm his men with lances. An annual jousting tournament was held at Chappell Hill at that time, and this (along with a lack of weapons available for Confederate troops) may have convinced Carter to raise lancers.[45]

Carter enlisted the help of two other prominent Methodist ministers, Frank Wilkes and Clayton C. Gillespie. Wilkes had taught at Soule University before becoming the general agent for the university. In addition to his duties at Soule, Wilkes practiced medicine and owned the only drugstore in Chappell Hill. Gillespie was a veteran of the Battle of San Jacinto in 1836. He had overseen the construction of the first Texas State Penitentiary at Huntsville and served as the first superintendent of that institution. In 1854 Gillespie had become editor of the *Texas Christian Advocate,* a Methodist paper published in Galveston. In his editorial capacity, Gillespie championed slavery within a Christian context. Gillespie also advocated striking John Wesley's general rule prohibiting Methodists from buying or selling slaves. In 1858 the Methodist general convention promoted Gillespie to edit the *New Orleans Advocate,* but when he heard of Carter's efforts to raise a cavalry regiment he rushed back to Chappell Hill.[46]

Carter, Wilkes, and Gillespie issued a call "To the Chivalry of Texas!" on November 1, 1861, to enlist for cavalry service. They instructed the recruits to provide their own mounts and equipment and rendezvous at Chappell Hill.[47]

Carter informed his potential recruits that the state would manufacture lances for them at Chappell Hill and that they should come to the rendezvous with the best horses they could procure. Carter also instructed the men to bring two suits of winter clothing, blankets, a Bowie knife, and the best firearms they could get, "if possible a double-barrel shot gun, and six shooter." Carter editorialized:

> We call upon our friends and the friends of Southern independence throughout the State, to assist our men in arming and equipping themselves. . . . This will be the only Regiment of Lancers in the service, and Lancers are the most formidable cavalry in the world. We have chosen this arm at the earnest solicitation of General Twiggs. The lance simply takes the place of the sword in a charge, and is much the most terrible weapon. Brave men of Texas, the South is

invaded; everything dear to us as men is at stake; there will be nothing to live for if we are conquered; this is the grandest contest in the world; who will not be emulous of the privilege of taking a part in the glorious strife!

Soon after the issuance of this ringing call to arms, Carter authorized those raising the men to recruit enough companies for an entire brigade. He enlisted the recruits for three years or the duration of the war and instructed them to meet at Hempstead on April 1, 1862. Carter's efforts proved very successful, and thirty companies of cavalry assembled.[48]

Governor Francis Lubbock caught wind of Carter's actions and complained bitterly to Confederate Secretary of War George W. Randolph, firing off a March 15, 1862, epistle inquiring as to whether or not Carter had authorization from the War Department to expand his command to brigade size. He then went on to reiterate his difficulty in filling the state's quota of fifteen infantry regiments, complaining that endeavors such as Carter's made it even more difficult. "I cannot understand why," whined Lubbock, "individuals should be placed on a more favorable footing in the raising of men than the State authorities. If cavalry is wanted," he wrote, "I could fill your requisition in twenty days. . . . I am exerting every influence and power to comply with the requisition made upon me, and were I left untrammeled and permitted to act independently of gentlemen having roving commissions my efforts would be successful." On April 8, Randolph replied that the Confederates had issued no authority to Colonel Carter, that the extra regiments remained an independent enterprise. Randolph went on to state that he had no power other than to discourage such undertakings by private individuals in the future.[49]

With the companies already raised, Carter received permission to reorganize his recruits into three regiments: the 1st Texas Lancers (designated the 21st Texas Cavalry) under Carter, the 2nd Texas Lancers (24th Texas Cavalry) under Frank Wilkes, and the 3rd Texas Lancers (25th Texas Cavalry) under Clayton Gillespie. Carter assigned the commanders of the ten companies in each regiment their alphabetic designation by lot, and the regiments moved into a camp on Clear Creek a few miles southeast of Hempstead. They dubbed this encampment Camp Hebert in honor of Department of Texas commander Paul O. Hebert.[50] In the 24th Texas, the soldiers elected Frank Wilkes of Waco colonel, with Robert R. Neyland of Nacogdoches lieutenant colonel and Patrick Swearingen major.[51] (See Appendix 2, "The 24th Texas cavalry.")

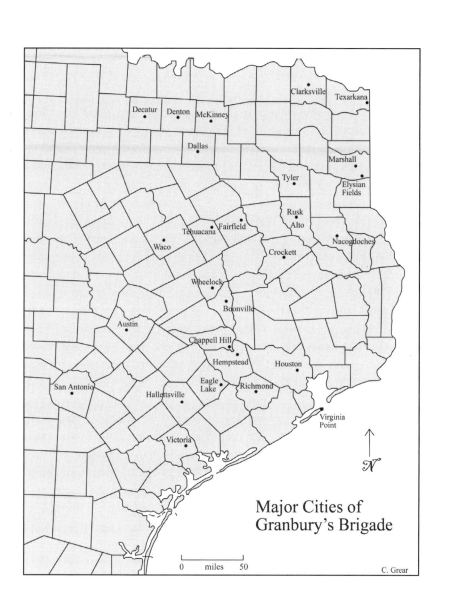

Major Cities of
Granbury's Brigade

| 0 | miles | 50 |

C. Grear

Wilkes's sister regiment, the 25th Texas, under Colonel Clayton Gillespie, also came from East and South Texas. The lancers chose William Neyland lieutenant colonel of the new regiment and J. N. Dark, of Company B, major. On April 15, 1862, Wilkes and Gillespie mustered the 24th and 25th Texas into Confederate service.[52] (See Appendix 2, "The 25th Texas Cavalry.")

Camp Hebert provided a central location for the new Texas cavalry recruits. Private J. P. Blessington of the 16th Texas Infantry, camped across the railroad tracks from Camp Hebert, visited the camp one day and recorded his impressions. "From this position," he recalled, "there was a magnificent view of the hills that gird the place, forming a sort of natural amphitheater; looking picturesque with their waving forests of trees, and innumerable white tents." Wandering through the camp, he noted the finery of the officers' tents and finally came to "The modest tents of the rank and file, arranged in streets. . . . The men around these are collected in groups . . . wearing their bell-spurs, while around each waist is dangling a huge knife, made by some village blacksmith, giving them the appearance of warriors, apparently ready for any emergency. Some are playing cards, pitch and toss, or a thousand other games known only in the army.'"[53] Despite the complaints of nearby infantrymen, the new Texan cavalrymen settled into camp to attend to training and equipping themselves for war.

The initial organization of the regiments that became Granbury's Brigade demonstrated the strength of devotion to the Confederacy among these men. As indicated by Lowe's and Lang's studies, Confederate nationalism sprang up early in Texas, stayed strong through the first months of the war, and swept up all classes of Texans. These trends manifested themselves clearly in the regiments that later became Granbury's Brigade. The early demonstrations of patriotic fanfare, even among the cavalry regiments that formed in early 1862, indicate that these men did not join up to avoid the Confederate draft, but rather to have their say in how, with whom, and where they fought. The demographics of the various regiments and the chronology in which they came into Confederate service laid the groundwork for their later contributions to the Confederate cause.

CHAPTER 2

FORT DONELSON

As other Texas regiments organized themselves, the 7th Texas prepared to see combat for the first time in the Fort Donelson campaign. The experiences of the 7th Texas Infantry in the campaign demonstrated the strength of Confederate nationalism among these Texan infantrymen. It also began their transformation into western Confederate soldiers. In the Donelson campaign, the 7th Texas enjoyed leadership by regimental leaders such as John Gregg, Jeremiah Clough, Hiram Granbury, and K. M. Van Zandt, who all demonstrated strong patriotism toward the Confederacy. Despite this stellar leadership at the regimental level, the men of the 7th Texas suffered a defeat in the surrender of Fort Donelson. But from their localized perspective, they fought well and won a victory, only to have it frittered away by the men in the high command. This poor high-level leadership and these events all fall perfectly into developing the paradigm set out by Larry Daniels in *Soldiering in the Army of Tennessee* regarding western Confederates, in which localized perspective mattered more than the strategic situation.[1] It is also noteworthy that despite their time in prison camps following the surrender, the men of the 7th Texas remained more willing than ever to lay down their lives for the Confederacy, a fact that belies the argument that Confederate soldiers lost faith in their cause in the face of adversity. In fact, if anything, the time in prison strengthened the resolve of the 7th

Texas and their officers to sustain the Confederate cause, a strength that allowed them to later become the heart and soul of Granbury's Brigade.

The struggle over Fort Donelson marked the first real campaign for any of the regiments that would one day become Granbury's Brigade. Only one of them, the 7th Texas Infantry, hastily thrown together and rushed to the front, took part in this first great campaign of the western theater. The fall of Donelson and her sister stronghold, Fort Henry, in February 1862 marked a significant turning point in the war in the West. In fact, some historians regard the capture of Forts Henry and Donelson as the Confederacy's most disastrous turning point.[2]

As constructed, Fort Donelson was a low, earthen embankment on the Cumberland River in Tennessee south of the Kentucky state line; Confederate engineers built Fort Henry as a similar structure scarcely a day's march to the west on the Tennessee River. In early 1862 Forts Henry and Donelson remained ill-prepared for a Federal campaign against them. Unfortunately for the Confederacy, they also occupied the most crucial points necessary to a defense of Tennessee up the main waterways from Kentucky. Lieutenant General Leonidas Polk, initially placed in charge of constructing Tennessee's defenses, largely ignored these important fortifications in lieu of building strong defenses along the Mississippi River. Polk served only as temporary commander of the forces in Tennessee pending the arrival of General Albert Sidney Johnston, but he did more than enough damage in the interim.[3]

When Johnston finally arrived in late 1861 he immediately set about constructing a line of defense across southern Kentucky and northwestern Tennessee. Henry and Donelson anchored this line, even though they remained inadequate. Such was the situation when the 7th Texas arrived in November.

Johnston initially assigned Gregg's regiment to General John B. Floyd's brigade. As soon as the regiment completed its organization it began drilling at Camp Alcorn near Hopkinsville. Floyd assigned the Texans a drill instructor named David Hirsch, a recent immigrant from Prussia. Gregg chose Captain Khleber Van Zandt as the second drill instructor. Hirsch, though trained as a soldier of the old school, succeeded in embarrassing himself several times in front of the Texans. Sinkholes pockmarked the ground in Kentucky over which the new infantrymen drilled. One day as Hirsch galloped back and forth, Captain Van Zandt lost sight of him. "The boys, with a look of astonishment on their faces, were pointing in one direction," recalled Van Zandt. "In a moment a horse came scrambling out of a large sinkhole. Close behind the horse came the rider, unhurt but much crest-fallen. When the boys realized that Mr. Hirsch was not hurt, they all started laughing. He turned to me and said, 'You are all dismissed for the day.'"[4] Despite this accident, Hirsch and Van Zandt succeeded in beginning to mold the Texans into soldiers on the plains of Kentucky.

Sickness served as the main enemy of the 7th Texas in these first few months. Measles, in particular, took their toll, "with accompanying lung and bowel troubles." Soon after arriving, the Texans made a forced march from Hopkinsville to Princeton and back during which they experienced cold rain and slept without any tents or food, equipped only with damp blankets. After this march the measles appeared in their ranks for the first time. This illness claimed the lives of a great many of the Texans. Lieutenant Colonel Clough wrote that more than 130 members of the regiment died of disease in the first few months, "a dreadful and almost unaccountable mortality." Clough explained that "from the beginning without agency of anyone, our men started from home predisposed to disease, that from a combination of unfortunate circumstances that could and should have been controlled, they arrived here well prepared to take all the diseases which hover over an army and to contract them with little prospect of getting well." Clough complained that the men took no care of themselves in camp. "They lie down with impunity on wet blankets and damp straw. They eat their food half-cooked. They are careless and unconcerned about the cleanliness of their persons or their clothing—they are irregular about their sleep and in fact wholly and injudiciously ignore all the sanitary and wholesome laws which in their comfortable houses they would not have dared to disregard." By late January the sick outnumbered the well and the hospitals overflowed with the first casualties of war.[5]

Soon the measles were not the only enemy the Texans had to fight. In late January, Brigadier General Ulysses S. Grant assembled a column of infantry and a fleet of ironclads at Cairo, Illinois, to move against Henry and Donelson. Grant made his first move against Fort Henry. On February 4 the ironclads appeared opposite Henry and began shelling the Confederate fortification that was already partially submerged due to poor construction. Two days later the Confederate commander, Brigadier General Lloyd Tilghman, surrendered the fort. In ironic witness to the fort's poor engineering, the Federal party accepting the surrender rowed over the outer wall of the fort, which was submerged beneath the Tennessee River. Tilghman sent all but eighty men of his command overland toward Fort Donelson while he remained to surrender the fort. With the capture of Fort Henry, Grant opened the Tennessee River all the way into the interior of Alabama.[6]

The attack on Fort Henry caught Johnston unawares. Since October he had concentrated on one thing—the Federal army of Don Carlos Buell along the Green River in central Kentucky. Johnston became convinced that any movement against his line would come from Buell. The fall of Fort Henry changed his calculations.

Johnston ordered Brigadier General Gideon Pillow at Clarksville, north of Fort Donelson, to gather all available forces at the fort. He also ordered Simon Buckner and John Floyd to Donelson with their brigades. Johnston then turned his attention to evacuating his remaining forces from Kentucky, leaving Floyd in command of Fort Donelson. On February 8 Johnston sent Floyd a note stating, "I cannot give you specific instructions and place under your command the entire force."[7]

In the first week of February, Colonel Gregg led his men south toward Fort Donelson. The Texans marched overland to Clarksville, where they boarded boats bound for Dover, a small hamlet near Donelson. The Confederates transported all the sick who could move south from Hopkinsville to Clarksville, and many of the Texans who could not continue remained behind in the homes Clarksville citizens.[8] After the regiment disembarked at Dover, Gregg led them on a lengthy march to their camp near Fort Donelson, where they arrived on the morning of Tuesday, February 11. Floyd assigned the Texans a position in the center of the Confederate left wing, overlooking a branch of Indian Creek. Part of Brigadier General Charles Clark's brigade, they were temporarily under the command of Colonel T. J. Davidson. They began digging in the next day. The entrenchments at Fort Donelson formed a rough semicircle protecting the land side of the fort. "They consisted," as one Confederate officer reported, "of small saplings, with which that country abounds, thrown lengthwise along the outside margin of ditches, dug some 5 feet wide and 2 feet deep, the dirt having been thrown upon the saplings, and giving us a protection of about 5 feet."[9] Without proper entrenching tools the Texans clawed at the earth, trying desperately to erect adequate defenses.

The Confederate situation at Donelson remained critical, due to the fact that the two officers whom Johnston had left at the fort proved incompetent.[10] To try to head off the advance toward Donelson, Johnston ordered Gideon Pillow to take his brigade out and strike the Union column in flank. Pillow moved slowly and then refused to carry through with the idea altogether. John Floyd, overall commander of the troops around Donelson, had no idea what Johnston wanted him to do. Floyd, a relative newcomer to the area, leaned wholly on his subordinates. These vacillating performances doomed Donelson from the outset.

Grant's forces appeared opposite the fort on February 13. As the Federal infantry moved into place, gunboats demonstrated in the river to attract the attention of the Confederate garrison. The next day a fierce duel ensued between the gunboats and the shore batteries in which Confederate cannons severely damaged some of the vessels. Meanwhile, the Confederate infantry remained idle. Because Floyd focused on the gunboats, he never attempted to keep a route of escape open for the garrison's twenty-one thousand Confederates. The Federal gunboats began shelling the position of Gregg's Regiment at 9 A.M. on February 13 and continued until 4 P.M. In this bombardment the first battle casualties of the regiment occurred with the death of Lieutenant E. B. Rosson of Company A and the wounding of Private Thomas Jordan of Company G.[11] After two days of inaction, Floyd received a telegram from Johnston instructing him to evacuate the fort if "untenable." Suddenly Floyd realized that Fort Donelson had become a trap and that he should evacuate. On the evening of February 14 he called a council of war and decided to try to break out the next day, down the Wynn's Ferry Road toward Nashville.[12] Ignorance of Grant's dispositions and the weather, which had suddenly turned bitterly cold, hampered the Confederate movements.

Floyd scheduled the assault on the Union right for dawn, February 15. The plan called for Davidson's Brigade, including the 7th Texas, to march from the center to the far left and spearhead the assault. If they succeeded, Davidson's men would pivot and force the Federals back across the Wynn's Ferry Road to open up a route of escape. Shortly after midnight Gregg put his men on the move south to join Floyd's Brigade to coordinate their attack. The dark night contrasted sharply with the white, swirling snow as the Texans marched toward their first real battle. Davidson's men reached their positions before dawn and formed their line barely a quarter-mile in front of Colonel Richard Ogelsby's Federal brigade of John McClernand's division.[13]

As dawn broke, Gregg ordered his regiment to right-face toward the hill to their front, where Ogelsby's Federals waited. With the early morning mists rising off the snow-covered ground the Texans rushed up the hill into the face of the defenders' fire. Just before they reached the crest of the hill, the fire increased, causing many casualties among the Texans. As they rushed forward Lieutenant Colonel Jeremiah Clough shouted, "Look ahead men, never look back. Our mothers, our wives, and our sisters are behind us and our enemies are in front of us." As he uttered these words a ball struck Clough in the head, killing him instantly, and he fell from his mount onto the frozen ground. Lieutenant Arch Adams rushed over to the body amid a hail of bullets and secured Clough's watch, memorandum book, and purse. Federal fire also killed Captain William B. Hill of Company H and Lieutenant J. W. Nowlin of Company A just below the crest of the hill, along with several other Texans. After half an hour, the 8th Illinois Infantry, directly in front of the Texans, fell back.[14]

Gregg continued the pursuit and broke a second line, capturing a six-pound cannon complete with ammunition and horses. The Texans kept going until they spotted a third line drawn up in a clearing. This, too, they routed, inflicting many casualties on the enemy in the pursuit. In the confusion Private George Blaine of Company G brought in Major John P. Post of the 8th Illinois, whom he had captured. Gregg reported that the fighting left twenty Texans killed on the field and thirty-four more disabled with wounds. Nevertheless, with the success of the Confederate assault, the Wynn's Ferry Road lay open.[15]

At this critical moment Gideon Pillow ordered his men to retreat to their entrenchments. Brigadier General Simon Buckner, third in command of the garrison, protested vehemently. Buckner rode off to find Floyd, who refused to do anything before he conferred with Pillow. Floyd made the mistake of listening to his second-in-command and ordered the troops back to their previous positions. Grant quickly repaired the holes in his line and re-encircled the garrison.[16]

That night Floyd held a conference of his subordinates at the Dover Hotel. There, they decided to surrender the garrison. Floyd abdicated responsibility, stating that the old charges of corruption brought against him when he had served as U.S. Secretary of War would make it even harder for him as a prisoner. Pillow declared that he too did not want to be the first Confederate general to fall into Federal hands. Floyd and Pillow both opted to escape. Only Buckner remained willing to stay and officially surrender the garrison. Numerous others escaped the trap, including Nathan Bedford Forrest, who with his entire command rode through the icy waters of a backwater of the Cumberland, and Captain Jack Davis, of Company E, 7th Texas, who got away on a flatboat.[17]

In the early morning hours of February 16, Buckner surrendered Fort Donelson and its remaining fifteen thousand-man garrison. In the surrender 379 members of the 7th Texas were captured, including Colonel Gregg and Major Granbury. Captain Van Zandt, Lieutenant Colonel Clough's brother-in-law, realized that the Federals would ship them north to prison camps, and he wanted to see to a proper burial for Clough. Major Granbury, whose wife, Fannie, remained at Clarksville, also wanted to see to her proper disposition before he departed. Therefore Van Zandt and Granbury went together to seek out help and found Colonel John A. Rawlins of Grant's staff, who advised them to petition Grant regarding their circumstances. The two Texans did so and Grant allowed Clough's body, accompanied by Granbury, to go to Clarksville under a special guard. Granbury saw to his wife, delivered Clough's body to friends in Clarksville, who interred him, and returned to the regiment at Fort Donelson.[18]

Grant shipped the fifteen thousand prisoners from Fort Donelson north to prisoner-of-war camps, primarily Camp Douglas in Chicago. Illinois officials had originally established Camp Douglas, a sixty-acre tract of land in the middle of Chicago, for the training of Illinois state militia troops in 1861. The camp received its name because the land originally belonged to Senator Stephen A. Douglas, the "Little Giant," who had taken such a prominent role in the politics that led up to the Civil War. The eastern edge of the camp ran along Cottage Grove, and its southern side bordered on the University of Chicago. With the surrender of Fort Donelson, the U.S. government needed a place to house the prisoners and appropriated Camp Douglas. The first of the prisoners arrived in Chicago in the third week of February 1862 to begin what would become a very long and for many a very lethal winter.[19]

The facilities at Camp Douglas were abysmal to say the least. Long rows of shacks housed the thousands of prisoners. Shelter proved scarce, and sanitary conditions remained terrible throughout the winter. The guards did not allow the prisoners to pass beyond a marked line around the edge of the stockade. The men called this the dead line, because the guards would shoot any man who crossed it. The massive number of prisoners from Donelson created overcrowded conditions that added to the misery.

After only a few days, Federal officials separated the officers of the 7th Texas from the enlisted men and shipped the former to Camp Chase, Ohio, west of Columbus. They arrived at Camp Chase on February 27, 1862, and remained there for about six weeks. Again at Camp Chase the conditions proved overcrowded. Ohio governor David Tod issued an executive order liberating the African American servants the Texan officers had brought with them from home.[20]

Federal authorities forwarded the field-grade officers from Fort Donelson on to Fort Warren in Boston Harbor. Colonel Gregg and Major Granbury found themselves among this number. John Gregg's wife, Mary, arranged transportation home after the surrender of Donelson, but Hiram Granbury's wife, Fannie, opted to accompany her husband to Boston. Gregg, Granbury, and Fannie boarded the train in Chicago for their journey to Massachusetts. At noon on March 4 the prisoners departed for Boston. That night they passed through Cleveland and reached Buffalo, New York, early the next morning. In New York the snow lay thick on the ground, presenting a dreary appearance for the Confederates. "We found crowds of Yankee people full of their kind of curiosity, at every town," Gregg wrote. "They gave us the hard and half-cooked meat and rye-o-coffee, which the government deals out to rebels, in their care. Hard words were to be heard at all our receptions; but there were many everywhere, who seemed disposed to argue 'the question' with us, and talked kindly enough."[21]

The officers reached Albany late in the afternoon and crossed the Hudson on the ice. Colonel Randall McGavock, one of the officers traveling with the party, remembered that "Maj. Granberry [sic] of Texas had his wife with him, a small and delicate woman, but she waded through the shock on the ice like a heroine, and seemed determined to cling to the fortunes of her husband." The officers reached Boston about 2 A.M. on March 6 and waited for six hours before being escorted to Boston Harbor. At the wharf the guards loaded them into the *Charles Fremont* and took them out to Fort Warren, on an island in the middle of the harbor. At the dock Hiram Granbury and his wife parted when the guards would not allow her to accompany him to the fort. Gregg and Granbury found Fort Warren a pentagonal-shaped brick edifice on George's Island, a twenty-eight-acre spit of land near the entrance to the harbor. The guards placed General Lloyd Tilghman, Colonel Adolphus Heiman, Gregg, and Lieutenant Colonel James Jackson in the same room. They furnished the quarters at Fort Warren with iron cots with mattresses and blankets. An anthracite fire in the stove kept them very warm. Sickness also affected the officers at Fort Warren, though in a different way. On April 22, Gregg wrote Captain Moody that Granbury had become badly afflicted with jaundice and "was moving about quite badly," but that he was getting better "I think." Due to a cold he had contracted, Gregg himself suffered from an attack of bilious fever.[22]

On April 9, 1862, the authorities had separated out a group of one hundred officers, including Captain Van Zandt, and taken them to Johnson's Island in Lake Erie near Sandusky, Ohio. The conditions at Johnson's Island, a prison almost exclusively reserved for officers, proved not nearly as severe as those at Camp Douglas or Chase. They quartered the officers ten to a room and the Rebels spent most of their time outdoors. Many of the prisoners had small knives and spent their time carving trinkets out of small pieces of bone and rubber buttons. The guards also allowed them to swim occasionally in Lake Erie.[23] It indeed seemed an idyllic life compared to the hell endured by the enlisted men at Camp Douglas.

The Federals placed Granbury in a room at Fort Warren with Dr. Charles MacGill, a physician from Hagerstown, Maryland, imprisoned for remaining a Southern sympathizer. MacGill befriended Granbury and offered to let Fannie stay at his home in Hagerstown until she could proceed farther south. Granbury accepted and Fannie traveled to Maryland. While at Fort Warren, Granbury wrote to Captain William L. Moody in late June that only a want of postage stamps and envelopes had prevented him from writing sooner. "We spend an hour of every day (Sundays excepted) playing football and pitching quoit. These are our principal outdoor activities. Chess, cards and whiskey occasionally vary the monotony of our indoor life, and upon the whole we get along as well as would be expected under the circumstances." Referring to Moody's imprisonment on Johnson's Island near Sandusky, Ohio, Granbury concluded his letter, "Give my warmest affections to all of Texas that 'summers it' at Sandusky." Though in prison, Granbury clearly had not lost his biting sense of humor.[24]

Conditions at Camp Douglas only worsened as the winter dragged on. The cold northern winds took a heavy toll on the health of the men in the

7th Texas. Sixty-two enlisted men of the regiment perished from illness in the harsh Illinois winter, while a handful more escaped from prison never to rejoin the regiment.[25] Finally in July 1862 Federal authorities organized a prisoner exchange, known as the Dix-Hill Cartel, for the officers at Johnson's Island and many of the enlisted men at Camp Douglas.

In the West the terms of the Dix-Hill Cartel called for an exchange of the Confederate prisoners at Vicksburg, Mississippi. They put both the officers at Johnson's Island and the enlisted men at Camp Douglas aboard trains and transported them to Cairo, Illinois. At Cairo guards placed them aboard boats bound for Vicksburg. At Vicksburg from September 12 to 14, 1862, approximately 1,300 officers and 2,600 enlisted men received exchanges.[26] The Federals exchanged all the members of the 7th Texas captured at Fort Donelson, and the Confederates began to reform their regiment at Port Hudson, Louisiana.

The experiences of the 7th Texas at Fort Donelson indicated early devotion to the Confederacy among the Texan infantry. Despite overwhelming odds, they stayed with their regiment and accepted capture and imprisonment. Disease took its toll, though, decimating the regiment. The Fort Donelson fiasco also highlighted a constant theme: stellar regimental leadership, which buoyed the spirits of the Texans in even the most trying of circumstances. The casualties suffered at Donelson and in prison served to bind the Texans closer together and strengthened their resolve. These facts support both Gary Gallagher's *The Confederate War* and Larry Daniels's *Soldiering in the Army of Tennessee* in delineating the role that Confederate nationalism and shared suffering played in forming devoted, diehard Confederates. This particular chemistry would later serve the Confederate cause well when the 7th Texas became the core of Granbury's Brigade.

CHAPTER THREE

SOJOURN IN ARKANSAS

As the 7th Texas dealt with capture and prison life, the other Texas regiments that would become part of Granbury's Brigade found themselves caught up in the mad scramble to get troops to the front. As a result, all of these regiments ended up in Arkansas, where they would get their first taste of war. Even in the earliest stages of the war, the Texas regiments stationed in Arkansas experienced trying circumstances, and for the cavalry regiments these experiences completely changed the nature of their service to the Confederacy. When the Confederate officials decided to dismount the cavalry regiments in Arkansas in 1862, it did not erase their loyalty to the Confederacy or their desire to defend the Southern way of life, it merely changed *how* and *where* they would fight. Mark Weitz in *More Damning Than Slaughter* posits that desertion destroyed any chances the Confederacy had for military victory, and massive desertions certainly occurred in the ranks of the dismounted Texas cavalry regiments, but Weitz ignores the fact that desertion was not a zero-sum game. Even though these Texans deserted their original regiments, most of them returned home and joined regiments in the Trans-Mississippi Department or in Texas itself. As Andrew Lang points out in "Victory Is Our Only Road to Peace," Confederate nationalism remained extraordinarily strong on the Texas home front in 1862, ensuring that these deserters could not stay out of the Confederate service for long without risking humiliation and ridicule. Losing their horses dealt a severe psychological blow to the Texan cavalrymen in Arkansas, and they returned across the Mississippi and back to Texas in droves in 1862, but the fact that so many others stayed with their original units in spite of the desertions and the deaths of others from disease so early in the war remains a mute testament to their devotion to the Confederacy.[1]

The fall of Forts Henry and Donelson greatly changed the complexion of the war in the West. The Confederate heartland now lay open all the way into northern Alabama, where the Tennessee River remained undefended. Albert Sidney Johnston abandoned Nashville after Donelson and retreated southward to Corinth, Mississippi, where he hoped to marshal enough forces for a counterstroke against Grant. In the meantime Richmond scrambled to find more troops to bolster the front lines.

On February 24, Secretary of War Judah Benjamin wired Brigadier General Hebert at Galveston to impress upon him the dire nature of the situation. Davis and Benjamin considered an imminent invasion of the Texas coast improbable, and therefore ordered Hebert to forward all units not needed for coastal defense to Arkansas. Benjamin ordered the Texas regiments to Little Rock, to report to Major General Earl Van Dorn, commander of Confederate forces in Arkansas. The "men," concluded Benjamin, "are to be pushed forward with all possible rapidity to Little Rock by such route as you deem best."[2]

Hebert instructed both the 6th Texas and 10th Texas to proceed to Arkansas. In early March he instructed Colonel Garland to move his regiment as soon as it reached the full complement of companies. By May 22 Garland had his regiment ready to move, and the companies of the 6th Texas formed into marching columns to head off to war. Departing Victoria, the regiment passed through Hallettsville and reached Eagle Lake after eight days of marching. At Eagle Lake Garland left his supply wagons behind and boarded his infantrymen on trains headed to Richmond and Houston.[3]

A disturbing incident involving larceny engaged the attention of the regiment during a stop at Navasota. One of the members of Company I stole a revolver belonging to his captain, C. P. Nanuheim. The thief attempted to sell the revolver the same day he stole it and authorities apprehended him. Garland assembled a court-martial, which tried and convicted the man. The regiment then drummed him out of the service, and two African American men paraded him through the streets with his head half-shaved riding a fence rail.[4]

Garland's men continued on through East Texas before they finally crossed into Arkansas and received their regimental colors. The Texans remained three days at Navasota before marching toward Tyler via Rusk. Garland kept his men at Tyler for a week before they resumed their march. In mid-July the regiment had crossed the Red River at Texarkana and moved into Arkansas. By that time the regimental banner had caught up with them. A Mrs. Owens from Victoria had sewn the flag of red merino with a white silk fringe. In the center of the red field was a twenty-eight-by thirty-six-inch blue shield with twelve white silk stars in a circle around a large white star representing Texas. She had stitched the letters "Sixth Texas Infantry Regiment" in white on the red flag.[5]

The piney woods of East Texas and southern Arkansas offered inhospitable terrain to the soldiers of the 6th Texas. "I like the people much better than I do the country," wrote Captain William Phillips of Company A. "The latter is too broken and sandy, and not enough of prairie." Private Franz Coller of Company H added, "Day after day we march in the woods and God only knows if we will ever come out again. I have never seen such a poor region as we see out here in east Texas and Arkansas." Private Benjamin Robertson came away unimpressed with either the terrain or the people of Arkansas. "A person cannot form any idea until they travel through the piney wood and rural district [of Arkansas] as I have seen one thousand women I think and I have not seen one that would wear less than a number eight pair of shoes."[6]

Garland's men moved through Washington and Antwine before reaching Rockport. There an outbreak of measles incapacitated many in the regiment before Garland elected to press on to Camp Holmes, ten miles from Pine Bluff. They stopped at Camp Holmes for several weeks to allow those left at Rockport to rejoin the regiment.[7] Thus by the middle of summer the men of the 6th Texas found themselves sweltering in the unappealing countryside of central Arkansas.

On March 23, Allison Nelson received orders from Hebert to move the 10th Texas to Little Rock. Nelson did not have his regiment ready to move until April 17. On that day the Texas infantrymen fell into line and began their march north. For the next two days the regiment marched first through Booneville and then Wheelock before making camp five miles beyond. By Wednesday, April 23, Nelson had reached Tehuacana, where he received orders to march through Alexandria, Louisiana, rather than

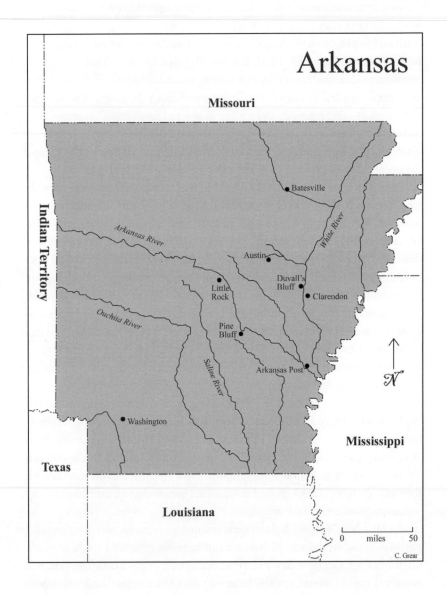

through Dallas. The next day a great many ladies came out to visit the Texans' camp and encourage the soldiers on their way. By May 7 the regiment had passed through Rusk, and Nelson received orders again to change his route of march to go through Shreveport. On May 12 they passed through Elysian Fields and crossed the Sabine River into Louisiana the next day. On the fourteenth they reached Shreveport and laid up ten days' provisions before continuing due north for the Arkansas line. Three days later the regiment crossed into Arkansas, and by June 6 it had reached Camp Texas and camped near a spring atop a ridge. On June 8 Nelson held an inspection of the regiment's equipment to see how it had passed the march, and the next day the Texans resumed the manual of drill. While here rumors circulated through the camp that the Federals had taken Memphis. Meanwhile, the Texans continued to anxiously await news from Corinth, Mississippi, where Henry W. Halleck and his Union army bore down on the town.[8]

Meanwhile, Union general Samuel Curtis initiated a Federal threat closer to home. With his offensive stalled in northwest Arkansas, Curtis called on Secretary of War Edwin Stanton to engage the navy in his aid. Stanton ordered several gunboats to enter and move up the White River in order to position themselves to assist and resupply Curtis.[9]

Soon after reaching Camp Texas, Colonel Nelson received orders to move his regiment north to Devall's Bluff, on the White River, to counter the Federal threat. On June 11 the regiment again took up the march and passed through Little Rock the next day. On June 17 the Texans reached Devall's Bluff and made camp. The following night Nelson received orders to have his men ready the next morning to intercept the Union gunboats. The enemy failed to appear the next day and Nelson ordered his men to sleep on their arms. Finally, on the twentieth, the Federals made their appearance and the Texans gave them a warm reception, killing several of the sailors and pilots. The gunboats soon turned around and headed back upriver. This skirmish served as an introduction to combat for the men of the 10th Texas. For the last ten days of June the Texans remained in camp amid swirling rumors of Union threats that never materialized.

Even though the 10th Texas had barely left home and had seen little combat, the regiment already showed signs of attrition. In a regimental muster dated June 30 it could count only 802 effectives—with the size of the companies varying widely, from sixty present in Company K to 104 in Company E. Thirty members of the regiment had died from disease in

Arkansas, while another 150 had received discharges due to illness and disability, or had simply deserted.[10] Even in the infantry regiments, the temptation to fight closer home often became too great, even early in the war.

In early July an outbreak of measles gripped the 10th Texas and many of the men became sick and died. From the beginning of July to the beginning of September 1862 regimental muster rolls indicate that 104 members of the regiment died of disease, a stiff toll for a regiment already reduced to 80 percent of its original strength. Railroad cars removed most of the sick to Little Rock to convalesce and recover—or perish—in the stifling Arkansas summer.[11]

In the third week of July, Colonel Allison Nelson took command of his own brigade and battled a mutiny among his men. The unit Nelson took command of contained his 10th Texas, plus the now dismounted 15th, 17th, and 18th Texas Cavalry regiments. Confederate authorities expected the lone infantry regiment to serve as an example to the cavalry, but at least in the beginning the Texan foot soldiers did a poor job. That same week a mutiny of sorts broke out among the Texans. On July 17 and 18 seven entire companies of the regiment threatened to mutiny and desert, complaining of hard discipline and inactivity. Lieutenant Colonel Roger Q. Mills made them a speech and most of the men returned to duty, but anywhere from forty to fifty held out to the last. Confederate authorities arrested these holdouts and took them to Little Rock, where Major General Thomas Hindman, newly appointed commander of Confederate troops in Arkansas, threatened to have every tenth man shot if they did not return to duty. This seemed to work, and the Texans returned to their commands the next day. Private Isaiah Harlan of Company G attributed the mutiny to the fact that they remained camped among "Arkansas troops, most of whom are said to be dissatisfied." Whatever the motive, the infantrymen returned to duty and averted a showdown.[12]

Despite the quelling of his first mutiny, desertion became more and more of a problem. On August 1 Nelson ordered the execution of four soldiers convicted of repeated desertion. The execution served as a stark awakening to the members of the 10th Texas. Ten days later Nelson had another five men executed. A week later Nelson's Brigade relocated to a camp near Austin, Arkansas, known as Camp Hope. Here at Camp Hope the 10th Texas whiled away the rest of the summer and early fall.[13] This early dissatisfaction makes it abundantly clear that a localized perspective almost entirely dictated whether or not a soldier chose to desert his original regiment.

Back in Texas, Colonel Middleton Johnson received orders on April 10 to move his brigade from Clarksville to Little Rock. By the third week in April the six cavalry regiments had reached Pine Bluff, Arkansas, after a rain-soaked march.

When they reached Pine Bluff the sun finally reemerged, drying the cavalrymen along with their horses and equipment. One of the things the sun also dried proved to be the leather scabbards containing the large Bowie knives they had brought from home. The Texans soon decided they could live without the knives and tossed them into the Arkansas River. After a few more days in camp the Texans moved on to Little Rock, where they went into camp on the grounds of St. John's College. Measles also broke out in the camp of Johnson's Brigade, incapacitating and killing many of the Texans.

While they were at Little Rock the Confederate Conscription Act of April 16, 1862, necessitated reorganization of the regiments. The law discharged all soldiers over thirty-five and under eighteen years of age, or those who owned twenty or more slaves. It also required the election of new officers. Approximately fifty members of the 15th Texas received discharges in May, most in compliance with the new law. Additionally, around thirty officers lost their bids for reelection to their previous positions. The story in the 17th Texas proved essentially the same; in the reorganization 137 men received discharges and half a dozen officers lost reelection. The 18th Texas suffered similar attrition during this time, losing fifty men and a dozen officers.[14]

Sickness also overtook the Texan horsemen. On May 13 Lieutenant Flavius W. Perry of the 17th Texas wrote his father, "We are getting along rather badly. Nearly half our company has the measles. We leave from four to six every day." The horses also suffered, as Perry related. "This is one of the poorest countries I ever saw. . . . Forage for our horses is very scarce and has been since we got in this state."[15]

The Texans remained at Little Rock until the middle of June, when Hindman placed Brigadier General Thomas Rust in command of the six cavalry regiments. Rust immediately set his new brigade in motion toward Batesville, Arkansas, to counter the thrust of Curtis's Federals, but after some fruitless maneuvers Rust returned with his brigade to Little Rock, leaving behind about 150 members of the 15th Texas to keep an eye on Federal movements. Among this detachment, newly elected Lieutenant Robert Collins, of Company B, noted that he and his comrades "put in all the bird-singing month of June in rollicking around over them high mountains, living high and making love to them pretty, honest Arkansaw girls."[16]

On July 8 the 15th Texas first tasted combat. A portion of the 5th Kansas Cavalry launched a foray south toward Batesville, and Colonel George Sweet decided to move out and capture the two hundred Yankees. The Texans engaged the Kansans, but soon fled the field, taking with them their first taste of defeat. In this skirmish they lost seven killed and seven wounded, including Captain Thomas Johnson, shot through the head and instantly killed.[17]

A few weeks later Hindman reorganized his forces. He folded the 15th, 17th, and 18th Texas Cavalry Regiments into a brigade with the 10th Texas Infantry under Colonel Nelson. His order also dismounted the Texas cavalry regiments. Protests long and loud accompanied this order, as the soldiers felt that since they had joined up as cavalrymen, they should serve out the war as such, an opinion apparently not shared by Hindman. Rather, the Texans became dismounted cavalrymen, destined to serve out the war essentially as infantry.

Mass desertions and resignations from the dismounted cavalry regiments followed this action. In the 15th Texas approximately eighty men deserted, while another dozen volunteered to take the horses back to Texas, never to return. Sweet discharged another fifty-six men and a half-dozen officers resigned their commissions. In all it appears that the 15th Texas lost 160 men due to the dismounting of the regiment. In the 17th Texas, 140 men deserted in July, with another sixty-two discharged the same month. Additionally, twenty-five members of the regiment died of disease in June and July. It appears that the 17th Texas lost close to 230 men during its reorganization and dismounting. In Colonel Nicholas Darnell's 18th Texas, a staggering 180 deserted shortly after the dismounting of the regiment. Another ten officers resigned their commissions, and Darnell lost a half dozen to sickness. Of the 3,697 men carried at one time or another on the muster rolls of these three regiments, 590 (16 percent) deserted or resigned rather than serve in dismounted cavalry regiments.[18]

Perhaps more than any other single factor, the dismounting of these cavalry regiments demoralized the Texans, and convinced them to serve the Confederacy somewhere other than Arkansas. Apart from the obvious disgrace of having to walk instead of ride, many of the horsemen brought their own mounts with them from home, and many of them shared strong emotional bonds with their animals, which now became the property of the Confederate government. The dismounting of these regiments drew a stark line between those who felt they could remain faithful to their original regiments and those who decided to go home instead. This desertion did not represent a lack of loyalty to the Confederacy, but rather a dissatisfaction with their own localized circumstances.

The Texans' frustration also spilled over into pranks played at the expense of their officers. Colonel George Sweet of the 15th Texas "had a hard time breaking five thousand wild Texans into the infantry harness," remembered Lieutenant Robert Collins. "Fact is, we were all mad because we had been dismounted, having had our hearts set on doing our soldiering on horseback, and the boys very unjustly charged all this misfortune and hard camp duty, drilling, strict guard duty, etc., to Col. Sweet." One night some members of the 18th Texas stole over to Sweet's headquarters and shaved off the mane and tail of his horse "Bay Bob." After that, according to Collins, whenever Sweet would ride into sight of the command, "the boys would commence hallooing 'Whoa, Bob,' at the top of their voices. This annoyed the colonel very much, as he was a proud, vain and very sensitive man."[19] This prank and other acts continued to occur as the Texans fought their new role as infantry.

While the disgruntled Texan cavalrymen of the 15th, 17th, and 18th Texas engaged in such behavior, Colonel George Carter received orders to march his three cavalry regiments north to Arkansas. Carter furloughed all of the men except thirty, whom he left behind to care for the wagons and supplies. He issued orders for the regiments to reassemble at Crockett in early May before proceeding to Arkansas. Apparently abandoning the idea of cavalrymen as lancers, the Texans left their long weapons behind. The regiments reassembled on the appointed day and proceeded northeast to Alto in Cherokee County, where they awaited Carter, who had stayed behind in Hempstead to take care of logistics. The men soon grew restless when Carter caught up with them but proved unable to provide their $50 enlistment bounty. Inactivity also began to bother the Texans, who had enlisted expecting to soon see combat.[20]

With no supplies or money to buy them, Carter's horsemen began to appropriate the needed items along the way, making a nuisance of themselves to the locals. On May 15 a resident of Alto wrote Confederate postmaster general John H. Reagan of the "notorious outrages . . . at this time being practiced in the way of plundering . . . from good citizens by an armed party of the citizens of Texas, professing to be Confederate soldiers and under the command of one Colonel Carter." The Texans remained in each neighborhood "just long enough to ravage the corn cribs and smokehouses of the defenseless surrounding country." According to this citizen the Texans had become the "hourly dread" of the locals. From Alto, Texas, Carter's Brigade marched to Rusk and then Mount Vernon. At this latter place measles broke out among the Texans, greatly adding to the sick rolls and causing several deaths.

Soon after this, Carter returned to Hempstead, leaving the brigade to dissolve in his absence. Carter had dispatched Colonel Wilkes to Richmond to requisition the enlistment bounties for the brigade. But upon arriving in Richmond, Wilkes informed the Confederate authorities that there existed no such entity as Carter's Cavalry Brigade. Wilkes then appropriated the brigade's money for his own regiment, the 24th Texas, and returned with orders stating that his and Colonel Gillespie's 25th Texas now comprised independent commands from Carter's 21st Texas. Despite these orders, for the moment the three regiments remained together in Carter's absence.[21]

Meanwhile the bad behavior continued. On June 24 a party of cavalrymen led by Captain William A. Taylor of the 24th Texas arrived in Alexandria, Louisiana, from Shreveport under the pretext of gathering supplies for the Confederate army. Governor Thomas O. Moore of Louisiana wrote Secretary of War Randolph of the outrages committed by Taylor and his men in ransacking the houses of private citizens and stealing property. Moore asked Randolph to remove both Taylor and his commander, Wilkes, and warned that if they returned he would have them shot. Randolph forwarded these complaints to Hebert, who promptly issued General Order No. 11, ordering the arrest and court-martial of any and all soldiers engaged in the stealing of private property. Hebert forwarded this order to Randolph and informed him of the impossibility of controlling the independent commands raised with orders directly from Richmond bound for posts outside the Department of Texas.[22] Despite these "outrages," none of the department commanders ever charged any of the Texan officers.

Largely because of a lack of forage for their horses, and a lack of pay, the Texans became increasingly angry with their officers. Thomas Elliott of the 24th Texas wrote to his wife on July 3, 1862, that "Pat Swearingen [Major Patrick Swearingen of the 24th Texas] went to Little Rock to try and secure arms and uniforms and get the bounty for the men. . . . Capt. Fly says they had no use for us up there. If we came we would be put on half rations for horse and men. He also states there is no arms and money in the place, so we will get no bounty or pay and Wilks [Colonel Wilkes] & Carter have so lied to the men that they have lost all confidence in them and it would not surprise me to hear that some one had shot them. Some of the western boys would just as soon do it."[23]

The issue of forage for the horses became critical, and led to the ultimate disgrace for the cavalrymen. General Theophilus Holmes issued instructions that reached the three Texas cavalry regiments at Pine Bluff, Arkansas, ordering that they dismount. Holmes had copies of the order posted at every street corner, instructing every officer to dismount his men and turn the horses over to the local quartermaster. In addition to the ignominy of dismounting, the Texans had provided their own mounts, making their horses private property that the Confederate government now wished to confiscate. According to one Texan, this produced "some large swearing, and small swearing, and any other kind you can think of." In fact, the dismounting so displeased the twenty members of the Alabama-Coushatta Nation that had joined the 24th Texas that Wilkes sent them back to Texas to await further orders. They never rejoined the regiment. Wilkes and Gillespie complied in dismounting the 24th and 25th, but Lieutenant Colonel DeWitt Giddings, commanding the 21st Texas, refused to do so, instead requesting that Colonel William H. Parsons incorporate Carter's Regiment into his brigade. Holmes relented, allowing the 21st Texas to remain mounted and join Parsons. Meanwhile, Wilkes and Gillespie began drilling their dismounted cavalrymen as infantry.[24] Soon orders arrived for the 24th and 25th Texas Dismounted Cavalry to join the 6th Texas Infantry at Camp Holmes, ten miles from Pine Bluff. Here the three regiments formed a brigade under Colonel Garland.

A surprisingly small number of cavalrymen from Wilkes's and Gillespie's regiments deserted after being dismounted. In the 24th Texas forty-one soldiers died of disease in the summer of 1862, while the Confederate Conscription Act forced the discharge of several dozen more, but only a handful appear to have deserted from Wilkes's Regiment in July or after. In Gillespie's 25th Texas anywhere from fifty to seventy-five men deserted shortly after dismounting, while a handful of officers resigned their commissions around this time. In addition, less than half a dozen cavalrymen died of disease. In all, it appears that the two regiments lost in the neighborhood of only 150 men due to the Confederate Conscription Act, dismounting, and disease.[25] Despite the grumblings of some of the men, the dismounting of these regiments apparently went much better because the units enjoyed officers who knew how to keep the morale of their men higher than in the other regiments. The commanders of the 24th Texas and 25th Texas had occupied themselves as Methodist ministers before the war, and it is very probable that a more compassionate approach, and preaching a religious devotion to the Confederacy, helped keep more of these men with their original regiments.

By July 1862 seven of the eight regiments that later comprised Granbury's Brigade had made their way to Arkansas and into two brigades under Allison Nelson and Robert Garland. The five regiments that had started out as cavalry now found themselves on foot as dismounted cavalry, while the infantry regiment in each brigade served as an example in the drill and manual of arms. Garland and the 6th, 24th, and 25th Texas settled down at Camp Holmes to spend the rest of the summer in boredom, while to the south Nelson and the 10th, 15th, 17th, and 18th Texas did the same at Camp Hope.

In early September General Holmes received intelligence that Union forces intended to attack Arkansas Post, a fortification on the Arkansas River upstream from the Mississippi. Accordingly, he dispatched Garland's Brigade to the Post. The 6th and 24th Texas began marching down the Arkansas River, with the 25th Texas a day's march behind. On September 18 the leading elements reached the Jourdan Plantation, eighteen miles above the Post, and the next day they reached Arkansas Post.[26]

A few weeks later Nelson's Brigade at Camp Hope experienced the first of their trying ordeals during the war. On the morning of October 1, Holmes dispatched Nelson's men north toward Clarendon on the White River to counter a perceived threat by Curtis, whom Holmes intended to confront. At midnight it began to rain, drenching the infantry and dismounted cavalry, who struggled through the mud for three days before reaching Clarendon on October 4. Here the sun finally reappeared—just in time for the Texans to turn around and head back to Camp Hope. The weather on the march back to camp proved even worse. Icy sleet and hail rained down on the hapless soldiers for days at a time. Mules and men alike dropped by the roadside from exhaustion, and their comrades left them there out of necessity. Finally, on October 11, the three regiments arrived back at Camp Hope.[27]

Even greater tragedy awaited them in the piney woods near Austin. Nelson, who had been promoted to brigadier general to date from September 12, fell ill with fever on September 27. The day after Nelson became sick, Holmes placed him in command of a division consisting of his own and Flournoy's Brigade, but it became a moot point. On October 7 Nelson died of fever at Camp Hope and received a burial in Little Rock. Four days later his 10th Texas and the other dismounted cavalry units arrived back in camp to find their leader dead. Lieutenant Colonel Mills took permanent charge of the 10th Texas and the men renamed their encampment Camp Nelson in honor of their fallen commander.[28]

To replace Nelson as brigade commander, Holmes appointed his chief of artillery, Colonel James Deshler. At twenty-nine years old, Deshler was a West Point graduate who had fought against Indians before the war. In 1861 he had found himself stationed at Fort Wise, Colorado, and left to join the Confederacy without ever officially resigning his commission. Appointed a captain of artillery, Deshler served as the adjutant to General Henry Jackson's brigade in the Cheat Mountain campaign. In a skirmish on December 13, 1861, a Union bullet pierced Deshler through both thighs, temporarily putting him out of action. He received an appointment as colonel of artillery and Confederate authorities assigned him to the staff of General Holmes in North Carolina. He served as Holmes's chief of artillery in the Seven Days campaign and accompanied his commander to the Trans-Mississippi Department. As a professional soldier, Deshler did not at first have the affection of the Texans under his command, but at length they reached an understanding and even formed a strong bond of friendship with the young, charismatic colonel.[29]

Deshler and his command remained at Camp Nelson until mid-November. At that time Holmes ordered him to take his brigade to Arkansas Post to reinforce Garland's Brigade and two regiments of Arkansas infantry already there. Deshler's men broke camp on November 21 and reached Little Rock the next day. From the capital they boarded steamers to head downriver to the Post. Each night the soldiers disembarked and camped on the riverbank, eventually reaching their destination on November 28.[30] Like Garland's men, they had no idea what awaited them.

The sojourn in Arkansas revealed a great deal about the regiments that would become Granbury's Brigade. Despite the fact that the 15th, 17th, and 18th Texas Cavalry Regiments suffered mass desertions due to dismounting, it appears that this desertion could be mitigated when compassionate officers devoted to the Confederacy replaced vain martinets like Colonel Sweet. This confirms the finding of Gary Gallagher in *The Confederate War*, that line officers had a tremendous role in influencing the men under their command. These experiences in Arkansas also helped winnow the ranks down to a hard core of men who remained devoted to their original regiments, officers, and above all the Confederacy. These experiences would later greatly influence the fighting prowess and devotion of Granbury's Brigade.

CHAPTER FOUR

ARKANSAS POST

As Union forces concentrated along the Mississippi River to capture that waterway, the Texans in Arkansas were caught up in this campaign and suffered a similar fate to that of the 7th Texas with their capture at Arkansas Post in January 1863. Arkansas Post would provide a crucial turning point in shaping the regiments that became Granbury's Brigade. The capture of the garrison and accompanying desertion reinforced the trends already set in motion in Arkansas. The Arkansas Post episode winnowed the ranks, taking one thousand Texans out of the rolls of the regiments that would later become Granbury's Brigade when these men fled to avoid capture at the surrender. Despite the fact that they deserted their original regiments, they did not desert the Confederate cause. As Charles Grear's study "Texans to the Front" suggests, these men deserted and remained near Texas, fighting closer to home. Grear asserts that the most desertion among Texas regiments occurred after the fall of Vicksburg, when the psychological barrier of the Mississippi River cut Texans off from their home. I would argue that in the particular case of Granbury's Brigade, most of the men who would have otherwise deserted later in 1863, 1864, and 1865 did so instead at the surrender of the Arkansas Post. It is worthy to note that the thousand men or so who made their escape at Arkansas Post gathered at Elysian Fields, Texas, later in 1863 and formed the 17th Texas Dismounted (Consolidated) Regiment. This regiment then fought hard in the trans-Mississippi theater, losing many of their men at the battles of Mansfield and Pleasant Hill in April 1864. Ultimately, the winnowing of the ranks at Arkansas Post produced among the Texans a shared experience of hardship, and a common suffering that made them fight harder to prove themselves later in the war.[1]

The fall of Forts Henry and Donelson opened the Mississippi, Tennessee, and Cumberland rivers to Federal incursion. In early March, Union forces overran New Madrid and Island No. 10, leaving the Father of Waters vulnerable all the way to Memphis. After the fall of New Orleans in April and Memphis in June, only two Confederate strongholds remained on the Mississippi: Vicksburg and Port Hudson. In late 1862, when General U. S. Grant first moved against Vicksburg, the Confederate authorities in Arkansas fortified the White and Arkansas rivers to establish a base along Grant's line of communications and defend the interior of Arkansas.

On September 28, Holmes dispatched Colonel John Dunnington, lately commander of the Confederate ram *Pontchartrain,* to command the Arkansas River defenses. Holmes provided Dunnington with two engineers and a company of sappers and miners to assist in constructing fortifications along the river. He also dispatched the 19th Arkansas Infantry under Colonel Charles Dawson and the 24th Arkansas Infantry Regiment under Lieutenant Colonel William A. Crawford. Simultaneously Holmes ordered Garland's Brigade to the defenses.[2]

On the Arkansas River, twenty-five miles from where it flows into the Mississippi, the engineers selected favorably high ground to construct an earthen fort. They situated it near the village of Arkansas Post, the seat of Arkansas County and the former territorial capital. Dunnington and his men began constructing the fort along the north side of the river at the head of a horseshoe bend that commanded the waterway for a mile in either direction. All through October and November the engineers and other troops assigned to the post continued construction on the fort, which eventually formed a square measuring one hundred yards on each side. The earthworks sloped up eighteen feet, fronting a ditch eight feet deep and twenty feet across.[3]

To equip the fort, Dunnington unloaded the armaments of his former ship, the *Pontchartrain.* He positioned the four heavy naval guns facing south along the river, including two 10-inch Columbiads. The fort, named Fort Hindman, also contained four ten-pounder Parrott rifles and four six-pounder smoothbore field guns mounted on artillery platforms. Three different layers of oak protected the artillery casemates at the corners of the fort, making Fort Hindman an imposing obstacle to any Federal ships proceeding up the Arkansas River. Dunnington and his men also constructed 720 yards of earthworks stretching in a westerly direction from the fort.[4]

By mid-November Colonel Deshler had arrived with his brigade, bringing the effective force at Arkansas Post to approximately six thousand men. To command the garrison, Holmes appointed Brigadier General Thomas J. Churchill. The garrison now consisted of Dunnington's Brigade (the 19th and 24th Arkansas Infantry and the river defenses), Garland's Brigade (the 6th, 24th, and 25th Texas), and finally Deshler's Brigade (the 10th, 15th, 17th, and 18th Texas Regiments).

The Federal authorities at Helena soon took notice of Confederate activity to the south at Arkansas Post. Brigadier General Alvin Hovey sent a memorandum to Department of Missouri commander Samuel R. Curtis on November 3 notifying him of the Confederate threat. Curtis declined to authorize an expedition, but his orders did not reach Hovey before he launched an excursion. On November 16 Hovey loaded his six thousand infantry and two thousand cavalry onto thirteen transports and headed for Arkansas Post. The transports had difficulty entering the mouth of the White River due to the low water level. The expedition eventually made it into the river and headed northwest toward the cut between the White and Arkansas rivers, which at that time was the only way to enter the Arkansas from the Mississippi. Farther up the river Hovey encountered an unmapped sandbar that allowed only thirty inches of clearance. He began preparing for an overland excursion against the Post, but before he could carry out this plan a courier arrived with Curtis's instructions not to proceed. Hovey then turned his soldiers and transports around and headed back to Helena. At least for the moment, Arkansas Post remained in Confederate hands.[5]

On December 20, 1862, Major General William T. Sherman set sail from Memphis bound for Vicksburg with four divisions of infantry. Nine days later he attacked the Vicksburg defenses at Chickasaw Bayou and was handily repulsed. On January 2, Sherman, now under the command of Major General John A. McClernand, reembarked his men on their transports and returned to the mouth of the Yazoo River. Meanwhile, on December 28 a part of Captain L. M. Nutt's Louisiana cavalry company from Arkansas Post sallied forth and captured the Union supply steamer *Blue Wing* as it made its way down the Mississippi from Memphis to Milliken's Bend. The

Confederates then sent the captured ship up the Arkansas River toward Little Rock. On January 2, Sherman met with McClernand and discussed the capture of the *Blue Wing*. They agreed that the Confederate garrison at Arkansas Post could not be left in the rear astride their line of communications. After meeting with Admiral David Dixon Porter two days later, McClernand set out with his four divisions to reduce and capture Arkansas Post. Porter dispatched the ironclads *Dekalb, Louisville,* and *Cincinnati* to accompany the expedition, which set sail from Milliken's Bend on January 5.[6]

On the morning of January 9, Churchill's pickets informed him that McClernand's Federals and three ironclads had just reached the cut between the Arkansas and White rivers. At this point Churchill had roughly twenty-eight hundred men fit for duty out of the six thousand present at the Post. Anticipating the Federal movements, Churchill placed his troops in a line of breastworks a mile and a quarter below the fort. He formed Deshler's Brigade on the right, with Dunnington's 19th and 24th Arkansas occupying the left. He dispatched three cavalry companies under Captains Denson, Nutt, and Richardson to watch the Federal movements and placed Garland's Brigade in reserve. Churchill also took five companies from the 6th and 24th Texas and placed them in front of the works as skirmishers under Lieutenant Colonel Phillip Swearingen of the 24th Texas and Major A. H. Phillips of the 6th Texas. Late in the afternoon the Union infantrymen disembarked several miles below Fort Hindman.[7]

At 9 A.M. on January 10 the Union gunboats advanced up the Arkansas River and opened fire on the fort. Churchill expected the heavy guns in the fort to return fire, but because of a defect in the powder they proved barely able to throw a shell beyond their own trenches, much less hit the Union fleet. Meanwhile, McClernand sent General Frederick Steele's division around the Confederate flank to force them out of their entrenchments. Around 2 P.M. Churchill discovered the maneuver and decided to pull his infantry back to the line of entrenchments directly adjacent to Fort Hindman.

As the Federals maneuvered, preparing to assault, Churchill and his brigade commanders made effective use of their time throughout the rest of the day. Churchill placed Dunnington's Brigade inside the fort itself, Garland's Brigade in the center of the entrenchments running inland from the fort, and Deshler's Brigade on the left, where the entrenchments stopped near the edge of a swamp. Garland placed the 6th Texas closest to the fort, with the 24th and 25th Texas to its left. Deshler placed the 18th Texas on

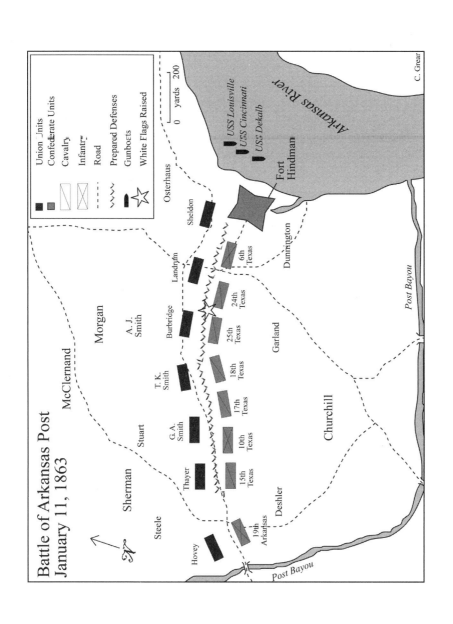

Battle of Arkansas Post
January 11, 1863

Legend:
- Union Units
- Confederate Units
- Cavalry
- Infantry
- Road
- Prepared Defenses
- Gunboats
- White Flags Raised

0   yards   200

McClernand

Sherman

Steele

Stuart

Thayer

G. A. Smith

T. K. Smith

Morgan

A. J. Smith

Burbridge

Landrum

Sheldon

Osterhaus

Hovey

19th Arkansas

15th Texas

10th Texas

17th Texas

18th Texas

25th Texas

24th Texas

6th Texas

Deshler

Churchill

Garland

Dunnington

Fort Hindman

USS Louisville
USS Cincinnati
USS Dekalb

Arkansas River

Post Bayou

Post Bayou

C. Grear

his right, followed by the 17th and the 10th, with the 15th Texas anchoring the left flank. Deshler realized that a two hundred-yard gap existed between his left and Post Bayou, an impassable swamp that protected the Confederate left. He informed Churchill of this weakness on the night of the tenth, but Churchill did nothing. Additionally, several log cabins that had served as the winter quarters of the 19th Arkansas sat directly in front of Deshler's position. Recognizing that these could be used by any attacking infantry for cover, Deshler ordered them razed and the logs used for breastworks. At dusk the Federal gunboats opened fire for a brief time on the Confederate entrenchments, effectively halting work for the night.[8]

That night Churchill tried desperately to augment his outnumbered garrison. He dismounted Denson's, Nutt's, and Richardson's cavalry companies for temporary infantry service in the trenches, and called on all available troops to rush to the Post. Later in the evening Captain Alfred Johnson's Texas cavalry company arrived along with part of the 24th Arkansas Infantry. Learning of the threat, General Holmes telegraphed Churchill that night to "hold out till help arrived or until all dead." As soon as he received this dire message, Churchill transmitted it to his brigade commanders.[9]

The next morning the Confederates continued to improve their position while McClernand prepared to attack. Meanwhile, Deshler still worried about his left flank. He had his regiments construct traverses at intervals and ordered Major V. P. Sanders, commanding the 15th Texas, to pull back his left flank. At daybreak McClernand ordered Hovey to take his Federal brigade forward on the right and ascertain the position of the Confederate left. Deshler observed these movements and sent eight companies, two from each of his regiments, to act as skirmishers in securing the gap between his left and Post Bayou. Seeing the skirmishers, Hovey halted his brigade and sent forward the 3rd and 17th Missouri to feel out the vulnerable flank. The skirmishers opened up and a fierce firefight developed. Churchill soon ordered Johnson's, Denson's, and Nutt's cavalry companies to cover the crossings over Post Bayou beyond Deshler's left flank. Sam Richardson's company remained dismounted in the front line with the rest of Deshler's Brigade. Churchill also dispatched the 19th Arkansas to take position between Deshler's left and the bayou. To cover the gap, the 6th Texas shifted its line to the right, covering the space between its right and Fort Hindman.

While Churchill shifted his men, McClernand massed his infantry beyond the open field in front of the breastworks and Admiral Porter prepared to renew his bombardment. At 1 P.M. the three gunboats opened fire. Soon, Porter's fleet had knocked out all of the fort's guns.

McClernand issued orders to his infantry commanders to launch their assault as soon as they heard the sound of Porter's bombardment. At 1 P.M. the blue coats swept forward. On the right the regiments of Hovey's Brigade advanced, only to be checked by fire from the Confederate snipers in Post Bayou on their flank and the 15th Texas in their front. To Hovey's left Brigadier General John Thayer's brigade advanced toward the center of Deshler's line. The regiments went forward in column until they approached the enemy breastworks, where Thayer formed them in line of battle with the 26th and 30th Iowa in front. The Iowans closed to within one hundred yards of the 10th Texas before the Texans opened fire, driving them back with heavy losses.[10]

As Hovey observed Thayer's men being repulsed, he ordered two of his regiments, the 3rd Missouri and 31st Iowa, to charge the 15th Texas. The Texans allowed the Missourians and Iowans to advance to within one hundred yards of their works before they opened fire. The Federals moved to the right, attempting to turn Deshler's flank. In response, Deshler moved up six reserve companies of the 19th Arkansas into the gap between the left flank of the 15th Texas and Post Bayou. The Arkansans took cover behind the trees and brush, repulsing Hovey's men.[11]

In the center, Sherman ordered the brigades of Giles Smith and Kilby Smith to attack. The two brigades moved forward until canister from Hart's Arkansas Battery checked their advance, forcing them to ground. Several Union companies worked their way forward until they could pick off the cannoneers. After a few minutes of sniping Hart's guns fell silent, and the Federals held themselves in position to storm the works held by the 17th and 18th Texas.[12]

Meanwhile, Deshler sent a message to Garland requesting reinforcements to shore up his left flank. The Federals had not made a serious demonstration on his front, so Garland ordered every other company in the 24th and 25th Texas and two companies from the 6th Texas to go to Deshler's aid. As the Texans worked their way to the left, they were exposed to a heavy fire, making it necessary to crawl on all fours until reaching their destinations.[13]

The advance of Thayer's Brigade on the Federal right served as the predetermined signal for the advance of Brigadier General Stephen Burbridge's brigade on the left. Burbridge's men moved forward until Confederate snipers arrested their advance. After emerging into a clearing in front of the works, Burbridge ordered his men to charge a small cluster of huts housing Confederate snipers. The 23rd Wisconsin swept forward, driving the snipers from their cover. The brigade attempted to advance farther, but Rebel fire checked it, causing heavy casualties and driving back Burbridge's men.[14]

By 4 P.M. the Confederate position had deteriorated. Porter's gunboats had silenced all of the guns in Fort Hindman and Dunnington called on Garland for reinforcements. Even though Garland had already detached over half his brigade to Deshler's aid, he now ordered Lieutenant Colonel Thomas Anderson of the 6th Texas to take two of his companies to the fort. For the next half-hour Porter's ships hammered the Confederate infantry with a saturation bombardment. At 4:30 Dunnington surrendered himself and thirty-six men of his Marine brigade to Porter. At this point the Federal infantry prepared themselves for one final assault.[15]

Just at that moment a weird and inexplicable incident took place. As he watched the approaching Federals, Colonel Garland heard the cry, "Raise the white flag, by order of General Churchill; pass the order up the line." Glancing to his left, Garland saw quite a few white flags displayed in the ranks of the 24th Texas, extending from the right company as far as he could see to the left.[16] No orders had reached Garland through official channels, and he hesitated about what to do next. Before he knew what was happening the Federal infantrymen to his front took advantage of the confusion and crossed into the breastworks to accept the surrender. Seeing the white flags, Sherman rode with his staff up to the Confederate works and demanded to know who commanded "at this point." Garland stepped up and Sherman instructed him to muster his brigade, have his men stack their rifles, and hang their belts on the stacked weapons.

Burbridge also spied the white flags and rode up to Fort Hindman, followed by McClernand. After initially being stopped by the sentries, Burbridge convinced them that their comrades had surrendered and instructed them to ground their arms. They complied and took him to Churchill's headquarters inside the fort. McClernand soon arrived and accepted the surrender of Arkansas Post from Churchill.

On the Confederate left Deshler remained in the dark and initially refused to surrender. Steele rode forward to confer with Deshler, and upon his approach the Confederate colonel demanded to know what the white flags meant. Steele informed him that it meant the Rebels had surrendered, pointing him to the U.S. flag now flying over the fort. Deshler still refused to believe it, stating that he had been instructed to hold out until the last man was dead. While the two continued to confer, Union infantrymen advanced until within pistol range of the breastworks. Seeing this, the twenty-nine-year-old West Pointer stated, "If you do not command 'Halt,' I will command 'Fire.'" Steele halted his men and continued to talk with Deshler for the next ten minutes. Finally he asked, "Will you surrender if I will bring General Churchill and he will command you to do so?" Deshler retorted, "I will obey Churchill's orders." When word reached Sherman of Deshler's refusal, he rushed with Churchill to the left to avoid a confrontation. When the two generals reached Deshler, they found the Confederates still crouching behind their breastworks. When Sherman inquired what this meant, Deshler said that "he had received no order to surrender." Churchill then interjected, "You see, sir, that we are in their power, and you may surrender." Upon hearing this, Deshler turned to his officers and commanded them to have their men stack arms.[17]

In Garland's Brigade where the white flags originated, the Confederates slowly got out of the ditch, staring around them as things became as quiet "as a meeting-house." Soon they spotted a long line of blue coats that approached within forty feet of the works. In one instance, a colonel approached Captain Samuel Foster of Company F, 24th Texas, and inquired, "'where are your men,'" to which Foster replied, "'Sir, from where you are, you can see them all.'" The Texans then began sticking their Bowie knives in the works and hiding their six-shooters in the dirt. The Federals ordered them to stack arms; some of them complied, while others simply threw their shotguns on the ground. Their captors then herded them down toward the river, where they posted guards in a semicircle.[18]

When the Federals reviewed the results of the battle, they found that they had captured 4,791 Confederates, along with numerous other spoils of war. When it became obvious that a surrender would take place, many of the Texans had escaped into the swamps and bayous rather than submit to capture. Lieutenant Colonel Thomas Anderson surrendered 589 members of the 6th Texas Infantry, while others escaped into the bayous. Colonel Frank Wilkes of the 24th Texas surrendered 652 members of his regiment, while another 130 or so slipped away at the time of the surrender. In Clayton Gillespie's 25th Texas, 555 members of the regiment surrendered and a little over 100 escaped into the woods. This brought the total number of men surrendered in Garland's Brigade to 1,796, while probably anywhere from 350 to 400 escaped capture. Additionally, the 6th Texas lost eight killed and twenty-four wounded, the 24th Texas suffered twelve killed and seventeen wounded, and the 25th Texas had two killed and eight wounded, for a total of twenty-two killed and forty-nine wounded.[19]

Deshler's Brigade suffered similar losses in the fighting and surrender. Mills of the 10th Texas surrendered 715 of his regiment, while about ninety either escaped capture or were left behind in Arkansas hospitals. In the 15th Texas only 478 men surrendered while another ninety escaped capture. The 17th Texas offered up 390 prisoners, and another 200 abandoned their comrades for the swamps. Finally, in the 18th Texas 533 became prisoners of war as another 250 escaped into the backcountry. Thus, it appears that in Deshler's Brigade 2,116 surrendered and 630 escaped capture in the Arkansas swamps and woods. The regiments in Deshler's Brigade failed to file individual casualty reports, but subtracting Garland's losses from the total yields a result of thirty-five killed and nine wounded in the four Texan regiments. Thus, of the 4,791 Confederates captured at Arkansas Post, 3,912, or 82 percent, belonged to regiments that would later comprise Granbury's Brigade. Meanwhile, a little over a thousand Texans escaped capture at the surrender.[20]

The Federal authorities should have sent the Confederate prisoners to Vicksburg for exchange under the terms of the Dix-Hill Cartel of July 22, 1862, but Ulysses S. Grant intervened. He argued that it would be criminal to send the prisoners to Vicksburg, where they could reinforce the garrison there even as he endeavored to capture the city. Instead, the day after the surrender McClernand herded the almost five thousand prisoners into three steamers, the *Sam Gatey*, *John J. Rowe*, and *Nebraska*, for transportation to northern prisoner-of-war camps.[21] Like their brethren in the 7th Texas, the rest of what would become Granbury's Brigade now found themselves prisoners of war.

The question of who was responsible for the surrender at Arkansas Post has remained the subject of debate among participants and historians since January 1863. In mid-July 1863, while the Texans were encamped near Tyner's Station, Tennessee, Garland called for a court of inquiry to investigate the matter. Despite this plea, the Richmond authorities denied his request, stating that "the exigencies of the service will not admit of assembling a court of inquiry at this time." Despite this rebuff, Garland apparently assembled an informal court of inquiry and summoned every officer who had been with the brigade at Arkansas Post to testify. They determined that the raising of the white flags and call to surrender started in the ranks of the 24th Texas, but as Captain Samuel Foster noted in his diary, "They came very near finding *where* it started; but not *who* started it. *Nor will it ever be known in this world*" (emphasis in the original). The call to surrender obviously began with one or more frightened enlisted men and/ or lower echelon officers, but exactly who started the panic will probably never be known.[22]

Historians have taken different stances on the Arkansas Post fiasco. For his part, historian Ed Bearss blames Colonel Garland for the surrender. Even though Garland did not issue the order, Bearss maintains that because the order reached him from the left while Churchill's headquarters stood to his right, Garland should have known that the order did not come from his commander. Furthermore, Bearss chastises Garland for his hesitation in allowing the Federals to cross into his works "with impunity" before he had determined the true state of affairs.[23] This analysis, while accurate as far as it goes, is probably not completely fair to Garland. In the chaos of battle it often becomes almost impossible to make snap decisions of such magnitude. On the other hand, Garland did receive formal military training and should have acted more decisively in time of crisis. If any one officer can be blamed for the surrender, it is most likely Robert Garland. Regardless of who was to blame, Arkansas Post set in motion a chain of events that would result in the formation of Granbury's Texas Brigade.

Arkansas Post provided a crucial turning point in shaping what became Granbury's Brigade. The surrender proved crucial to reinforcing a loyalty to the Confederacy and to each other. This shared experience of surrender and prison reinforced a hatred of the Union and defiance toward the United States that stayed with them. It also maintained the fighting effectiveness of Granbury's Brigade later in the war, when other Texas regiments began hemorrhaging men at an alarming rate, because those who might have deserted later in the war had already made their escape at Arkansas Post. However, it is abundantly clear by their later behavior that these men who escaped did not desert the Confederacy, but merely chose to fight closer to home, in the trans-Mississippi theater.

CHAPTER FIVE

FIGHTING FOR VICKSBURG

The campaign for Vicksburg began the second phase of the war in the regiments that became Granbury's Brigade, testing the 7th Texas Infantry after their surrender and imprisonment following Fort Donelson. The fighting for Vicksburg gave these Texans the first chance, after surrender, to prove their loyalty to the Confederacy. Although the 7th Texas underwent reorganization after the death or departure of many of their field officers, those officers who stepped up filled the gaps well, keeping the morale of the regiment high. From the almost suicidal charge at Raymond to the boredom of trench life at Port Hudson, the 7th Texas conformed perfectly to the type of Confederate nationalism and devotion to the cause outlined in Jason Phillips's *Diehard Rebels* and Gary Gallagher's *The Confederate War*. The 7th Texas would serve as the heart and soul of Granbury's Brigade, and their fierce devotion to the Confederacy and fighting prowess in the Vicksburg campaign set in motion these results.[1]

Vicksburg held the key to the western Confederacy. By 1863 the hill city alone blocked Union control of the Mississippi. One other Confederate garrison at Port Hudson also remained, but Vicksburg remained the key; as Vicksburg went, Port Hudson would follow. Since December 1862, U. S. Grant and his Federal forces had attempted to capture the city, with the first foray at Chickasaw Bluffs on December 29, where Sherman met with a bloody repulse. In January, McClernand succeeded in diverting a good portion of Grant's forces to Arkansas Post, but by the beginning of spring Grant again prepared to take the "Gibraltar of the Confederacy."

In the spring of 1863 the 7th Texas once again found itself at the center of action in the western theater. After the exchange of the officers and men, the regiment began to reform at Port Gibson. Major Granbury received promotion to colonel on August 29, 1862, to replace John Gregg, who had been placed in command of a brigade in Mississippi. The 7th Texas was assigned to the brigade of General Lloyd Tilghman. Captains K. M. Van Zandt and William L. Moody were the two senior captains in the regiment, and Tilghman decided that they should draw lots to determine who would become lieutenant colonel and major. Moody drew the lot for lieutenant colonel, while Van Zandt became major. Gregg received a promotion to brigadier general on September 27, placing him in permanent command of a brigade. Later in the year Major General Frank Gardner transferred the 7th Texas to the brigade of Brigadier General Samuel Maxey.

While the Texans remained at Port Gibson, their officers turned their attention to recruiting, so as to fill out the thinning ranks. On October 11 Gregg placed an advertisement in the *Marshall Texas Republican*. "The recruiting officers of the 7th Texas Infantry are among you," it read, "to fill the thinned ranks of the veterans . . . we call upon you to join us, as you expect to enlist in maintaining our liberties." In mid-October Granbury, Van Zandt, and Captains E. T. Broughton and C. N. Alexander all departed for Texas to recruit.[2] From October through January they busied themselves enrolling volunteers and conscripting those who did not enlist willingly. The recruiting paid off, with 216 men added to the regiment from October 1862 to March 1863. This number included eighty-seven conscripts and volunteers that Van Zandt formed into Company K.[3]

While the officers recruited, they left the 7th Texas almost leaderless. On October 23, Lieutenant Colonel Moody fell ill at Holly Springs, Mississippi. Van Zandt and Granbury remained in Texas, leaving Captain W. H. Smith of Company F in command. Finally, in January, Van Zandt and Broughton returned to Port Gibson. Granbury elected to stay in Texas a little longer, placing the major in temporary command of the regiment.

In early January Gardner ordered the brigades of Sam Maxey and John Gregg to defend Port Hudson. On the evening of January 5 the 7th Texas boarded the steamer *Charm* in Vicksburg for the trip downriver to Port Hudson. By the next morning the Texans had reached Natchez, Mississippi, where they stopped for a few hours. From there they moved down the river, passing the mouth of the Red River and arriving at Port Hudson around 10 P.M. At Port Hudson, Gardner placed the 7th Texas in the entrenchments to await any possible Federal threat.[4]

In Louisiana the Texans spent the spring months, gathering strength and enduring constant rain. On February 15, Van Zandt wrote his wife, "We are surprised that Col. Granbury has not reached here before this. . . . We have had a great deal of rainy weather within the last week or so, in fact, it rains a great deal of the time here. We have had but very little weather that is suitable for drilling." Van Zandt went on to complain about the quality of water available to the regiment and suggested that as soon as Granbury arrived they should move the camp closer to the Mississippi to utilize the river water.[5] While at Port Hudson the Texans again received a brigade transfer, this time to the command of John Gregg.

Granbury rejoined his regiment in time to celebrate his thirty-second birthday on March 1. On March 3 Van Zandt held a birthday party for his commanding officer, serving the cake Mrs. Van Zandt had baked for the occasion. Captain Charles Talley's wife had also sent some preserves and a jelly cake, which the officers consumed along with sausage, biscuits, and real coffee. Gregg, Moody, and several other officers also attended the gathering. At the end of his letter, Van Zandt hinted at a developing tragedy in the life of Hiram Granbury when he said, "Colonel Granbury is trying to get off to go see his wife, but I don't hardly think he will succeed."[6]

While Granbury had been away recruiting in Texas, his wife, Fannie, fell very ill with ovarian cancer. Soon after his arrival in Port Hudson, Granbury again departed the regiment for Mobile, where doctors were attempting to treat Mrs. Granbury. With her husband at her side, Fannie passed away on March 20 and was interred in Mobile. Eight days later a depressed Granbury rejoined his regiment at Port Hudson.[7] From that point on, Hiram Granbury focused his energy and attention solely on the men of his regiment and the prosecution of the war.

Back home, the wives of men in the 7th Texas continued to express concern in their letters. On March 26, 1863, Minerva again wrote her husband, Major Van Zandt, "Oh my Darling how could I stand it I never felt half as uneasy about you at Donelson as I do today. . . . But Dear, how could I content my mind if we hear of anything happening to you[?]"[8]

While the 7th Texas remained idle at Port Hudson and Hiram Granbury mourned his wife, Ulysses Grant concocted a plan to capture Vicksburg. Grant intended a bold flanking maneuver; instead of attempting to fight his way through the strong Confederate fortifications along the Yazoo River north of the city, he intended to bypass the defenders and attack from the south. Marching along the west bank of the Mississippi, Grant could recross the river at Grand Gulf and strike north toward the city.

To take the attention off of his plans, Grant dispatched Colonel Benjamin Grierson with several thousand cavalrymen to distract Lieutenant General John C. Pemberton and the other defenders. On April 17 Grierson and his troopers left La Grange in northern Mississippi and struck south. The plan worked perfectly, and Pemberton shifted many of his units north to deal with the raiders. In late April Pemberton ordered Gardner to send some of his units toward Woodville, Mississippi, to prevent Grierson's reaching the command of Major General Nathaniel Banks in Louisiana, his presumed destination. Gardner ordered Granbury's regiment and a section of Bledsoe's Battery toward Woodville on April 28.[9]

On May 1 Grant crossed the Mississippi at Grand Gulf and immediately drove away the Confederate defenders of Port Gibson. Learning of the crossing, Pemberton ordered Gardner to send Gregg's Brigade to Jackson. Gardner complied and that same day the Texans were startled with their new orders to rejoin the rest of the brigade at Osyka before proceeding to Jackson. The march took Granbury and his men through a part of Mississippi untouched by the war, and after eight days and 160 miles they reunited with Gregg's command, arriving in Jackson on Saturday, May 9.[10]

By May 11, Pemberton had recovered somewhat from his shock at Grant's river crossing and began issuing orders to defend central Mississippi. Grant intended to strike first toward Jackson, but Pemberton mistakenly assumed his goal was the Big Black River Bridge west of the city. Therefore on the eleventh Pemberton instructed Gregg to take his brigade southwest toward Raymond and strike the Federals in flank as soon as they turned north toward the Big Black. Pemberton decided that Grant intended the move toward Jackson merely as a feint, and informed Gregg of his suspicions. He also dispatched Brigadier General W. H. T. Walker's brigade to aid Gregg in this assignment. John Gregg and his small brigade marched into Raymond on the afternoon of May 11, raising a cloud of dust. The locals hailed them as heroes because rumors had reached them of Grant's approach via the Utica Road.[11]

Near dawn on May 12 a courier awakened General Gregg to give him news of the approach of a Federal column. Gregg naturally assumed the column a small force intended to carry out the feint toward Jackson. A short time later another courier reached Gregg and informed him that the Union force consisted of no more than twenty-five hundred to three thousand, and Gregg naturally assumed he faced only a brigade. In fact, it proved to be the van of Major General James McPherson's XVII Corps of Grant's army.[12]

Gregg immediately decided to confront the Federals as they advanced up the Utica Road, and at 9 A.M. he began deploying his brigade. To anchor the position he placed Hiram Granbury and the 7th Texas in the center, at the junction of the Port Gibson and Utica roads a mile southwest of Raymond. Granbury deployed his men on the forward slope of a hill to the right of the Utica Road, one hundred yards south of the intersection. To the left of the Texans Gregg placed the 3rd Tennessee Infantry, with a gap of about one thousand yards between their right and Granbury's left. To the left of this unit Gregg placed the 10th and 30th Tennessee Infantry Regiments, and finally the 50th Tennessee straddling the Gallatin Road. In reserve Gregg held the 1st Tennessee Battalion and 41st Tennessee to serve wherever needed. Finally, he placed Hiram Bledsoe's battery atop a knoll in the rear of the Texans.[13]

When the 7th Texas reached its position, Granbury detached Captain Thomas B. Camp to gather volunteers from Companies A and B to serve as skirmishers at the Fourteenmile Creek Bridge. Camp and his skirmishers crossed the dry creek bed and took position in some brush at the northern edge of a wide field that stretched south for another three hundred yards. Soon Federal skirmishers appeared at the other end of the field, and at one hundred yards Camp ordered his men to open fire. The Yankee skirmishers went to ground and Bledsoe opened fire on the opposing Union artillery.[14]

In front of the Confederate position, Fourteenmile Creek formed an oxbow curving toward Gregg's position. Gregg realized that Bledsoe couldn't stand up long against McPherson's artillery, and he decided to take the initiative and attack. He hoped to pin down the Yankees with a frontal assault while the Tennesseans on the left swung around the Federal right.

The bold Texan hoped that this could result in the capture of the entire enemy force.[15]

At noon Gregg set his left into motion, with the Tennessee regiments moving diagonally southwest toward Fourteenmile Creek. Once they were in place, Gregg personally led the 7th Texas forward, ordering the attack to commence from right to left. Brandishing his sword, Gregg led the Texans toward the dry creek bed. Granbury pulled back Camp's skirmishers to cover his right flank and sent out another line of skirmishers under Captains W. H. Smith and J. H. Collett one hundred yards in advance of the main line.[16] To their front the Texans faced the Second Brigade, Third Division, of the XVII Corps under Brigadier General Elias Dennis. The Texans surprised Dennis's men, and at the approach of the gray line the men of the 20th Ohio, in Dennis's center, grabbed their muskets and rushed into line along the dry creek bed, which they utilized as a trench. From here they opened fire on Granbury's men, only to discover that the 68th Ohio, instead of taking position in the creek on their right, had run the other direction. Nothing stood between the left flank of the 7th Texas and the rear of the Ohioans' position.[17]

Dennis had placed his skirmishers at the base of the hill north of the creek, and as the Texans approached they opened fire. Granbury ordered his men forward at the double-quick, and when they neared the creek they rushed forward "with a shout."[18]

To the right of Dennis's brigade, its division commander, Major General John A. Logan, had placed his 1st Brigade, under Brigadier General John E. Smith. In response to the Confederate advance, Smith tried to lead his brigade forward to come into line beside Dennis. A dense belt of thickets intervened, though, breaking up formations and badly delaying all of Smith's regiments except the 23rd Indiana, which was thus left to fend for itself. Soon the 3rd Tennessee popped out of the woods to the Hoosiers' front and drove them back. Van Zandt encountered some of the Indianans as he led the left wing of the 7th Texas. Captain Alonzo Tubbs of the 23rd Indiana took a swing at Van Zandt with his sword before being disarmed and captured by Sergeant J. M. C. Duncan of Company K. To the left, the 20th Ohio witnessed the Hoosiers' plight, and their line began to waver as the Texans lapped around their flanks.

At that moment Logan himself rode up and began rallying the Ohioans with his presence, riding up and down the line, shouting encouragement.

Some of Granbury's men succeeded in crossing the creek, but the thin blue line held against repeated assaults. One Union soldier remembered how the Texans tried to advance "just as you may see a lot of dead leaves in a gale of wind, eddying to and fro under the bank, often rising up to fly away, but never able to advance." The Federal also noticed a Texas officer who stood no more than ten yards away, calmly smoking a meerschaum pipe and emptying his revolver into the blue ranks.

The left-flank companies of the 7th Texas fought their way across the creek, only to be driven back in a counterattack by the 20th Illinois of Smith's Brigade, which had finally beaten its way through the thickets. By this time the 3rd Tennessee and 7th Texas had nearly fought themselves into exhaustion, and Gregg puzzled over the lack of fire from his left, which indicated that something had gone awry with the assault.[19]

On the left, the commanders of the Tennessee regiments had realized the true nature of their enemy. From atop a rise they could plainly see at least an entire Federal division on the field, marshaling against the lone Confederate brigade. In light of this discovery the Tennesseans halted where they were and sought further instructions from Gregg. To get the attack moving again, Gregg ordered up his reserves.[20]

Meanwhile Colonel Manning Force of the 20th Ohio urged his regiment forward and counterattacked the 7th Texas and 3rd Tennessee. The Tennesseans retreated across the creek first while Hiram Granbury tried desperately to hold his regiment in place. Colonel J. C. Clack of the 3rd Tennessee sent word to Granbury that his left was in trouble. Accordingly, Granbury ordered Moody to take the three rightmost companies of the regiment out of line to aid the Tennesseans. Upon investigating the situation for himself, Granbury decided the left could be held and sent a runner to Moody ordering him to hold his position. An errant ball killed the runner en route and Moody withdrew per the earlier order. Reaching the field they had previously charged across, Moody and the three companies glanced around for where they might be needed most. They spotted a Confederate line of battle to the east and began marching to join it. The Confederates turned out to be Colonel Randall McGavock's 10th and 30th Tennessee, which had just arrived in position.[21]

Granbury and the remaining companies of the 7th Texas found themselves assailed in front and both flanks and at approximately 1:30 P.M. fell back to the cover of Bledsoe's Battery.[22] The battle continued to rage as the

Federals pushed their advantage, and McGavock's Regiment, plus the three Texan companies, attempted to stem the tide.[23] At length Gregg realized that he in fact faced McPherson's entire corps and ordered a retreat through Raymond, ending the battle.

That night Granbury attempted to reorganize his regiment as the Texans licked their wounds. The 7th took 306 men into the fight and Granbury reported his losses as 22 killed, 73 wounded, and 73 missing, for a total of 158. The Compiled Service Records of the 7th Texas indicate that the regiment lost 29 killed, 86 wounded, and 40 captured, a total of 155. Raymond proved a bloody lesson for John Gregg and his brigade, who reported a total of 73 killed, 252 wounded, and 190 missing, for an aggregate of 515 casualties. McPherson reported his losses at 68 killed, 341 wounded, and 37 missing, for a total of 446. Interestingly enough, 154 of those casualties, or 34 percent, occurred in the 20th Ohio and 20th Illinois, the two regiments primarily engaged with the 7th Texas during the battle. This means that the Texans inflicted almost equal losses on their more numerous opponents, an unusual feat for a Civil War regiment on the attack.[24]

In the aftermath of the battle Gregg withdrew his brigade into Jackson to await orders. Grant decided to concentrate his forces in Jackson before turning west toward Vicksburg, and beginning with McPherson's XVII Corps, Grant's entire army marched on the Mississippi capital. The day after Raymond, General Joseph E. Johnston, whom Jefferson Davis had dispatched to central Mississippi, arrived in Jackson to take command of the defense of the city. Davis had also admonished General P. G. T. Beauregard to send troops from the East Coast to aid Johnston. On May 6 Beauregard dispatched the brigades of W. H. T. Walker and the improbably named States Rights Gist to Jackson. Johnston could also expect Samuel Maxey's brigade from Port Hudson the next day.

After conferring with Gregg, Johnston decided he could not defend Jackson against Grant's army—probably the only time during the war when Johnston justifiably abandoned an important military target—and ordered Gregg to take charge of the defenses until the withdrawal could be effected. While his own brigade retreated north toward Canton on the morning of May 14, Gregg placed Gist's and Walker's men west and south of Jackson to fight a delaying action. The massive blue columns overpowered the outnumbered Confederate defenders, and by 3:30 P.M. Gregg and the rear guard had begun their retreat north toward Canton.

From Jackson Grant turned west toward Vicksburg, bludgeoning Pemberton's forces back into the fortifications of the city by means of victories at Champions Hill and the Big Black Bridge. By the third week in May Grant had laid siege to the Gibraltar of the Confederacy, and it fell to Joseph Johnston and his small force near Canton to find a way to raise the siege.

If Jefferson Davis and John Pemberton expected quick, decisive, aggressive movements from Joseph Johnston, they placed their hopes in the wrong man. Obsessed with caution and his reputation as a strategist, Johnston proved unwilling during the course of the Civil War to risk his army where any doubt existed as to the outcome of the battle. On the Virginia Peninsula in the spring of 1862 Johnston retreated almost all the way to Richmond before finally being forced to fight at Seven Pines. Had he not been wounded and replaced by Robert E. Lee, Richmond might have fallen in June 1862 instead of April 1865. At Atlanta in the spring of 1864 Johnston abandoned more than one hundred miles of territory into the interior of Georgia without launching a counterattack. Had Davis not replaced Johnston that July, Atlanta would have fallen then rather than six weeks later. Finally, in central Mississippi in the summer of 1863 Johnston proved unwilling or unable to do anything in relief of Vicksburg.

Though he would not take decisive action, Johnston kept his twenty-three thousand men busy marching and countermarching along the Big Black River during the siege of Vicksburg. While thus marching back and forth, Granbury passed through many of the haunts of his childhood. Proceeding first toward Calhoun, Gregg led his brigade west toward the Big Black, passing near Adelle and the farm where Hiram Granbury had grown up. By May 29 the Texans arrived back in Canton, and then proceeded north to Yazoo City by May 31. They spent the first twelve days in June in the vicinity of the Yazoo before heading south to cross the Big Black again on June 13. The next day the brigade made camp very near the old brick church where Hiram Granbury's father had served as a minister. They stopped for six days near the old Granberry farm and by July 4 had reached a point again very near the Big Black.

Many of the Texans fell ill during the march, due to the unhealthy conditions and Mississippi summer heat. Van Zandt began to suffer from the sun and by July 4 wrote his wife from the home of a Mr. Davis in Brownsville, Mississippi, where he was recuperating. Davis proved to be Hiram Granbury's brother-in-law (his first wife had been Granbury's sister), and so he was more than glad to host any of the ailing soldiers from the 7th Texas. Meanwhile the march continued. Moody wrote his wife that he and Granbury had procured a cart in which to carry their baggage and that at the moment they were getting enough to eat.[25]

On the Fourth of July Johnston's soldiers received word of the fall of Vicksburg. The men in the ranks were stunned—not only that the Gibraltar of the Confederacy had fallen on Independence Day, but also that they had done nothing to relieve the siege. Disheartened by their losses at Raymond and Vicksburg, Gregg and his weary brigade prepared to march wherever their next orders might take them.

After accepting the surrender of Vicksburg, Grant dispatched William T. Sherman to capture Jackson and defeat Johnston's army. Johnston rushed his men into the trenches outside the Mississippi capital, and on July 9 Sherman arrived and laid siege to the city. During the siege of Jackson the 7th Texas saw relatively little action, while snipers made their position sometimes unbearable. During this time the regiment lost a half-dozen men to the sun and snipers' bullets. On July 12 a sniper struck Moody in the small of the back near his hip, putting him temporarily out of the war and sending him back to Texas. At length Van Zandt recovered from his sun-related illness and rejoined the regiment. In Moody's absence he was second to Granbury in command of the regiment. Finally, on July 16, Johnston ordered a cautious retreat out of Jackson, once again leaving the city to the Federals.[26]

For forty-eight grueling hours the Confederates marched east along the railroad until they reached Morton Station, Mississippi. Here Johnston elected to rest his troops and conferred with Lieutenant General William J. Hardee, who ordered Gregg's Brigade to detach from the army and march north to Enterprise, Mississippi, south of Meridian.[27]

The Texans were only too happy to get out from under Johnston, and on July 29 they reached Enterprise. There Granbury situated his regiment near the Chickasawhay River, affording plenty of clear, pure water. The men's health began to improve, and they began constructing temporary shelters from pine poles covered with pine boughs.[28] For the moment Granbury and his regiment found time to rest and recuperate after their adventures in Mississippi.

The exploits of the 7th Texas in trying to rescue Vicksburg exemplified both the plight and courage of western Confederates. Even though the

Texans saw the larger picture, the fall of Vicksburg, they maintained their courage and determination through a faith in their line officers like Hiram Granbury and John Gregg, and a localized perspective. From the perspective of the 7th Texas, they had taken on a much larger force at Raymond, acquitted themselves well, and escaped capture at Port Hudson. They had fought as hard as possible and maintained a faith in themselves and their officers. In the campaign for Vicksburg, the 7th Texas began to exhibit all of the qualities of western Confederate soldiers as outlined by Larry Daniels in *Soldiering in the Army of Tennessee* and Richard McMurry in *Two Great Rebel Armies*. Their faith in their officers and their perspective would carry them through the rest of the war.[29]

CHAPTER SIX

PRISON

The shared experience of incarceration affected the Arkansas Post prisoners much like it had the 7th Texas; for those that survived, it served to deepen their loyalty to the Confederacy and to each other. It also culled the ranks, as disease took its toll and some men made the decision to take an oath of allegiance to the United States rather than risk dying in prison. This latter group, though, formed a small percentage of the prisoners as a whole. Among the Arkansas Post garrison, prison actually served to strengthen the Confederate cause and provided a common experience of suffering that these Texans carried with them through the rest of the war. As suggested by J. Tracy Power in *Lee's Miserables* and Larry Daniels in *Soldiering in the Army of Tennessee,* the common suffering of prison brought the survivors closer together and began the process of molding them into first-class fighting men.[1]

While the 7th Texas fought to save Vicksburg, the Arkansas Post garrison made its way toward Northern prison camps. On the morning of January 12, 1863, the Texans and Arkansans awoke to the reality that they had become prisoners of war. Many of the men had not eaten anything for two days, and Sergeant William Heartsill reported that he had a breakfast made entirely of river water. Finally, in the evening, the Federals transferred Heartsill's men to the *Sam Gatey* and issued the Texans "a good supply" of pork and hardtack. After dark the Federals began bringing other prisoners aboard, until at last over eight hundred men—a bevy of Arkansans along with Texans from the W. P. Lane Rangers—had boarded the ship.[2]

The Federals loaded the *John J. Roe* and the *Nebraska* in similar fashion. As Captain Samuel Foster walked up the gangplank of the *John J. Roe*, a sentinel stopped him at bayonet point at the top and demanded his name, rank, company, and regiment. As the Texans boarded the boat, rumors circulated among them that they would be exchanged at Vicksburg.[3] While Dunnington's Arkansans and the W. P. Lane Rangers boarded the *Sam Gatey*, Deshler's Texans climbed aboard the *Nebraska* and Garland's Texans made their way onto the *John J. Roe*.[4]

After they had boarded the *Nebraska*, the captain of the boat invited the Texas officers to dine with him and the other Union officers aboard while the enlisted men occupied the lower decks. To the chagrin of the Union captain, the officers and men of the Texas regiments dressed alike, making it impossible to distinguish enlisted men from officers, and before the dinner was over the captain began cursing, shouting that he didn't know all of the men aboard were officers or he wouldn't have offered to feed them. After this prank, the captain of the *Nebraska* never again offered to feed the Texas officers.[5]

All day on January 12 the three boats stood still, completing preparations for the voyage, and several men took the opportunity to escape over the gunwales and into the river. Some made it to safety, but the guards shot a few and the others drowned. Finally, at 1 P.M. on January 14 the lead vessel gave the signal and the three transports started down the Arkansas. After three hours the steamers passed into the White River, and by 9 P.M. they had entered the Mississippi. "And to our surprise," wrote Sergeant Heartsill, "we head up stream, so the Vicksburg exchange business has 'played out' and many are sorely disappointed, for we did not have any idea of being taken North." Captain Foster wrote, "Now what's what—Vicksburg is down the river and we are going up the river. All speculation and calculation is guess work, as to where we are going. We are going north and that is about all we do know."[6]

A blinding snowstorm met them as they traveled up the Father of Waters. In these deplorable conditions, pneumonia broke out among the soldiers, and soon sick men covered the floor in every room, "two rows of them with their heads toward the center and their feet toward the state room doors." On January 16 the transports reached Memphis, and anchored opposite the city on the Arkansas shore. The next morning the ships remained in place while rumors of exchange at Memphis floated about the decks and holds of the ships. On the *Sam Gatey*, Lieutenant Heartsill wrote, "we are all very anxious to get out of this filthy hulk, for there is a great danger of it going down at any moment." Apparently the captain of the ship promised Heartsill and his compatriots that he would procure a new vessel at Helena, but this never materialized, and the lieutenant hinted darkly that perhaps the Yankees intended a more sinister fate for the prisoners. While at Memphis sixteen Confederates slipped over the side and escaped. William Oliphant of the 6th Texas wrote of their stop at Memphis: "Of food, there was plenty to spare, and no unkindness was shown by the guards, but the cold was intense. . . . The kind citizens of Memphis were not permitted to give the clothing they so generously offered to keep us warm, notwithstanding a frozen Confederate had been that day carried to the wharf; and, as the men were not allowed to enter the cabins, the scarcity of overcoats and blankets caused great suffering."[7]

On January 21 the three boats passed Cairo, Illinois, on their way north. The next day the paddle wheel on the *Sam Gatey* broke for the second time during the voyage, and on January 23 the *Nebraska* ran aground. The *John J. Roe* and the *Sam Gatey* unloaded their prisoners under guard, then ferried the prisoners of the *Nebraska* off the ship. By 11 P.M. the crew had freed the *Nebraska* and the journey proceeded. On Saturday, January 24, the Texans and Arkansans reached St. Louis and the guards put them ashore on Arsenal Island, south of the city. There, a home guard unit, the 37th Iowa, policed the prisoners for the next few days. After this interlude the prisoners continued to Alton, Illinois, just above St. Louis, where they boarded trains for prisoner-of-war camps.[8] The Federals sent the enlisted men of the 6th, 24th, and 25th Texas regiments to Camp Butler, near Springfield, Illinois. The enlisted men of the 10th, 15th, 17th, and 18th Texas went to Camp Douglas in Chicago, and the officers of all the regiments shipped out for Camp Chase, near Columbus, Ohio.[9]

Established in August 1861 six miles east of Springfield, Camp Butler originally served as a depot for soldiers from Illinois. Located on the Great Western Railroad half a mile from the Sangamon River, the camp provided an ideal location for housing enemy prisoners. A wood fence surrounded the camp's fifteen acres and enclosed the wooden, tar paper-roofed shacks that served as barracks. In late February 1862 several thousand captured

Confederates from the Donelson garrison arrived, and throughout the rest of the war Camp Butler served as a prisoner-of-war camp.[10]

As at other camps, the men at Camp Butler spent much of their time plotting to escape. Some bribed guards, while others dug tunnels. Joseph Hinkle of the 30th Tennessee Infantry served time in Camp Butler after his capture at Donelson. He wrote: "We didn't go to that prison to stay if we could get away, we agreed among ourselves [to] use one of the large outhouses, back of the barracks. The idea was to dig out under the high fence back of this building, which was guarded. This we began to do not long after we got there. We had men in the outbuilding digging, & pulling the dirt back, & in order to keep back suspicion we would play marbles & engage in other amusements, around the building." Ultimately, though, the guards discovered the tunnel and put an end to it. Some prisoners managed to escape in coffins meant for their dead comrades. The guards would take the "dead" man in the coffin to an outbuilding a short distance outside the walls, where they would deposit it, unguarded. After a while, the live man would emerge from the coffin at night and make his escape. In this way many of the Tennesseans escaped, and of course the Texans tried the same things.[11]

In their letters, Texans expressed contentment with the treatment they received. Private Franz Coller of the 6th Texas wrote that the provisions issued him at Camp Butler exceeded those he had received in the Confederate service. William Oliphant of Company G remembered that the barracks "were comfortable. . . . Stoves were set up for us and we were furnished with plenty of fuel." Despite these statements, hygiene remained poor in the camps and measles, coupled with smallpox and pneumonia, appeared soon after the Texans arrived. By the end of February 1863, 103 deaths had occurred among the Texans at Camp Butler.[12]

Boredom also stalked the prisoners, and the men reacted in various ways. Some bought rubber buttons and carved them into rings, while others whittled whistles and pipes from wood, which they sold to guards and visitors. The Texans also played marbles, chess, cards, wrote letters, sang songs, and in general whiled away their time as best they could.

One day seventeen-year-old Austinite William Oliphant of Company G, 6th Texas, found himself lying outside his barracks when a Federal surgeon passed. Oliphant paid him no attention, and the officer demanded to know why he had not saluted. At this, Oliphant suggested that the surgeon "emigrate to a country where the climate was much warmer than any to be found in America." The enraged surgeon returned with some guards and threw Oliphant into the smallpox ward to serve as a nurse in the hope that he would catch the disease. Unbeknownst to the surgeon, Oliphant had already suffered through and acquired immunity to the disease, and he cared for the sick as best he could for ten days. After this period the surgeon, disgusted that Oliphant had not contracted the illness, ordered him back to his barracks.[13] This act of defiance suggests that many of these Texans were unbowed by prison and maintained their loyalty to the Confederacy.

Taking the oath of allegiance to the United States became the only way to escape from Camp Butler with the blessing of the commandant. Petitions outlining the process constantly circulated through the ranks, reminding the men of this alternative. In all, seventy-three members of the 6th Texas took the oath at Camp Butler, including thirty-seven from Company I alone. After the exchange, Company I, 6th Texas, ceased to exist because of this massive desertion. Thirty-eight members of the 24th Texas took the oath, as did twenty-six men of the 25th, bringing the total amount at Camp Butler to 137, approximately 8 percent of the men from these regiments captured at Arkansas Post, a small proportion considering their situation.[14]

To an even greater degree sickness ravaged the ranks at Camp Butler. Of the 1,693 enlisted men in the three regiments captured at Arkansas Post, approximately 57 members of the 6th Texas, 112 members of the 24th Texas, and 137 members of the 25th Texas died of disease at Camp Butler, bringing the total to 306, roughly 18 percent of those imprisoned. Thus, the three Texas regiments near Springfield lost 443 to disease or desertion in just four months' imprisonment, 26 percent of their total number.[15]

The Texans at Camp Douglas had a decidedly worse experience than those at Camp Butler. Located in Chicago, the camp lay barely three hundred yards from Lake Michigan. A fourteen-foot-high fence surrounded the compound, which contained wood-framed barracks situated on piers due to the low, marshy nature of the ground. Because of the low elevation, whenever it rained the streets turned into quagmires. This factor, along with the harsh Chicago winter, made Camp Douglas an unhealthy environment for the Arkansas Post prisoners. The camp contained a hospital within the walls and another outside the walls for smallpox patients. Camp Douglas also contained all of the customary guard towers and a "dead line" that ran all the way around the camp inside the walls. The sentries had orders to shoot any prisoner who passed the dead line.[16]

The enlisted men of the 10th, 15th, 17th, and 18th Texas boarded the Chicago, Alton & St. Louis Railroad in Alton when they disembarked from the *Nebraska* in January 1863. Along the way they passed through places like Springfield and Joliet before reaching Chicago near the end of January. Roughly 1,939 enlisted men from the four Texas regiments entered Camp Douglas, minus the few men who died on the way or escaped off the *Nebraska*.[17]

Hundreds of these Texans had already fallen ill by the time the regiments reached Camp Douglas. Dr. George Park, regimental surgeon of the 65th Illinois, took care of the sick, and several Texan medical officers assisted him. This group included D. F. Stewart and Thomas C. Foster, surgeon and assistant surgeon of the 10th Texas, and James W. Motley, assistant surgeon of the 17th Texas. With almost no protection from the bitter winds and snow off Lake Michigan, hundreds of Texans died within the first month of incarceration. In that first month the temperature dipped to 40 degrees below zero, and in one night forty prisoners froze to death. Food also proved scarce; rats, cats, and even dogs disappeared from the camp and into the stomachs of the hungry Confederates. To while away the boredom, the prisoners composed a song called "Camp Douglas by the Lake," set to the tune of "Cottage by the Sea." One Texan who escaped, Private Niles Beeler of Company E, 18th Texas, made it over the walls and traveled back to Texas disguised as a civilian.[18]

As at Camp Butler, taking the oath of allegiance offered an attractive way out. Seventeen members of the 10th Texas took the oath. Forty-two members of the 15th Texas deserted in this way, as did two members of the 17th Texas. Eighteen members of the 18th Texas did the same. This brought the number of Texans at Camp Douglas who took the oath of allegiance to seventy-nine, 4 percent of the total. As at Camp Butler, the Union officials at Camp Douglas used the oath to pull on the heartstrings of the homesick Texans. Despite this situation, an astonishing 96 percent of the Texans at Camp Douglas refused to take the oath, indicating their continued loyalty to the Confederacy.

Death from freezing, pneumonia, smallpox, and other illnesses took a slightly higher toll at Camp Douglas than at Camp Butler. Eighty-five members of the 10th Texas died, as did ninety-five soldiers of the 15th

Texas. One hundred and three men of the 17th Texas also expired in the harsh winter, as did 105 soldiers of the 18th Texas. This brought the death toll at Camp Douglas to a staggering 388, 20 percent of those imprisoned. Added to those who took the oath of allegiance, this brought the attrition rate to 24 percent.[19]

While the enlisted men suffered and died at Camps Douglas and Butler, railroads transported the 308 officers of the seven Texas regiments from Alton, Illinois, to Camp Chase, near Columbus, Ohio. From Alton the Federals loaded the officers on common stock cars for a bitterly cold ride to Cincinnati. That night, Lieutenant William F. Rogers of Company F, 15th Texas, froze to death. At Cincinnati they changed cars for Columbus, and on the way the Texans had to endure the constant singing of "We will hang Jeff Davis on a sour apple tree" by the guards. At midnight on January 30 the officers reached Columbus, exited the cars, and "were formed into two ranks on a broad street in front of a hotel. The ground was frozen stiff and the north wind bit 'shrewdly,' the skies were as clear as a bell, and the bright fires in the hotel, and well-dressed people moving around was quite in contrast with the condition of the 300 rebel officers standing out and shivering in the cold." While they stood in line, some ladies of Columbus went through the ranks distributing food, which the famished Confederates gladly accepted. At 1 A.M. the guards ushered their captives out onto the National Pike, and at 3:30 they reached Camp Chase in the midst of "a blinding snow storm."[20]

At Camp Chase the first order or business became registering and searching the prisoners. The sentries led each officer into "a kind of ante room" one at a time, where a clerk recorded his name, rank, regiment, and state, and then a big Federal soldier would search him, "in order to be sure that we had no gunboats, torpedoes, shotguns, or mountain howitzers in our old clothes." By the time this process reached completion, the "snow was coming down in full-grown flakes." The Confederates found two rows of buildings within the walls of the camp, with a street between them. Each building measured about three hundred feet by fifteen feet, divided up into rooms approximately twelve feet by fifteen feet. The Federals had furnished each room with a stove, cooking utensils, and blankets, with bunks "something like the shelving in a store with room for two."[21]

About fourteen men lived in each room, and life soon became monotonous for the officers. Captain Foster complained of no reading material, "no books—no newspaper except one little negro loving paper published at Cin. O. blackest of the black." In Foster's mess, they began to carve out chess pieces from carrots, and someone got hold of a deck of cards with which they played euchre. Foster noted that they led a lazy life; cooking, eating, sleeping, playing chess and euchre, and carving out small rings. One of the Texas officers, Lieutenant James Selkirk of the 6th Texas, had relatives living in New York State, and they furnished him liberally with money and clothing, which he generously shared with his compatriots.[22]

Theological debates, discussions, and sermons also occupied the time of the officers. Lieutenant Collins remembered: "We had two Methodist preachers with us, Rev. [Clayton] Gillespie, Colonel of the 24th Texas, and Rev. [Frank] Wilkes, Colonel of the 25th Texas. They would preach for us on Sunday when not hushed up by the officer of the day." Collins recalled that "one nice, bright Sunday morning we were all on the ground in rows like chickens on a bean pole, and the Rev. Gillespie was dishing out some good gospel from a text, where some lecherous, broken down king was making war on some one who was leading a rebellion against him. Colonel Gillespie was lifting the king's scalp in an artistic manner, and the lines of comparison he was running seemed to point in the direction of Washington City. We were drinking it down like good medicine. The Federal officer soon got enough of it and ordered us to disband and go to our quarters."[23]

The foregoing example shows that religion encouraged the Confederates in their cause, as Steven Woodworth has argued in *While God Is Marching On*. The religious leadership of officers like Wilkes and Gillespie gave the Confederate prisoners reassurance that God remained on their side.[24]

The officers, like the enlisted men, also turned their attention to escape. Beneath the barracks they began a tunnel that had reached forty feet in length before a lieutenant from Arkansas reported the attempt to Captain Edwin Webber, commandant of the camp. Captain Foster reported of the Arkansan, "if they had not took him out as quick as they did we would have hung him. . . . There were about 150 of us going out, and our plans were to capture all the arms here at this place, then open the prison, turn all the balance out, and arm the whole lot—make our way as fast as we could to the Ohio river and cross over into Ky. and get with Gen'l Morgan."[25]

One day in March, three visiting dignitaries paid a visit to Camp Chase to see the prisoners, especially the highest ranking officer, General Churchill. Military Governor Andrew Johnson of Tennessee, Governor

David Tod of Ohio, and Senator Jesse Bright of Indiana composed the triumvirate who intended to call on Churchill. As Webber welcomed the three governors, a group of Confederate officers gathered outside Churchill's quarters. When the three dignitaries arrived, Webber conversed with the Rebel commander, who refused to see them. A cheer erupted from the prisoners, and according to Lieutenant Collins, "Andy Johnson turned around and gave us a look of contempt and withering scorn that would have made ordinary mortals quake in their boots." After this incident, Johnson, Tod, and Bright departed.[26]

To pass the time, the officers regularly discussed the subjects of politics and religion. Around Colonel John T. Coit's mess, theological debates took center stage, while around Roger Q. Mills's politics became the subject of the day. Even literary discussion found a place at Camp Chase in Deshler's mess. The theological discussions proved particularly heated, with Coit a devoted Presbyterian. To counter this view, Captain Sebron Sneed of the 6th Texas had once studied for the Catholic priesthood. Lieutenant Collins remembered spending many enjoyable hours listening to these discussions.[27]

In contrast to the attrition rates at Camps Douglas and Butler, very few fatalities occurred at Camp Chase. There is also no record of any of the officers taking the oath of allegiance to the United States. Many of the officers hoarded clothing and blankets, despite orders not to do so, and several of the prisoners at Camp Chase even gained weight during their incarceration.[28]

As winter thawed into spring in the Midwest, the enlisted men and officers of the Arkansas Post garrison whiled away their time, making the best of their circumstances. The time would soon come, however, when they would be reunited and again fighting for the Confederacy, this time east of the Mississippi in the decisive theater of conflict between that river and the Appalachians.

The time in prison did several things for the Arkansas Post prisoners. First, it winnowed the ranks through disease, but it also displayed their loyalty to the Confederacy as the men mouthed off to Union officers, refused to see U.S. dignitaries, preached religion from a pro-Confederate point of view, and attempted to escape at every opportunity. It also strengthened the resolve of those who survived it, because they found themselves the toughest of those still alive. They had their opportunities to desert, but only a paltry few took them, indicating that those who came out of prison would ultimately prove the most devoted to the Confederate war effort. Desertion also dropped off noticeably after their exchange, reinforcing the idea that the time in prison became the watershed moment for these Texans, like the closing of the Mississippi River later became for other Texans, as suggested by Charles Grear in "Texans to the Front." Adverse circumstances would continue to dog them, but those who made it out of prison alive and fit for duty found themselves destined to become Granbury's Texas Brigade.

CHAPTER SEVEN

A NEW START

Like most prisoners captured relatively early in the Civil War, the Arkansas Post prisoners would soon find themselves exchanged and back in the Confederate ranks in time to participate in the Tullahoma campaign—a disaster for the South that nonetheless gave these Texans a new start and a chance to prove themselves. Following their exchange, the Confederate war effort continued to fare badly, but this did not seem to dampen the morale of the Arkansas Post prisoners. Rather, local matters captured their attention, underscoring the importance of perspective as outlined in *Soldiering in the Army of Tennessee,* "Texans to the Front," and other literature. The issue that bothered the Texans most after exchange became the ignominious consolidations, in which authorities folded regiments in with each other due to reduced numbers. It was this issue that preoccupied their letters and diaries most of all. Also, after the exchange a small number of Texans opted to leave their original regiments and head back to Texas to fight, especially in the later summer and early fall of 1863, supporting Grear's argument in "Texans to the Front" that the Mississippi River served as a psychological barrier between these Texans and their homes, encouraging them to desert in order to fight closer to home. However, also after the exchange the Texans finally began experiencing effective leadership at the brigade and division level in the form of James Deshler and Patrick

Cleburne, ensuring that those who stayed in the ranks deepened their devotion to the Confederacy and to the Confederate cause.[1]

By spring, Federal officials had arranged an exchange of the Arkansas Post prisoners. Normally the exchange would have taken place at Vicksburg, but because of the ongoing efforts of Grant to capture the city, Quartermaster General Montgomery Meigs decided to send the Arkansas Post regiments to Virginia. Around the first of April the Federals loaded the first contingent of five hundred prisoners onto trains for their journey east. The westerners first traveled by train to Indianapolis and Columbus. All along the way, hostile crowds hurled rocks, insults, and beer bottles at the passing Confederates, forcing their Yankee guards to protect them from harm. In several shipments of five hundred each, they sent the prisoners to Pittsburgh, Pennsylvania, and Elmira, New York, before reaching the Susquehanna River. Here the guards loaded them aboard steamers and sent them downriver into the Chesapeake Bay and thus to Fort Monroe, on the tip of the Virginia peninsula. At Fort Monroe the Federal authorities arranged an exchange for the prisoners with the Confederate War Department. After their exchange, the former prisoners sailed upriver to City Point, Virginia, where they again set foot on dry land and continued by rail to Model Barracks, near Petersburg, Virginia. At Model Barracks they awaited the rest of the prisoners and their officers.[2] The Texans and Arkansans spent their time quietly at Model Barracks as the Confederate War Department decided what to do with them. Despite this tranquility, events in northern Virginia soon interrupted their repose.

On May 5, Confederate officials suddenly shipped the former prisoners north to Richmond to act as part of the city's home guard during the Battle of Chancellorsville. After arriving, the former prisoners merely marched to the city square to await further orders. There they spent the night in a church on Canal Street, and the next morning they moved out onto the Ashland Road to picket the roads leading into the Confederate capital. That morning as they moved northeast out of the city, "a young lady came to the window to ask what soldiers we were, and we told her Texans, and she screamed to her mother not to be uneasy, that the Texans were there."[3] A little later on, the Texans encountered Hood's Texas Brigade, a part of James Longstreet's corps, hurrying to the front to rejoin Lee. An emotional reunion ensued in which friends and relatives enquired about one another.

After the emergency of defending Richmond passed, Confederate officials transported the Texans and Arkansans back to Petersburg and from there to Tennessee. From Model Barracks on May 9, Colonel Robert R. Garland placed his brigade on cars bound for the Army of Tennessee, followed some days later by the rest of the Arkansas Post garrison, the brigade of Colonel James Deshler. On May 12, while Deshler's men awaited transportation, Sergeant Andrew Murphey of Company H, 17th Texas Cavalry, marched as a part of the honor guard accompanying the body of General Thomas J. "Stonewall" Jackson as it lay in state in the Confederate capitol. "His countenance was lovely to look upon," commented Murphey, "although asleep in death."[4] The former prisoners traveled by rail to Knoxville and then on to Chattanooga, where they boarded trains for Tullahoma, and finally marched from there to Wartrace to join the Army of Tennessee.

Months before the Arkansas Post prisoners arrived, the high command of the Army of Tennessee had degenerated into chaos. The year 1863 had not begun well for the army commander, Braxton Bragg. Following his retreat from Kentucky and defeat at Murfreesboro (Stones River) in December 1862, events began to spin out of control. Almost immediately after Murfreesboro the Confederate press and some of Bragg's subordinates began to criticize the general for his retreat. A number of his subordinates, including Major Generals Leondias Polk and John Breckenridge, became his chief detractors. In addition, the Confederate government began stripping the Army of Tennessee to reinforce the more threatened parts of the country. In April, Bragg could count nearly fifty thousand effectives. The following month Davis redirected John McCown's and John Breckenridge's infantry divisions to reinforce Joseph Johnston in Mississippi. At that time Johnston had the task of raising the siege of Vicksburg. This, coupled with the detachment of much of his cavalry, left Bragg with barely thirty thousand men. Consequently, he took up a defensive stance behind the Highland Rim in Middle Tennessee.[5]

Adding to his problems, at this juncture Bragg had to deal with the question of what to do with the Arkansas Post garrison. When they arrived at Wartrace, the Texans and Arkansans promptly caught "*fits*" from several veterans, according to Captain Samuel Foster of the 24th Texas. "These old soldiers came into our camp," he explained, "and want to know all about that surrender over in Ark. Want to know why we did'n't fight &c

and as we pass their camp or any of them pass us they hollow at us 'Who raised the white flag in Ark.' *'We don't want you here if you can't see a Yank without holding up your shirt to him'*—'Lie down I am going to pop a cap—don't pull off your shirt it won't hurt you'—and more—it was constant. We could never get out of some old fool making fun of us about that fight at Ark. Post."[6] Rumor had it that only one division commander, Major General Patrick Cleburne, stood willing to "try" the Texans and Arkansans, and so Churchill's Brigade became a part of Cleburne's Division in Lieutenant General William J. Hardee's corps.[7]

The Texans repaid this show of faith by Cleburne time and again as they served under his command for most of the rest of the war. This loyalty to Cleburne underscores the importance that popular officers played in reinforcing devotion to the Confederate cause.

When they arrived in Tennessee, Bragg ordered Churchill to consolidate the Texans and Arkansans from three brigades into one, due to the loss of men during incarceration. Churchill formed the seven Texas regiments into two and the two Arkansas regiments into one. He consolidated the 6th and 10th Texas Infantry Regiments along with the 15th Texas Dismounted Cavalry into the 6th, 10th & 15th Texas under Colonel Roger Q. Mills of the 10th Texas. Churchill formed the second Texas regiment from the 17th, 18th, 24th, and 25th Texas Dismounted Cavalry Regiments into the 17th, 18th, 24th & 25th Texas under Colonel Clayton C. Gillespie of the 25th Texas. Finally, he consolidated the 19th and 24th Arkansas Infantry Regiments into the 19th & 24th Arkansas under the command of Colonel A. S. Hutchinson. At first Churchill attempted to organize the regiments according to company designation, but the men universally protested this method. Instead, he organized each of the original regiments into separate battalions, composed of three or four companies apiece, to act together in the field as a regiment. The Texans sorely resented these consolidations and longed for a return to their original regiments. Colonel Mills wrote his wife, "I have now a very fine command, but it is not my old tenth . . . I had rather command my old one, though small, than a half-dozen blended . . . it makes me sorrowful, every time I think of my old Rgmt. having lost its identity."[8] Similarly, Captain Bryan Marsh of the 17th Texas wrote, "The old 17th regiment is no more. She was buried at Tullahoma on the 23rd of last month [May] by Parson C.C. Gillespie of the 25."[9] Because of these new consolidations, Churchill found he now had too many officers and reassigned them west of the Mississippi, adding to the dissatisfaction of the men in the ranks. These command assignments also temporarily excluded the ranking officer of the brigade, Colonel Robert R. Garland, whom Bragg reassigned pending a court martial hearing into his role in the surrender at Arkansas Post.

On June 1 Cleburne decided to assemble his division in the vicinity of Wartrace. Accordingly, Churchill moved his brigade to the designated rendezvous spot, meeting with the other units of the division on June 3. As soon as the division had assembled, Cleburne began whipping the Arkansas Post brigade into shape. "We are under the most stricked disspling that I ever saw; we drill seven hours evry day," wrote Private A. L. Orr of the 18th Texas. "Gen. Clayborn is our drill officer and the tites one you ever saw." Similarly, his brother Private J. N. Orr wrote, "Gen. Claybourn (our Division Commander) drilles us very hard; we will soon be as well drilled as any troops in the servis."[10] Captain Bryan Marsh of the 17th Texas wrote his wife, "it used to make me mad to hear the Trans Miss Army called the ragamuffin army but I am compell now to acknowledge it to be so. We ner knew what soldiering ment until since we have bin hear."[11]

For the Confederacy, Vicksburg remained the preeminent point of interest in gauging the progress of the war in this summer of 1863. Lincoln knew it, Davis knew it, and perhaps as significantly the men in the ranks knew it. On June 20, Marsh wrote his wife from Wartrace: "The too armys are lying hear fasing each other waiting the result of affairs at Vicksburg. It is generally believed hear that if Vicksburg surrenders that Bragg will fall back but if Grant should be whiped that Rosecrans will either have to fight or fall back."[12] Private J. N. Orr of the 18th Texas wrote home on June 13, "It is generally thought here that thare wont be any engagement here untill the battle is decided at VixBurg."[13] Despite these uncertainties the morale of the Texans in Deshler's Brigade remained high, reinforcing the idea that although the Texans remained cognizant of larger events around them, their localized circumstances played a much larger role in their morale. Sergeant William Heartsill of the 6th, 10th & 15th Texas wrote on June 15 that at night, "when the bands strike up 'Dixie' or the 'Bonnie Blue Flag' the boys make these Tennessee Beech groves ring with their Texas yells, all as happy and as merry as if on a pic-nic excursion."[14]

The general perception among the Texans that nothing would happen in their front until the fall of Vicksburg turned into a false hope. Because of its focus on Vicksburg, the Lincoln administration began prodding and push-ing Major General William Rosecrans to make an advance with his Army of the Cumberland before Bragg could reinforce Johnston in Mississippi. For several months Lincoln put a great deal of pressure on Rosecrans to move forward. Finally, on June 23, Rosecrans prepared to move.[15]

That day Brigadier General David Stanley and his Federal troopers rode out against Lieutenant General Leonidas Polk's Confederates around Shelbyville, initiating the Tullahoma campaign. Early the next morning Major General George Thomas moved his Federal corps against Hoover's Gap and soon captured the pass. With Hoover's Gap secured, Thomas pos-sessed an almost uncontested avenue to the railroad bridge over the Elk River, Bragg's only line of retreat to Chattanooga.[16]

The increased activity soon affected Churchill's Texans and Arkansans. On the afternoon of June 25, the 19th & 24th Arkansas and the 17th, 18th, 24th & 25th Texas departed their camp near Wartrace for Liberty Gap, in the center of the Confederate position. Early the next morning Mills, with his 6th, 10th & 15th Texas, followed the rest of the brigade and over-took them just south of the town of Bell Buckle, below Liberty Gap. When Churchill and his men arrived that morning he ordered Mills's 6th, 10th & 15th Texas, along with Douglas's Texas Battery, to relieve two regiments of Brigadier General S. A. M. Wood's brigade posted in the gap.[17] Churchill kept back the rest of his brigade as a reserve.[18]

When Mills's regiment arrived to replace two of Wood's regiments posted in the gap, the Texans decided to play a prank on the unsuspecting Missis-sippians. The men of Wood's Brigade had become some of the most vocifer-ous detractors of the Texans when the Arkansas Post brigade first joined Cleburne's Division, and the Texans determined to exact some revenge. The "mud-heads," as the Texans referred to them, had taken up positions a bit further down the hill from the Texans, on ground which, according to Lieutenant Robert Collins, was covered with a "sort of iron ore pebbles." As Collins described it, "the Texans would flip these pebbles right over the heads of the Mississippians in such a manner as to make them sing like a minnie ball, and they stuck their heads so close to the ground that their mustaches took root and commenced to grow. We had fun enough for all until they caught us in the trick."[19] Instead of becoming angry, however, the Mississippians simply laughed along with the Texans and grudgingly acknowledged the rectification of past injustices. After replacing Wood's regiments, Mills's men skirmished for most of the rest of the day with the advancing Federals.

With the bulk of the Yankee infantry moving down almost upon the rear of the Army of Tennessee, and with Bragg still unaware of Rosecrans's intentions, it appeared as if the Federals might cut off the Army of Tennessee from Chattanooga and destroy it. At that moment, nature intervened on behalf of the Confederates. Early on June 25, a heavy rain commenced in Middle Tennessee, turning the roads into nearly impassable quagmires. This substantially slowed the advance of Rosecrans's infantry. The rain continued for three straight days, allowing Bragg to react. By June 27, Bragg had started withdrawing his men toward Tullahoma by rail.

Hardee chose Cleburne's Division to serve as rear guard, and Cleburne placed Churchill's Brigade in the rear, personally accompanying the Texans and Arkansans. Hardee ordered the westerners to protect the rear of the division as well as valuable military supplies. The veterans of Arkansas Post, accompanied by Cleburne, withdrew slowly, crossing the Duck River on the afternoon of June 27. They then continued several more miles into the night before dropping, exhausted, on both sides of the road for some rest. That night the rain came down like a "mill tail" as Churchill ordered his men into an old field to sleep on their arms.

At Tullahoma Bragg planned to make a stand against Rosecrans, but the rapidity of the Federal advance completely unnerved the Confederate commander and, added to his enfeebled physical condition, convinced him that he could not hold Tullahoma. Two days later Bragg learned that Rosecrans had started concentrating the entire Army of the Cumberland at Manchester, and he decided to withdraw to the south bank of the Elk River.[20] South from Tullahoma the Texans of Churchill's Brigade slogged along. "Hour after hour we marched through the mud," complained Heartsill, "so tired we can scarcely put one foot before the other, every few hundred yards may be seen one, two or half a dozen men by the road side sick or too tired to go further without rest."[21]

On July 1 Churchill's Brigade, still acting as the rear guard of the army, crossed the Elk near Allisonia over the Bethpage Bridge. No sooner had the Texans and Arkansans sat down to rest on the south side of the river than Churchill ordered them to double-quick back across to fend off the pursuing Federals. The infantrymen went for two miles at a run before halting and forming a line of battle. By this time the rain had ceased, and

Churchill's men stood in the hot sun for several hours during sporadic skirmishing with the enemy.

With the 8th and 11th Texas Cavalry Regiments on either flank of Douglas's Texas Battery, Colonel Mills halted to give his men a rousing speech. "Texas cavalry on the right; Texas cavalry on the left; a Texas Battery in center," he bellowed, "who dare come against us."[22] Despite this pronouncement, nothing happened, and in the evening the rear guard recrossed the Elk. At Cowan, Tennessee, ten miles south of Tullahoma, Bragg halted to oppose Rosecrans. As at Tullahoma, the Confederate commander, pressured by Polk and Hardee, ordered a retreat, this time all the way across the Tennessee River to Chattanooga. As Churchill's Brigade began to scale the northern face of the Cumberland Mountains, men began dropping from the ranks due to exhaustion. Though the pursuing Federals remained close on their heels, many simply could not go any farther and fell by the wayside. Expressing his discomfort, Heartsill, one of the "dismounted" cavalrymen, wrote on July 3, "never in my life . . . was I as completely worn out, I cannot make anything out of this infantry business; it beats me decidedly," he continued, "my feet are almost one solid blister and my shoulders are worn out."[23]

As the Confederate cavalry fended off their pursuers, Churchill's men continued marching south, crossing the Tennessee at Kelly's Ford, five miles west of Chattanooga. Here, on July 6 along the banks of the river, a humorous event occurred between a Texan in Churchill's Brigade and General Hardee. Lieutenant Robert Collins of the 15th Texas had fallen ill and become separated from his command. When Collins approached the Tennessee River, the brigade had not come up yet, but several men from different commands, some of them Texans, had already arrived. On the banks of the river the Confederate provost guard refused to allow anyone to cross the pontoons until their respective commands caught up with them. Collins remembered, "Our Corps commander General Hardee was there; a long keen Texas soldier said he was going over anyhow; when he started, General Hardee drew his sword and made a dive for him. The fellow jumped into the river and the General plunged in after him on horseback. This created some excitement and no little amusement for the boys."[24] With this diversion, Collins simply walked across the bridge. The rest of the Texans and Arkansans crossed the river a short time later and went into camp on the slope of Raccoon Mountain. As a precaution, Churchill ordered Gillespie's

17th, 18th, 24th, and 25th Texas back to Kelly's Ford to perform guard duty all night. Three days later Churchill's Brigade moved by rail to Tyner's Station, twelve miles east of Chattanooga, to join the rest of Cleburne's Division.

In a matter of less than two weeks Rosecrans had forced Bragg to evacuate all of Middle Tennessee, and at the same time even greater events had transpired in Pennsylvania and Mississippi. Captain Samuel Foster wrote in early July, "We hear that Vicksburg has fallen and on the 10th Jackson Miss was attacked and Charleston S c also, by land and by water and that Lee has fallen back, and the Yanks are advancing on this place with a view to going into Georgia and Alabama."[25] The terrible truth about Confederate reverses began to circulate through the ranks of the Army of Tennessee. On July 4 Pemberton had surrendered Vicksburg to Grant. Five days later Port Hudson had also surrendered, giving the Federals full control of the Mississippi. Following Vicksburg, Grant and Sherman had turned part of their forces on Johnston at Jackson. On July 1–3 Robert E. Lee and his Army of Northern Virginia had fought George Meade and the Army of the Potomac to a bloody standstill in southern Pennsylvania around Gettysburg. Meade gained a slight advantage, and after the loss of twenty-eight thousand casualties Lee withdrew back into Virginia on July 4, ending his invasion of Pennsylvania. Charleston, South Carolina, also remained under siege by Federal land and naval forces, but it continued to hold out.

From Vicksburg to Chattanooga to Gettysburg the fortunes of the Confederacy waned during the summer of 1863, lowering the morale of the men in the ranks and focusing the attention of both governments on the armies in Tennessee. Despite these reverses, it is a testament to their devotion to the Confederacy that the vast majority opted not to desert their original regiments. For Braxton Bragg the Tullahoma campaign nearly undid him. Sick and suffering from an attack of boils, the Confederate commander checked himself into a hospital in Ringgold, Georgia, south of Chattanooga, to recover. With Bragg once again at a loss, the initiative passed to Rosecrans.

In the camp of the Arkansas Post brigade changes and controversy followed closely on the heels of their arrival at Tyner's Station. On July 9 Churchill requested a transfer to the Trans-Mississippi Department. A few days later, on July 14, Colonel Garland requested a court of inquiry because the report about Arkansas Post submitted by Churchill had "seriously impeached" his reputation as a soldier. William Mackall, the chief of staff of the Army of Tennessee, respectfully forwarded the request to Adjutant and Inspector General Samuel Cooper in Richmond. Cooper replied, "The exigencies of the service will not admit of assembling a court of inquiry at this time."[26] To satisfy Garland, Churchill called for an informal court in the brigade camp at Tyner's Station. "All the investigation could not ascertain who gave the order to raise the white Flag on the Fort, at Ark. Post," wrote Captain Foster. "They came very near finding *where* it started but not *who* started it. *Nor will it ever be known in this world.*"[27]

In addition to these disruptions in brigade leadership, on July 14 Bragg transferred Hardee, at his own request, to serve under Johnston in Mississippi. Hardee felt that after the dismal Tullahoma campaign he could no longer serve under Bragg. In his stead, Davis appointed Major General Daniel Harvey Hill to the rank of lieutenant general and ordered him to take command of Hardee's Corps around Chattanooga.[28]

The poor weather and retreat from Wartrace seriously damaged the condition of Churchill's men, but with their semi-permanent encampment around Tyner's Station, Cleburne managed to return discipline and morale to the westerners. The men spent the last of July and the first few days of August constructing brush arbors for shelter from the Tennessee summer sun. This type of shelter became necessary because before leaving Tullahoma they had burned their tents as impediments to their withdrawal.[29] The regularized discipline implemented at Tyner's Station helped to revive the morale of the men, but the arrival of bad news on other fronts counteracted these trends. On July 22 the westerners learned that Johnston had abandoned Jackson, Lee had fallen back into Virginia, and Charleston remained under siege. Sergeant Heartsill wrote, "take it all in all, these are the 'dark days' of the Confederacy, but all will come out right in the end, we WILL succeed in this strife for independence."[30] Heartsill's declaration is somewhat startling considering the bad news, but it highlights the loyalty to the Confederacy displayed by these diehard Confederates. During this period the Texans also fared well in foraging the surrounding countryside. On July 28 Heartsill noted ruefully in his diary, "Col. Mills is trying to guard all the corn fields in this County, one hundred from this Regiment on guard today, I am thinking," he mused, "the remedy will prove more fatal than the disease; for the guards will bring an armful into camp every time they come and will manage to have considerable business on hand that will require their presence quite often."[31]

On July 31 Cleburne paraded Churchill's men in front of their new corps commander, D. H. Hill, who had arrived two weeks earlier. Richmond granted Churchill's request for a transfer, and on August 18 James Deshler, who had received a promotion to brigadier general on July 28, took command of the Arkansas Post brigade.[32] Deshler came with the recommendation of none other than Robert E. Lee, and the appointment of this professional soldier suited most of the westerners well.

Colonel Roger Q. Mills, commanding the 6th, 10th & 15th Texas, was not so sure. On August 16 he wrote his wife, "Garland has applied for the place I now hold on the ground that he is my senior. . . . General Churchill refused to permit him to command and stated in writing to General Bragg that I was the best officer." Mills's concern centered on the fact that Deshler favored Garland for command of the regiment, and Mills felt that if Garland applied under this new commander Deshler "will give it to him." Despite the ruminations of Mills, and regardless of Deshler's preference for Garland, events in late August precluded such a change in command. Despite Mills's claims that he remained the best officer, some of the men of his regiment did not think highly of him. On the night of August 14 a Texan in Mills's command raised a hearty yell, which others took up and echoed along the whole regiment. Soon afterward Mills issued orders, as one soldier remembered, "for every man to be quiet or suffer severe punishment . . . the men cannot engage in a little merriment occasionally without displeasing our RULER, petty tyranny now reigns over this Regiment." Their displeasure with Mills notwithstanding, the Texans knew that Colonel Garland had a propensity for stricter discipline, so they indulged the occasional "petty tyrannies" of "King Roger."[33]

On August 15, after six weeks of inaction, William Rosecrans prepared to strike. Impressed with his own success, he planned to cross the river west of Chattanooga and flank the Confederates out of the city. The next day he set his army in motion. In conjunction with the movement by the Army of the Cumberland, Rosecrans instructed Major General Ambrose Burnside with his IX Corps in East Tennessee to hold Confederate lieutenant general Simon Buckner and his divisions in place, keeping them from reinforcing Bragg. The plan got off to a good start, and it appeared as if Rosecrans would again dupe Bragg.[34]

Though Bragg did not know the location of the Army of the Cumberland, he began pushing Richmond to send him reinforcements. He also appealed for aid directly to Joseph Johnston, who had eighteen thousand Confederates in Mississippi. Johnston agreed to send two divisions to the Army of Tennessee. On August 23, Major General W. H. T. Walker with his three brigades of infantry departed for Chattanooga by rail. Two days later, Major General John Breckenridge departed Mississippi with his three brigades. Though Breckenridge became an outspoken Bragg detractor, for the moment Bragg welcomed him and his men.[35]

Meanwhile, Bragg's ignorance regarding Rosecrans's movements held the Confederate general inactive. On August 21 he ordered all noncombatants to leave Chattanooga while he remained purely reactionary in his plans. By the morning of August 29 the first of the Federals set foot on the east bank of the Tennessee, and by the night of September 2 all but Thomas Crittenden's XXI Corps had gotten across the river. Early the next morning Rosecrans issued orders for his troops to start crossing the mountains into the Confederate rear. Meanwhile a lack of intelligence coupled with the effective demonstrations by Colonel John Wilder's Union brigade north of Chattanooga kept Bragg and the Army of Tennessee in place. Not only did Wilder begin lobbing shells into the city, he also had his musicians mimic the bugle calls and drum beats of an entire corps. Amazingly, a single brigade on the north bank of the Tennessee held the entire Confederate army in place.[36]

Finally, on August 30, Bragg's fortunes began to turn. On that day a Confederate sympathizer from Stevenson, Alabama, near where the Federals crossed the Tennessee, arrived at Bragg's headquarters in Chattanooga. He reported the Federal movements, and Bragg responded by ordering his cavalry to protect the mountain gaps. Confederate cavalry commander Joseph Wheeler ignored his orders, however, depriving Bragg of the information needed to act.

Then on September 5 a copy of the *Chicago Times* made its way to the headquarters of the Army of Tennessee. The paper detailed Rosecrans's plan of action, including the diversions north of Chattanooga and the crossing of Crittenden's corps northwest of the city. The Confederate commander immediately decided to abandon Chattanooga and march south toward Rome to catch Rosecrans crossing Lookout Mountain. On the night of September 6 Bragg pulled out of Chattanooga and headed south after the Army of the Cumberland.[37]

The withdrawal from Chattanooga did not sit well with the Texans of Deshler's Brigade. Lieutenant Collins expressed his dismay at the abandonment of the town because the idea "of our army giving up the city of Chattanooga, the gate to the center of the Confederacy, was trying on our confidence in General Bragg and all others in authority over us." As the Texans marched along they despaired among themselves with the reflection that "'If we can't check them and whip them with the advantages of the river and the mountain-locked passes on the right and left of Chattanooga, where is the place we can?'"[38] Sergeant Heartsill similarly noted, "This may not be a retreat, but it looks very much like one; but if General Johnston (as reported) is in command; then we have no fears, if however Bragg is maneuvering, then we will not be surprised to wake up one of these September mornings and find the entire army at or near Atlanta."[39]

Rosecrans believed that Bragg was leading a badly demoralized retreat toward Atlanta. Based on this assumption, he planned to push his three corps as rapidly as possible over the mountains and catch the Army of Tennessee in the flank as it retreated southward. His principal subordinate, George Thomas, advised against such a plan. Rather, he suggested that the army move to Chattanooga to regroup before heading south in pursuit. Rosecrans, flushed with his recent successes, decided to push ahead.[40]

In the early morning of September 8, Major General William Negley's division of Thomas's XIV Corps pushed across Stevens Gap in Lookout Mountain into McClemore's Cove, a semi-enclosed valley formed by Lookout Mountain to the west and Pigeon Mountain to the east. At the southern end of the cove, the two mountains converged, while a single sluggish stream, Chickamauga Creek, ran through the valley. Ten miles further north up this creek Bragg had established his headquarters at a place called Lee and Gordon's Mill. On the afternoon of the next day, September 9, Brigadier General William Martin, whose cavalry brigade Wheeler had reluctantly assigned to guard the gaps in Pigeon Mountain, reported to Bragg that a part of Thomas's Corps had descended into McClemore's Cove and remained there, vulnerable to defeat.[41]

Negley's isolation in McClemore's Cove presented just the opportunity Bragg had waited for to crush a part of the Army of the Cumberland. He immediately sent orders to Major General Thomas Hindman to move his division into place at Davis's Crossroads in the north end of the cove.

Meanwhile, he ordered D. H. Hill to send Cleburne's Division to Dug Gap in Pigeon Mountain, south of Negley's right flank. At the sound of Hindman's attack from the north, Bragg instructed, Cleburne was to attack from the south, catching Negley in a pincer movement and destroying him. Hindman received his orders shortly after midnight on September 10 and moved his men quickly toward Davis's Crossroads. Meanwhile Hill did not receive Bragg's orders until 4:30 A.M., and when he did get them he fired off a list of reasons to his commander why he could not spare Cleburne. When he received Hill's reply, Bragg ordered Simon Buckner to move up two of his divisions to compensate for the absence of Cleburne. By daylight Hindman began to grow cautious. As his men stood poised within striking distance of McClemore's Cove, he convinced himself to do nothing until he heard from Bragg or Hill. Meanwhile, Hill had changed his mind about sending Cleburne, and the Irishman had his men on the road by 1:30 P.M. on September 10. By dusk Bragg had moved his headquarters to Lafayette, closer to the front, and shortly after midnight on September 11 he ordered Hindman to attack "at the earliest hour that you can see . . . in the morning. Cleburne will attack in front as soon as your guns are heard."[42]

The Georgia sun rose on September 11 with Negley still in McClemore's Cove and the Confederates in a perfect position to crush him. By dawn the lead elements of S. A. M. Wood's Brigade of Cleburne's Division began picking their way through Dug Gap, closely followed by Deshler's Texans and Arkansans. At the top of the gap Cleburne posted Wood's Alabamans and Mississippians on the left, Deshler's Brigade on the right, and Lucius Polk's Tennesseans in reserve. Meanwhile, to the north, Hindman received his orders from Bragg at 4 A.M. but did nothing. He sent a courier to headquarters, and though Bragg explained his plan to the courier, Hindman later claimed that he understood his orders as discretionary. At 11 A.M. one of his staff members pointed out that it appeared as if Negley's supply wagons remained in a compromised position at the foot of Stevens Gap and could not escape. This spurred Hindman into action, and he quickly moved toward Davis's Crossroads until his men arrived just a few hundred yards north of Negley's left flank. At that moment he received instructions from Bragg indicating that if he found the enemy "in such force so as to make an attack imprudent" he could fall back to Lafayette.[43] Hindman sent a courier to Bragg to find out whether his orders required him to attack. Finally at 4 P.M., as the sun began to set behind Lookout Mountain, Bragg's reply came: "The attack which was ordered at daybreak must be made at once or it will be too late." Hindman then advanced Brigadier General Patton Anderson's brigade into the cove, only to find Negley and his Federals gone. Wood's Brigade simultaneously advanced and met Anderson's men near Chickamauga Creek. Earlier in the morning when the Federal skirmishers encountered Wood's men coming through Dug Gap, Negley grew wary and withdrew his division back through Stevens Gap onto Lookout Mountain. The opportunity had passed. When Bragg met Hindman in the cove the Arkansan received a severe public tongue lashing from his commander. Though Bragg had the perfect opportunity to crush a part of the Federal army, his plan had failed because Hill and Hindman failed to carry out his orders.[44]

Bragg then spotted another opportunity. Crittenden had allowed his XXI Corps to become dangerously spread out along the Lafayette Road, and Bragg decided to strike him in front and flank on September 12. Bragg ordered Polk to spearhead the assault, but Polk whined about not having enough reinforcements and refused to carry out his orders. While Polk hesitated, Rosecrans realized Crittenden's danger and began concentrating his forces.[45]

Then on September 15 Bragg received intelligence that reinforcements had started his way. Evander McNair's brigade had just arrived from Mississippi, and Bragg expected Brigadier General John Gregg's brigade, including the 7th Texas, to arrive momentarily from the same quarter. In addition, Lee had detached two divisions of his army under James Longstreet, whom Bragg expected to arrive within forty-eight hours. These reinforcements would bring the total Confederate strength on the field to sixty-eight thousand to face Rosecrans's sixty-three thousand Federals. Bolstered by this news, the Confederate commander decided to resume the attack.[46]

On the morning of the fifteenth, Bragg called his corps commanders together and informed them of his decision to assume the initiative once again. He intended to push his divisions across the Chickamauga and cut Rosecrans to pieces. He had to postpone the attack two days, but before 1 A.M. on September 18 his orders went out for Walker and Buckner to cross Chickamauga Creek at 6:30 A.M. while Polk continued to divert Crittenden around Lee and Gordon's Mill.[47]

That night the temperatures in northern Georgia fell to near freezing, and after the scorching weather of the past month soldiers on both sides sought blankets to keep warm. "If I am not greatly mistaken," wrote William Heartsill on the night of September 17, "this time tomorrow will see many a lifeless form strewed over these valleys, whose hearts now pulsate with life and great expectations for the future. We know not our future and would not if possible, but leave all to the great I AM; who governs the life of one man as carefully as he rules the destinies of a World. It is true that when I reflect that this may possibly be the last days entry in my journal; I feel a strange and inexpressible dread of the morrow."[48]

A localized perspective, effective leadership at the regimental and brigade level, and an undying loyalty to the Confederate cause are the only logical explanations for the steadfastness of the Arkansas Post brigade in the spring, summer, and fall of 1863. Although the Confederacy suffered major setbacks at Vicksburg, Gettysburg, and Chattanooga, and although the Texans suffered through consolidation, most of them stayed with their regiments because of a faith in the Confederate cause and effective leadership by Cleburne and Deshler. Even though a few of the Texans deserted to fight closer to home, the vast majority did not, showcasing the motives set out for western Confederates in Daniel's *Soldiering in the Army of Tennessee* and Grear's "Texans to the Front." Though the fortunes of the Confederacy appeared dim, these Texans relied on a faith in themselves, their leaders, and the Confederate cause to carry on.[49]

CHAPTER EIGHT

CHICKAMAUGA

The coming battle of Chickamauga would offer the Arkansas Post prisoners their first taste of combat since their exchange, and put the 7th Texas through a crucible of fire. During the battle, the Texans would perform extremely well, maintaining good discipline and performing everything asked of them while suffering many casualties. From a strategic point of view, Chickamauga would be a pyrrhic victory for the Confederacy, as Bragg would fail to follow his success with a quick strike at Chattanooga; but from the perspective of the men in the ranks, the battle would prove an unqualified success. This phenomenon demonstrates the importance of a localized perspective to the morale of the western Confederates. At Chickamauga, the Arkansas Post brigade would first display the fighting prowess that would make them, along with the 7th Texas, into the shock troops of the Army of Tennessee.

At dawn on September 18, 1863, Brigadier General Bushrod R. Johnson's division, including Gregg's Brigade and the 7th Texas, initiated the Battle of Chickamauga when they began pushing toward Chickamauga Creek. They encountered stiff resistance from the Federal cavalry posted there but by mid-afternoon had gained a foothold on the west bank.[1] John Bell Hood soon arrived on the field, taking command from Johnson, and in the gathering darkness pushed ahead with Gregg's and Jerome Robertson's brigades until they reached the Vinyard house on the Lafayette Road.

On the morning of September 19 a firefight developed around the Vinyard house, and soon the 7th Texas found itself engaged. Rosecrans ordered the Union brigadier general Jefferson C. Davis to turn the Confederate left around the Vinyard farm, and Davis in turn sent the brigade of Colonel Hans Heg across the Lafayette Road into the dense forest. Moving without skirmishers, the Yankees soon ran into the Confederate skirmishers of Gregg's Brigade, who had not been engaged since the day before. Heg's men loosed a volley into the Confederate ranks, but Gregg soon had his brigade advancing.[2] The 7th Texas under Granbury marched on the left flank of the brigade. Gregg and his men drove Heg back before running into Federal reinforcements along the Lafayette Road, and there the Confederates halted.[3]

Brigadier General William Carlin's brigade of Davis's Division joined Heg in a counterattack that drove back Gregg's Brigade.[4] During this period the 7th Texas suffered heavily. Granbury took a hit when a ball struck him in the lower abdomen, not penetrating the skin but leaving extensive bruising that produced a painful wound.[5] Major Khleber M. Van Zandt replaced his fallen colonel as commander of the regiment.

To the north, fighting around the Brotherton farm in the middle of Rosecrans's line gradually spread south toward the northern end of the forces engaged around the Vinyard farm. Near dusk Colonel Emerson Opdycke, leading the 64th and 125th Ohio Infantry Regiments, ran into the battered Tennesseans of Gregg's Brigade amid the tangle of woods east of the Lafayette Road. The Tennesseans repulsed the attack, and as a silence fell over the field Gregg himself rode out to reconnoiter in front of his brigade. Advancing too far, he ran into the skirmish line of the 64th Ohio, which ordered him to surrender. Refusing, Gregg instead turned his horse to ride for safety before a ball struck him in the neck, knocking him from his saddle. The Ohioans gathered around the fallen Texan and divested him of his spurs and sword. Suddenly, from out of the woods, a group of Texans from Robertson's Brigade charged forward and recovered the unconscious officer and his horse. Colonel Cyrus Sugg of the 50th Tennessee took command of Gregg's Brigade.[6]

While Gregg's Brigade saw heavy action, Deshler's Texans had not yet engaged the enemy. The morning of September 19 found Cleburne and his division still at Pigeon Mountain, several miles south of the main action north of Lee and Gordon's Mill. At noon, Cleburne received orders to move his men north toward Bragg's headquarters near Thedford's Ford over the Chickamauga. The Irishman started his troops northward, and they marched at the "quick" and the "double quick" for six miles before they reached Thedford's Ford around 4 P.M. Here the soldiers had the "pleasure" of wading the Chickamauga. Cleburne immediately reported to Polk, who ordered him to move his division toward the battle and form a line behind Brigadier General St. John Liddell's division near the Youngblood farm. On the way to the front the men of Deshler's Brigade passed the 7th Texas, badly cut up from the fighting around the Vinyard farm. By 5:30 P.M. Cleburne had his division in place in the steadily darkening woods.[7]

When Cleburne arrived in the rear of Liddell's Division, Liddell urged him to attack immediately with his division before the Confederate offensive lost its momentum. Cleburne was understandably reluctant to try anything of the sort because of the gathering darkness and the unfamiliarity of the ground. Polk soon arrived and Liddell pled with their corps commander to order Cleburne forward. He succeeded in persuading him, and Polk ordered Cleburne to advance. The Irishman carefully aligned his brigades, with Lucius Polk on the right, Wood in the center, and Deshler on the left. At 6 P.M. Cleburne ordered his men forward.[8]

By this time night had fallen, and the Confederates could do little but aim at the muzzle flashes in the dark as they groped forward. On the right Polk's Brigade encountered and routed two Federal regiments, while in the middle Wood's Brigade did not advance with any enthusiasm, halting periodically to reform its ranks. To break the stalemate, Cleburne ordered up his artillery under Major T. R. Hotchkiss, who opened on the Union troops with double-shotted canister. The Federals began to flee, and Cleburne ordered his men to pursue. In the darkness and confusion the Federals captured the skirmishers of the 17th, 18th, 24th & 25th Texas before their charging comrades coming up from behind freed them. Climbing over the improvised enemy fieldworks, Cleburne ordered his men to halt for the night around 9 P.M.[9] During the fighting the 17th, 18th, 24th & 25th Texas captured over one hundred prisoners, including many officers from the 77th Pennsylvania and 79th Illinois. Colonel Wilkes and his regiment also captured the colors of these two regiments, along with 150 stands of small arms.[10] During this engagement the Texans suffered limited casualties, including Colonel Frank Wilkes of the 17th, 18th, 24th & 25th Texas, who received a slight wound. Lieutenant Colonel John T. Coit replaced Wilkes as commander of the regiment.[11]

Deshler's men settled down for the night in a captured Union camp. Lieutenant Collins noted, "The dead and wounded were all about us all night we could hear the wounded between ours and the Federal lines calling some of their comrades by name and begging for water. The night was cold and crisp, and the dense woodland was dark and gloomy; the bright stars above us and flickering light from some old dead pine trees that were burning in an old field on our left and in front, giving everything a weird, ghastly appearance."[12] Adding to the unpleasant conditions, many of the Texans remained damp from crossing the Chickamauga in a hurry with their boots on. In addition, throughout the night Cleburne shifted his lines, so his soldiers got little if any sleep. Some of the Texans collected the arms and ammunition of fallen Federal soldiers. In this miserable state Cleburne and his division passed the night of September 19.[13]

At long last the fighting on the first day of Chickamauga came to an end. The two armies had fought one another to a stalemate. Rosecrans still controlled the Lafayette Road, but the Confederates had come very close to breaking through at several points.

The next morning Bragg intended to renew the assault from the north with Cleburne's Division and move south with the left wing under Longstreet to make the final attack on the Federal right. The sun rose at 5:47 A.M. on Sunday, September 20. The morning dawned cool and frosty for the soldiers of both armies, and more than a few men reflected on the great conflict. Sergeant Heartsill wrote, "and now must another Holy Sabbath day see two mighty Armies meet in fierce and deadly strife; to measure arms of glistening steel with each other upon the aggravated issues of this once glorious country. Will this day . . . see the struggle end in our defeat or in our triumph, we put our trust in Him who is ever on the side of Justice, Truth and Right."[14]

The day began with delay and confusion on the Confederate right. Bragg listened in vain for the sound of the attack. Hearing nothing, he sent a courier to find right-wing commander Leonidas Polk and order him to attack immediately. The courier found Polk subordinates Hill, Cleburne, and Breckinridge a few hundred yards behind the front line a little after 6 A.M. Earlier in the morning, Polk had instructed Hill to attack as soon as he was "in position," and Hill did not consider his men yet in position because of an angle that existed between Cleburne's left and the right of Major General Frank Cheatham's division. He decided that he should correct the alignment before he could advance. In light of these circumstances, he declined to advance. By the time the courier found Polk, Bragg had almost reached him as well, impatient at the delays. Polk, seeing the situation, rode off in search of Hill. Finding his recalcitrant subordinate, he ordered him to attack immediately. Meanwhile, Bragg, having corrected the alignment of Cheatham's Division, also found Hill at 8 A.M. and demanded that he attack at once. Finally, Cleburne's and Breckinridge's men began to file into place for the assault.[15]

By 9 A.M. the sun was well up, ending any possibility of catching the Federals off guard.[16] The assault, planned to proceed from left to right, began with Breckinridge's three brigades on the north flank. The former vice president's men charged, but Union troops repulsed them with heavy losses. Breckinridge's assault ground to a halt due to a lack of support.

Meanwhile, Cleburne prepared his division to advance. For many of the men in Deshler's Brigade, breakfast that morning had consisted only of blue (or raw) beef, cornbread, and cold water, and as the sound of the fighting reached them they grew anxious to join the fray.[17]

At 9:30 Cleburne's men started forward. The division advanced with Lucius Polk's brigade on the right, Deshler's in the middle, and S. A. M. Wood's command on the left. Deshler and his men moved past Jackson's Brigade of Cheatham's Division and then ran into the rear of Brigadier General Alfred Vaughn's Tennessee brigade. Frustrated, Deshler awaited orders from Cleburne. Meanwhile, Wood's Brigade advanced into the fight after some hesitation on the part of its commander, for which he received an upbraiding from Cleburne. Wood's men did attack, though, before fierce musketry pushed them back out of the field in front of the Union works. As the Mississippians and Alabamans streamed back through the field, Cleburne ordered Deshler's Brigade to take their place.[18]

The Texans advanced six hundred yards through the woods until emerging into an open clearing directly in front of the breastworks of George Thomas's entrenched veterans. Before entering the clearing, the Texans had to pass through the ranks of the broken Mississippians, the same men who had made so much fun of the Texans a few months before. Lieutenant Collins remembered, "The boys seemed to enjoy it as a good joke on the mud-heads," but soon found it no joking matter as they crested the ridge. As they cleared the tree line, Federal batteries opened on them with grape and canister. "The rain of lead that the Federals poured into our lines was simply terrific," wrote Collins, "our loss in officers and men for the first few minutes was alarming in the extreme. . . . We were ordered to lie flat down and hold it." On top of the ridge they took prone positions and stubbornly traded fire with the Federals.[19]

As they advanced toward the top of the hill, Private George Cagle of Captain L. M. Nutt's company in the 6th, 10th & 15th Texas picked up four or five discarded muskets and carried them with him, hoping to increase his firepower. As the Texans reached the top of the ridge and lay down, Cagle kept his guns loaded and firing, giving commands to himself such as, "Attention CAGLE'S BATTERY, make ready, load, take aim, fire."[20] Despite "Cagle's Battery," Brigadier General William Hazen's Union brigade continued to pour a heavy fire into the ranks of the exposed Confederates.

For the next two hours Deshler's men held their ground, but then began to run low on ammunition. Captain James Formwalt ordered Collins to inform Mills of the dwindling cartridges. Collins carried out his orders, and Mills instructed him to report the fact to Deshler. Collins headed toward the right, where he discovered Deshler on his hands and knees, as if trying to peer under the smoke. As Collins approached within ten feet of his commander, a shell ripped through the general's chest, killing him instantly. About the same time a piece of shrapnel struck Colonel Wilkes of the 17th, 18th, 24th & 25th Texas in the right leg and put him out of action. Collins reported these facts to Mills, who assumed command of the brigade as the ranking officer present.[21]

Roger Mills's first problem as commander of the brigade was the lack of ammunition. Just after he took command, the Texans and Arkansans reported their ammunition completely spent. He ordered his men to strip the cartridges off the dead and wounded and fix bayonets. Soon, Lieutenant Colonel Thomas Anderson of the 6th, 10th & 15th Texas sent Lieutenant Matthew Graham of Company C, 10th Texas, to inform Mills that the left companies of his regiment still had plenty of ammunition. Because they had been too far from the enemy works, these four companies had preserved almost all of their bullets. Mills ordered the companies to the front to maintain a steady fire while he saw to the acquisition and distribution of new cartridges for the rest of the brigade. No sooner had he accomplished this than a courier from Cleburne approached and informed him of the imperative to hold the hill at all costs. To preserve the lives of his men, Mills ordered the brigade back twenty paces beyond the crest of the ridge.

He left behind sharpshooters in the trees atop the hill to maintain a steady fire on the Yankees.[22]

But the fight had not quite ended. Lieutenant Colonel John Coit, who had assumed command of the 17th, 18th, 24th & 25th Texas when Wilkes fell, sent word to Mills that the Federals had moved out from behind their works and had started trying to turn his right flank. Mills ordered Coit to throw out a company of flankers to check their advance. Coit soon sent word that the Federals had pushed the flankers back, and Mills ordered Lieutenant Colonel Asa Hutchison to send a company from the 19th & 24th Arkansas to shore up the right flank. The Arkansans likewise failed to stem the advance, and Mills ordered Captain John Kennard of the 6th, 10th & 15th Texas to take his Company A and reinforce the other two companies. Kennard obeyed and succeeded in halting the enemy skirmishers. After this action, the Texans exchanged only desultory fire with the Federals for the rest of the day.[23] The end of the Texans' attack marked the final act of Cleburne's assault.

Meanwhile, James Longstreet had prepared his left wing for action, arranging an assault column five brigades deep. At 10:00 A.M. the last of his units arrived and took its place in line. Longstreet had eight brigades, eleven thousand men, packed into seventy acres east of the Lafayette Road. The front line, composed of Fulton's and McNair's brigades of Johnson's Division, stretched roughly five hundred yards. On the left of the first line lay Gregg's Brigade under Colonel Cyrus Sugg. Sugg arranged his regiments with the 7th Texas, 1st Tennessee Battalion, and 50th Tennessee in the first line and the remaining regiments in the second line of battle.

Meanwhile, chaos enveloped the Union position directly in front of Longstreet's massed columns. In the afternoon, Rosecrans mistakenly ordered Brigadier General Charles Woods to fill a gap in the Union line that did not exist, thereby creating an actual hole in the line. As a result, at 11:15 A.M. Longstreet's columns, with Johnson's Division in the lead, swept through the hole created by Wood's departure. Caught out of position, Wood's Division and the units immediately around them disintegrated into a mob of panicked blue coated soldiers running for their lives with the Confederates on their heels, chasing them west and north toward Rosecrans's headquarters and the rear of Thomas's men.

Johnson's Division advanced through the woods for six hundred yards before they crossed the Lafayette Road. After crossing the road, the 7th

Texas and the Tennessee regiments passed on either side of the Brotherton farmhouse. The Confederates drove off the Union troops around the farmhouse and outbuildings. Advancing farther, the right of Johnson's Division encountered stiff resistance from behind a makeshift line of breastworks in the woods west of the Brotherton field. Under heavy fire, they succeeded in driving the Federals from their position in the woods east of the Dyer farm. Moving on, the Confederates emerged into a vast field five hundred yards deep and fifteen hundred yards wide. "The scene that now presented itself," wrote Johnson, "was unspeakably grand. The resolute and impetuous charge, the rush of our heavy columns sweeping out from shadow and gloom of the forest into the open fields flooded with sunlight. The glitter of arms, the onward dash of artillery and mounted men . . . made up a battle scene of unsurpassed grandeur."[24]

By this time the entire right and center of Rosecrans's army had started retreating. Thousands of Federals streamed back toward Chattanooga as Thomas's left wing held fast throughout the day and then slowly withdrew that evening, staving off complete disaster.

Moving into the Dyer field, Johnson directed Sugg to charge a battery of eight cannons to his right. Sugg complied, and the 7th Texas and 1st Tennessee Battalion and 50th Tennessee rejoined the brigade before they rushed forward and overran the battery, capturing the guns. Johnson then directed Sugg to charge a heavily wooded ridge to his front, which the Confederates also captured. From this eminence Sugg observed the Union wagon trains, which the Federal gunners and teamsters soon abandoned. The Confederates took the wagons and used the captured ammunition to replenish their cartridge boxes. Finding that yet another ridge commanded his brigade's position to the front, Sugg ordered his men up the slope, where they drove away the defenders. No sooner had he placed a battery of artillery in position to secure the ridge than the Union troops counterattacked, contesting the ground with "obstinacy." The left wing of the brigade fell back, exposing the guns, but the 50th Tennessee and 7th Texas held their ground, protecting the cannons and allowing the other units to regroup. Sugg reformed his brigade and remained in possession of the ridge until another brigade relieved them at approximately 5 P.M.[25] This ended the fighting for the 7th Texas at Chickamauga.

On the right, Polk ordered Cleburne to advance his division at about 3:30 P.M. He instructed the Irishman to leave his left flank unit, the Texas

Brigade, in place, while advancing his right and center brigades. Lucius Polk's brigade advanced, carrying several lines of breastworks before halting. By this time twilight had fallen on the field, with the Federal army in full retreat, while the exhausted Confederates celebrated their first major victory in the western theater.

Chickamauga took a severe toll on the eight Texas regiments that would soon become Granbury's Brigade. In addition to the death of General Deshler, Colonel Wilkes of the 17th, 18th, 24th & 25th Texas sustained a wound along with Colonel Granbury of the 7th Texas. Major Khleber Van Zandt then took command of the 7th Texas in Granbury's absence. Both of the Texas regiments in Deshler's Brigade also suffered staggering losses. The 6th, 10th & 15th Texas went into action on the morning of September 19 with 667 men and lost 21 killed, 94 wounded, 1 mortally wounded, 2 captured, 2 missing, and 2 deserted, for a total of 122 casualties, a loss of 18 percent of their force. Lieutenant Colonel Thomas Anderson, commanding the regiment after the battle, reported that the roll call showed 524 present on the morning of September 21.[26] Wilkes's 17th, 18th, 24th & 25th Texas suffered even worse, carrying 767 men into battle and losing 28 killed, 150 wounded, 7 mortally wounded, 1 captured, and 2 deserted, for an aggregate loss of 188 men, or 25 percent of the unit. The regiment also lost four of ten company commanders. Together, the seven original regiments lost 310 men in the vicious two-day battle. In Gregg's Brigade the 7th Texas did not fare any better. The regiment went into battle on the morning of September 19 with 177 men and lost 8 killed, 81 wounded, and 1 deserted, for a total of 90, or 51 percent of those engaged. This brought the total loss of the eight regiments to 57 killed, 325 wounded, 8 mortally wounded, 3 captured, 2 missing, and 5 deserted, for a total of 400 casualties. This represented 25 percent of the 1,611 men carried into action.[27]

One anomalous feature of Chickamauga that showed the ferocity of the fighting was the number of men who reported receiving wounds from multiple rounds almost simultaneously. William Oliphant of Company G, 6th, 10th & 15th Texas, reported three bullets striking him in quick succession, "first in the mouth, breaking my jaw . . . then in the right arm and then in the left hand." William Boyce of Company F, 17th, 18th, 24th & 25th Texas, wrote of the pain caused by a ball that passed through his shoulder while another pierced his skull. Finally, G. G. Gardenhire of Company B, 6th, 10th & 15th Texas, received seven wounds during the battle, including one ball that knocked out the vision in his left eye and destroyed the hearing in his left ear. Despite these wounds, he remained with his regiment until the end of the war.[28]

"The blood red sun has gone down over beyond the great range of mountains," wrote Lieutenant Collins, "deep darkness has spread its mantle over the field of Chickamauga, and the heart sinking silence that prevailed after the great battle, is disturbed only by the groans of the wounded and the hum of many voices as the soldiers would in deep tones inquire for missing comrades, and earnestly congratulate each other upon the success of the day." Deshler's men moved back a little way toward Chickamauga Creek and made camp there, with "the dead in blue and gray" all around them. "Strange as it may seem . . . ," wrote Collins, "we spread our home-made blankets and slept sweetly and soundly on the field of death that Sunday night."[29]

The fighting at Chickamauga provided a heartening triumph for the men in the ranks, although strategically it was an isolated, pyrrhic victory. The victory also revealed the fighting prowess of the Arkansas Post brigade for the first time, even as they lost their beloved Deshler. However, despite Deshler's demise, the Texans retained faith in Cleburne and their regimental commanders that buoyed their spirits and maintained their devotion to the Confederacy. In terms of combat prowess, however, Chickamauga provided for the Texans merely a prelude of things to come.

CHAPTER NINE

CHATTANOOGA

The aftermath of Chickamauga united all of the regiments of Granbury's Brigade. The addition of the 7th Texas aided the other Texans. The excellent regiment served almost as an example, and brought with them Hiram Granbury, the most effective leader the brigade would possess throughout the war. When Granbury and the 7th Texas joined the Arkansas Post brigade, it became Granbury's Brigade, and touched off the third and penultimate phase in the history of these Texas regiments, a chapter in their history that would establish them as the best combat brigade in the Army of Tennessee, the diehard Texas Confederates. The fact that Granbury and the 7th Texas added so much to the history of the brigade indicates the preeminence of effective leadership and localized perspective that many other works, such as *Soldiering in the Army of Tennessee,* have extolled as so prominent in soldiers of the western Confederacy.[1]

Victory at Chickamauga nearly undid the Army of Tennessee and brought changes to the Texas Brigade. After two days of brutal fighting the soldiers had to rest and reorganize, especially Deshler's Brigade, which had lost nearly half its men and its commander. On September 21, Bragg issued orders for his units to pursue the beaten Army of the Cumberland to Chattanooga.

Late in the afternoon of September 21 Cleburne received verbal orders to move his division north toward Chattanooga. This slight delay cost the Confederates in morale, giving the soldiers time to wander about the battlefield. Lieutenant Robert Collins of the 6th, 10th & 15th Texas borrowed a horse and spent five or six hours riding about, inspecting the field. To his horror the lieutenant discovered a dead Confederate still sitting against a tree with his eyes wide open. He discovered dead rabbits and birds and one man with his brains between his feet where a cannonball had decapitated him. Captain Samuel Foster of the 17th, 18th, 24th & 25th Texas found himself part of a detail detached from the brigade to bring in the dead and care for the wounded. He performed this duty for several days after the others had left. Benjamin Seaton of the 6th, 10th & 15th Texas reported in his diary on September 21, "I went over the battlefield and found a grate many dead Yankees and a good many of ours." The shock of their first big battle of the war certainly unnerved the Texans, who were relieved when "at dark, we took up line of march and went som 10 miles and camped for the night."[2] Cleburne had his men back on the road by 7 A.M. on September 22 and that same afternoon the division reached Missionary Ridge outside Chattanooga. Instead of attacking Rosecrans within the city, Bragg decided (with little choice) that he should lay siege in hopes of forcing the Federals' hand.[3]

On Missionary Ridge the Texans went about the task of recovering from Chickamauga. The first challenge involved adjusting to a new commanding officer as they mourned their late commander's death. "Our beloved Gen. Dashler [Deshler] was killed," lamented A. L. Orr of the 17th, 18th, 24th & 25th Texas. Similarly, on October 8 Henry Curl of the same regiment wrote, "You can imagine the gloom that has been cast on this brigade, for there was not a man who did not love him, and they are satisfied they will never get another Brigadier who will treat them so kindly." Cleburne wrote of Deshler, "It was the first battle in which this gentleman had the honor of commanding as a general officer. He was a brave and efficient one. He brought always to the discharge of his duty a warm zeal and high conscientiousness. The army and country will long remember him."[4] In the immediate aftermath of the battle, Colonel Mills of the 6th, 10th & 15th Texas had retained command of the brigade, but Confederate authorities had other ideas. On September 30 the Confederate Congress promoted Colonel James A. Smith to brigadier general and Bragg assigned him command of the Texas and Arkansas brigade.

Like Deshler, Smith had graduated from West Point in the Class of 1853. He served only briefly on the frontier and in 1861 resigned his commission to join the Confederacy, eventually becoming colonel of the 5th Confederate Infantry. Smith fought at Perryville and in subsequent engagements at the head of his regiment, assigned to Lucius Polk's brigade, in Cleburne's Division. After repeated urging, the Confederate Congress promoted him, and he officially took command of the Texas and Arkansas brigade on October 6.[5] With Smith now in command of the brigade, Colonel Mills resumed command of the 6th, 10th & 15th Texas while Major William A. Taylor (originally of the 24th Texas) took command of the 17th, 18th, 24th & 25th Texas in the absence of Colonel Wilkes, who was wounded at Chickamauga, and Lieutenant Colonel John T. Coit, who had fallen ill.

The siege of Chattanooga soon turned sour for the Confederates as privations and hardships played on the men in the ranks, although these circumstances do not seem to have dampened the spirits of the Texans. Bragg placed his army in a wide arc, with the left flank resting atop the towering prominence of Lookout Mountain, southwest of Chattanooga. From there the line curved north up Missionary Ridge to Tunnel Hill, so named because the Chattanooga & Cleveland Railroad ran through it. Though hypothetically Bragg intended to starve the Federals out of Chattanooga, it turned out that his own men had to subsist on short rations outside the city. Bragg kept Cleburne's Division in the center of the line near the crest of Missionary Ridge, where they lived off a little "corn pone." By this time the fall weather had turned cold, adding misery to the boredom of the siege.

Many of the Texans took the opportunity of a lull to write home about Chickamauga and their current circumstances. Captain Bryan Marsh of the 17th, 18th, 24th & 25th Texas wrote his wife on October 15, "We are still at the foot of Missionary Ridge in front of Chattanooga. . . . I am on picket at the present time within 175 yards of the Yanky lines." Fraternization often occurred in these situations of close proximity, and Marsh reported, "Some of the boys are out between the lines at this time exchangin newspapers with them. We have orders not to fire at each other unless they attempt to advance." But memories of prison prompted the captain to relate, "We can talk to each other, but when I think of Camp Chase I can hardly keep from ordering the boys to fire at the Scoundrels." He went on to write that when President Davis visited the army and passed by the Texas Brigade, "The boys gave him a regular Texas yell as he passed. He made some of them a short speech congratulating them on the Battle of Chickamauga." Furthermore, he reported, "The Army is in fine sperits and the best health I have ear [ever] seen them."[6]

Despite the high spirits described by Marsh, vice and the occasional desertion also stalked the bored Texans. "The peculiar circumstances of a life in the field give such latitude to pillage and other wanton mischief that it is almost impossible to suppress the grossest violence even among our own people and upon our own soil," lamented Second Lieutenant Henry V. Smith of the 17th, 18th, 24th & 25th Texas. "Several have deserted from our Regt since the fight," he continued. "Look out for Tom Richards he is among them."[7] Lieutenant Collins busied himself writing letters home, "or to two or three Georgia girls at the same time," or going down to "Hell's half acre. Now this was a place in front of and near the center of our main line, and just in rear of the picket line, it being some three quarters of a mile in front of our line of battle. Here the thugs, thumpers and gamblers from our army as well as from Atlanta and other cities collected to gamble, and you could get a square up and up whack at any kind of game from faro, monte, draw-poker, seven-up, down to thimble ring poker—dice and three card monte." Collins related that he had never seen so much gambling at one time in one place anywhere since, nor any more hard-looking characters. In addition to gambling and fraternizing between the lines, the Texans also amused themselves by observing the daily artillery duel between the Confederate guns atop Lookout Mountain and the Federal cannons in Chattanooga. In this way they wore away the monotonous siege.[8]

Bragg decidedly lost his advantage on October 18 when Abraham Lincoln appointed Grant commander of the newly created Military Division of the Mississippi, giving him jurisdiction over the army at Chattanooga. Five days later Grant arrived in the besieged city, replacing William Rosecrans, and began devising a way to break the siege. Even before Grant's appointment, Lincoln had dispatched two corps from the Army of the Potomac to reinforce Grant and the Federals had established the "cracker line" by capturing Brown's Ferry on October 27, bringing supplies into Chattanooga across Raccoon Mountain. The capture of Brown's Ferry gave the Federals control of Lookout Valley, effectively breaking the siege and allowing Grant to replenish the army's food stores. Though theoretically the Confederates continued to besiege Grant and his Federals, in reality it appeared more the reverse, with the Army of Tennessee starved for provisions and warmth on the hills outside the city.[9]

Meanwhile, trouble began brewing in the ranks of the 7th Texas. Ever since joining John Gregg's brigade, which consisted entirely of Tennessee regiments except the 7th Texas, the Texans had felt slighted regarding their accomplishments. After the wounding of Gregg at Chickamauga, it appeared certain that Confederate authorities would break up the brigade. On November 13, Hiram Granbury, who had recently recovered from his wound at Chickamauga, sat down to write a letter to G. Moxley Sorrell, the Assistant Adjutant General to Lieutenant General James Longstreet, then detached from the Army of Tennessee in East Tennessee. Granbury wrote Sorrell, a fellow Texan, in hopes of having the 7th Texas transferred to Hood's Texas Brigade in Longstreet's Corps. Granbury related:

> The Brigade in which I now serve is composed entirely of Tennesseans with the exception of my Regiment—it is known wherever you go as a Tennessee Brigade, and it is the earnest wish of all the officers and men of my Regiment to be brigaded with troops from their own State. In an account of the operations of Gregg's Brigade in the Battle of Chickamauga, published in an Atlanta paper, the writer being a Tennessean, every Regiment was mentioned except the 7th Texas, and my losses in the battle were greater than those of any other Regiment of the Brigade in proportion to the numbers present. . . . It is true that we can do as much and as good service here, as elsewhere, but we are not insensible to the praise of our fellows and wish to have credit at least in our own State for whatever sacrifices it may be our duty to make, and whatever deeds it may be our good fortune to achieve. We have friends, neighbors and relations in Robertson's Brigade and in many respects the change solicited would be agreeable to us.

Two days earlier, Brigadier General Jerome Robertson, commanding Hood's Texas Brigade, had written a letter to Major Van Zandt, whom he believed to still be in command of the 7th Texas pending Granbury's return, expressing the desire of himself and the men of his brigade that the 7th Texas should join them as well. However, instead of listening to the appeals of Granbury and Robertson, Braxton Bragg officially dissolved Gregg's Brigade via Special Orders No. 294 on November 12 and assigned the 7th Texas to the Texas Brigade in Cleburne's Division.[10]

Thus, all of the Texas regiments of Granbury's Brigade finally came together. On November 12, Bragg also transferred the 19th & 24th Arkansas from Smith's Brigade to Daniel Govan's Arkansas brigade, making room for the 7th Texas. Now Smith's Brigade consisted of the 6th, 10th & 15th Texas under Colonel Roger Q. Mills, the 17th, 18th, 24th & 25th Texas under Major William A. Taylor, and the 7th Texas under Granbury.[11]

The standoff outside Chattanooga continued until Grant prepared to move in the third week of November. At midnight on November 22, Bragg ordered Cleburne to take his division and proceed south to Chickamauga Station, where he would take command of his own and Bushrod Johnson's divisions and proceed to East Tennessee to reinforce General James Longstreet. At dawn on November 23, Cleburne moved his division south toward the rendezvous point. Learning of the movement, Grant ordered two divisions of the Army of the Cumberland forward, and they captured Orchard Knob, an isolated Confederate outpost a mile in front of Missionary Ridge. In response, Bragg recalled Cleburne's Division and placed it in reserve near the center of the Confederate line.[12]

Once his troops captured Orchard Knob, Grant went about planning an assault on Bragg's left, atop Lookout Mountain. On November 24 he dispatched Major General Joseph Hooker with several divisions to capture the prominence. By mid-morning the Federals had taken the summit. At the same time Bragg learned that several Union divisions had begun to advance against his right around Tunnel Hill. Immediately he dispatched Cleburne with his division to the right, to shore up that flank.[13]

With James Smith and his Texas Brigade in the lead, Cleburne's Division headed for Tunnel Hill at the same time that three Federal divisions under William T. Sherman also converged on the hill. Just as Bragg dispatched Cleburne, a courier arrived from Hardee, who had recently returned from Mississippi and to whom Bragg had assigned command of the right wing. Hardee's messenger indicated that Sherman's columns had arrived within striking distance of the tunnel. He indicated that Hardee's engineer, Major D. H. Poole, would meet Cleburne at the summit and direct him where to place his brigades. Cleburne spurred ahead of his men and found Poole as promised. The engineer quickly explained that Hardee wished Cleburne to cover the ridge beyond Tunnel Hill, known as Billy Goat Hill, as well as Tunnel Hill itself. Cleburne protested that this was too much to cover with his three brigades (earlier he had temporarily detached Polk's Brigade), and that Poole should go back and tell this to Hardee. Despite his protest, events soon spun out of control as the skirmishers from Sherman's three divisions began ascending the opposite slope of Billy Goat Hill. Immediately Cleburne ordered Smith to take his men and charge the hill. The Texans rushed down into the valley and up the slope of Billy Goat Hill, toward the Federal skirmishers who by then had already taken possession of the crest. Together three Union regiments, the 4th Minnesota, 30th Ohio, and 6th Iowa, fired down into the ranks of the Texans. At this time Smith realized that it would be impossible to drive off the attackers with his lone brigade. Precipitously, the Texans fell back to Tunnel Hill, where Cleburne placed them along the crest.[14] No sooner had they regrouped than the Union troops began toward them, up the slope of Tunnel Hill. Smith and his men easily repulsed the assault and Sherman declined to press the matter that night.

During the night, Cleburne placed his brigades in position to defend the hill. He organized his line in the shape of a fishhook, with the Texans anchoring the center of the line. On the brigade left, Mills's 6th, 10th & 15th Texas faced due west, while to their right Granbury and the 7th Texas fronted north. Finally, on the right flank, the 17th, 18th, 24th & 25th Texas under Taylor faced northeast. Cleburne placed Lowrey's Brigade on the Texans' left, extending the line south. He sent Govan's and Liddell's Brigades to the right, directing Govan to occupy a low ridge on the right, north of the railroad. At 4 P.M. Hardee arrived on Tunnel Hill and directed two regiments of Lowrey's Brigade to occupy another low-lying ridge on the right, east of Govan's line. Meanwhile, he promised to send reinforcements to shore up this new extended line.[15]

Cleburne made little effort to shore up this new line, apparently because he assumed that Bragg would abandon Missionary Ridge with the fall of Lookout Mountain. He ordered all but two guns of his artillery to the rear, and though he directed the men to make breastworks, he left their supervision to one of his staff members. Cleburne sent his aide, Captain Irving Buck, to Bragg's headquarters to learn the state of affairs, and Buck returned at midnight with the unsettling news that Bragg had decided to stay and fight it out. At this news, Cleburne gave orders to bring back the artillery. He personally placed Swett's Battery in Smith's line and Key's Battery so as to command the approaches from the west. He also issued axes to his men to construct breastworks.[16]

On top of Tunnel Hill the Texans made the best they could of the situation: "We . . . slept but little . . . having been engaged in felling trees, entrenching and erecting breastworks," wrote Sergeant Albert Jernigan of the 6th, 10th & 15th Texas. The Texans could not build fires and had to endure the cold night without blankets, no one speaking above a whisper. Shortly after midnight a lunar eclipse occurred, creating inky blackness atop Tunnel Hill. About 3 A.M. Major Taylor ordered Captain Foster to take his company and relieve the pickets in front. "The night [was] very dark," wrote Foster, "and here along these high mountains and steep hill sides, and tall timber, and thick undergrowth of course it was very *very* dark." Foster groped his way forward until he found one end of the picket line and then proceeded along it, placing a man every ten or fifteen feet behind trees to give them more cover, and then the captain "Stood perfectly still till day light." "We threw up temporary works, such as we could make of old logs, loose rocks, etc., from where we were," wrote Lieutenant Collins. "But," concluded Sergeant Jernigan, "the morning found our works but frail, and along portions of the line none at all, on account of the scarcity of implements with which to work."[17]

November 25 dawned hazy. Sherman would attack Tunnel Hill from the north and northwest. The nature of the position allowed room to use just two of the nine brigades at his disposal. In addition, on the left he ordered one regiment of Colonel Joseph Lightburn's brigade to support the attack. Lightburn selected the 30th Ohio, and quickly Colonel Theodore Jones had his Ohioans moving toward the crest of Tunnel Hill. They quickly ran into Captain Foster and his skirmishers. As soon as it became light enough to see, one of Foster's men said, "Capt. I see one. Can I shoot at him." Foster replied to wait until it got a little lighter, and then "blaze away." That man fired the first shot of the day a minute later, and soon the entire skirmish line opened up on the Ohioans. Amazingly, the Texans lost only one man in this firefight, George Woods, who took a bullet through the neck that cut his windpipe. The Texans continued to fire from behind their trees until Foster passed the word down the line to "fall back slowly, but keep firing from tree to tree as we fall back." The skirmishers fell back, contesting every inch of ground until they reached the main line of the brigade.[18] The Ohioans continued until canister from Swett's Battery forced them back down the ridge into some abandoned breastworks.

Furious because of the lack of support, the Ohioans fell back to John Corse's brigade, where they prepared for another attack. Corse arrayed his regiments and advanced with companies from the 40th and 103rd Illinois, 46th Ohio, and 6th Iowa. On their left the 30th and 37th Ohio, supported by the 4th West Virginia, also went forward, intent on dislodging the Texans. After his deployment as a skirmisher, Sergeant Jernigan of the 6th, 10th & 15th Texas fell back on the main line as Corse's men pressed him,

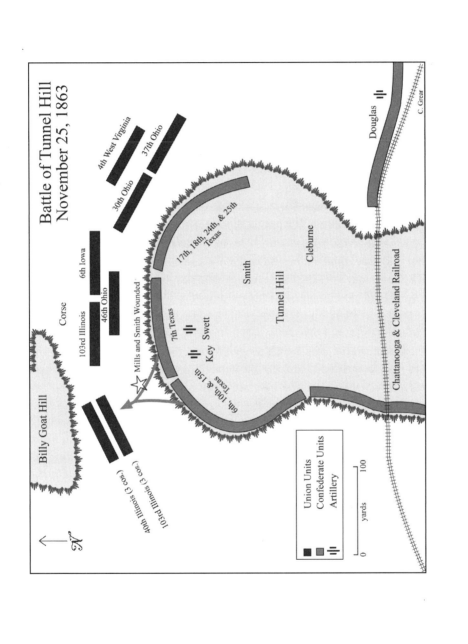

Battle of Tunnel Hill
November 25, 1863

Billy Goat Hill

N

Corse

4th West Virginia

30th Ohio

37th Ohio

6th Iowa

103rd Illinois

46th Ohio

Mills and Smith Wounded

40th Illinois (3 cos.)

103rd Illinois (3 cos.)

17th, 18th, 24th, & 25th Texas

Smith

7th Texas

Key

Swett

6th, 10th, & 15th Texas

Tunnel Hill

Cleburne

Douglas

C. Grear

Chattanooga & Cleveland Railroad

Union Units
Confederate Units
Artillery

yards

0   100

and "as the first rays of the morning sun look over the eastern hills, light-ing up a most beautiful, picturesque, autumn landscape, long blue lines of the enemy, with bayonets gleaming in the sun light and banners floating on the breeze, are seen marshaling themselves in battle array." Soon the battle commenced in earnest and the Federals wavered and fell back, leav-ing the bodies of the slain in their wake. They reformed and came again, only to fall back in the face of the fierce musketry. A third time Corse's men reformed and advanced up the slope.[19]

Massing directly in front of Swett's Battery, the blue coats came on, clambering up the side of the rocky hill until they reached a point where the Mississippians could not depress the cannon enough to hit them. The Yan-kees advanced from behind boulders and trees, making one final rush for the Texans. "His front rank is mowed down at one fell swoop," wrote Jerni-gan. "Their places are filled immediately as if by the spirits of the lifeless bodies at their feet; these share a similar fate to those who have gone before. But still they come, more, and still more. In many places they are within a few feet of our line. The dead and dying lie heaped upon the ground; while their blood commingles and runs in streams down the steep hill-side."[20]

In desperation, Smith thought he detected the Federal lines beginning to waver and asked permission of Cleburne to launch a counterattack. Cle-burne consented, and Smith lunged forward with the right flank of the 6th, 10th & 15th Texas and the left flank of the 7th Texas. "Some fly, others surrender, while others, for a brief space continue to fight, but they are soon overcome," wrote Jernigan. "We sailed into them," wrote Lieutenant Collins, "captured many prisoners, six stands of colors and many guidons." Collins had unbuckled his sword earlier. As he charged, he "left it, grabbed a rock and went in." As he later wrote, "A good many of the Yankees played dead that had not been touched." Collins "captured a whole company that had taken shelter behind a big chestnut log; they were more than willing to surrender." Mills and Smith led the charge on horseback, and bullets soon felled them from their saddles, both badly wounded. The Texans pursued their foe to the foot of the ridge before Cleburne recalled them.[21]

Almost all of the Confederates fell back immediately, and in good order, but some lingered to return fire. "I was torn to leave without giving them a parting salute, I fire at them, load and fire a second shot, and now I find myself all alone, my comrades having obeyed the order to fall back," remembered Jernigan. The Union troops soon discovered him and took aim. "I step behind a pine," he wrote, "and concluded to load, and give them one more shot before retiring. While loading, a ball grazed the tree striking my gun and splintering the stock. I am putting on a cap, a shrapnel explodes near me, my right arm falls paralyzed to my side, Am shocked by the concussion, feel dreadful pain in my elbow, my gun falls to the ground, a momentary dizziness comes over me." Still able to walk, Jernigan stumbled back to the crest of the ridge.[22]

Back on Tunnel Hill, Cleburne gave command of the Texas Brigade to Colonel Granbury. Granbury assigned command of the 7th Texas to Captain Charles E. Talley, while Captain John R. Kennard took charge of the 6th, 10th & 15th Texas in place of the dangerously wounded Mills.

Corse fell back to the cover of a ravine at the base of the hill and decided to try again. The two rear regiments of his brigade had not been engaged and the fighting Iowan decided to try a little farther to his left, along the front of the 17th, 18th, 24th & 25th Texas. "Here they come again for about the sixth time," wrote Captain Foster, "and they come like they are going to walk right over us—Now we give them fits. See how they do fall, like leaves in the fall of the year. Still they advance and still we shoot them down—and still they come. Oh this is fun to lie here and shoot them down and we not get hurt. Ark. Post was not like this." Corse's Federals took cover under the crest of the hill and proceeded to pick off the gunners of Swett's Battery. The Mississippians took such heavy casualties that Granbury detached some of the infantrymen of the 7th Texas to man the guns.

Meanwhile, Cleburne tried to dislodge the determined attackers by placing Douglas's Texas Battery on Govan's flank to enfilade them. "This is business," remembered Foster, "when they get in about 50 yards of us they halt, commence wavering, some keep coming, others hang back, some are killed in 20 ft of our works." Finally, without orders, the Texans jumped over the works and, "yelling like only Texans can," charged into them, killing many and driving the others back again. "I was standing on top of the logs yelling like an Indian," recalled Foster, when a ball caught him in the right leg, passing under the knee. Several of his men cried out, "Capt. you are hit," as they rushed to his aid. They helped the wounded captain rip open his pants to find the wound, as litter bearers came to carry him to the brigade hospital. This wound did not keep Foster out of action for long, though. Meanwhile, the men of the 17th, 18th, 24th & 25th Texas drove Corse's attack back to its starting point.[23]

By noon the Texans had driven back their attackers, and Sherman decided not to renew the assault, but he still pushed several of his brigades close enough to snipe at the Confederates from the bottom of the hill. Meanwhile, Cleburne called for reinforcements, receiving first the 2nd, 15th & 24th Arkansas from Govan's Brigade and then Alfred Cumming's Georgia brigade. Cumming massed his three regiments behind Granbury's Brigade, while Cleburne orchestrated a counterattack with the 2nd, 15th & 24th Arkansas, the 6th, 10th & 15th Texas, and two of Cumming's regiments. At 3:30 P.M., after arranging the regiments in column, Cumming led them forward down the hill. At first the attack stalled, but the Georgians, Arkansans, and Texans regrouped and tried again, this time sweeping the pesky Federals from their positions. The Confederates again pursued to the bottom of the hill before returning, forcing the Union troops to give up their attack altogether. At 5 P.M. Cleburne sent out skirmishers; the Federals had withdrawn, ending the fight for Tunnel Hill.[24]

Despite the performance of Cleburne and his Texans, the rest of the Confederate army had not fared so well. To take attention off Sherman, Grant had ordered several divisions of the Army of the Cumberland forward up Missionary Ridge in the center of the Confederate position, and the attack punched a huge hole in the middle of the Confederate lines. Taking advantage of poorly sited Confederate breastworks, the Federals put the Rebels to flight and forced Bragg to abandon Missionary Ridge.

The defense of Tunnel Hill had come to naught. For over seven hours Cleburne's men defended the hill against determined attacks. The Texans acquitted themselves particularly well, participating in no less than three counterattacks. They also repulsed their attackers over and over. But all their fighting became a moot point with the rout of the rest of the army. "Soon after night," wrote Cleburne, "Gen. Hardee ordered an immediate retreat across the Chickamauga . . . and Smith's (Texas) brigade should remain in position and bring up the rear." By 9 P.M., all the wagons were across the Chickamauga, and Cleburne "ordered Smith's brigade to move in retreat. Sadly, but not fearfully," wrote Cleburne, "this band of heroes left the hill they had held so well and followed the army across the Chickamauga."[25]

Meanwhile, the wounded from Granbury's Brigade languished in the brigade hospital. "Each brigade had its hospital," remembered Sergeant Jernigan, "say half a mile in rear of the army, to which the wounded were conveyed by the litter corps." The surgeon in charge of the hospital would give them whatever attention he thought proper and then ambulances would take them farther back to the division hospital. Jernigan did his best to describe the scene: "A cloudy night.—a pine forest, with but little undergrowth.—A long row of the blazing fires on each side of which lie a host of torn, mangled and bleeding forms in gray jackets, the features of most of whom are distorted and writhing in agony. . . . Attendants flittering about, casting ghostly shadows on the dark forest background— Moans, groans, cries, prayers, curses, screams and wailings of anguish all commingled." Around midnight word reached the hospital that the army had suffered defeat and that the reversal would force them to withdraw as quickly as possible to Chickamauga Station.[26]

Granbury's Texans paid a heavy price for their steadfastness. The only definite casualty figures for the Texas Brigade come from the 6th, 10th & 15th Texas, which suffered 16 killed, 59 wounded, and 4 missing, for a total of 79. Cleburne reported the loss of his entire division at 42 killed, 178 wounded, and 2 missing, for a total of 222, meaning that the losses in the 17th, 18th, 24th & 25th Texas and the 7th Texas must have been much lighter than those of their counterparts. It appears that Mills's regiment accounted for roughly 36 percent of the divisional casualties, a staggering proportion. As trophies for their sacrifice, the 6th, 10th & 15th Texas held four enemy battle flags at the end of the conflict. More importantly, however, the brigade lost its two senior commanders, Smith and Mills, leaving the regimental leadership to junior officers and the brigade command to Colonel Granbury.[27]

As the rear guard of Texans made its way down Tunnel Hill and south through the night, Lieutenant Collins and Captain Jack Leonard tramped along at the head of the column. Collins turned to Leonard and said, "This, Captain, is the death-knell of the Confederacy, for if we cannot cope with those fellows over the way with the advantages we have on this line, there is not a line between here and the Atlantic ocean where we can stop them." "Hush, Lieutenant," Leonard replied, "that is treason you are talking." With this utterance, the column fell back into abject silence. After catching up with the rest of Cleburne's Division, the Texans laid down to rest for a few hours before resuming the march. At daylight on November 26 they reached Chickamauga Station on the Western & Atlantic Railroad.[28]

At Chickamauga Station, Cleburne ordered his men to destroy all the supplies they could not bring off, to deny their use to the Federals. Some of the division took advantage of the situation and helped themselves to all they could before lighting the bonfires. Some filled sacks with hardtack, and others slung sides of bacon over their shoulders before heading south.

At 10 P.M. Cleburne and his men reached South Chickamauga Creek, and here they halted before proceeding. Just after midnight the Irishman received orders from Bragg to position his division in Ringgold Gap until all of the army's wagons had escaped south. At 2:30 A.M. on November 27, reveille sounded for the tired soldiers, and they assembled in what one remembered as the coldest morning he had ever experienced during the war. "By this time it was cold and frosty," wrote Lieutenant Collins, "the moon was bright and clear, and seemed to cast an extra sheen of bright light over everything. We could even see the diamonds of frost as they fell through the cold, crispy air." Cleburne ordered his men to strip off their uniforms and wade the creek while others built large bonfires on the south side. At this point the creek stretched about thirty yards wide and came up to their waists as the soldiers began to cross. Some of them obeyed orders and stripped down to nothing but their shirts, while others "went in like horses, with all their rigging on . . . the former fared better, even if we did have to climb the wet frozen banks with bare feet." Once across the creek the Texans continued south through the town of Ringgold and into the gap.[29]

Ringgold Gap was a virtual Thermopylae: the defile allowed barely enough room for a small stream, a wagon road, and the Western & Atlantic Railroad to pass through. Liddell's Brigade commanded by Govan arrived first, and Cleburne, because a single regimental front literally filled the defile, posted the four regiments one behind the other in the gap. Granbury's Texans arrived next and Cleburne sent the 6th, 10th & 15th Texas to protect the right (north) side of the gap. He then placed the 17th, 18th, 24th & 25th Texas to their right further up the side of the ridge. Finally, the Irishman sent the 7th Texas to the high ground in the rear of the other two regiments with orders to watch the right flank. Lowrey's Brigade arrived last, and Cleburne put three of his regiments behind Govan's men in the gap, sending the 16th Alabama to the left (south) side of the gap to guard that flank. He also positioned two twelve-pound Napoleon cannons concealed behind brush on the left side of the 6th, 10th & 15th Texas to enfilade any attackers.[30]

No sooner had the last of Lowrey's regiments arrived than the Federal pursuers appeared on their heels. Major General Joseph Hooker, in command of the Union pursuit, decided to attack the Confederates defending the pass in the hope of breaking through and completing the destruction of the Army of Tennessee. The Confederate gunners and the Texans hidden in the brush concealed their presence until the 17th and 31st Missouri Infantry Regiments approached within a few paces. At nearly point-blank range the 17th, 18th, 24th & 25th Texas opened on its quarry a few minutes after 8 A.M., shattering the ranks of the Missourians. The Federal brigade commander, General Charles Woods, sent forward another regiment, the 29th Missouri, which almost succeeded in slipping around the flank of Taylor's regiment. At the last second Taylor bent back his right flank and posted a line of skirmishers at right angles to the line. He also dispatched two companies to occupy a swell that jutted out from the mountain due east of Ringgold. To reinforce this flank, Granbury dispatched two companies from the 6th, 10th & 15th Texas to bolster Taylor's two detached companies. As the 29th Missouri clambered up the slope, Taylor surprised them by leading three companies in a wild charge that swept the Missourians back down the mountainside into the valley below, capturing their colors in the process. The other two regiments also caught the panic and followed the example of the Twenty-ninth.[31]

With the repulse of his front-line regiments, Wood ordered up the 76th Ohio, 13th Illinois, 3rd Missouri, and 12th Missouri. He directed the Illinoisans to advance toward the left-center of the Confederate position and instructed the Ohioans to try to get around the Confederate right. To hold the Texans' attention, Woods pushed the 3rd and 12th Missouri toward the center of the 17th, 18th, 24th & 25th Texas. The 13th Illinois advanced straight toward the two camouflaged Napoleons. The Federals approached within a few yards before Cleburne gave the order to fire. Blasts of grape and canister ripped through the ranks of the Illinoisans and their advance rapidly came to a halt. The 3rd and 12th Missouri also moved forward, before the relentless fire from the Texans to their front pinned them down. While these Missourians held the attention of Granbury's men, the 76th Ohio slipped around their right flank. Seeing the danger, Cleburne dispatched the 1st Arkansas, which trapped the Ohioans in a defile and checked their advance with a destructive fire.[32]

With the failure of Woods's attack, Hooker advanced several more brigades forward, again hoping to turn Cleburne's right. Seeing the threat, Cleburne shifted most of Lowrey's and Polk's brigades to meet the attackers. The action on Granbury's front quieted, so the Texans merely added enfilade fire to aid their comrades on the right. For the next five hours the Confederates made a tough defensive stand, holding the Yankee brigades in check against repeated assaults. Around noon Cleburne received a note from Hardee that he could safely withdraw: he had secured the passage of the army's wagons. At 2 P.M. Cleburne ordered the brush camouflage resurrected in front of the cannons and cautiously withdrew his men, leaving skirmishers behind to provide warning of any new advance. Cleburne had nothing to worry about, Hooker had had enough. No attack came and Cleburne and his men escaped south to rendezvous with the rest of the army near Dalton, Georgia.[33]

Cleburne and his division received accolades for their important defense of Ringgold Gap, juxtaposed with a relatively slight price in casualties. The Confederate Congress passed a resolution of thanks to Cleburne and his division for saving the army's wagons, and even the normally acerbic Bragg praised the Irishman in his official report. The 6th, 10th & 15th Texas lost a mere nine wounded and three missing, while the 7th Texas had five wounded. The heaviest loss in the brigade came from Taylor's 17th, 18th, 24th & 25th Texas, which lost five killed, twenty wounded, and twenty missing, bringing the total brigade loss to five killed, thirty-four wounded, and twenty-three missing, for a total of sixty-two casualties, compared to 507 for the Union.[34]

The accomplishments of Cleburne, Granbury, and their men provided a bright spot in the otherwise grim atmosphere following the defeat at Missionary Ridge. Bragg, despondent and discouraged in the wake of the disaster, tendered his resignation to Jefferson Davis on November 27, and the president readily accepted. Davis placed Hardee in temporary command of the Army of Tennessee while he looked for a permanent replacement. On December 2, Bragg departed the army for the last time, to the relief of Patrick Cleburne, Colonel Granbury, and many of its soldiers. North of Dalton, Cleburne and his men went into winter encampments, while Grant and his Federals did the same near Chattanooga. It proved the final act in an eventful year for Granbury's Texans. "The present year is about to close," mused Benjamin Seaton of the 6th, 10th & 15th Texas, "and will close leaving many a widow and orphan to moan the loss of the brave hoo have falen on the battlefields to rise no more—O[h] that this war wold end and let peace raign again."[35]

Although the Texans of Granbury's Brigade had shown a strong devotion to the Confederacy and the Confederate cause prior to November 1863, the addition of Hiram Granbury and the 7th Texas took that devotion to a whole new level. The 7th Texas and the rest of the Texas regiments benefitted from being brigaded together, and even after the death of Deshler at Chickamauga they enjoyed unparalleled leadership at the regiment, brigade, and division level. Despite the fact that Chattanooga and the surrounding battles proved largely disastrous to the Confederate cause, the Texans saw them as unqualified victories. Twice against overwhelming odds they had met and repulsed larger Union forces, increasing their confidence in each other and their leaders. A very few Texans did desert in the wake of Chickamauga, but these desertions largely came, as suggested in "Texans to the Front," due to the closing of the Mississippi in July. Overall, Chattanooga and Ringgold Gap showed that even as the Confederacy crumbled around them, the diehard Confederates of Granbury's Brigade would continue to uphold the Southern cause with their perspective and their leaders to guide them.[36]

CHAPTER TEN

CAMP LIFE

In early 1864, the instatement of Hiram Granbury and Joseph Johnston to command the Texas Brigade and the Army of Tennessee provided a major boost for the Confederate war effort. The morale of the western forces of the Confederacy might have dissipated without these charismatic leaders in command. From the perspective of the historian, even though Johnston did not perform well as an army commander, the men in the ranks adored him, and that fact in itself prolonged the Confederate war effort by keeping men in the field. This phenomenon further illustrates the primacy of a localized perspective when understanding the morale of the men in the western Confederate armies. The rise of Granbury to command of the brigade and the leadership he displayed also helped increase the devotion of the Texans to the Confederate cause. While the Confederacy crumbled around them, Granbury's Texans went forward heartened.

In spite of the waning fortunes of the Confederacy as a whole, New Year's Day, 1864 dawned with hope for the Confederate Army of Tennessee. Their new commander, General Joseph Johnston, had renewed the spirits of the weary soldiers. Despite their prospects, the end of the war remained uppermost in the minds of many of the soldiers in this western army. "In comes a new year and no prospect of peace," wrote Private Benjamin Seaton of the 10th Texas Infantry on January 1, "O that peace may be made before the end of the present year may close."[1]

At the highest levels of Confederate command, Jefferson Davis had confronted a hard task in finding a new commander for the Army of Tennessee. Hardee had made it clear that he did not want the responsibility of commanding the army permanently, and circumstances had forced Davis to search for another replacement.[2] The only suitable candidate had been General Joseph E. Johnston. The appointment of Johnston proved the last desperate option for Jefferson Davis. A bitter feud existed between Davis and Johnston that had begun when the Confederate Congress commissioned Johnston a full general, but fourth on a list of five in order of rank in the old U.S. Army. Johnston believed himself entitled to the number-one spot, due to his staff ranking.[3]

Davis wrote Johnston in December, advising him of the general condition of the Army of Tennessee prior to his arrival. He informed him that the army remained relatively well supplied and had plenty of ammunition and artillery on hand. He also mistakenly informed him that the army possessed high spirits despite the earlier defeat. Under these circumstances, he expected Johnston to take the offensive at the earliest possible opportunity. On December 27, Johnston reached Dalton and assumed command the next day, replacing Hardee. When he arrived, he encountered little that resembled what Davis had described. Johnston quickly saw that he had his work cut out for him.[4]

As Johnston helped to make the Army of Tennessee an effective fighting force and raise its morale, just to the north of Dalton the division of Major General Patrick Cleburne attended to business as usual. Bragg had posted Cleburne's Division six miles north of Dalton, near Tunnel Hill. This distance allowed the Irishman to keep his division somewhat separate from the decay that attended the rest of the army. Experience made Cleburne a stickler for drill, and though the rest of the army fell into poor condition, he kept his men attending to discipline regularly. He conducted classes on military matters for his brigade commanders, who in turn instructed their regimental commanders, and so on down to the men in the ranks.[5] Colonel Hiram Granbury's Texas Brigade made its camp on Tunnel Hill with the rest of the division.

The Texans fashioned an elaborate camp that contained all the comforts of good winter quarters. For some, shelter consisted of dug-out ditches with pine boughs for cover. For others, winter quarters were log huts replete with fireplaces, bunks, and shelves. Some Texans even created chimneys from barrels with the bottoms knocked out. Lieutenant Robert M. Collins of the 6th, 10th & 15th Texas Dismounted Cavalry noted that "in our winter quarters there was as great a variety of architecture as there is to be found in any city or town in the country."[6] Many of the men excavated rectangular pits in the ground upon which they erected wood framing. They covered these frames with planks and finished out their winter cabins by roofing them temporarily with dog tents, which they eventually replaced with sod roofs, completing their winter quarters. The Texans made their doors from pine, creating a more homey feeling for many of the Confederates. The men dubbed the area around them Pine Ridge, due to the abundance of pine trees that soon disappeared in the erection of winter quarters. This left the Georgia topsoil exposed, and when it rained the camp of the Texas Brigade turned into a quagmire.[7]

Meanwhile Joseph Johnston remained hard at work repairing the army. To deal with the dwindling Confederate manpower, Johnston asked the men to reenlist "for the duration." Perhaps because of the boost in morale that they had recently experienced, most of them complied. On Tunnel Hill, Granbury's Texans faced a substantially more difficult decision about reenlisting. They harbored two main complaints against the army. The first was that they could not be transferred or get to the trans-Mississippi to be closer to their homes. Expressing this regret, Captain Bryan Marsh of the 17th Texas Dismounted Cavalry wrote his wife that the troops had commenced "reinlisting [sic] for the duration of the War—I have not yet but expect too. You need not look for me at home until the war ends"[8] The second complaint they held remained the status of their consolidated units. The brigade contained the remnants of eight original regiments, consolidated into three: the 6th, 10th & 15th Texas, the 17th, 18th, 24th & 25th Texas, and the 7th Texas. The men had supposed these consolidations were temporary but now began to fear they were permanent, and they did not like it. As Erasmus E. Marr, originally of Company F, 10th Texas Infantry, wrote his sister, "There is a strong movement here to get us to reinlist for the war as is the case with the entire army here. I presume," the Texan mused, "that we will all reinlist and be kept here as long as the war lasts for we cannot be sent across the river but," he insisted, they would "be taken out of this consolidation and be put to our selves again." He concluded, "there is considerable discontent with this brigade owing to consolidation."[9] Similarly, A. L. Orr, originally of the 18th Texas Dismounted Cavalry, wrote his mother on January 29, "There is a write smart of excitement over hear a bout reinlisting or going in for the war. Our boys is very much disatisfyed and says they never will reorganise on this side of the river—We have sent some 300d petitions to the War Department to come west of the river, boath by our officers and privates, but we have never got a hearing from them yet—There is one thing serting—we will never reorganize on this side of the river unless we are drawed out of this consolidation."

The Texans held a meeting, related Orr, and concluded, "If we could have our camp and field officers and men which is west of the River brought to this Department and be mounted, we would bee contented over hear." On January 27, the officers of the 10th Texas Infantry petitioned Granbury to break them out of their consolidation with the 6th and 15th Texas. Granbury promptly forwarded the petition to Cleburne, but nothing came of it immediately.[10] Though the majority of the Texans in the brigade reenlisted for the duration of the war, their dissatisfaction increased as the weeks went by.

Apart from their complaints, the Texans were also forced to endure the discomforts of camp life. Lieutenant Robert M. Collins of the 6th, 10th & 15th Texas wrote that "while on picket duty we were required to keep on all of our clothing and accoutrements, and while we were permitted to have some fires on the line, yet our suffering from cold was great." He went on to relate that as soon as he would "sail off into a good snooze, about twenty-nine big body lice commence prizing up Hades down about" his "hips or between" his "shoulder blades, or away somewhere where" he "could not scratch without getting up and saying a great many unladylike words."[11]

In early February, events conspired to disturb Granbury's men from their winter encampment. In command of the Army of the Tennessee in Vicksburg, Union general William T. Sherman decided to advance east and capture Meridian, Mississippi, demonstrating his brand of hard war. As soon as Sherman began advancing, General Leonidas Polk pleaded with Johnston to send reinforcements from the Army of Tennessee to help counter the threat. Johnston refused, maintaining that the Federals around Chattanooga had started advancing and that if he reinforced Polk, Atlanta would surely fall. Polk appealed to Davis, and the president, sensing the danger, ordered Johnston to send reinforcements. Benjamin F. "Frank" Cheatham's division of Hardee's Corps departed for Mississippi first. Next, Hardee ordered Cleburne to march his division into Dalton to board trains headed west.[12] Before daylight on February 22 the men of Granbury's Brigade abandoned their log huts and cabins around Tunnel Hill and marched south to Dalton, where they boarded boxcars bound for Atlanta. From Atlanta they continued to Montgomery, Alabama. Meanwhile, Sherman, finding no military stores of use, returned to Vicksburg.

General George Thomas, acting in accordance with Grant's orders to keep the Confederates on his front occupied, sent a reconnaissance in force south to probe toward Dalton.[13] In their advance the Federals overran the log huts and cabins that had housed the Texas Brigade during the winter. While waiting to board another train in Alabama, word reached Cleburne to return to Dalton at once. Johnston wrote: "The enemy is advancing; is now in force at Tunnel Hill. Lose no time."[14] With no other choice Cleburne ordered his men back onto the trains for the return trip to Dalton. Several Texans enjoyed the trip back immensely. Attaching pieces of paper with their names on them to sticks and rocks, they tossed them out of the train in the direction of any young women who might be near the depot. In this way some of them gained pen pals with whom they corresponded for many months.[15]

Upon reaching Dalton on February 25, Johnston ordered the Texans to retake Dug Gap. With the first light of dawn on February 26 they charged up into the gap, driving away a regiment of mounted infantry. The next day they marched down into the valley at the foot of Dug Gap and went into bivouac. Soon drizzling rains drenched the Confederates. Granbury's men, who had expressed discontent before, now approached a state of near mutiny.[16]

Hiram Granbury in early 1864 had two main rivals for command of the Texas Brigade. The first was Colonel Robert R. Garland of the 6th, 10th & 15th Texas. Garland held a senior position in rank to Granbury even though the latter had taken command of the brigade following Chattanooga. However, Confederate authorities had temporarily assigned Garland to the post of provost marshal in Dalton, removing him from the brigade and placing Granbury (who held the favor of both Hardee and Cleburne, not to mention the men of the brigade) in an advantageous position.

The next obstacle Granbury faced came from Brigadier General John Gregg, at that time in command of Hood's Texas Brigade in East Tennessee and seeking a way to rejuvenate the brigade. On February 25, 1864, Brigadier General Jerome Robertson received a court-martial, placing Gregg in permanent command of Hood's Brigade. Gregg proposed a plan whereby

Confederate authorities would consolidate the Texas Brigade with Hood's Brigade and give him command of the hybrid command. Gregg approached Confederate Secretary of War James Seddon through his friend Congressman Malcolm D. Graham of Texas. However, Major Sam W. Melton, the assistant adjutant general of the Army of Tennessee replied briefly, "The consolidation at this time would seem to be impracticable." Samuel Cooper, the adjutant and inspector general of the Confederacy, then appealed Gregg's proposal to General Bragg, then serving as Jefferson Davis's chief military advisor. Displaying loyalty to his old army, Bragg replied, "I do not see how the proposed union of two brigades could well be made at this time, though there is ample room in the depleted Texas and Arkansas organizations, in the Army of Tennessee, to absorb all of Gregg's and thus increase the efficiency of both. This action would render one of the brigadiers [Gregg or Granbury] a supernumerary. . . . This application comes in the form to which I have heretofore expressed an emphatic objection and reaches the Department in violation of orders and regulations." With Bragg's denial and threat to fold Gregg's Texans in with Granbury's instead of vice versa, Gregg dropped all attempts at consolidation.[17]

While the drama in the highest Confederate echelons unfolded, in the Army of Tennessee Johnston appeased the Texans on March 5 when he gave Colonel Granbury permanent command of the brigade and the Confederate Congress promoted him to brigadier general. As his first act in command, on March 6 Granbury decided to rearrange the consolidation of his brigade to the satisfaction of the men. He removed the 10th Texas Infantry from the 6th & 15th Texas and allowed it to remain independent, per the petition previously filed by the officers of the 10th Texas. He formed the old 6th Texas into six companies and the 15th Texas into four and designated them the 6th & 15th Texas. He did the same with the 17th & 18th Texas, removing them from the 24th & 25th Texas. Granbury also designated these latter consolidated regiments. The 7th Texas, like the 10th, remained independent. Jim Turner of Company G, 6th Texas, wrote: "Everybody was pleased with the arrangement. 'Old Pat' (as we called our Major General) gave every man in the brigade a big drink of whiskey and good humor once more reigned."[18] Granbury's reorganization of the brigade stands out as a prime reason his men felt such loyalty to him.

Instead of returning to the old encampments near Tunnel Hill, Cleburne moved his division to Mill Creek, where they entrenched along the Middle

Springs Place Road three miles east of Dalton. Here the Texans spent the remainder of the winter encampment.[19] For the first time, Brigadier General Hiram Granbury came into permanent command of the brigade that would bear his name.

Far away in Washington, D.C., unfolding events altered the course of the war. On March 9, 1864, President Abraham Lincoln appointed U. S. Grant lieutenant general to command all Union armies, and Grant ordered William T. Sherman to take his Union forces to Chattanooga and confront Joseph Johnston and the Confederate Army of Tennessee.

Granbury's Texans spent the rest of their winter encampment in peace. While camped around Dalton, Johnston detached some of the Texas Brigade for the purpose of provost duty in town. Lieutenant Thomas Stokes of the 10th Texas Infantry wrote his sister, Missouri, on March 15, "We are now in Dalton doing provost duty (our regiment), which is a very unpleasant duty. It is my business," wrote the Texan, "to examine all papers whenever the cars arrive, and it is very disagreeable to have to arrest persons who haven't proper papers. The regulations about the town are very strict. No one under brigadier general," he related, "can pass without approval papers. My guard arrested General Johnston himself, day before yesterday. Not knowing him," the Texans "wouldn't take his word for it, but demanded his papers. The old General, very good-humoredly showed them some orders he had issued himself, and, being satisfied, they let him pass."

Stokes went on to inform his sister, "There is a very interesting meeting in progress here. I get to go every other night. I have seen several baptized since I have been here. There are in attendance," he wrote, "every evening from six to seven hundred soldiers."[20] What Stokes in fact described were the massive revivals occurring in the Army of Tennessee. Lieutenant Stokes took an active role in the revival in Cleburne's Division. On April 5 he wrote Missouri, "Sabbath night we had services again, and also last night, both well attended, and to-night, weather permitting, I will preach. God help me," wrote the devout lieutenant, "and give me grace from on high, that I may be enabled, as an humble instrument in His hands, to speak the truth as it is in Jesus, for 'none but Jesus can do helpless sinners good.'" He went on to relate that he "preached last Sabbath—two weeks ago to a large and attentive congregation. There seemed to be . . . much seriousness, and although much embarrassed, yet I tried, under God, to feel that I was but in the discharge of my duty; and may I ever be found battling for my Savior. Yes, my sister, I had rather be an humble follower of Christ than to wear the crown of a monarch. Remember me all times at a Throne of Grace that my life may be spared to become a useful minister of Christ. I have never seen such a spirit as there now is in the army. Religion is the theme." He concluded that the cause of this change must be "manifestly the working of God's spirit."[21]

Religious revivals were not an uncommon occurrence in Civil War armies. After the Second Great Awakening, Christianity played an important role in American life, and this spilled over into the ranks of Civil War armies. Manifestations of Christian belief appear nearly everywhere in the letters and diaries of most Civil War soldiers, and the men of Granbury's Brigade were no exception. The mass revivals such as those described in the camp of the Army of Tennessee here usually occurred during periods of inactivity. It would be hard to overestimate the importance of these revivals in maintaining the morale of soldiers on both sides of the war. Just as much as (if not more than) camaraderie with the men in the ranks beside them, religious faith motivated Civil War soldiers to keep fighting for the cause they felt God had sanctioned.[22]

Early on the morning of March 22 an event occurred that stuck in the minds of nearly all who witnessed it. Before daylight the Texans' officers awakened them and ordered them into line. A heavy snow had fallen, and amid the swirling snowflakes in the dark Cleburne ordered his division to form three sides of a square. A solemn procession approached toward the open end of the square consisting of a hospital ambulance with two people in it: the driver and a man sitting on a coffin with an armed guard marching slowly behind the wagon. The man belonged to the 1st Arkansas Infantry. He had been sentenced to death for repeated desertion.[23] The wagon and guard halted at the open end of the square, and the condemned man descended. The guard placed the coffin in the snow and the wagon drove away. Jim Turner recorded his impressions of the scene. "The silent guard stood at attention" as the "chaplain's voice could be distinctly heard." The clergyman "offered up prayers for the man about to die. The guard bound the prisoner's arms, bandaged his eyes and caused him to kneel on the snow beside his coffin. Then the officer—commanding the guard, or firing party, gave the commands, 'Ready, Aim, Fire!' A puff of smoke, a crashing sound, and the condemned man lay stretched out on the ground. The volley did not leave him dead, and the firing party reloaded their guns and fired another volley at the prostrate form, this time killing him instantly."[24] Lieutenant Robert Collins noticed the "contrast between the dark, gloomy, condemned man and the black coffin he was sitting on, and the white, whirling, whispering snow-flakes as they came from above."[25] According to Turner, the men "marched silently back to camp, and soon had great log fires burning, around which we clustered and quietly discussed the terrible scene we had just witnessed."[26]

A little later in the day the mood lightened and, perhaps as a psychological escape from the earlier execution, some of the more mischievous members of the division began throwing snowballs at one another. Soon, the engagement became general, and the troops moved out in formation with battle flags waving and officers at their head to attack neighboring brigades. Polk's Brigade attacked Daniel Govan's brigade in their camp. Cleburne led the brigade into battle due to Polk's illness. The "enemy" soon captured the division commander and paroled him. Cleburne could not stand this inactivity though, and he once again entered the action at the head of Polk's men. The Arkansans soon routed the Tennesseans and chased Cleburne back to his tent with gleeful threats of a court-martial and punishment by dunking him in the nearby creek. His men knew Cleburne to make offending parties in his division "carry a rail" for a mile before rejoining their unit, and one of the men yelled out, "Arrest that soldier and make him carry a fence rail." In the end, the Arkansans let their commander go on the pretense that it proved the only time "he had been known to break his word to them."[27] While the other two brigades of Cleburne's Division battled it out, Granbury's Brigade attacked the Alabamans of Mark Lowrey in their encampments, charging "right up to their dog tents." After battling for some time, according to Jim Turner, "one half of the division was arrayed against the other half, and a regular battle of snowballs began, which kept up until late in the afternoon."[28] Despite this revelry, not all of this grand battle consisted of fun and games. Some of the men began packing snow around rocks and ice, then hurling them at their opponents. A "big, red-headed freckled-face Mississippian" captured Lieutenant Collins and carried him quite a distance to the rear on his shoulders. When the Mississippian let go of Collins, the Texan bolted for his own line, and one of his own men hit him "in the left eye with a big half ice and half snow ball, and laid one Confederate out." His comrades carried him to the tent of a nearby officer and he remained so blind at the end of the battle he had to be led back to his quarters. Collins reported that he could not see well out of that eye "to this day," writing in 1892.[29] Cleburne, sensing that the conflict was getting out of hand, ended the snowball battle with the call of, "'Come up boys and draw your whiskey.'" According to Jim Turner, "Old Pat had sent a quantity of whiskey to each regiment, and before very long the men were standing around the fires in steaming groups, yelling at the tops of their voices. This was kept up until midnight."[30]

The month of March slipped into April as Joseph Johnston continued to build on the drill and morale of the army. Many Texans gained furloughs to return home, and others put on displays for civilians. On Thursday, April 5, the Army of Tennessee staged a "sham fight," to the great delight of the local crowd in attendance. Lieutenant Overton Davenport of Company K, 10th Texas, wrote his father about the display: "On Thursday last they took us to Dalton & put us through a sham battle. . . . Our Corps was all engaged & you ought to have seen us running from the Goober grabbers. They whipped us badly. I believe there was no blood spilled. It was a pretty representation of a real battle," mused the Texan, "but lacked the screaming of the shells & the whistle of the balls & the nervous system was not so seriously effected."[31] On April 19, Johnston held a grand review of the army, again much to the delight of the civilians. Captain T. J. Key commanding Key's Arkansas Battery, wrote that the "whole army was out for review, Gen. J.E. Johnston was the inspector, with hundreds of ladies. The army presented itself in the best condition I have ever witnessed, and the thousands of hardy soldiers marching to the notes of the shrill fife and bass drum or the harmonious melodies of brass bands looked grand and cheering."[32]

Meanwhile, the revivals continued. On April 28 Tom Stokes wrote Missouri, "The revival in our brigade has continued now for four weeks, nearly, and many have found peace with their Savior. If we could remain stationary a few weeks longer," he stated, "I believe the greater portion of the army would be converted. This is all the doings of the Lord, and is surely the earnest of the great deliverance in store for us. It is the belief of many that this is the 'beginning of the end.'"[33] As Stokes scribbled these words from the camp of the Texas Brigade, Sherman prepared to advance. The young lieutenant had no way of knowing how prophetic his words would prove to be.

The Confederate war effort received a major boost from the instatement of Hiram Granbury and Joseph Johnston to command the Texas Brigade and the Army of Tennessee. Even though Johnston was a terrible strategist and tactician for the Army of Tennessee, the men in the ranks admired and trusted him, and that fact in itself prolonged the Confederate war effort. In the case of the Texas Brigade, Hiram Granbury played much the same inspirational role, and his Texans loved him so much they always would remember themselves as Granbury's Texas Brigade.

Lieutenant Colonel Robert B. Young, 10th Texas Infantry,
killed at the Battle of Franklin, November 30, 1864.
(Courtesy Jenece Waid-Hurst.)

Private Calloway Reid, Company B, 7th Texas Infantry,
killed at the Battle of Franklin, November 30, 1864.
(Courtesy Dave Noble Collection, ex: George Esker III.)

First Sergeant James I. Darter, Company C, 24th Texas Dismounted Cavalry, severely wounded at the Battle of Atlanta, July 22, 1864. (Courtesy Martin Callahan.)

Private John S. Pickle, Company B, 18th Texas Dismounted Cavalry, escaped capture in the confusion at Arkansas Post, January 11, 1863. (Courtesy Austin History Center, Austin Public Library.)

Private William J. Oliphant, Company G, 6th Texas Infantry, wounded at the Battle of Chickamauga, September 20, 1863, wounded at the Battle of Pickett's Mill, May 27, 1864, and wounded and captured at the Battle of Atlanta, July 22, 1864. (Courtesy Austin History Center, Austin Public Library.)

Major General Patrick R. Cleburne, killed at the Battle of Franklin, November 30, 1864. (Francis T. Miller, *The Photographic History of the Civil War* (New York: Review of Reviews Co., 1911.)

Brigadier General Hiram B. Granbury, killed at the Battle of Franklin, November 30, 1864. (New York: Review of Reviews Co., 1911.)

Battle flag of the 17th & 18th Texas Dismounted Cavalry, captured at the Battle of Atlanta, July 22, 1864. (Courtesy Texas State Library and Archives Commission.)

Private Malcolm M. Hornsby, Company B, 18th Texas Dismounted Cavalry, captured at the Battle of Atlanta, July 22, 1864. (Courtesy Texas State Library and Archives Commission.)

Cleburne's Repulse of Sherman at Missionary Ridge, by Alfred R. Waud
(Joseph M. Brown, *The Mountain Campaigns in Georgia; or, War Scenes on
the W. & A.,* 5th ed. [Buffalo, N.Y.: Matthews, Northrup & Co., 1890].)

Battle of Pickett's Mill—First Volley by the Confederates, by Alfred R. Waud
(Joseph M. Brown, *The Mountain Campaigns in Georgia; or, War Scenes on
the W. & A.,* 5th ed. [Buffalo, N.Y.: Matthews, Northrup & Co., 1890].)

First Lieutenant Joseph R. Garza, Company K, 6th Texas Infantry, escaped in the confusion at Arkansas Post, January 11, 1863, rejoined the 17th Texas Dismounted (Consolidated) Cavalry, killed at the Battle of Mansfield, April 8, 1864. (Courtesy Martin Callahan.)

Private Henry Elms, Company F, 6th Texas Infantry, captured at Arkansas Post, January 11, 1863. (Courtesy Mrs. Mark Kerr Collection, U.S. Army Military History Institute.)

CHAPTER ELEVEN

FROM DALTON TO PICKETT'S MILL

As the Confederates sat in camp that winter, little did they know that their situation would soon change. As spring began they would find themselves retreating into the interior of Georgia, hounded by blue-coated troops and the timidity of their own beloved General Johnston. But even as Johnston retreated toward Atlanta and the Confederate cause grew dim, the spirits and fighting prowess of Granbury's Texans grew brighter than ever. In the fierce fighting the Texans again began losing strength due to battle casualties, but the survivors carried on in spite of their odds. The Confederate war effort weakened, but continued for Granbury's Brigade because of a devotion to the Confederacy and effective leadership on the part of Hiram Granbury, Patrick Cleburne, and others. This situation underscores the arguments made by Gary Gallagher in *The Confederate War* and Jason Phillips in *Diehard Rebels* that the Confederate cause did not fail due to a lack of commitment on the part of the men in the ranks, but rather ultimately only military defeat and overwhelming numbers forced the Confederates to abandon their dream of an independent slaveholding society. More specifically, Granbury's Texans carried on because of their localized perspective and effective leadership, qualities found most often in western Confederates.[1]

On May 4, 1864, the aforementioned spring campaign commenced as Grant ordered Sherman to advance. Two days later, Sherman began moving his columns south against Johnston's two corps (approximately forty thousand men) around Dalton. Johnston placed the I Corps under Lieutenant General John Bell Hood, and the II Corps under Lieutenant General William J. Hardee, "Old Reliable." In addition to these two corps, Polk's twenty thousand men remained at Tuscaloosa. Though available, President Davis preferred to keep them in Alabama to guard against a possible Federal thrust south from Memphis.

Marching south from Chattanooga, Sherman had at his disposal approximately 110,000 soldiers in three armies. The first was the Army of the Ohio under Major General John Schofield. James McPherson's command, the Army of the Tennessee, constituted Sherman's second army. Third in line came the Army of the Cumberland under Major General George Thomas, the "Rock of Chickamauga."

Johnston at first deduced Sherman's target as Rome, southwest of Dalton. Sherman, rather than striking toward Rome, devised a different plan. He decided to send McPherson's Army of the Tennessee south through Snake Creek Gap to cut Johnston off from the rear at the town of Resaca, while his other two armies kept the Confederates' attention at Rocky Face Ridge.

On May 6, Joseph Wheeler's cavalrymen reported McPherson moving south. In Johnston's mind this confirmed Rome as Sherman's target. Consequently, he did nothing to secure Snake Creek Gap. Of the two gaps immediately south of Rocky Face Ridge, Snake Creek Gap remained unguarded and Dug Gap remained protected by only two regiments of dismounted Kentucky cavalrymen from Colonel John Grigsby's brigade.[2]

On May 8 Sherman put his plan in motion. That morning, Federal infantrymen demonstrated against Rocky Face Ridge and Buzzard's Roost Gap. Meanwhile, Thomas ordered Joseph Hooker, commander of the XX Corps, to demonstrate against Dug Gap. Hooker chose John Geary's division for the task and instructed him to take the position if he could. Just before 4 P.M. Geary's Division approached the gap. He advanced on the dismounted Kentuckians with his forty-five hundred infantrymen, only to be repulsed three times. Before long, however, it appeared that Geary would capture the defile by sheer force of numbers.[3]

Soon reinforcements began rushing to the point of danger, and they turned out to be none other than Mark Lowrey's and Hiram Granbury's brigades of Cleburne's Division. Hardee had been holding Cleburne and his men in reserve at Dalton. At the sound of heavy firing from Dug Gap, Johnston ordered Hardee to see to its defense. As the Confederates moved swiftly south, Johnston, Hardee, and Cleburne rode ahead to reconnoiter.

The Texans, with Granbury at their head, marched as fast as they could toward the point of danger. Upon reaching the base of the ridge, they discovered to their delight the horses of the Kentucky cavalrymen that had been left in the rear. Here the Texans left their knapsacks and blanket rolls. Several of them leapt into the saddle and rode at top speed to the crest of the ridge. One Confederate wrote, "Mounted in the saddles once more, they felt war's delirium and seemed to catch the spirit of the chainless winds that swept across the prairies of their state, and shouting and yelling they galloped forward at a breakneck speed to the succor of their hard-pressed comrades on the mountain top."[4] Hardee and Cleburne positioned their men at the top of the pass as a young Texan galloped up, threw himself off his mount, and asked, "Where am I most needed?" This incident at once reduced the two generals and their staffs to laughter as the rest of the brigade, huffing and puffing, reached the crest of the ridge.[5] When he saw the approach of Granbury's Brigade, Hardee shouted, "Here are my Fighting Texans!" He then departed, leaving Cleburne's men to hold the position. For a while the Federals shelled the gap, making their projectiles "just graze the top of the ridge." This cannonading became "frightening" according to Captain Sebron Sneed of the 6th & 15th Texas. One shell that exploded in the midst of the regiment knocked Sneed unconscious, took off the finger of Private Daniel Cryer, and momentarily stunned Lieutenant Collins.[6] Despite the shells Geary did not attempt another assault. The bombardment ceased as night closed in on the first battle of the Atlanta campaign.

Still puzzled on the morning of May 9, Johnston endeavored to divine Sherman's intentions. The Federals still remained in force in front of Buzzard's Roost Gap and Rocky Face Ridge, and yet the attack at Dug Gap had shaken him. He ordered Cleburne to send out skirmishers to learn whether the Yankees remained in his front. Upon moving forward, the Texans found only Geary's dead and wounded from the day before. Though Johnston still assumed that Rome was McPherson's target, as an added precaution he ordered Grigsby's tired cavalrymen to ride south to Snake Creek Gap to reconnoiter in that direction.[7]

On the morning of May 9, Grigsby's troopers arrived at Snake Creek Gap and found to their surprise and dismay the whole Army of the Tennessee coming through the mountains. Just as McPherson prepared to cut the Western & Atlantic Railroad at Resaca, he hesitated, allowing Johnston to react.

Johnston had no idea of Sherman's plan as he received conflicting messages from Brigadier General James Cantey and others. Johnston still felt Sherman intended to take Rome, but he decided to send two divisions plus Granbury's and Lowrey's brigades toward Resaca. There Hood, whom he had sent to reconnoiter, would command them.

Around midnight Cleburne started his men south. When they reached the foot of Dug Gap the Texans found to their disgust that the Kentucky cavalrymen, before departing, had emptied their knapsacks of all food and coffee. Disgruntled, they set out on their long march. Cleburne's brigades in the lead reached Resaca after five hours of heavy marching, and there they stood at ease for a little while.[8] Not realizing the danger to Resaca, at 8 A.M. on May 10 Hood telegraphed Johnston, "Resaca all right. Hold onto Dalton." With this mistaken intelligence, Johnston continued to regard Rome as Sherman's target and ordered Cleburne's Division to march back to Dug Gap. He also halted the other two divisions and ordered them to retrace their steps as well.[9] Captain Samuel Foster of the 24th & 25th Texas wrote disgustedly, "After remaining here [Resaca] about half an hour, just long enough to rest we started back the road we came by night we are back at Dug Gap on top of the mountain to the left of the gap at the same place we left this morning, after having traveled 38 miles today—all hands being tired."[10]

Only after nightfall on May 10 did Johnston finally realized what was happening at Resaca. He began to respond to the threat, and Sherman's window of opportunity closed in front of him.[11] That night a thunderstorm poured rain on the hapless soldiers of Cleburne's Division. In fact, it rained so hard that, according to Captain Foster, "blankets were of no use at all in trying to keep ourselves dry." He remembered that "after marching all day yesterday I squatted down with my back to a tree, and a little oil cloth haversack on top of my head, and kept awake all night, and was just as wet as if I had swam a river."[12]

On the morning of May 11 Cantey telegraphed Johnston and informed him that the Federals were advancing on Resaca in force. In light of this revelation Johnston prepared to move Cleburne's Division back to Resaca while he ordered Cheatham's command to slide south and take Cleburne's place at Dug Gap. He also telegraphed Polk and exhorted him to move his forces with all speed to Resaca. Later in the day Hood telegraphed John ston from Resaca and informed him of no enemy within "four miles" of the town.[13] As Polk began to arrive at Resaca, Johnston countermanded his orders to Cheatham and Cleburne. He remained hesitant to abandon Rocky Face Ridge because he feared that Sherman would pounce on his rear as soon as he did. In the meantime, learning that McPherson had failed to take Resaca, Sherman started the rest of his forces toward Snake Creek Gap to try to take the Confederates from the rear. Johnston quickly detected Sherman's advance and issued orders to his corps commanders to abandon Dalton and move south to Resaca with the entire army.[14] Sherman had turned Johnston for the first time and the maneuvering for Atlanta officially got under way.

On the morning of May 13 Union skirmishers entered Buzzard's Roost Gap and Rocky Face Ridge to find the Confederates gone. Empty campfires still burned and scouts reported Johnston's wagon train heading south. Sherman believed that Johnston intended to retreat south of the Oostanaula, and he ordered his army to pursue and occupy Resaca as soon as the Confederates had crossed. This assumption worked to the advantage of Johnston, who planned to make a stand at Resaca.[15]

As the Army of Tennessee withdrew from Dalton, Cleburne's Division served as the rear guard. At 4 A.M. on May 13, Hardee ordered the division to march to the left, toward the main body of the army. In doing so it had to cross over Chattooga Ridge. One of the pickets thrown out by Granbury, Captain Foster, wrote that the skirmishers advanced until they could hear Federals from the cover of some blackjack bushes talking and laughing.[16] This proximity with the Yankees on the ridge proved dangerous. "While we were marching by the flank to our position," wrote Lieutenant Collins, "the Federals fired on us. We could hear the balls strike our men." A sniper's shot killed Lieutenant J. N. Nash of the 6th & 15th Texas during this encounter, while Lieutenant William Barton of the 10th Texas Infantry had his arm splintered by a ball. Other casualties in the brigade included Private "Pink" Robertson of the 10th Texas, who received a leg wound that necessitated amputation, and Private J. P. Fullingham of the same regiment, who lost an eye.[17]

When Johnston arrived at Resaca, he finished deploying his forces. The right flank of the Army of Tennessee rested on the Connasauga River, while he anchored the left on the Oostanaula west of the town. In the center he placed Hardee's Corps. Hardee positioned Cleburne's Division in the middle of his line. Cleburne in turn arranged three of his four brigades from south to north, Granbury, Lowrey, and Polk, with Govan in reserve.

Johnston's position at Resaca proved a naturally strong one, and he hoped to hold Sherman there at least for a while. The crossing of the Oostanaula at Lay's Ferry four miles west of Resaca, near Calhoun, remained the one weakness in the line.[18]

The valley at Resaca held memories for some in Granbury's Brigade. Tom Stokes had grown up in Georgia near Resaca, and he wrote his sister, Missouri, that "it grieved my very soul" when coming through the valley "to think of the sad fate which awaited it when the foul invader should occupy that 'vale of beauty.' We formed line of battle," continued the Texan, "at the old Eads place. . . . Right here, with a thousand recollections of bygone days crowding my mind, in the valley of my boyhood, I felt as if I could hurl a host back."[19]

Ironically, Sherman intended to do exactly what Johnston feared: cross the Oostanaula at Lay's Ferry. He remained sure that Johnston would retreat, and when he did Sherman wanted to be there to crush him. With some of his units crossing at Lay's Ferry, he intended to keep pressure on Johnston in front of Resaca.

To keep Johnston pinned down, Sherman ordered two of his divisions to make a diversion in the center. On the morning of May 14 he ordered the divisions of Absolom Baird and Benjamin Judah to attack the Confederate right in the hopes of turning the Rebel flank adjacent to the Connasauga. The two divisions advanced toward the center-right of the Confederate position and rushed down the slope into Camp Creek at the foot of the ridge under heavy fire from Cleburne's men. Here in the marshy creek the badly coordinated frontal assault ground to a halt. The Yankees proved unable to extricate themselves from the base of the ridge, and it took another attack to rescue them. Subsequent to the failure of their infantry attack the Yankees began a fierce bombardment on the ridge. The shells hissed and exploded all around Cleburne's men as they tried their best to avoid the deadly projectiles.[20]

Throughout the next two days the two armies sparred back and forth with first Sherman, then Johnston launching limited sorties. Shortly after dark on May 16, Johnston assembled his corps commanders and informed them that the Army of Tennessee would retreat to the south bank of the Oostanaula that night. He explained that a strong Federal force had taken position to strike Calhoun and cut the Western & Atlantic. During the day at Lay's Ferry, however, though Brigadier General Thomas Sweeney faced only a weak resistance from one brigade, he failed to advance on Calhoun, believing Walker's entire division present. Sweeney's hesitance, like McPherson's before him, kept the Army of Tennessee from disaster.

Beginning around midnight, Hardee's weary infantry crossed the Oostanaula on the railroad bridge, followed by Hood and Polk. Cleburne awakened his men at 10 P.M. and then told them to lie down and go back to sleep again. An hour later the officers roused them and again told them to go back to sleep with their accouterments on. At 1:30 A.M. the Texans "were ordered up again, told to be very quiet not to speak above a whisper" as they moved south and crossed the river. By daylight the whole army had crossed and they continued in full retreat. "About an hour before day this morning," wrote Foster, "we could see the light of the burning bridge that we had crossed."[21] As the Confederates moved south, the artillery on the ridges north and west of Resaca remained silent—a tribute to the fact that Sherman believed Johnston would not yet evacuate his position.[22]

By the time the Union soldiers discovered the empty trenches in their front, Johnston had already busied himself laying plans for another defensive position. Once the army crossed the Oostanaula, Johnston resupplied his troops and started them toward Adairsville, seven miles to the south. Once there, Johnston discovered that the narrow valley marked on his map proved much wider than expected. This convinced him not to offer battle at Adairsville. Rather, he came up with an alternative.[23]

His plan called for Hardee's Corps to march southwest toward Kingston while Hood and Polk withdrew southeast toward Cassville. He hoped that this maneuver would force Sherman to split his armies to pursue both columns. Once this happened, Hood and Polk could ambush and destroy the eastern column while Hardee made a forced march east from Kingston and completed the trap before the column pursuing him could come to the aide of their comrades.[24]

For the men of Granbury's Brigade, the night of May 18 brought little rest. They had gone almost three days with virtually no sleep, making it hard to remain alert. Many of them dozed listlessly as they watched the stunning display of lightning and thunder off to the northwest. Rumblings of thunder that resembled artillery rent the night air as the flashes of lightning played upon the stragglers of the army moving down the road.[25]

The next day Johnston attempted to spring his trap, but through a series of bungles and hesitation Hood waited too long to attack. Johnston realized his plan to destroy Sherman had now become impracticable and ordered Hardee to make a demonstration to his front while he established a new defensive position southeast of Cassville. As Hardee's men skirmished, Johnston aligned his other two corps along a 140-foot-high ridge east of Cassville. This position proved naturally strong and protected the Western & Atlantic at Cass Station. With his dispositions completed, Johnston ordered Hardee to withdraw and to take up a position on the left of the line. Polk's Corps held the center and Hood's the right as the Confederates hunkered down and waited for Sherman's next move.[26]

That night, Johnston and his three corps commanders met at his headquarters to discuss the situation. Hood and Polk argued stringently for withdrawal. They felt their lines badly exposed, as evidenced by the damage done to the artillery of Major General Samuel French's division by the bombardment. After three hours of discussion, Johnston ordered the Army of Tennessee to abandon its position and march south of the Etowah River, where he hoped to make a stand at Allatoona Pass. On the night of May 19 the veterans started south. In his official report, Johnston wrote of the withdrawal from Cassville as a mistake he had "regretted ever since."[27] As they moved out, French issued axes to his men and ordered them to fell trees, masking the noise of the retreat.[28] This retreat marked the second time Johnston allowed Sherman to turn his flank, an alarming trend.

On May 20 the Confederates withdrew south of the Etowah on pontoon bridges. At Cartersville, Cleburne's men had stopped to eat breakfast before continuing on. After lying in line of battle for two hours in the hot sun, they proceeded to cross the river. They then marched three miles to the west, camping on Pumpkinvine Creek.[29]

After retreating once more, Johnston positioned his army at Allatoona Pass, a narrow gorge through which the Western & Atlantic ran. This position proved the strongest that he had yet occupied, stronger even than

Rocky Face Ridge. He hoped that Sherman would be brash enough to attack him here, south of the Etowah. At this point, President Davis began corresponding with Johnston, expressing his displeasure at the army's retreating.[30]

As Sherman planned his next move, the men of Granbury's Brigade enjoyed a break from the campaign. For the "first time since we left Resaca," wrote Captain Foster on May 20, "the Yanks did not shoot at us today." The next day he recorded that after remaining in camp all night, he had a "good rest." They were not, he continued, "disturbed last night This morning we are ready for any thing that may turn up and expecting to move every minute; but no move."[31]

Before sunup on May 22, Granbury ordered his men into line and instructed them to discharge their muskets, clearing them. This respite from battle afforded the opportunity for many of the Texans to write home, while others read the Atlanta papers or slept.

Having ridden through Allatoona Pass as a young officer in 1844, Sherman realized that Johnston's position was too strong to be assaulted. Instead, he decided to move southwest, toward the crossroads of Dallas. From there he could strike out toward Marietta, Johnston's base of supplies. With this in mind, the Federal commander changed his supply depot to Kingston and ordered his subordinates to be ready to move out on May 23. The wet weather came to an end and gave way to sweltering heat. In the heat, the muddy roads of North Georgia turned to dust, encumbering Union movements.

Johnston, divining Sherman's intention to capture Dallas, rapidly started Hardee's and Polk's corps west. Dallas lies sixteen miles south of the Chattahoochee River and sixteen miles west of Allatoona Pass. Despite the Federals' head start, because no river or heavy wagon train impeded the Confederate forces they had the advantage over Sherman's columns. At midnight on May 23 the commissary issued Granbury's Texans two days' rations consisting of "corn bread and bacon," and at 3 A.M. they began west toward Dallas. They had become so tired of retreating that according to Captain Foster they became sarcastic and began to muse, "Some say we are going to Florida and put in a pontoon bridge over to Cuba, and go over there. While others contend that some Yank would put a torpedo under it and blow it up."[32] Rather than heading for Florida, however, Hardee and Polk had orders to hold Dallas against the Federals, whom Johnston assumed merely intended to launch a feint. Johnston believed that Sherman intended to oppose him at Kingston, north of the Etowah.

However, Wheeler's cavalry, busy operating in Sherman's rear, reported that they had advanced from Cartersville to Cassville and sighted no Yankees except a large wagon train. Johnston realized that Sherman had started his entire army toward Dallas, and he immediately put Hood's Corps into motion west from Allatoona.

The morning of May 24 found the Army of Tennessee in position to protect Dallas. Johnston formed Hardee's Corps, including Granbury's Brigade, on the left in front of Dallas. Polk held the center and Hood's men took up positions around New Hope Church on the right.[33] West of Allatoona and south of the Etowah the terrain became rough and broken with thick underbrush and forests, coupled with steep ravines and ridges that made it difficult to maneuver under ordinary circumstances, and even more so under fire. This difficult terrain would play a factor in the battles ahead.

Sherman believed that Johnston would not make a stand north of the Chattahoochee. He remained convinced that the Confederates had only a small delaying force in the environs of Dallas. On May 25 he sent forward Hooker's XX Corps to overwhelm any resistance at New Hope Church and capture the crossroads there. About 5 P.M. Hooker instructed his division commanders to go forward, where the Confederates heavily engaged them. Hooker discovered Major General A. P. Stewart's veteran division of Hood's Corps entrenched in front of the crossroads. The battle raged throughout the evening until 7:30 P.M., when a torrential downpour and the coming of darkness ended the fighting. The Confederates had bloodily repulsed Hooker's men, and as they withdrew Stewart's troops sent up victory yells.[34]

At 10:30 P.M., in response to the action around New Hope Church, Johnston ordered Cleburne's Division to move north and bolster Hood's Corps. Clogged roads blocked Cleburne's men, who did not go into bivouac until 4 A.M. After a brief respite, they continued their march north, where Hood placed them in rear of Thomas Hindman's division, the extreme right of his corps.[35] During the march Granbury's Texans passed directly behind Brigadier General Matthew Ector's Texas brigade, busy skirmishing with the Federals. Lieutenant Collins took the occasion to locate his old friend Captain Sam Lusk of Company A, 14th Texas. Collins wrote that when he found him, "Something had gone wrong" and Lusk "was cussing like a Norwegian sailor."[36]

When Cleburne's Division reached the right, Johnston ordered him to report directly to Hood. Cleburne placed Lucius Polk's brigade[37] on the right of Hindman's Division and positioned eight cannons under the command of Captain Thomas J. Key on Polk's right. Cleburne detached one Arkansas regiment from Govan's Brigade to guard the guns. Cleburne then placed the remainder of Govan's, Lowrey's, and Granbury's brigades in reserve to support Hindman's right.[38] As soon as Granbury had his men in place, some of them went forward to explore the troops in their front, "for they have no confidence in any of them but the Arkansas troops." They "found Georgia troops to our front," wrote Captain Foster, "and our boys tell them that if they run that we will shoot them, and no mistake, and as soon as they find out that the Texans are in their rear, they believe we will shoot them sure enough."[39] Granbury sent out the 6th &15th Texas as skirmishers to bolster the Georgians, while the rest of the brigade took position in an old, rutted wagon road to the rear.[40]

All day on May 26 Johnston remained content on the defensive while Sherman brought up the rest of his troops. Sherman still did not believe Johnston's entire army was in front of him, and he ordered Thomas to try to turn the Confederate right northeast of New Hope Church. At daylight on May 27, Major General Oliver O. Howard, commander of the IV Corps, ordered General Thomas Wood to withdraw his division from the front and march north to flank the Confederates.[41]

At 11 A.M. Wood's and Johnson's divisions set out, an hour behind schedule, with Howard and his staff accompanying them. During the march, because of the heavy foliage, Colonel William Gibson, who commanded one of Wood's brigades, ordered his buglers to guide the troops by blowing frequent blasts on their instruments. The noise alerted the skirmishers of Cleburne's Division to the presence of Howard's column. One Federal inquired, "If we are expected to surprise the enemy, why don't they stop those damned bugles?"[42] Several hours later, after marching a mile and a half, Howard supposed himself beyond the Confederate flank. To make sure, he sent out skirmishers. When they reached the edge of a large field, the skirmishers could plainly see Polk's Brigade, entrenched and ready for battle. Howard resumed his march east. After marching another mile he again moved south to reconnoiter. In the meantime he halted his men along a tributary called Pickett's Mill Creek. Coming to a clearing, Howard observed entrenching Confederates, this time Govan's Brigade, on the right of Cleburne's line. There were no troops to the left of these Confederates and Howard decided to attack. He ordered Wood to place his division facing south, and instructed Johnson to do the same on the left. He next placed General Nathaniel McLean's brigade on the right to protect Wood's other flank. Howard remained busy deploying his men at 3:35 P.M. when he sent a note to Thomas notifying him that "I am now turning the enemy's right flank, I think."[43]

In the center, Wood narrowly aligned his division with his three brigades situated one behind the other, with William Hazen's command in the lead. At 4:30 P.M. precisely Wood ordered Hazen to attack. Accompanying Hazen was his young topographical engineer, Ambrose Bierce, who would gain prominence as a writer after the war. "We moved forward," wrote Bierce. "In less than one minute the trim battalion had become simply a swarm of men struggling through the undergrowth of the forest, pushing and crowding. The front was irregularly serrated, the strongest and bravest in advance." For the first two hundred yards or so the course of Hazen's men "lay along the left bank of a small creek in a deep ravine, our left battalions sweeping along its steep slope." He remembered that the regiments became, "inextricably intermingled, rendering all military formation impossible. The color-bearers kept well to the front with their flags, closely furled, aslant backwards over their shoulders. Displayed they would have been torn to rags by the boughs of the trees." Hazen and his staff officers dismounted and sent their horses to the rear as they struggled through the dense undergrowth.[44]

Meanwhile Cleburne had recognized the Federal attempt to turn his flank, and a little before 4 P.M. he sent an urgent message to Granbury to move his brigade to the right and extend Govan's flank. At 4:00 the courier rode up to Granbury under a large oak tree and handed him the dispatch. He did not even have time to brief his regimental commanders on the situation and immediately gave the command, "Attention Brigade!" In a few seconds the entire Texas Brigade rushed into line and Granbury gave the command "Right Face! Forward! Double quick march!" They were "off at a run" and moved the full length of the brigade to the right before the officers gave the command to place percussion caps on their weapons.[45] Granbury led his men to the west, toward a steep ravine that separated two farms. As the Texans approached the edge of the defile, Granbury sent out skirmishers from the 24th & 25th Texas. No sooner had the skirmishers disappeared into the

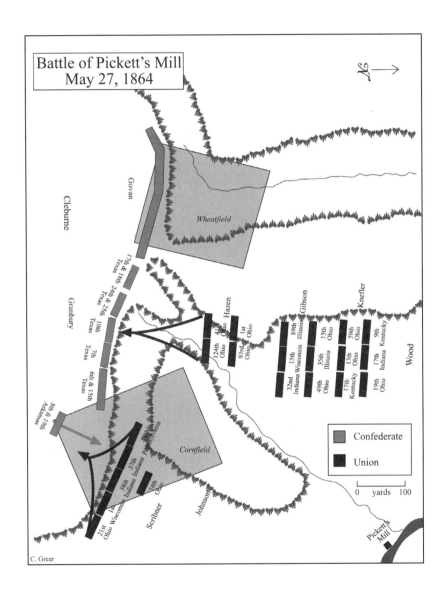

Battle of Pickett's Mill
May 27, 1864

N →

Govan

Cleburne

Wheatfield

Granbury

17th & 18th Texas

24th & 25th Texas

10th Texas

7th Texas

6th & 15th Texas

8th & 19th Arkansas

Hazen

124th Ohio

41st Ohio

93rd Ohio

1st Ohio

Gibson

89th Illinois

15th Indiana

35th Illinois

15th Ohio

Knefler

59th Ohio

9th Indiana Kentucky

32nd Indiana

49th Ohio

13th Ohio

17th Indiana

Wood

17th Kentucky

19th Ohio

Cornfield

79th Pennsylvania

37th Indiana

38th Wisconsin

1st Wisconsin

21st Ohio

24th Ohio

Scribner

Johnson

Pickett's Mill

Confederate

Union

0   yards   100

C. Grear

shaded gorge than they came running back after encountering the enemy. In fact, some of them reported the whole northern race on their heels.[46]

As the Federals approached the bottom of the ravine, the Texans, lying concealed at the lip of the crevasse, suddenly stood up and delivered a point-blank volley into Hazen's startled men. "Suddenly there came the familiar rattle of musketry," wrote Bierce. All the spaces of the forest were immediately blue with smoke as "Hoarse, fierce yells broke out of a thousand throats . . . the edge of our swarm grew dense and clearly defined as the foremost halted, and the rest pressed forward to align themselves beside them, all firing." The roar from the battle was incessant and "the frequent shock of the cannon was rather felt than heard, but the gusts of grape which they blew into that populous wood were audible enough, screaming among the trees and cracking their stems and branches."[47] Seeing Granbury's men without breastworks, many of the Yankees rushed forward shouting, "Ah! Damn you, we have caught you without your logs now!"[48] Lieutenant Stokes wrote his sister that as they mowed down their attackers you could "see a pleasant smile playing upon the countenances of many of the men, as they would cry out to the Yankees, 'Come on, we are demoralized!'" During the intense fighting Major John Kennard of the 10th Texas kept busy encouraging his men by saying, "Put your trust in God, men, for He is with us." In spite of his initial piety, Kennard soon changed his tune and began taunting the Federals by yelling, "Come on! We are demoralized." Just then a spent Minié ball struck him between the eyes. Not wounded seriously, he raised himself up, saying, "Boys, I told them a lie, and I believe that is the reason I got shot."[49] With Govan's Arkansans enfilading the Federals' flank and Granbury's Texans leveling a destructive fire into them from the front, Hazen had little choice but to withdraw the survivors of his brigade to the other side of the ravine to seek shelter. In just a few minutes of fighting Hazen's crack brigade had lost over five hundred men.

Howard began having trouble coordinating his attack as the Texans bloodily repulsed Hazen's Brigade. Insisting that his men needed rations, McLean promptly marched his brigade to the rear in disobedience of orders. Howard did not immediately order Johnson's Division into the fight either, leaving only Wood's men to carry out the assault. Despite Hazen's exhortation to attack immediately, it took forty-five minutes before William Gibson had his brigade ready to go forward.

Gibson's men rushed down into the ravine among the survivors and casualties of Hazen's Brigade and began up the opposite side. No sooner had they started up the slope than they met an invisible wall of iron and lead from the Texans, a barrier that Bierce described as the "dead line." In an impetuous charge, Sergeant Ambus Norton, color-bearer of the 15th Ohio, planted his flag at the line of the Texas Brigade, only to have the Confederates kill him, along with three of his comrades, in hand-to-hand combat.[50] Private Andrew Gleason, also of the 15th Ohio, wrote of a man in his regiment leaning against a tree who would not lie down. The Ohioan did not fire, remembered Gleason, and "in a few minutes a ball came from the left and struck him squarely in the temple with that peculiar 'spat' which, once heard, is at once recognized as the passage of a bullet through flesh and bone." The impact splattered Gleason with the blood and brains of the Ohioan as his shattered unit began to seek shelter.[51] Gibson's veteran brigade suffered close to seven hundred casualties in the first few minutes. The survivors sought shelter behind rocks, trees, and the corpses of their comrades at the base of the ravine.

As Gibson's men met their fate, William Johnson finally had his men ready to advance. As the division went forward, they threatened to overrun Granbury's right, at the southern edge of a large cornfield. The men of the 6th & 15th Texas on the right began to get anxious as Johnson's Federals pushed the skirmishers of the 24th & 25th Texas back out of the cornfield. Granbury begged Cleburne for reinforcements, and Cleburne sent the 8th & 19th Arkansas from Govan's Brigade. Granbury's assistant adjutant general, George Hearne of the 10th Texas, personally led the 8th & 19th Arkansas and 6th & 15th Texas in a savage counterattack through the cornfield that halted the Northerners in their tracks. As he led the two regiments onto the field, several bullets struck Hearne and instantly killed him. After this counterattack Cleburne posted Lowrey's Brigade to the right of the Texans, extending their flank east of the cornfield.

At 6:30 P.M. Howard decided to send in Wood's last unit, Colonel Frederick Knefler's brigade. Knefler's men advanced down into the ravine, where they took cover, not daring to advance up the opposite slope. They remained content to tend to the wounded and dying and keep the Texans occupied with their presence.

Night closed in on the gruesome scene in the ravine. Private Iver O. Myhre of Company G, 15th Wisconsin, wrote, "The first night after we were wounded several hundred of us lay in an open field. The night was cold and those who were strong enough started to light some fires. Then the Rebels started to shoot at us, and the atmosphere among us was depressed. Some of the men asked politely that the fires be put out, others used foul language."[52] As the wounded suffered, Knefler's men remained quietly in the ravine, less than twenty yards from the Texas Brigade.

After dark Granbury realized that the Texans could not live in peace with the Yankees in such close proximity. He sent Captain Richard English of his staff to Cleburne's headquarters to request that he allow Granbury to order a bayonet charge to clear the ditch. Cleburne responded by saying that no one had authorized him to order a charge, but that he would inquire with Hood about it, and that in the meantime Granbury should do as he saw fit.[53] This provided enough authorization for Granbury, who aligned the 7th, 10th, and 24th & 25th Texas at the edge of the ditch and ordered them to fix bayonets. He held the 6th & 15th and 17th & 18th Texas in reserve in case the charge failed. Before the assault Captain Foster remembered everything being so still "that the chirp of a cricket could be heard 100 feet away—all hands lying perfectly still and the enemy not 40 yards in front of us. While waiting (all this time none had spoken above a whisper) we could hear the Yanks just in front of us moving among the dead leaves on the ground, like hogs rooting for acorns; but not speaking a word above a whisper. To make this charge in the dark," he remembered, "and go in front at that; and knowing that the enemy were just in front of us, was the most trying time I experienced during the whole war."[54]

At 1 A.M. the bugles sounded and the three regiments rushed down into the pitch-black ravine screaming a "regular Texas yell, or an Indian yell, or perhaps both together" as they swooped down on the unsuspecting Federals. The Texans could not see anything at all as they plunged into the blackness until muzzle flashes lit up the darkness like flashes of lightning. Confusion reigned as the Yankees fled for their lives. One of them grabbed a member of Company F, 24th & 25th Texas, and told him "to fall in quick as Co. C was gone already."[55] At times the Texans would ask what regiment a man belonged to, and sometimes the man in question would answer the 40th and the Texans knew they did not have a 40th regiment in their brigade. They would then shoot the man in question.[56] The Texans charged so impetuously that many of them injured themselves in their advance. Tom Stokes exemplified this trend as he tripped and fell from a rock outcropping while charging into the blackness. Granbury's boys rushed down to the bottom of the ravine "still Yelling like all the devils from the lower regions had been turned loose." The Confederates found several fallen trees with fifteen or twenty Federals behind them pleading, "don't shoot, don't shoot."[57] When the troops reached the base of the hill Granbury ordered the Texans to the crest of the ridge until daylight. "It needed but the brilliancy of this night attack," Cleburne wrote, "to add luster to the achievements of Granbury and his brigade. I am deeply indebted to them both."[58]

Dawn on May 28 revealed a gruesome sight. Captain Foster, whom Granbury had sent out with his company as pickets on the previous night, recorded that as he returned to the main lines the next morning, "I beheld that which I cannot describe and that which I hope never to see again, dead men meet the eye in every direction." He described how the Federals lay "just as they had fallen, and it seems like they have nearly all been shot in the head, and a great number of them have their skulls bursted open and their brains running out, quite a number that way." The sight made the staunch captain sick to his stomach, and he stated that "if a soldier could be made to faint I do believe I would have fainted if I had not passed on and got out of that place as soon as I did." Both sides kept the fire so hot during the battle that they had shot away many of the trees and nearly all of the underbrush, and the dead lay in thick piles. That day Johnston, with Hood, Granbury, and Cleburne, rode out to view the battlefield. Johnston and Hood both commented that they had never seen dead lay so thick, and then Johnston, turning to Granbury, said, "This shall no longer be known as Granbury's, but shall be known as Johnston's Brigade."[59] Johnston, by making this pronouncement, essentially claimed Granbury's Texans as his own, an honorific title indicating that the Texans had become the color (or best) brigade in the army in Johnston's opinion. Hood quietly remarked, "Texans did this and Texans can do it again."

The casualties revealed the ferocity of the fighting. Gibson's Brigade of Wood's Division suffered 687 casualties. Wood's Division as a whole lost 212 killed, 927 wounded, and 318 missing. Gibson's 49th Ohio lost 203 of 400 men engaged, while the 89th Ohio of the same brigade suffered 154 casualties. One company of the 41st Ohio lost 20 of 22 men engaged. The Texas Brigade suffered 32 killed and 114 wounded. Cleburne's Division as a whole suffered 85 killed and 363 wounded.[60]

In the aftermath of Pickett's Mill, Granbury's men reoutfitted themselves. Many of the Texans had gone into battle armed with Austrian-made

Lorenz rifles issued to them early in the war. Taking advantage of their momentous victory, they stripped the Union dead of their Enfield rifles, uniformly rearming the brigade.

Sherman, who omitted any mention of Pickett's Mill in his memoirs or his official report, decided to bypass the Confederates and slide back east toward the railroad. On May 28 Johnston received erroneous information about the Federals at Dallas moving north. He acted quickly to try to turn Sherman's right. That afternoon William Bate's division of Hardee's Corps attacked, and the Yankees, still very much in place around Dallas, soundly repulsed them.[61] Both sides then settled down for a standoff as Johnston awaited Sherman's next move.

For the next several days the two armies remained in place, skirmishing and sniping at one another. On May 31, Sherman ordered McPherson to march the Army of the Tennessee to the northeast, heading back toward the Western & Atlantic. The Confederates remained in place as Sherman slowly shifted.

Even as Johnston retreated toward Atlanta and the Confederate cause grew dim, the spirits and fighting prowess of Granbury's Texans grew brighter than ever after Pickett's Mill. Almost every collection of Texan letters and diaries from the men of Granbury's Brigade mention Pickett's Mill in detail, detailing the prominence it held for them in their minds. While the battle had little strategic importance, it did keep Sherman from flanking Johnston's army, and earned the Texans accolades from Johnston, Hood, and others. To the Texans, Pickett's Mill was a huge triumph, proving to them in their minds that they could win no matter what the odds, especially if other Confederates would just perform as well as they did. This demonstrates the preeminence of local perspective when examining the motives of western Confederate soldiers. Although the Confederacy itself was dying, to Granbury's men the war had never gone better. They continued to win, in their minds, huge victories, trusted their leaders implicitly, and carried on with a loyalty to the Confederate cause, which they believed could still succeed.

CHAPTER TWELVE

STUCK IN THE THICKETS OF NORTH GEORGIA

After the dramatic events of May, the Texans would soon find themselves engaging in tedious marches and countermarches as both sides attempted to outmaneuver each other in the thickets of North Georgia. From a strategic standpoint, the marching and countermarching in Georgia weakened the Confederate war effort because Johnston retreated farther toward Atlanta, but the spirits of Granbury's Texans remained high. Despite the constant marching and countermarching the Texans did not lose faith in themselves, their leaders, or the Confederate cause, reinforcing the idea that a lack of Confederate nationalism did not affect the Confederate war effort, even as late as 1864, and that a localized perspective and effective leadership remained the key to keeping the Army of Tennessee together as a coherent fighting force.

The maneuvering began in June. The beginning of the month found both armies still bogged down in the tangled thickets. Johnston realized that the Federals had withdrawn from Dallas, but he could not discern Sherman's intentions. At first he suspected that Sherman might be retreating. He soon ruled this out and began to suspect a turning movement toward his right. To counter this threat, he ordered Cleburne's Division to march across the rear of the army from the left to the right flank.[1]

In fact, in the early days of June Sherman began to execute just such a maneuver. On June 1, Federal cavalry seized Allatoona Pass and Acworth on the Western & Atlantic and Sherman began slowly shifting his forces east toward Acworth. He hoped that this flanking maneuver would force Johnston to retreat across the Chattahoochee, the last natural barrier before Atlanta.

Meanwhile, on June 3, in the ranks of Granbury's Brigade the monotony of trench life continued. The rain continued unabated, and Captain Foster remarked, "All our dog tents and Oil Cloths that we picked up on the battle field are now of use to keep us dry."[2] Captain Edward Broughton of the 7th Texas wrote his wife on June 3 and told her that from what he could ascertain "our army seems to have the best morale possible. The soldiers are all in high spirit, buoyant and confident of success."[3]

On June 3 Johnston realized that Sherman had chosen Acworth as his objective. Consequently, he decided to move the Army of Tennessee east into position behind a previously prepared line of fortifications along Pine, Brush, and Lost Mountains. This line, though farther south, remained north of Marietta and the Chattahoochee. That night he issued orders to his corps commanders to move out.[4]

Just as the Confederates were poised to move, Hiram Granbury took leave of his brigade, complaining of ill health. It is probable that Granbury was suffering from a bout of clinical depression, owing to several factors. Around this time he learned of the death of his brother at the Battle of Mansfield, Louisiana. June 3 also fell close to the one-year anniversary of the death of his wife, Fannie. The stress from the campaign and the slight head wound he sustained at Pickett's Mill also combined to produce the breakdown to which the lanky Texan succumbed. To recover, he retired to an Atlanta hospital.[5] In the interim, Colonel Mills of the 10th Texas took command until Brigadier General James Smith again assumed command of the Texas Brigade. As Granbury made his way to Atlanta, Johnston set his army in motion. On the evening of June 4, the Confederates quietly withdrew from their fortifications and headed southeast.[6]

Another shakeup in the command of Granbury's Brigade occurred on June 6, when Colonel Robert Garland arrested Colonel Frank Wilkes of the 24th & 25th Texas. Wilkes then preferred charges against Garland, and Johnston sent both officers to Atlanta. The source or outcome of the altercation is not known, but Garland forced Wilkes to resign on July 30, leaving Lieutenant Colonel William Neyland (originally of the 25th Texas) in command of the regiment. With Garland also gone, Captain Rhoads Fisher assumed command of the 6th & 15th Texas.[7]

Because of their position on the extreme right of the army, Cleburne's men waited all through the dark, rainy night of June 4 as the entire army passed behind their camp. Finally, at 11:30 P.M. on June 5, Granbury's Texans received their orders to move southeast. At midnight they began their mud march through the rain-soaked woods of North Georgia. "We are in the very thick of the timbered country," wrote Captain Foster, "and thick undergrowth, makes it darker than it would be in open country, and so very thick cloudy, and raining very hard all combined, makes it the darkest night of all dark nights."[8] The Georgia mud became so thick that it sucked men's shoes off their feet. Foster remembered that "occasionally a man would stumble and fall flat in the mud, get up, and go on again." Even these conditions could not dampen the spirits of the Texans, who remained "all in good humor, passing their jokes as usual, as though it was noon instead of midnight and clear instead of raining and muddy."[9] The high spirits of the Texans revealed their attitudes toward the war, and their devotion to the Confederate cause and their leaders.

In the dark woods and drenching rain the two armies shifted and sparred, vying for position. When Johnston ordered the Army of Tennessee south, he positioned his men on a line running from Gilgal Church southwest to Lost Mountain. After Sherman completed his concentration at Acworth, Johnston shifted his units to a line running from Gilgal Church east to Brush Mountain, directly north of Marietta. Hardee occupied the left of the new line, Polk the center, and Hood the right. At Acworth, Sherman waited to concentrate all of his units before beginning his advance against the Confederates, who remained entrenched north of the Chattahoochee.[10] On June 10, Sherman began his advance. As his first move, he decided to push some of his units forward against the bulge in the Confederate line on Pine Mountain.

On June 13 Cleburne decided to have a look at the Federals and rode to the crest of Pine Mountain with a staff officer. Cleburne sought to satisfy his own curiosity and began to peer over the logs of the redoubt. Before long a shell whistled overhead and then another, just a few feet above his head. Satisfied with his reconnaissance, Cleburne and his staff officer hurriedly withdrew from the top of the mountain.[11] The next day the rain stopped, and the Union artillery fire cost the Army of Tennessee one of its corps commanders when a solid shot killed Leonidas Polk atop Pine Mountain.

With the return of sunny weather Sherman began maneuvering around the Confederate left. On June 15, John Schofield discovered that Cleburne's line around Gilgal Church formed a salient vulnerable to enfilade fire. Expecting an attack, all day on the fifteenth Granbury's men dismantled the walls of Gilgal Church to strengthen their earthworks. Soon after they finished the Federals moved several batteries to within three hundred yards of their position and began firing canister and solid shot at them.[12] During this fight a spent ball struck Captain Foster "just to the right of my nose" and produced a superficial wound that split the skin of his face "for some distance." He soon withdrew to the rear to seek medical attention.[13] As Schofield's artillery blasted away at the fortifications, some of his infantrymen worked their way around to Cleburne's left. There, only Brigadier General Lawrence Ross's dismounted cavalrymen stood between them and turning the Confederate flank. Cognizant of the threat, Johnston ordered Hardee to withdraw his corps to a line running along the south bank of Mud Creek.[14]

As Cleburne's Division withdrew on the afternoon of June 16, a shell exploded near Lucius Polk, one of Cleburne's brigade commanders, killing his horse and inflicting a serious wound. The wound necessitated the amputation of Polk's leg, ending his active field service. Cleburne divided Polk's regiments among the other three brigades of the division. Two of Polk's regiments, the 5th Confederate and 35th Tennessee, went to Granbury's Brigade. The Texans quickly became fond of the 5th Confederate and soon informally titled the Irishmen the "5th Texas."[15]

On the night of June 16 the rain returned. Lieutenant Collins remembered "trying to sleep in water half side deep. The undertaking was all right until we would move and let in a lot of cold fresh water, then sleep would quit our eyes, and slumber flee from our eyelids. We had the consolation of knowing, however, that each one of us was drowning several hundred 'graybacks.'"[16]

That night the rain continued as the Army of Tennessee abandoned its trenches and moved three miles to the south. The army took position on a line that slanted from Kennesaw Mountain south to Little Kennesaw and Pigeon Hill. As before, Hood's Corps occupied the right, Polk's (now under Loring) the center, and Hardee's the left. In this new line, Cleburne posted Granbury's Texans on the right, along the Dallas-Marietta Road.

No sooner had the opposing armies taken their places than skirmishing resumed. On June 19, as Granbury's Texans kept busy constructing earthworks, a shell exploded in the midst of a pile of rails. The concussion threw several members of the brigade into the air, including Private Frank Cook of the 6th & 15th Texas, who came down "running." Despite this shock Cook remained unhurt, and soon went back to firing in the direction of the Federals. That night his regimental commander placed Lieutenant Collins in command of the brigade pickets. When Lieutenant James McCracken came to replace him, a sniper fired a ball at Collins, singeing his mustache and knocking him to the ground. With the constant skirmishing, such narrow escapes were common. Every morning the whistling of Minié balls overhead greeted the soldiers.[17]

On Tuesday, June 22, the drenching rains again ceased, and the Georgia countryside began to dry. That day Sherman ordered Thomas to take Hooker's Corps and move west on Marietta down the Powder Springs Road to feel out the Confederate left. Johnston realized that his lines had become too long to adequately defend, and when he received word of the Federals moving toward his left, circumstances forced him to make a decision: either order another retreat or find some way to stop Sherman. Although Johnston launched a sortie against Sherman around the Kolb farm on June 22, it did little to change the strategic situation.

The third week of June proved monotonous for the two armies facing each other down around Kennesaw Mountain. That week saw a continuation of the skirmishing that had become the constant companion of both sides for several weeks. Captain Foster scribbled in his diary on June 25 that the musketry exchanged with the Yankees amounted to a constant "bang bang bang, like water dropping off the eaves of a house. The bullets go zip zip over our breastworks day and night, making the men bow their heads."[18]

Sherman grew increasingly frustrated in his month-long stalemate with Johnston. He decided in the last week of June to attack the center of the Confederate line. On June 25, he ordered Thomas to assail the Confederate center south and west of Kennesaw while McPherson made a feint toward the Confederate right.[19] He scheduled the attack for Monday, June 27.

At 8 A.M. on June 27 Federal infantrymen of the IV, XIV, and XV Corps began their attack on the Confederate works. On the south end of the Confederate line Cleburne and Cheatham's men repulsed the second prong of the attack. John Newton's division of the IV Corps struck the left of Cleburne's line north of Cheatham's Hill. Nathan Kimball's, George Wagner's, and Charles Harker's brigades advanced due east into the mouth of Cleburne's guns. Cleburne had posted Granbury's Brigade north of the assaulting columns. No attacks fell directly on their front, so the Texans kept up a withering enfilade fire into the left flank of Kimball's Brigade. Night finally ended the Battle of Kennesaw Mountain. Federal losses came to nearly three thousand killed, wounded, and captured, while the Confederates suffered just seven hundred casualties.[20]

Seeing that his frontal assault at Kennesaw Mountain had failed miserably, Sherman reverted to his old strategy of moving by the Confederate left. On June 30, McPherson's Army of the Tennessee swung around to the right flank and began advancing down the Sandtown Road to Nickajack Creek, beyond the Confederate left and closer to the Chattahoochee. Johnston realized that he dared not extend his line any farther—with his right flank already stretched to the breaking point. On the night of July 2, unwilling to do anything else, he ordered a retreat south of the Chattahoochee.

By this point the campaign had started to wear down the men in the ranks. On June 8, Lieutenant Sebron G. Sneed of Company G, 6th & 15th Texas, wrote humorously, "In this army one hole in the seat of the breeches indicates a Capt.—two holes a Lt.; and the seat of the pants all out . . . indicates a private."[21] Lieutenant Collins wrote that the Texans, "Not having had a change of food or raiment for sixty days, we were not to say very clean, and scurvy broke out amongst us, some of the boys' legs were as black and brown as navy tobacco." To remedy this problem Johnston had tomatoes shipped in from Florida and Alabama. Another ever-present pest facing the Texans remained the huge body lice that infested their clothing. They soon discovered that the lice could not stand heat or smoke, and so, "Just before turning in at night each fellow would rake him up a pile of dry leaves, set fire therein and hold his shirt over the smoke and heat, and the big, fat lice would drop into the fire and pop like popcorn popping in the skillet back home."[22] Despite their discomforts, the soldiers retained implicit faith in the decisions of "Old Joe" Johnston.

For the moment, however, "Old Joe" changed his mind and decided not to retreat south of the Chattahoochee just yet. Rather, he chose to place his army in a line of fortifications guarding the Western & Atlantic Railroad bridge on the north side of the river. Brigadier General Francis Shoup, who designed the fortifications, had constructed the "Shoup line" with slave labor. On the morning of July 5, the Confederates took position and began to improve Shoup's works.

In the first week of July Hiram Granbury made an appearance in the camp of his brigade. On July 8, Private F. E. Blossman of the 6th & 15th Texas wrote, "Gen. Granbury is in camp today. He has been quite sick, but says he can take command in eight or ten days. None of us like Gen. Smith . . . he is brave as a lion but mean as a hyena. I am the only private he has spoken to in the brigade. We will be glad to get rid of him. A petition is to [be] sent to 'Old Joe' to let us have Granbury."[23] Blossman's letter indicates the devotion the Texans felt to Granbury, and this devotion encouraged them to stay in the ranks and continue the fight for Confederate independence.

The impasse along the river proved short lived. On July 8 Federal units crossed the Chattahoochee north of the railroad at Cavalry Ford, beyond the Confederate right. Johnston had not expected Sherman to move by his right. Fearful of being cut off from Atlanta, he ordered a retreat south of the Chattahoochee on July 9. The following day the Confederates crossed the river and moved three miles south.[24]

In Richmond, news that Johnston had crossed the Chattahoochee reached Jefferson Davis on July 10. With the Army of Tennessee south of the river, the fate of Atlanta hung in the balance. Bragg insisted that Johnston needed offensive action to halt Sherman. Davis agreed and felt that Johnston had not done enough in this regard. When Johnston retreated across the Chattahoochee, he changed his base of supplies from the Five Points in Atlanta to Macon. Davis clearly saw this as a sign that he would abandon Atlanta. Hurriedly, the president cast about for a suitable replacement. Throughout the campaign, Hood had kept up a steady correspondence with Davis outlining Johnston's shortcomings in the conduct of the campaign. At every opportunity Hood related to Davis a "better" course of action that he supposedly favored instead of retreating. Bragg recommended Hood to replace Johnston, and eventually (influenced by Bragg and Hood's appraisals of the situation) Davis came to agree. When he wrote Robert E. Lee about the dilemma, Lee replied that the timing was wrong to replace an army commander at so critical a juncture. Lee also intimated that his choice for command would be Hardee. Finally, Lee informed Davis that "Hood is a bold fighter. I am doubtful as to the other qualities necessary."[25] Whatever he decided, Davis felt that it should be done soon.

Regardless of Hood's deficient experience and temperament, he would at least favor offensive action to stop Sherman. In any event, Davis decided not to fall prey to haste. He concluded to await developments in the near future before making his final decision.

Although Johnston's marching and countermarching ultimately weakened the defense of Atlanta as he retreated south, the men in the ranks had a very different perspective. Rather than resent the retreating, the Texans seemed to revel in the idea that Johnston was outsmarting and outmaneuvering Sherman—and that he would not waste their lives needlessly in battle. From the historians' perspective and that of Jefferson Davis, Johnston committed terrible blunders in retreating toward Atlanta without a fight, but from the localized perspective of Granbury's Texans he was taking the right course of action.

CHAPTER THIRTEEN

HOOD TAKES COMMAND

In July 1864 a high-level command decision would set in motion a series of bloody battles as both sides vied for possession of the Gate City of Atlanta. This dramatic shift in the campaign would shake the Texans to their core and send many of them to their graves. The fighting around Atlanta reinforces the idea that a localized perspective dictated the morale of Granbury's Texans. Even though the Confederate government made unwise decisions in their eyes, and even though the fighting took a heavy toll, they continued to remain optimistic about their chances for success because of the example set by Hiram Granbury, Patrick Cleburne, and their regimental officers. The fact that the Texans also remained in the ranks during the terrible bloodletting around Atlanta also underscores their devotion to the Confederate cause.

With the two armies at the very gates of Atlanta, Davis and Johnston set the stage for an unexpected shift in the campaign. On the morning of July 12, Johnston telegraphed Davis and advised him to "distribute" the Federal prisoners from Andersonville, south of Atlanta. Davis took this as direct proof that Johnston planned to abandon the city, and the pressure on Davis to replace him mounted. In Atlanta, Bragg wired Davis and advised against appointing Hardee to army command because he would continue the same policy that Johnston had implemented. Left with no other choice, Davis decided to remove Johnston from command and replace him with John Bell Hood on July 17.

The appointment of Hood shocked and outraged the soldiers of the army. Captain Foster wrote in his diary on July 18: "In less than an hour after this fact becomes known, groups of three, five, seven, ten or fifteen men could be seen all over camp discussing the situation. Gen. Johnston has so endeared himself to his soldiers, that no man can take his place. We have never made a fight under him that we did not get the best of it." Foster continued, "For the first time we hear men openly talk about going home, by tens (10) and fifties (50). They refuse to stand guard, or do any other camp duty, and talk open rebellion against all Military authority. All over camp, (not only among Texas troops) can be seen this demoralization—and at all hours of the afternoon can be heard Hurrah for Joe Johnston and God Dn Jeff Davis."[1]

Lieutenant Collins and his company were amusing themselves by playing cards underneath a large oak tree when Adjutant John Willingham of the 10th Texas Infantry arrived and read them Davis's order replacing Johnston. "The boys all threw down their cards," remembered Collins, "and collected in little groups discussing the new move they were all dissatisfied, but soon dismissed the whole with the remark hell will break loose in Georgia sure enough now." John Bell Hood was "a bulldog fighter from away back," concluded the Texan, "and President Davis could not have suited Gen. Sherman better, had he commissioned him to have made the appointment."[2] Private William Oliphant of Company G, 6th & 15th Texas, remembered that after an officer read the order announcing the instatement of Hood, "absolute silence" reigned. "Not a word was spoken for several minutes after," wrote Oliphant, "and then one of the boys, as brave a soldier as ever lived or died shrugged his shoulders and said with a sigh, 'Well boys, we're going to catch hell now.'"[3] These exchanges demonstrate that even though the Texans felt the Confederate government had made a poor decision, as Gary Gallagher points out in *The Confederate War*, this did not dampen their devotion to the Confederate cause.[4]

The removal of Johnston seems to have cast a heavy shadow over the spirit of the Texans, but they kept going just the same. Again, their loyalties lay not with the Army of Tennessee or even so much with Johnston, though admittedly he remained very popular. The soldiers thought Davis had made a mistake, but this did not cause them to desert the cause or give up. Cleburne, Granbury, and other officers accepted the change in command and set an example for their men by staying the course and not voicing displeasure. This leadership is what helped keep the spirits of the Texans high as they prepared to defend Atlanta.

The day he took command, Hood began to develop a strategy to save Atlanta. On July 18 Hood had 48,750 effectives (33,000 of whom were infantry) with which to launch the offensive. The Texas Brigade could count one thousand effectives at this same date. Thomas had his Army of the Cumberland astride Peachtree Creek, north of Atlanta, with McPherson's Army of the Tennessee and Schofield's Army of the Ohio moving east toward Decatur. Sherman intended to trap the Confederates in a pincer movement from the north and east, but in their current disposition Hood saw an opportunity to strike back. While Thomas crossed Peachtree Creek, Hood intended to attack with Hardee's and Stewart's corps in the hope of destroying the Army of the Cumberland before Sherman could bring up support.

While Sherman completed his dispositions on the evening of July 19, Hood met in Atlanta with his corps commanders and announced his decision to take offensive action the next day. He directed Stewart and Hardee to take their corps out of the Atlanta defenses and strike Thomas before his men had time to prepare breastworks on the south bank of Peachtree Creek. Hood scheduled the attack for 1 P.M. While they crushed the Army of the Cumberland, Cheatham's Corps, supported by the Georgia militia under General Gustavus Smith, would hold Atlanta against Schofield and McPherson.[5]

The next day the Confederate attacks stalled against a tough defense along Peachtree Creek. Several hours of hard fighting spent the Confederates, and they lacked resolve to go forward again. There remained a little daylight, and General W. W. Loring maintained that with reinforcements his division could make another attack. Hardee sent word back to Cleburne to move forward and align his division for an advance.[6] When the order arrived, Cleburne and his command were near the Peachtree Road with an open field about four hundred yards wide to their front. Granbury's Texans (still under Smith) occupied the left of the division, with Govan's Arkansans in the center and Lowrey's Alabamans and Mississippians on the right. Cleburne advanced his men to the northern edge of the farm field, and here they came up against a post and rail fence. The entire line took hold of the fence and "bodily lifted it from its foundation."[7]

Just at that moment, a twenty-pound Parrott shell exploded in the midst of the 6th & 15th Texas. Lieutenant Collins wrote, "a blinding flash right in our front and a shell explodes. It seemed to be filled with powder and ounce balls. It laid a good many of the boys out and among the number was Capt. Ben Tyus, and the writer." The round wounded Captain Tyus in the ankle, while Collins "received an ounce ball in the upper third" of his left thigh.[8] Private Charles Leuschner of Company A recorded, "One 18 pound gun ball came within 3 feet of me & killed four men & cut one man's leg off. I and Mike Shivits & 4 more were be spatter [bespattered] with blood and flesh."[9] Lieutenant Collins recalled that as he fell he "noticed that about two inches square of our gray Georgia jean pants had gone in with the shot." He took this as evidence that part of the shell had gone through his thigh, cutting the femoral artery, and that he would be a dead Confederate in three minutes. (As the Texan understood it, that was the time allotted to bleed to death with such a wound.) Four "big stout fellows" picked up Collins on a stretcher and began carrying him to the rear. At length, he summoned the courage to ask one of his litter bearers whether or not he had lost much blood. "He was a witty Irishman and replied 'Not a drap of the ruddy current to be seen, Lieutenant.'" These words brought back hope to the young Texan for recovery, and he "chuckled" in his sleeve "when the thought occurred that maybe this wound will win a good furlough and if it does, won't we have fun with those Georgia girls." He continued, writing in his memoirs, "This may all sound like a strange line of thoughts to run through one's mind in so short a time and under such circumstances, but all this is sound common sense compared to some things we are guilty of doing during our natural lives."[10] Hardee's position placed him within eyesight when the shell exploded, and he ordered Granbury's Brigade to charge the battery.[11]

Just as Hardee ordered Cleburne's men into action, he received a message from Hood directing him to send reinforcements at once to the east side of Atlanta. With Stewart and Hardee busy trying to destroy Thomas along Peachtree Creek, McPherson and Schofield had advanced toward Atlanta and begun to push back Wheeler's dismounted cavalry east of the city. Wheeler had informed Hood that if he did not send infantry support soon, his dismounted troopers would not be able to hold the Federals at bay. Wheeler remained particularly concerned with the prominence known as Bald Hill. As the highest elevation on the low-lying flatlands east of the city, whoever controlled the elevation would command the entire plain.

Because Cleburne's Division remained unengaged, Hardee ordered the Irishman to take his command and march at the double-quick south into Atlanta and then east to bolster the dismounted cavalry on Bald Hill. "Five minutes more," wrote Captain Irving Buck of Cleburne's staff, "would have been too late, and would have found this command heavily engaged."[12] The withdrawal of Cleburne's Division ended any hope for further offensive action at Peachtree Creek. Despite this order, the fighting had already claimed two Texans killed and eighteen wounded.[13] Hood's first test of command had failed, at a cost of nearly five thousand Confederates killed, wounded, or captured.[14]

Quietly withdrawing his men, Cleburne marched south down Peachtree Road into Atlanta. At 7:15 P.M. Hood advised Wheeler of the reinforcements on the way and instructed the embattled general to "communicate this to the men, and *urge them to hold on*."[15] After resting in the suburbs, Cleburne's men continued south on a route parallel with the Georgia Railroad until they reached the line of breastworks east of the city occupied by Wheeler's tired horsemen. After marching south for about a mile and a half the division found itself opposite Bald Hill. They found the hill a "lozenge-shaped" prominence about a half-mile in length from north to south. The eastern (or front) side of the hill angled up rather steeply, while the west side and either end tapered down gradually into the surrounding woods. The promontory had little vegetative cover, and any layman could see that it would become a key position in any attempt to take Atlanta from the east.[16] Cleburne reported to Wheeler about midnight, and immediately deployed his troops. On the left of the division he placed Mark Lowrey's brigade just south of the Georgia Railroad. On Lowrey's right he placed Govan's Arkansans, and last Cleburne placed the Texas Brigade under Smith just north of Bald Hill. On the far left of the brigade, Smith placed the 7th Texas. To their right he put the 6th & 15th Texas, 5th Confederate, and 10th Texas. Finally, sloping up the northern end of the hill, he positioned the 17th & 18th Texas followed by the 24th & 25th Texas to hold the right flank.[17] Because Smith's flank did not reach all the way to the peak of the hill, Wheeler volunteered to place the dismounted cavalry brigades of Alfred Iverson and William Allen on the right flank of the Texas Brigade. Cleburne completed these dispositions about an hour before dawn.[18]

The first rays of light on July 21 revealed to the Texans atop Bald Hill why their comrades had been so eager to abandon the position. Less than a mile to the east, on a parallel ridge, Captain Francis Degress had situated his 1st Illinois Light Artillery. At 7 A.M. the battery of twenty-pound Parrott guns opened up on the exposed defenders atop the hill.[19] Soon the Illinoisans gained the range and began to plaster the Texan breastworks with a very accurate fire.[20]

Degress and his gunners laid down one of the most fierce and destructive cannonades sustained by Granbury's Brigade during the war. Soon after it opened up, a shell entered an angle of the works occupied by the 17th & 18th Texas. The shrapnel ricocheted along the ditch, decapitating six Texans of the company and severely wounding twelve others. Captain Foster wrote that the explosion "knocked one man into a hundred pieces—one hand and arm went over the works and his cartridge box ten feet up in a tree."[21] Only one member of the company escaped death or injury. Private W. W. Royall of the 17th & 18th Texas recalled with horror that "a cannon ball hit the breastworks and struck a man on the head, his head struck me in the breast and knocked me down and covered me with his blood. His name was Bill Sims."[22] Captain Foster had just finished work on the breastworks to his front when, "as I was lying down resting on my elbow and another man in about the same position with our heads about two feet apart and our feet in opposite directions, a shell (schrapnel) exploded just between us blowing me one way and him the other hurting neither one of us but killing three men about 10 ft. from us eating their breakfast."[23] During this terrific bombardment the hapless Texans suffered forty killed and over one hundred wounded.[24] Though the shells continued to fly fast and thick, they proved only a prelude to the main thrust against Bald Hill—an infantry assault.

After the bombardment had softened up the defenses, McPherson ordered Brigadier General Mortimer Leggett's division of the XVII Corps to attack the Texans on Bald Hill. McPherson ordered Leggett to draw support from Brigadier General Giles Smith's division. Leggett's men advanced out of the wood line a little to the south of the Texas Brigade, directly against the dismounted Confederate cavalrymen. The scared horsemen of Iverson's Brigade could not wait any longer, and rising where they stood they fired a ragged volley into the advancing Federal line. This premature fire forced the Texan skirmishers to lie down to avoid being hit from the front and rear. The Yankees then swept forward and captured the majority of these Texans. After they had discharged their weapons, the cavalrymen broke and ran, exposing the right flank of the 24th & 25th Texas. After reaching the summit of Bald Hill, Leggett halted his Federals, awaiting the support from Giles Smith's division.

Soon, Colonel William Hall's Iowa brigade of Smith's Division emerged from the woods north of Leggett's men and hit the right flank of the Texas Brigade, threatening the right flank of the 24th & 25th Texas. Lieutenant Colonel William Neyland, commanding the regiment, quickly swung around his right wing to the rear at a right angle. Neyland led the right wing of the regiment in a fierce counterattack against the Federals sweeping north up the breastworks. John Langley, the color-bearer of the regiment, led the charge as a bullet cut his flagstaff in two. He rescued the flag before it touched the ground and continued with it a few steps further before another round shattered his arm.[25] The combatants made the fighting so intense that Joe Harrison of the 24th & 25th Texas ran "up to a Yank who was cursing a wounded Confed, put the muzzle of his gun to his back and blew him up."[26] A wound to the groin felled Neyland, but his men swept on, using bayonets and rifle butts to force the invaders from close to three hundred yards of entrenchments. As soon as they retook the works, geography forced the Texans to swing back north and force out the enemy, who had taken possession of their old line during the counterattack. After Giles Smith's men retired to the cover of the woods south of Bald Hill, Smith placed the Texas Brigade in a single rank to hold the position vacated by Iverson's and Allen's dismounted cavalrymen. Though Degress and others kept up the artillery bombardment until dark, McPherson made no further attempt to advance toward Atlanta because Leggett's left flank remained in the air, potentially vulnerable to attack from the Texans. Nightfall put an end to the fighting around Bald Hill.[27]

Though they held their position throughout the day on July 21, this steadfastness came at a heavy price for the Texas Brigade. The regiment most heavily engaged, the 24th & 25th Texas, lost the most during the day. Neyland's regiment suffered nine killed, twenty-five wounded, and nine captured during the intense fighting. The 17th & 18th Texas lost twelve killed and thirty-nine wounded, and the losses decreased further north. The 10th Texas lost eight killed and twelve wounded, while the 7th Texas lost two killed and seven wounded. On the far left of the brigade, the 6th

& 15th Texas lost six killed, eighteen wounded, and six captured. Smith reported the losses of his brigade on July 21 as forty-seven killed, 120 wounded, and nineteen captured.[28] Though they had repulsed Giles Smith's men, Leggett's Federals remained atop Bald Hill, compelling the Texans to stay in their position and await further developments.

As night fell, Hood busied himself concocting another flanking maneuver. He knew from intelligence sources that McPherson had positioned his left flank unprotected south of Bald Hill, and Hood planned to have Hardee's men make a forced march around the Federals and get in their rear. To accomplish this, he instructed Hardee to go as far east as Decatur if necessary. Once he had turned McPherson's left, he planned to sweep north and attack the Federals in flank as Cheatham's men hit them from the west. Though sound in theory, in reality two days of constant fighting had exhausted Hardee's men and it would be difficult at best for them to execute a circuitous twenty-plus-mile march to gain McPherson's left-rear. Whatever the odds, Hood saw his strategy as being the equal of Jackson's or Lee's, and set his men in motion to try.

After nightfall, the Texas Brigade abandoned its works and marched to the rear to rendezvous with the rest of Cleburne's Division. Once the Irishman had assembled his division they marched west into the city for a short respite before continuing south as the rear of Hardee's column. Hardee's exhausted men made their way back into Atlanta and then south and east in search of McPherson's rear. As they staggered along, the third night without rest began to tell on the progress of the march.

While the Confederates executed their flanking maneuver, Sherman did not remain idle. Around 3 A.M. Schofield sent him a message that the Confederates had started withdrawing from their entrenchments. Sherman ordered his units to pursue and occupy the city, assuming Hood had decided to retreat. But at first light Sherman could see that Hood did not intend to abandon Atlanta. Instead, he could clearly see the Confederates strengthening their breastworks east of the city. Hurriedly, he cancelled the pursuit order and instructed his three army commanders to lay siege to the city from the north, east, and west. He also ordered McPherson to deploy Greenville Dodge's XVI Corps toward Decatur to destroy the railroad there. McPherson had his other two corps deployed facing west. Logan's XV Corps stretched from well north of the Georgia Railroad all the way down to the northern edge of Bald Hill, with Major General Frank Blair's XVII Corps to its south. Blair in turn deployed Leggett's Division atop Bald Hill and shifted Smith's command around to their left, south of the prominence.

Though Sherman remained unconcerned about the possibility of a Confederate attack, McPherson's personal reconnaissance suggested otherwise. He also observed the Confederates strengthening and building breastworks parallel to and south of his southern flank. Hence, when Sherman ordered Dodge's Corps to begin the railroad destruction, McPherson intervened and convinced Sherman that the pioneers could do the work as well as infantry. This left Thomas Sweeney's division in place, already deployed north of Terry's Mill Pond facing south. At 1 P.M. Sherman ordered McPherson to send John Fuller's division back toward the railroad to aid in the destruction.[29]

Meanwhile, on the Confederate side, confusion and a lack of intelligence regarding the terrain contributed to the fact that Hardee did not have the first of his men in position to attack until almost noon. At the head of his column, Hardee designated William Bate's division to attack farthest east. Bate fretted about a lack of knowledge of Federal deployment as his men struggled through thick undergrowth and briar patches. Because of the rough ground, straggling reduced the division to a little over a thousand effectives. West of Sugar Creek, Walker and his men floundered through a large briar patch before confronting the massive pool of water and rotting foliage known as Terry's Mill Pond. Becoming irate at the prospect of the impassable morass, Walker threatened to shoot his guide before the scout informed him that the pond could be circumvented to the west. About a quarter past twelve, Walker, riding ahead of his division, emerged into a prominent clearing in front of Sweeney's Division. A Federal picket, seeing him, fired, and the outspoken Georgian fell to the ground dead, still grasping his field glasses.[30] Walker's and Bate's divisions quickly moved up and assailed Sweeney's and Fuller's atop the ridge to their front.

As the two Confederate divisions advanced, withering Federal fire beat them back, and to the west Cleburne's and Maney's divisions emerged from the thick, entangling undergrowth directly on McPherson's left. Rather than finding an exposed flank, Hardee found Colonel William Hall's Iowa brigade bent back at a right angle to the main line, facing south. Directly in front of the Iowans lay a cleared field of fire fifty yards deep, and beyond that an entangling abatis the Iowans had constructed by chopping down trees and facing their interwoven branches outward.[31] Because of the

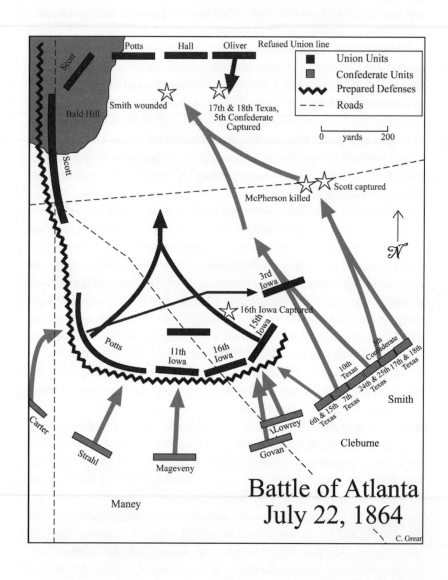

Potts   Hall   Oliver   Refused Union line

Scott

Bald Hill

Smith wounded

17th & 18th Texas,
5th Confederate
Captured

Union Units
Confederate Units
Prepared Defenses
Roads

0   yards   200

Scott

Scott captured

McPherson killed

3rd
Iowa

16th Iowa Captured

Potts

15th
Iowa

11th
Iowa

16th
Iowa

5th
Confederate   17th & 18th
Texas

10th
Texas

24th & 25th
Texas

Lowrey

6th & 15th
Texas

7th
Texas

Smith

Carter

Strahl

Govan

Cleburne

Mageveny

Maney

Battle of Atlanta
July 22, 1864

C. Grear

grueling combat and marching of the past several days, as well as the heat and lack of sleep, many of the Confederates fell prey to heat stroke and exhaustion as Hardee's men neared the enemy.

While Maney's Division advanced on the left, Cleburne's Division formed on the right. Cleburne placed Govan's Arkansans on the left, with the Texas Brigade on their right, supported by Lowrey's and Carter's brigades in reserve. The advance of the Texas Brigade took them over rough ground interlaced with rivulets of brackish water and choked with underbrush until they emerged into the cleared field in front of the Iowan breastworks.[32]

The Federals opened on Govan's and Smith's men with devastating effects. Scores of Confederates went down as their first line crumpled to the ground. A second line came up only to suffer the same fate, while yet a third battle line advanced to within several yards of the blazing entrenchments and there traded fire with the enemy for several minutes. Soon, incoming fire forced the attackers to go to ground, and several of them raised white flags.[33] The situation had become critical for the Arkansans and Texans. At that moment, to the right, the rest of the Texas Brigade swept around Hall's flank, capturing nearly the entire 16th Iowa with its colors and two guns of Battery F, 2nd U.S. Artillery. Almost completely alone, the Texans surged forward, far outdistancing the Arkansans on their left and Lowrey's Brigade to their right.[34]

Just as the Texans surged through the gap and captured scores of prisoners, an encounter occurred that would spawn much controversy in the decades to come. Federal general James McPherson, upon hearing the first shots of the battle, rode out to the left to appraise the situation for himself. He found himself in the woods directly in front of the Texas Brigade just as they broke through. Riding toward Blair's Federals, Captain Richard Beard of the 5th Confederate halted McPherson and his orderly. Beard found himself so close in fact that he could "see every feature of his face" as he raised his sword and demanded McPherson's surrender. The Federal commander merely doffed his cap, checked his horse, and turned to gallop away. Just as he did a volley from the skirmishers cut him down, mortally wounding him.[35] The smashed watch of one of McPherson's aides preserved the time of the encounter as 2:02 P.M. Though Beard's account is the most compelling, for years after the war controversy existed as to exactly who fired the shot that felled James McPherson.[36] In any event, the men of the Texas Brigade proceeded to divest his prostrate form of valuables.

Advancing farther, the Texans captured numerous ambulances, artillery pieces, and enemy battle flags in their precipitous charge. The Texans also included in these prizes of war Colonel Robert Scott, commander of the 2nd Brigade, 3rd Division, XVII Corps, who was riding along the road just behind McPherson.[37] After overrunning a second line of breastworks and capturing several prisoners, the Texans pressed on. However, because of their "ungovernable enthusiasm," the rough terrain they had passed, and exhaustion, the brigade front had become little more than a skirmish line. The enthusiasm of the 24th & 25th Texas put them out in advance of the rest of the brigade before they passed over a small ravine with a creek running through it, beyond which lay the line of works held by Leggett's Division atop Bald Hill. Here the Texans captured the colors of the 3rd Iowa.[38]

The rest of the brigade accumulated at the foot of the hill, and in an ironic twist of fate the Texans charged wildly up the hill from the same direction that the Federals had charged them the day before. The Federals, who had built their breastworks facing Atlanta, quickly jumped over to the other side of the works and leveled a murderous fire against the Texans. The Confederates swept up the hill and engaged them in hand-to-hand combat. The combatants used both rifle butts and bayonets in this fierce contest before the Federals forced the Texans back into the open field.[39] Caught in the field in the middle of a horrendous fire, the Texans began to waver. Smith called desperately for reinforcements, but none came. After ordering a withdrawal, Smith himself fell with a painful wound.[40] Brigade losses for the day had remained relatively light up to this point, but now they went down by the dozens, and enemy fire killed or wounded every single regimental commander.

At this critical moment Colonel John Oliver's brigade of Harrow's Division, XV Corps, swung around from its position facing west and struck the Texas Brigade in the right flank. After the wounding of Smith, command of the Texas Brigade went to Colonel Roger Q. Mills of the 10th Texas until incoming fire wounded Mills during the counterattack. Because of difficulties in communication concerning the order to fall back, on the right flank of the brigade the 99th Indiana and 15th Michigan cut off and captured half of the 17th & 18th Texas and the entire 5th Confederate under Major R. J. Persons. During the struggle the Midwesterners also captured the battle flags of the two regiments.[41] Sergeant Major Andrew La Forge of the 15th Michigan wrote, "With revolver in hand, I jumped upon the breastworks and demanded surrender of the flag, at the same time reaching for the top of the flagstaff. In the meantime my regiment came to the rescue and captured the flag."[42]

Several more Confederate assaults also failed to overrun Bald Hill. Sadly depleted, the remnants of the exhausted Texas Brigade under Lieutenant Colonel Robert B. Young of the 10th Texas fell back to the second line of Union works. As the Texans licked their wounds, Lowrey's men moved through their ranks and attacked the Yankees, only to be thrown back. Otho Strahl's brigade of Maney's Division also charged, only to be pushed back as well.

As Hood watched apprehensively from his vantage point near Oakwood Cemetery on the outskirts of Atlanta, he received word at 3 P.M. that Hardee's men had failed to roll up the Federal flank. Hardee also indicated that his men desperately needed assistance. In response, Hood decided to have Cheatham's Corps advance east out of Atlanta and strike the Army of the Tennessee from the front. Because Hardee had apparently failed, Hood ordered Cheatham to do nothing more than make a "demonstration" against the Union front. As Cheatham made his preparations, Hood received word at 4 P.M. that Hardee now had his men driving the Federals in front of them. This report proved partially true in that Govan's Arkansans and Strahl's Tennesseans had renewed their attacks on Giles Smith's division and proceeded to roll up the Federal position south of Bald Hill. Subsequently, Hood ordered Cheatham not merely to make a demonstration but to launch an all-out assault against the Yankees.[43]

Cheatham arrayed his corps from north to south with Henry Clayton's division on his northern (or left) flank, John Brown's division in the center, and Carter Stevenson's division on the right flank, opposite Bald Hill. Cheatham designated Stevenson's Division to advance first on the right. Because the attacks of Govan and Strahl had somewhat died down by this time, Leggett's men merely jumped back over to the other side of their works and easily repulsed the Confederates, who made only a half-hearted attempt before retiring. Meanwhile, Brown's Division advanced with two brigades north of the Georgia Railroad cut and two south of it against the blazing guns of Morgan L. Smith's division of the XV Corps. The Federal commander posted the four Parrott guns of Francis Degress's Battery H, 1st Illinois, on one side of the cut and the guns of Battery A, 1st Illinois, on the other.

The Confederates took advantage of two weaknesses in the Federal line: the deep railroad cut and a large white house known as the Troop Hurt house north of the railroad cut. From the cover of these two positions, Brown's men rained down fire on the Federals in the breastworks and broke open a huge hole in the middle of the XV Corps line. Only swift action by Logan and Brigadier General Charles Woods sealed off the gap in the line with massive artillery fire and a savage counterattack. Under pressure, Brown ordered a retreat. Though Clayton rushed two of his brigades to the front, the counterattack had already done enough damage. Woods's Division, urged on by "Black Jack" Logan, himself, pushed forward in a counterattack, and Brown ordered a complete withdrawal. This ended the fighting in front of the Troop Hurt house.[44]

As Cheatham's attack fizzled out, the savage fighting around Bald Hill continued unabated. By this time Leggett's and Smith's Union divisions had refused their line at right angles to the first line. In one last desperate attempt, Hardee assembled Cleburne's Division on the left and two of Maney's brigades on the right to attack the refused line.[45] At 5 P.M. Cleburne gave the order to charge, and once again the survivors of his division swept forward toward the rail barricades hastily erected by Leggett's men. The Arkansans and Texans charged up to the very muzzles of the defenders, and there ensued a bitter hand-to-hand fight. Ensign Hosea Garrett led the charge of the 10th Texas and got within "10 paces of their works with the colors of the 10th Texas Regt. but could not stay there." Garrett discovered upon looking around that he could not even find a dozen of his comrades around him and hastily retreated. He blamed the lack of support on the fact that the men "were badly scattered and many exhausted from the lack of sleep and warm weather and long marching."[46] Despite their efforts, the odds were against them and Cleburne's Division slowly withdrew to its previous position south of the improvised Federal line, ending the Battle of Atlanta. As the sun set on the evening of July 22, a lull in the action finally allowed the men of the Texas Brigade to rest after three days of nonstop marching and fighting.

Roll call the next morning for Granbury's Texas Brigade revealed the toll taken by the previous day's fighting. Smith's command had suffered 19 killed, 107 wounded, 25 missing, and 160 captured, for an aggregate of 311.[47] In the 6th & 15th Texas, artillery fire wounded Captain Rhoads Fisher on the twenty-first, and Captain Matthew M. Houston replaced him before he, too, went down with a wound. Captain S. E. Rice led the regiment into the Battle of Atlanta only to have the Federals capture him in the fighting. Finally the regiment fell to the command of Lieutenant Thomas Flynt. The regiment as a whole suffered five killed, twenty-four wounded, and fifteen missing during the day's fighting. On July 22 Captain J. W. Brown commanded the 7th Texas, which numbered a mere one hundred rifles at the start of the battle and suffered thirty killed, wounded, or captured. Colonel R. Q. Mills led the 10th Texas into action until he ascended to brigade command and received a wound himself. Captain James Formwalt took command of the small regiment and led it through the rest of the battle. The 10th Texas lost five killed and fifteen wounded during the day. Captain William H. Perry led the 160 rifles of the 17th & 18th Texas into the contest. The regiment lost approximately twelve killed, twenty-nine wounded, and eighty-seven captured, for a total of 119. Because of the wounding of Lieutenant Colonel William Neyland the day before, Major William A. Taylor led the 24th & 25th Texas into combat and the regiment suffered a loss of four killed, twenty-one wounded, and three captured. The 5th Confederate went into battle with ninety-two rifles under Major R. J. Persons. The enemy captured Persons and the regiment lost seventy-one casualties, many of them captured.[48] Though the casualties of the brigade proved high, they did not suffer completely in vain. During the fighting, the Texans captured fifteen pieces of artillery, two stands of colors, numerous ambulances, and a brigade commander. They could also take credit for the demise of James McPherson at the hands of the 5th Confederate.[49]

On the morning of July 23, Granbury's Brigade under Colonel Young made the best they could of their situation with roughly 750 effectives in the ranks. Captain Foster wrote, "Our men are getting boots hats &c watches knives &c off of the dead Yanks near us in the woods, lots of them." He also wrote of the return of two of the men of his regiment who had fallen out the previous day due to being overheated. "We cook and eat," continued the captain, "talk and laugh with the enemy's dead lying around us as though they were so many logs."[50] Private Charles Leuschner of the 6th & 15th Texas wrote that after the battle, "we seen knapsak's piled up as high as a house; & all of our boys taken all the clothing they wanted; & the rest we destroyed. Nearly every one of us had 3 or 4 daguerotype's from the yankey's." The day after the battle the Texans went about burying the Federal dead by throwing them "in their own made fortification & covered them up." Meanwhile they buried their own dead "each one in a separate grave."[51] Shortly after the battle, General Granbury returned to resume permanent command of his brigade. On July 23 the Texans erected fortifications almost on top of where the Federals had placed their breastworks prior to the battle, and here the tired veterans remained through the night of July 26. On that summer night, Captain Foster wrote in his diary of the shells the Yankees were throwing over their lines. "At night they can be seen like a rocket going through the air. They seem to go a mile high," he mused, "and it must be four or five miles from where they shoot into the city."[52]

After failing to break the Federal advance either north or east of the city, Hood resigned himself to a siege and began pulling his men into the city's fortifications to await Sherman's next move. At 10 A.M. on the morning of July 27 Granbury's men moved off toward Atlanta. At noon they stopped at a creek in the woods to rest for about two hours. The veterans then marched closer to the city and took position in the outer line of defense. As soon as they positioned themselves, the Federals initiated a fierce bombardment of the position, though with little effect. Captain Foster wrote defiantly, "Shelling don't scare us as it used to and if they pass us before they burst there is no danger in them. All they do is to make men bow their heads as it passes over."[53]

In the wake of the Battle of Atlanta, Sherman sought another way to sever Hood's lifeline and force him to abandon the city. The Federal commander decided to send the Army of the Tennessee, now under Major General Oliver O. Howard, from the far left to the far right, to strike at the Macon Railroad north of East Point and sever the Confederate supplies. Sherman erroneously assumed that Hood would not dare sally out in opposition to Howard and risk his troops in yet another engagement.

Sherman withdrew the Army of the Tennessee and sent it north and west around Atlanta. On July 28 a reconnaissance in force by Hood west of the city turned into the Battle of Ezra Church, where Howard's veterans repulsed several Confederate assaults.

It had been a bloody ten days for the Army of Tennessee. Of the 48,750 effectives available on July 18, now over ten thousand had become casualties. The losses equaled roughly a third of the thirty-three thousand infantry available on July 17. In this harsh fighting Granbury's Texans suffered almost six hundred casualties, having begun the battle with a little over one thousand men. It proved a rough start for Hood.

The fighting around Atlanta showcased both the dedication of the Texans to their leaders and their cause. The three days between July 20 and July 22 involved some of the heaviest combat of the war, but with effective regimental leaders in command, Patrick Cleburne, and the eventual return of Hiram Granbury, the Texans demonstrated loyalty to the Southern cause based on those qualities unique to western Confederates outlined by Larry Daniels and others. The Texans also demonstrated their loyalty to the Confederacy when they proved that even with uninspiring leaders in command for a short period of time (i.e., Smith and Hood), they would still remain with the Confederate cause, regardless of the cost.

CHAPTER FOURTEEN

THE FALL OF ATLANTA

Despite the hard fighting for Atlanta, the city would soon fall into Union hands, dimming hopes for the survival of the Confederacy. As these events transpired, Granbury's Texans clearly understood the dire circumstances facing their cause in August and September 1864, but they stayed with their regiments anyway. From a localized perspective, their steadfastness makes sense in light of the stellar leadership they enjoyed from Hiram Granbury and Patrick Cleburne. Loyalty to the Confederate cause also kept them going. As Jason Phillips points out in *Diehard Rebels*, the Confederate cause engendered a loyalty sufficient to carry men through the most trying circumstances, conditions such as those that confronted Granbury's Texans in the waning days of the war.[1]

As the dog days of July turned into August, Granbury's men tried to fight the heat, boredom, and constant barrage of bullets and shells that rained down on them day and night. On August 2 Captain Foster recorded in his diary that he had "done a big days wash today. 2 prs Drawers 1 pr Socks 1 Shirt and 1 Pocket handkerchief, and it was all decently done."[2]

During the first week of August an event occurred in the 7th Texas that further endeared its men to their division commander, Pat Cleburne. One day with a company of the regiment on picket duty, a cow belonging to a local farmer wandered near the picket line. Even though the Texans knew they were violating regulations, their hunger for beef took over and they shot and butchered the cow. Each company took a part of the meat back to camp and began to cook it over open fires. Private T. O. Moore recalled that just as the beef began to sizzle, "one of the company looked up and saw old Pat coming down the line on a tour of inspection. We had no time to hide the beef, and knew we were in for it." Thinking quickly, one Texan jumped to his feet, walked up to Cleburne, saluted, and said, "General, we have some nice, fat beef cooking and it is about done; come and eat dinner with us." The wise commander stared for a long moment at the Texan and then replied, "Well it does smell good. I believe I will." He sat down and his men handed him a piece of sizzling beef and a piece of cornbread and he "ate quite heartily." After dinner Cleburne lighted his pipe, chatted with the men, and passed down the line with Granbury's boys cheering him on. Private Moore later recalled, "How could we help admiring him?"[3]

The first two weeks in August kept the Texans busy with constant shelling, false alarms, and marching back and forth behind their defenses. East of the city, Sherman began to shift his units southwest to try to get at the railroad near East Point. Because of this, the Texans' commanders constantly shifted them back and forth. On August 1 Captain Foster recorded a false alarm, "but from some cause or other we did not move." Two days later Hardee moved Cleburne's Division two and a half miles to the right along the railroad in the midst of constant skirmishing. On the night of the sixth the Texans received orders to move left and support Bate's Division, against whom the Federals had made a small demonstration, but they arrived too late to take part in the fighting. Two days later they moved several hundred yards to the right and the next day marched back to their previous position. From August 10 to August 18 Foster reported at least four more separate movements of a few hundred yards apiece back and forth behind the fortifications.

Every new threat forced Hood to spread his already sparse garrison even thinner. On August 13 Captain Foster scribbled in his diary, "Our Brigade are put in one rank about 3 feet apart, but I believe we can hold our position against any force that can be brought against us." This optimism obviously sprang from the strength of the works the brigade occupied, which included a line of stakes fifty yards in front of the trenches, "drove down in the ground, firmly slanting from us and made sharp at the top and so close together that a man can not get thru, and high enough to strike him little above his waist. It will be very difficult for men to get to us."[4]

As Sherman shifted his forces south toward the railroad, Hood decided to take matters into his own hands. On August 10 Wheeler set out with six thousand troopers on a raid to tear up the railroad and destroy Federal communications as far north as Marietta. Hood ordered only a few cavalry commands to remain in the vicinity of Atlanta, including Jackson's Division. As scattered reports of Wheeler's raid began reaching Sherman, he exhorted his garrison commanders to crush the raiders. Other than this, he remained unconcerned. His supply wagons carried enough supplies for at least two weeks. In fact, Sherman decided to launch a cavalry raid of his own. On August 15, he ordered Brigadier General Judson Kilpatrick to make a thrust toward Fairburn on the West Point Railroad. Kilpatrick easily captured Fairburn, and his success emboldened Sherman. Rather than have his infantry make a circuitous march to get at and destroy the Macon Railroad, he planned to have his cavalry do the job. On the night of August 18 Kilpatrick set out from Sandtown toward the railroad, near Jonesboro. Though he met with some initial success, Kilpatrick ultimately failed in his mission to permanently disable Hood's supply line.

This failure forced Sherman to consider the option he had hoped to avoid. The Confederates contradicted Kilpatrick's exaggerated claims of railroad destruction by the night of August 21, when trains again began rumbling into Atlanta from the south. Sherman decided that he must swing south of Atlanta with the main body of his infantry and cut Hood's lifeline. On August 23 he asked his three army commanders when they could be ready to move. His commanders replied that with some preparation they could have their men ready by the night of August 25.

On August 25 the Federals abandoned their trenches and marched south. The next day Sherman started the Army of the Tennessee south. On August 27 Captain Foster took thirty men and ventured out "seven or eight miles" to bring in twenty head of much-needed cattle to the Confederate lines. The Texans accomplished all this before night, "and no one got hurt."[5] Because Cleburne posted Granbury's Texans so far to the right, August 29 had dawned before the Yankees finally abandoned the trenches in their front. The next morning some Texans inspecting the abandoned works found pieces of paper tacked to trees that read, "Goodbye Johnny Rebs. . . . Don't Follow us, if you do you will catch H——ll."[6]

On August 30 Major General William "Red" Jackson informed Hood that the Federals had begun moving toward Jonesboro. A mere twenty-five hundred dismounted Confederate cavalrymen stood between the Army of the Tennessee and Jonesboro on the night of August 30. In the gathering twilight, Howard opted not to attack. Instead, he entrenched on a ridge west of the town where his artillery could dominate the railroad. Hood believed this gave him just the stroke of luck he needed. At 6 P.M., after receiving desperate messages from Brigadier General Frank Armstrong, one of his cavalry commanders, he ordered Lee's and Hardee's Corps to Jonesboro. As a precautionary measure, Hood ordered Stewart's Corps to remain northwest of Atlanta. Hood planned to have Hardee and Lee move south and drive the Federals into the Flint River the next day.[7]

In the early morning of August 31, Hardee's and Lee's men marched through Jonesboro to confront the enemy. At 10 P.M. on August 30 Granbury's Texans had moved out of their entrenchments and marched south. Just after dawn they had marched through town and formed a line of battle facing west.[8] Hardee positioned his own corps, now temporarily under Cleburne, on the left (or southern) flank of his attacking force. To their right he placed Lee's Corps. Hardee planned to attack en echelon from left to right, with Lowrey, commanding Cleburne's Division, to lead off, followed by the other two divisions of his corps. When Lee heard the sounds of battle, Hardee instructed him to launch his own assault.[9]

The men whom Hardee went up against on August 31 were members of the XV Corps under John Logan. Logan had drawn his men up in a semicircle with their right flank resting on the Flint River, and their left protected by a tributary of the river. Dislodging these veteran soldiers would be a difficult task.[10]

At 3 P.M. Hardee's artillerymen commenced their bombardment, prior to launching the infantry assault. After about ten minutes, Cleburne's skirmishers started forward. To the north, Lee, mistaking the fire of the skirmishers for the beginning of the main assault, ordered his corps forward. Lee's men advanced, driving in the Federal skirmishers before they ran into a wall of lead from Logan's veterans. Many of Lee's men turned and fled after first coming under fire. Others tried to advance, but soon the entire corps degenerated into a disorganized mob and refused to go forward. One Union officer thought it the least determined assault he had ever seen Rebels make. The Federals slowed their fire with deliberate aim, slaughtering the Confederates.

Meanwhile, to the south, Cleburne's Division fared little better. Granbury's Texans occupied the extreme left of the division and hence the extreme left of the army. As they began their assault, the left of the brigade came under fire from Kilpatrick's Federal troopers to the right of Logan's infantry. Instead of following orders and swinging north, the Texans continued due west. They charged impetuously across an open field toward the dismounted cavalrymen. Captain Foster wrote that because of their repeating rifles the Yankees "just fairly made it rain bullets as long as they had any in their guns, but as soon as they gave out, and we getting closer to them every moment, they couldn't stand it but broke and ran like good fellows."[11] The Texans chased the enemy across Anthony's Bridge over the Flint River. They pursued them "as long as we could find any to follow" before they returned. It proved a perfect way to divert an entire Confederate brigade away from the battlefield. Cleburne rallied and reformed his division by 5 P.M. only to find the battle over. The fighting at Jonesboro had been one-sided in the extreme. Logan's men suffered 172 casualties of all sorts, while the Confederates sustained twenty-two hundred dead and wounded.

Meanwhile, at his headquarters in Atlanta, Hood had received erroneous intelligence of a large Federal force heading for the city. He decided that he should bring Lee's Corps back to counter the threat. At 6 P.M. he issued a dispatch instructing Hardee to send Lee's Corps back to Atlanta. He also instructed Hardee to hold the railroad around Jonesboro against Sherman's "feint." Hardee recognized Sherman's move as not merely a feint, but he felt he had to obey his orders. On the evening of August 31 Lee's tired veterans marched north toward Atlanta.

Hood at last received a dispatch from Hardee in the early morning of September 1. The news proved exactly what the Confederate commander feared: Hardee had failed to drive the Federals across the Flint. Immediately, Hood decided to abandon Atlanta. With a large part of Sherman's army bearing down on his supply line at Jonesboro, Hood had little choice but to retreat toward Macon. With no other options, he instructed Hardee to hold the railroad.[12]

At Jonesboro, Hardee made his defensive dispositions. At 3 A.M. he ordered Cleburne's Division to the extreme right, extending his line northward and eastward toward the railroad. Cleburne stretched his men so thin that they stood about a yard apart, with elbows "not quite touching."[13] Lowrey's Brigade occupied the left of the line, with Granbury's Texans in the middle and Govan's Arkansans on the right. As soon as Cleburne put them in place the Texans and Arkansans began strengthening their posi-

tion in dangerous proximity to the enemy, who had begun to mass immediately beyond the tree line to their front.[14]

At first light Cleburne and his men could see the danger of their position.
As they watched, the Army of the Cumberland massed to their front and right
to deliver the final, crushing blow. In the early afternoon Hardee learned
of the threat gathering on his right and ordered Govan's Brigade back to
a more secure position. He also sent two brigades to extend its right.[15] In
the meantime, the soldiers could clearly see the fate about to befall them.
Captain Foster wrote in his diary, "All the forenoon we can see the Yanks
passing to our right—Regt after Regt of the blue coats going to the right.
The report by noon is that they are massing their troops in our front."[16]

A little after 4 P.M. the Federal columns started southward against the salient occupied by Govan's Brigade. William Carlin's division of the XIV Corps
advanced first. The two brigades that Carlin had on the field had to force
their way through brush so thick it became difficult to maintain contact
with one another. Because of this Carlin's men emerged piecemeal from the
underbrush. The first of the Northerners pushed forward to a ridge from
which they beheld the Confederate works. A storm of canister and bullets
forced the hapless Federals to fall to the ground. After advancing a little
further, it soon became obvious that they could not take the Confederate
position without reinforcements. Carlin's third brigade advanced, only to
suffer the same fate as their comrades. At the same time Carlin decided to
renew the assault with George Este's brigade of Absolom Baird's division.[17]

At 5 P.M. Este's eleven hundred veterans moved forward to the top of
the ridge. Unlike their predecessors, they flopped to their stomachs just
in time to avoid the opening volley of the Arkansans. Then they jumped
to their feet and charged straight into the middle of Govan's line, held by
the 6th & 7th Arkansas. Using their bayonets freely, the Midwesterners
overwhelmed the Arkansas regiments and punched a hole in the middle
of Govan's position. Este's men exploited the gap by moving the 10th Kentucky and 74th Indiana behind the Confederates. Govan's men fought tenaciously until completely engulfed by the enemy. In the fierce struggle,
the attackers clubbed down the Confederates or forcefully took their rifles
from them. The Union troops soon overwhelmed Key's and Swett's batteries as well, bayoneting one of Swett's officers when he refused to surrender.
The Federals captured Govan and most of his Arkansans, who wept and
cursed, because they had never before been whipped in battle.[18]

As soon as Granbury saw the fate of the Arkansans not more than forty paces to his right, he ordered the right of the brigade back at an angle to protect his flank. At this moment, Hardee saw the Texans apparently falling back. Immediately, he and Lowrey rode toward the Texans and began trying to rally them before Granbury approached them. The supposition that his men would fall back without orders hurt the Texan, and he said to Hardee, "General, my men never fall back unless ordered back." Hardee assured him that he had ordered up Cleburne with reinforcements to shore up his right. With this new information Granbury led his men forward, quickly retaking their breastworks.[19] During this action an errant ball wounded Captain Sebron Sneed of Granbury's staff in the breast while he served as a messenger.[20] Soon, Cleburne rode to the front at the head of John Gordon's brigade of Brown's Division. Sweeping forward, the Tennesseans stemmed the onrush of Federals through the gap in the line.

Sherman took personal command on the field and felt that one final push by David Stanley's division east of the railroad could crush Hardee's line. Seeing the movement, Hardee shifted the rest of Brown's Division east to counter the threat. Because of the stiff resistance and gathering darkness, Sherman decided not to attack, ending the battle of Jonesboro.

The aftermath of the two-day battle revealed the ferocity of the fighting. On August 31 Granbury reported his losses as sixteen killed and thirty-two wounded. For September 1 the casualties of the small brigade amounted to eighteen killed and eighty-nine wounded.[21] After dark, Hardee began withdrawing his men south toward Lovejoy's Station, to rendezvous with the other two army corps. Atlanta had fallen. After four months of hard fighting and campaigning, Sherman could at last report, "Atlanta is ours and fairly won!"

In the late night hours of September 1, 1864, the weary soldiers of Hardee's Corps grudgingly abandoned their trenches around Jonesboro and moved south along the railroad toward Lovejoy's Station. As the foot soldiers moved through the pre-dawn darkness, they could distinctly hear explosions coming from the north—from Atlanta. They knew it as the sound of defeat. Before abandoning the city, Hood ordered his rear guard to destroy whatever munitions and supplies could not be brought off, to deny their use to the Federals. In addition, the soldiers could see the northern horizon lit with the bright blaze of the munition cars in the Atlanta railway yard. Lieutenant O. P. Bowser of the 17th & 18th Texas recalled,

"Many a soldier in the brigade regarded the dismal sounds as the death knell of the Confederacy."[22]

Despite their fading prospects, the spirits of the Texans in the Army of Tennessee remained high as they skirmished with the pursuing Federals. On the morning of September 2, Granbury's Texans reached Lovejoy's and began throwing up breastworks in anticipation of a renewed assault. Samuel Foster recorded in his diary the nature of the breastworks. "By the middle of the day we have made a ditch about 4 feet deep and put the dirt in front so as to mak[e] a bank about a foot high but slants off about 10 feet," he wrote. On the evening of September 2, Yankee skirmishers approached within 250 yards of the Confederate breastworks before withdrawing for the night. On September 3 and 4, they continued to skirmish with the Confederates, and the next day, Foster wrote, "Picket firing and artillery are making music all day today."[23] Finally, on September 6, the last of the fighting in the Atlanta campaign came to an end when Sherman opted to withdraw his forces back to Atlanta.

As Sherman and Hood planned their next moves, word reached the family and friends of Texans who had fallen defending Atlanta. On September 17, from a hospital in Barnesville, Georgia, Lieutenant Sebron Sneed penned a letter to Mrs. Susan Piper of Austin. He wrote her regarding the fate of her son Benjamin, who had received a severe wound at Jonesboro. Sneed began by citing a letter he had written to her nine days earlier in which he "could give you but little ground to hope for the recovery of your son Benjamin. Our fears were realized—on the night of the 14th inst. The pure spirit of your brave and noble soldier boy, fled from this world of suffering and strife and took refuge in the bosom of its God. I know my dear Madam," Sneed continued, "this will be a severe blow to you, and feel incompetent to offer a word of comfort, save, it would be to assure you, that Ben has always done his duty to his Country and Companions. I remember your last words to me," Sneed concluded, "when our Company of lively, handsome boys left Onion Creek, 'Seb, take good care of my baby boy.' I have ever tried to do my duty to Ben, and had hoped to one day see you meet him in all the pride of his manhood. . . . Let us not weep, his trials and troubles are over—May he rest in peace."[24]

Granbury's Texans understood the importance of the loss of Atlanta. From a strategic standpoint the defeat crippled the Confederacy's ability to win the war, but the Texans did not see it that way. Atlanta had fallen.

Yet they had also experienced the losses of Vicksburg and Chattanooga and still the war continued. To the Texans, the fall of Atlanta was demoralizing, but they still believed they could win the war. This spirit in the face of overwhelming odds is evidence of their devotion to the Confederacy, and the conduit through which that devotion passed: their field officers. To the men in the ranks, field officers like Granbury and Cleburne represented the Confederacy and the Confederate war effort, and they adored them. As Jason Phillips posited in *Diehard Rebels,* the ideological devotion to the Confederate cause among these soldiers would never die as long as they lived—the men would become in a sense "unconquered losers" after the war. But until then, a chance to win the war would remain as long as their field officers were there to lead them.[25]

CHAPTER FIFTEEN

THE INTERLUDE

The willingness of Confederate troops to stay with the Southern cause late in the Civil War, despite their obviously dire situation, is the strongest argument in favor of a strong nationalism that provided the backbone of the Confederate war effort. Authors such as Mark Weitz in *More Damning Than Slaughter,* and others, do not have a reasonable explanation for the strong dedication displayed by the common Confederate soldiers even late in the war. The steadfastness of Granbury's Texans after the fall of Atlanta can only partially be explained by a loyalty to their leaders and their localized perspective. Just as important to the equation in explaining their dedication was their devotion to the Confederate cause.[1]

As they abandoned the Gate City of the Confederacy, some Confederate soldiers made dire predictions for the future in their letters and diaries. Others remained optimistic while recovering from the campaign. The Army of Tennessee had reached a critical juncture in its history. Captain Foster recorded his apocalyptic remarks: "This army is going to do something wrong—or rather it will undertake something that will not be a success, if the future is to be judged by the past." In contrast to Foster's dire prediction, William Henderson of the 7th Texas wrote that "although Atlanta has been taken by the fed I am in as good a spirits as ever, I will live in hopes if I die in despair." Henderson also took this lull to clean up. He wrote to his parents that "I have just finished washing some very dirty clothes it was very hard work I assure you. For we had been lying in the ditches ever since we came to Atlanta."[2]

After the fighting of the Atlanta campaign, on September 6 the Confederates awoke to find quiet. After over one hundred days of constant fighting and skirmishing from May through September, they could not hear a single gun. Samuel Foster wrote, "Every body astonished this morning. No shooting in hearing of us, everything is as quiet as a meeting house. Whats up."[3] Charles Leuschner wrote, "We wake up at daylight and we could not hear a single gun fired. Our Gen. soon sent scout's out to see whether yankey were gone, & they soon come back & reported them gone."[4] Sherman had in fact withdrawn to Atlanta and remained content to let Hood's army stay at Lovejoy's Station.[5] This signaled the beginning of a lull in the fighting.

As Sherman and Hood retreated to their respective corners, Hood began to push some of his units north toward Jonesboro to feel out the Federals. Hood cautiously advanced his men north in the early morning of September 8, where, along the road of advance, the Confederates encountered the offensive odor of "dead horses, decaying men, and the debris of the battlefield."[6] It became a most unwelcome and disheartening sight to the Confederates who had so recently fought over the ground they now camped upon.

The Confederate army stayed at Jonesboro for ten days, during which they experienced beautiful weather. One of the Texans camped at Jonesboro with his regiment in early September 1864 was Lieutenant Thomas J. Stokes, commanding Company I, 10th Texas. Thomas Jefferson Stokes hailed from Georgia, but had moved to Texas before the war. Having voted for secession, Stokes felt it his duty to fight in the war. He had worked as a schoolteacher in Johnson County, Texas, before the war and proved a deeply religious man, and as such he helped bring about the mass revivals in the Army of Tennessee preceding the Atlanta campaign. In April, Stokes had written his sister, Missouri Stokes, and confided to her almost prophetically that many believed this "the beginning of the end." He had had no way of knowing how events would prove him right.[7]

During this period Mary A. H. Gay of Decatur, Georgia, visited the troops of Granbury's Brigade. Gay, the half-sister of Lieutenant Stokes, visited the Texans to see her darling brother "Thomie," but also in anticipation of the winter privations she knew would come. Before the commencement of spring campaigning, several men of Granbury's Brigade, including Stokes and Granbury, had left their heavy winter coats in the possession of Miss Gay for safekeeping. With the return of fall, she decided to return the coats. In doing so she exhibited quite a bit of ingenuity. She first approached the Federal provost marshal in Decatur with a request for a wagon to go to her sister's house in Augusta with bedding items. The provost marshal granted the request, and Gay requested the use of some large grain sacks lying unused at the Federal depot. Returning home, Gay sewed the sacks shut with the coats inside them. The next morning, a Federal soldier arrived, loaded the bundles into the wagon, and drove her south to Atlanta, where Gay met some of her friends evacuating the city in compliance with Sherman's orders. She continued south with the Federal wagon as far as Rough and Ready, and then the rest of the way to Jonesboro.

While at Jonesboro, Mary Gay wrote that events seemed to have altered the spirits of the Texans. She noted this change particularly in General Granbury, whose fatalistic remarks to her during their conversation led her to realize that in the wake of the fall of Atlanta, though cautiously optimistic about success, these Texans knew their chances for ultimate victory had become bleak.[8] The fact that in spite of the realization of their dire situation the Texans stayed at their posts exhibited their dedication to the Confederacy.

Also while at Jonesboro, the Federals exchanged General Daniel Govan and six hundred Arkansans, who returned to Cleburne's Division. The Arkansans found themselves the fortunate beneficiaries of an unusually quick prisoner exchange. This exchange brought the strength of Cleburne's Division to 3,290 men. The Arkansans, after returning to the camp of the division, immediately put out a petition to the camp of Granbury's Brigade to see whether or not the Texans had lost confidence in them. If they had indeed lost confidence in them, the Arkansans stated that they were prepared to request a transfer, rather than serve with men who would not accept them on an equal footing. The Texans for their part heartily welcomed back the Arkansans, and went so far as to turn out en masse in the camp of Govan's Brigade to express their confidence.[9]

On September 15, Governor Joseph Brown of Georgia set aside a day of prayer and fasting, and General Hood required that the Army of Tennessee observe the holiday. Accordingly, they held a worship service in a "grove of gigantic poplars and oaks where seats made of logs covered almost half an acre." General Mark Lowrey, commander of one of Cleburne's brigades, had served as a Baptist minister before the war, and he agreed to preach a sermon from Psalms, "'He teacheth my hands to war, so that a bow of steel is broken by mine arms. . . . I have pursued mine enemies, and overtaken them: neither did I turn again until they were consumed."[10] Lowrey, with his flowing beard, appeared the epitome of an Old Testament warrior, a contemporary Joshua or Gideon. In this way, religion also continued to encourage the Confederates, who had obviously not lost faith in the idea that God was on their side.

On September 16, the Confederates started west toward Palmetto, Georgia, the first leg of a trip designed by Hood to cut Sherman's supply line. At 1 A.M. on September 16 they started westward, periodically resting and marching until they reached the West Point & Palmetto Railroad at Palmetto during the night of September 19. After they arrived, their officers formed the men in line of battle and allowed them to rest. On the morning of September 20, around 3 A.M., Cleburne ordered Granbury's Texans to make breastworks, during "considerable rain," with their right flank across the railroad and their left flank across the Chattahoochee River.[11]

Here at Palmetto, Georgia, the Army of Tennessee stayed for nine days, resting and gathering supplies as President Jefferson Davis and his staff traveled to Georgia to visit the army and consult with Hood. President Davis, accompanied by his aides Custis Lee and ex-Governor Francis Lubbock of Texas, departed Richmond for Palmetto on September 20. On September 25, Davis reached Hood's headquarters. He intended his visit to gauge the morale of the Army of Tennessee as well as to discuss strategy with Hood. Davis and Hood agreed that the army should cross the Chattahoochee and strike the Western & Atlantic Railroad in order to draw Sherman north from Atlanta. But Davis instructed Hood that if Sherman moved south from Atlanta, Hood should follow him as far as necessary, to the Atlantic Ocean if need be.[12] On September 26, President Davis, accompanied by General Hood and Francis Lubbock, reviewed the troops of the army. Lubbock took this opportunity to visit the Texas troops. On his visit, however, he embarrassed himself, as Samuel Foster recorded in his diary. "He stopped in front of an Irish (Brigade) Regt. Just on our right before he got to us," wrote Foster. Lubbock, thinking that he had found the Texans, "rode square up about the centre pulled off his hat and says 'I am Governor Lubbock of Texas' and just when he expected to hear a big cheer, an Irishman says 'An who the bloody H——l is governor Lubbock?' with that peculiar Irish brogue, that made the Governor wilt." Lubbock, mortified, then turned his horse and galloped on to catch up with Davis and party, and passed by the Texans without even so much as a glance.[13]

General William J. Hardee took advantage of the visit by Davis to personally request a transfer from the Army of Tennessee. Hardee had felt slighted, as the senior corps commander, when Davis appointed Hood to army command. In addition to this, Hardee and Hood did not get along well together. Considering these circumstances, Davis permitted Hardee's transfer, assigning him instead to the command of the defenses of Savannah, Georgia, on September 27. In his stead, Hood appointed Major General Benjamin F. "Frank" Cheatham, one of Hardee's divisional commanders, to lead the II Corps, and elevated Brigadier General John C. Brown to command Cheatham's Division. The inexperience of these leaders certainly boded ill for the battles ahead.

As he visited the Army of Tennessee and returned to Richmond, President Davis in his speeches spoke of the plan he and Hood had formulated. In a speech at Macon, Georgia, on September 24, Davis indiscreetly revealed a hint of the plans that he had concocted to draw Sherman north from Atlanta. He even went so far when addressing some Tennessee regiments at Palmetto Station as to hint that they might soon march toward their homes. In subsequent speeches that he gave at Montgomery, Columbia, and Augusta, Davis broadly hinted at the possibility for an invasion of Tennessee.

On September 29, the Army of Tennessee began its northward trek through Georgia and Alabama to try to draw Sherman out of Atlanta. That day Granbury's Brigade moved west through Palmetto and along the south bank of the Chattahoochee. That night, Hood summoned the regimental commanders of the army to his headquarters to discuss the invasion of Tennessee, the specifics of which remained as of yet largely unknown to the rank and file. The following day the soldiers of Cleburne's Division crossed the Chattahoochee River. That night the Texans made camp eight miles north of the Chattahoochee and waited for daylight before resuming their northward progression. On October 1, the rest of the army crossed the river, and the Confederates started northward, though as Captain Foster noted, "but no one knows where." On October 2, Hood had drawn the army up west of Marietta, Georgia, and here the regimental commanders briefed the men on what the days ahead had in store. Hood requested that the colonels instruct their men that they would attempt to flank Sherman out of Atlanta, and that while maneuvering, the rations might get short, but that he would do everything he could to ensure the welfare of his men. Captain Foster recorded, "He expected there to be some fighting and some hard marching, and wanted an expression of the men upon it. Of course every man said go."[14]

On the night of October 2, a bolt of lightening struck a stack of rifles in the Texans' camp, throwing the guns about before bouncing between two trees, "knocking the bark off both of them." The blast knocked one man of Company F, 24th Texas, temporarily unconscious, and another man lounging around the camp suddenly died. The bolt carried Captain Foster, he wrote, "about five feet forward, apparently like a rail had struck both my legs from behind, below the knees and carried me forward without throwing me down." The lightning momentarily stunned nearly every man in the 24th & 25th Texas. The blast killed at least three men from the 6th & 15th Texas and the 24th & 25th Texas, and a number suffered breathing difficulties, and remained generally disconcerted and dumbstruck from the abnormal occurrence.[15]

As the Army of Tennessee continued northward, the Federals under Sherman did not remain idle. Leaving the XX Corps to hold Atlanta, Sherman started north along the railroad to rescue his garrisons along that route as well as to stop Hood from cutting his supply lines. As an additional precaution, Sherman sent General George H. Thomas to Nashville to guard against the suspected invasion of Tennessee.

During the march north, one of Hood's predictions came true: rations became short. Because of this situation, inevitable foraging occurred, despite Hood's constant warnings regarding respect for private property. While riding ahead of his soldiers with part of his staff, Cleburne came upon a half-dozen soldiers who had stripped a nearby apple orchard of its contents, and now nearly six bushels of apples lay at their feet. Cleburne, with a grim expression, ordered the men to move the apples to the roadside. Then, lighting his pipe, Cleburne waited for the head of his division. Soon General Granbury arrived at the head of his troops, who happened to be the head of Cleburne's column that day. As Granbury rode up, Cleburne addressed him: "General Granbury, I am peddling apples today." Granbury replied, "How are you selling them, General?"

"These gentlemen," Cleburne replied, motioning toward the foragers, "have been very kind. They have gathered the apples for me and charged nothing. I will give them to you and your men. Now, you get down and take an apple, and have each of your men pass by and take one—only one, mind—until they are all gone." Smiling, Granbury selected an apple and sat on his horse munching while the entire Texas Brigade passed by in single file and each selected an apple. Cleburne then ordered the guilty foragers to carry a rail for a mile before rejoining their units.[16]

The night of October 2, while encamped near Powder Springs, Georgia, some of the men of Cleburne's Division serenaded him, and in the warm night Cleburne decided to address his men. He expressed the importance of the current offensive and urged every man to do his duty. In Ireland, Cleburne said, the downtrodden masses had suffered from oppression, but if the North prevailed against the South, the condition of Southerners would become much worse. Then he paused, looked toward the sky, and with a resolute expression on his face said, "If this cause which is so dear to my heart is doomed to fail, I pray that heaven may let me fall with it, while my face is toward the enemy and my arm still battling for that which I know to be right."[17]

Cleburne's theatrics indicate that in many ways the Confederate Army of Tennessee continued to function this late in the war through the sheer determination of the officers and men in the ranks. This was especially important regarding the officers, who often dictated the morale of the men under their command, but undeniably devotion to the idea of Confederate nationalism played just as important a role in keeping men in the ranks. Granbury and Cleburne, despite their occasionally unguarded remarks, continued to display high spirits and a loyalty to the Confederacy that inspired the men in the ranks.

CHAPTER SIXTEEN

FLANKING SHERMAN

During the march into North Georgia and beyond, the Texans of Granbury's Brigade exhibited a bravado that remains a testament of their devotion to their leaders and the Confederate cause. They also rejoiced at the end of the Atlanta campaign. Although they had lost Atlanta, to the Texans it was no different than having lost Chattanooga, or other cities before it. As long as they retained strong confidence in their leadership, their morale soared, demonstrating the effect their leaders had on them and their fidelity to the Confederate cause. During this time, it is apparent that the Confederate cause was held together through the fealty and sheer determination of the men in the ranks. This display so late in the war is the best argument for the kind of devotion to their leaders and the Confederacy that other historians have come to recognize both for the Confederacy as a whole and the western theater in particular.

The morning after Cleburne gave that rousing speech to his men, Hood set into motion his plan to cut Sherman's supplies by severing the rail lines. That day Stewart's Corps captured Big Shanty and its garrison of 175 men. On October 4 the Federal garrison at Acworth, Georgia, surrendered with 250 officers and men. Meanwhile, the Confederate army halted and threw up breastworks west of Big Shanty.[1] On October 5, Major General Samuel French and his division assaulted the Federal garrison at Allatoona Pass and made limited gains in the face of high losses until reports of Union reinforcements forced French to withdraw.

As the weary veterans of French's Division made their way back to rejoin the army, Hood formulated his next move against Sherman. On October 5, A. L. Orr, of the 18th Texas Dismounted Cavalry, wrote his sister, Mary, "Gen. Hood says we will go to Tennessee, that we will never turn back." Should Sherman try to bypass the Confederates, "we will still flank him." Orr also wrote of the visit from "Olde Jeff" Davis, who, according to Orr, told the Texans, "If we would run the Yanks out of Georgia, that he would furlow us this winter. We Texans," he wrote, "are a going to doo all we can, all though there is but few of ous."[2] At 4 A.M. on October 6, the bugle sounded for Granbury's Texans to rise and renew their northward trek. Rain made the marching miserable on this particular October day. Captain Foster recorded in his diary, "Mud over our shoes and every little gully had to be waded. About 12 Oclock the rain stoped and we camp— build fires and dry our clothes blankets &c."[3] The next day Captain Foster wrote in his diary that at noon, as the Texans rested, "Genl Hood passed us, and told us 'that the Yanks were leaving Atlanta in a great hurry.'" In their enthusiasm at this remark all the Texans yelled "Hurrah for Genl Hood" as he tipped his hat and rode on. At 2 P.M. the Texans reached Cedartown, Georgia, where they went into camp with all "in high spirits." According to Captain Foster this boost in morale resulted from the Confederates "Running the Yanks out of the State of Ga. Without a fight." Foster surmised that Hood intended "evidently making for Tenn. and perhaps Ky." This action, hypothesized the Texan, would force Sherman to retreat and "go into East Tenn. and go across Cumberland gap, and if we can get there first they will have to go into Ky. This army," Foster wrote enthusiastically, "has done wonders! Flanked the Yanks out of Atlanta without firing a gun."[4] Hood withdrew to Cedartown, Georgia, to regroup and communicate his intentions to Richmond of destroying the Federal railroad from Kingston to Tunnel Hill. The lanky Kentuckian remained highly optimistic about the results of his flanking maneuvers thus far. He wired Bragg, then serving as military advisor to President Davis: "In truth, the effect of our operations so far surpassed my expectations that I was induced to change my original plan." At this point, Hood intended to draw Sherman out in the rough terrain near the Tennessee River and offer battle.[5] On October 9, the Texas

Brigade departed its camp around 1:30 P.M. and proceeded nine miles to Cave Spring, Georgia, where they moved through the town and, according to Captain Foster, "camped on a high hill—or rather a mountain." That night the Texans experienced the first frost of the season while passing through the mountains.[6] At Cave Spring Hood met with General P. G. T. Beauregard, departmental commander, regarding his proposed railroad wrecking scheme. Beauregard concurred with Hood, and on October 10 the army crossed the Coosa River, near Rome, Georgia.

For the next few days the Confederates wrestled with tough Federal garrisons along the railroad. Hood, deciding the Union garrison at Rome would be too strong to assault, bypassed it and instead continued north along the Oostanaula River, reaching Resaca on October 12. The Federal commander, in replying to Hood's demand for an unconditional surrender of the seven hundred-man garrison, wrote, "If you want it come and take it." Deciding that he could just as easily bypass the position, Hood continued up the railroad.[7] On October 12, Cleburne's Division formed the rear of the army, even behind the wagon trains, and the going proved slow for the impatient Texans.[8]

During this delay the impatient Cleburne and Granbury made the best of their situation. At noon on October 12 Cleburne wrote complainingly in his diary, "We are being delayed almost as provokingly as on yesterday by the troops in front and have to rest long and frequently." To pass the time, he and Granbury "scratched a draft board [checkers] on the road. Marked the black squares with green leaves. I took red dogwood berries for men. Gen. Granberry [sic] took puff balls." The two generals played two games, both of them draws. They then turned their attention to feats of athleticism. "Had a jumping match," wrote Cleburne. "I won at a running jump, he at a standing." This kind of playfulness between Cleburne and Granbury doubtlessly heartened their men, who saw their leaders as something of peers as well as superiors.[9]

At Dalton, fifteen miles north of Resaca, the Confederates encountered another small force of Federal troops, including General John Schofield, who barely slipped away north along the railroad ahead of the Confederates.[10] Hood formed Cleburne's Division directly in front of the 751-man Dalton garrison, primarily composed of the 44th U.S. Colored Infantry under Colonel Lewis Johnson. Johnson, severely outnumbered, talked nervously with Hood under a flag of truce, seeking assurances that if he surrendered the Confederates would treat his African American troops as prisoners of war. Hood declined to make any such promise.[11] Many of the men of Granbury's Brigade had already made up their minds, shouting, "Kill every damn one of them." Johnson, nevertheless, in no position to bargain, reluctantly surrendered his garrison. After Johnson's men had stacked arms, the Confederates pounced on them and divested them of their shoes and clothes. Many of the Confederates threatened the lives of the African American prisoners, incessantly haranguing and taunting them. Instead of killing them, though, they put the prisoners to work tearing up the railroad.[12]

On October 13, the Army of Tennessee struck the railroad below Dalton and put their hands to destruction. The first rail, however, proved extremely difficult to pull up. Consequently, Cleburne aligned his division along the railroad in a single rank and called out, "Attention Men! When I say ready, let every man stoop down, take hold of the rails and when I say 'heave ho!' let every man lift all he can and turn the rails and crossties over." And so when Cleburne called out, "Heave," the three thousand men of his division all lifted at once, and removed the first rail.[13]

Captain Foster wrote in his diary on October 13 of the manner in which the Confederates destroyed the railroad track. With the first rail that Cleburne's Division removed, wrote Foster, "we prize them up as fast as we can handle it." Following this, the Confederates piled up the wooden crossties on top of the track along with kindling until the piles reached "as high as a mans head," at which time they set them on fire. On top of each of these bonfires the "iron rails are then balanced," and "they soon get red hot." After the iron had reached this point, four men (two on each end) would take each rail to the nearest telegraph pole and "bend it double—by walking around until they meet. Have considerable fun," wrote the Texan. They dubbed these bent rails "old Mrs. Lincoln's Hair pins."[14]

The Confederates continued to tear up railroad tracks until midnight on October 13, at which time the commissary issued meager rations, and the troops settled down for the night. On October 14 the railroad mischief continued until around 10 A.M., when the entire Confederate army began to move off in a southwestern direction, toward Lafayette, Georgia. Hood and his army had succeeded in vandalizing the railroad from Resaca to Tunnel Hill, just south of Chattanooga. The Confederates became exuberant about their chances for success. Captain Foster described this feeling:

"The whole army are in high spirits," noting they had "torn up the R.R. 100 miles in the rear of the Yankee army and cut off their supplies." In light of this, theorized the Texan, "their only chance of now to live is to disband and scatter over the country, and make their way back north as best they can." Because of this seeming success, the Army of Tennessee began to gain confidence in their new commander. Foster wrote that the Texans began "to think that Jeff Davis and Hood made a ten strike, when they plan[n]ed this thing. It beats fighting 'all hollow.'"[15]

Unfortunately, the destruction of the railroad only worsened the situation for the Georgian populace. Sherman, in typical sarcastic fashion, wrote, "We find [an] abundance of corn and potatoes out here. They cost us nothing a bushel. If Georgia can afford to break our railroads, she can afford to feed us. Please preach this doctrine to men who go forth and are likely to spread it." With Sherman's soldiers spread out in North Georgia in an attempt to protect the railroads, he put ten thousand men to work repairing the more than eight miles of railroad that the Confederates had destroyed. The repairs required thirty-five thousand railroad ties and six miles of iron, and yet in the space of a week they had the railroad up and working again.[16]

As Sherman and his Federals repaired the railroads, the Confederates continued north. On the morning of October 15, Cleburne's Division marched fifteen miles over the mountains and bivouacked near Lafayette. The next day, Cleburne's men moved a few miles down the Lafayette and Rome road and bivouacked on the exact ground that they had occupied prior to the Battle of Chickamauga.[17] On October 17, Hood started his army west toward Alpine, Georgia. For the next few days the march continued west, heading for Alabama.

During this leg of the campaign communications with the rest of the South remained uncertain at best. Only occasionally did a piece of mail get through. On October 18, Lieutenant Thomas Stokes wrote his sister, Missouri Stokes, "I am tried of confusion and disorder—tired of living a life of continual excitement. You spoke of passing through a dark cloud. 'There is nothing true but Heaven,' and it is to that rest for the weary, alone, to which we are to look for perfect enjoyment." He went on, "I think we will cross the Tennessee river and make for Tennessee." Many of the Texans, like Stokes, remained guarded in their hopes for success and thoroughly tired of the war.[18] Others, though equally weary, stayed confident of success. Wiley Donothan of the 24th Texas wrote to his sister on October 18, "Our prospects were never brighter for a great change has been wrought within the last two weeks."[19]

On October 20, Hood reached Gadsden, Alabama, on the Coosa River, and here he again met with Beauregard, who agreed with Hood's evolved plan to invade Tennessee. Beauregard only stipulated that Hood leave General Joseph Wheeler's cavalry in Georgia to watch Sherman, whose forces remained spread out in North Georgia and Atlanta. In Wheeler's stead, General Nathan Bedford Forrest would move from West Tennessee to accompany Hood and the Army of Tennessee in their advance north. On October 21, Hood started his men toward Decatur, Alabama. The Confederates moved across Sand Mountain, a huge plateau in northern Alabama. For five days, according to Captain Foster, the Confederate army trekked across the plateau before descending toward the Tennessee River on October 25. On the night of October 27, a drenching rain began, soaking everything and creating mud and knee-deep water in the pitch-black darkness. On October 28 the Confederates reached Decatur, but found the town strongly garrisoned by Federal troops. Instead of assaulting the garrison, Hood decided to move to Tuscumbia, Alabama, one hundred miles west of Decatur, where he might construct pontoon bridges to ferry his men across the Tennessee. At Tuscumbia, while gathering supplies for the invasion, Hood waited for Forrest to arrive.[20]

This delay along the Tennessee River cost Hood dearly in time, as it gave Federal general George H. Thomas time to organize his defense. Thomas gave command of the IV and the XXIII Corps to General John Schofield, who established his headquarters at Pulaski, Tennessee.[21]

While the Federals made their defensive preparations, the Army of Tennessee under Hood remained idle. The Confederates had reached Tuscumbia on October 30, and here they stayed for the next sixteen days. Because of the nature of the march, Hood's army had been cut off from any good source of supplies. Therefore, many members of Granbury's Texas Brigade resorted to foraging. On the night of November 2, the Texans found a pen with a large number of hogs. While one Texan distracted the guards, another made a gap in the fence and drove out two hogs, which the Texans subsequently butchered. The Texans cleverly buried the meat in the camp, then distributed it throughout the brigade while the officers had their backs turned.[22]

As a part of Hood's invasion, the Confederates gathered up all of the able-bodied men from the various hospitals in northern Mississippi and Alabama and ordered them to report to their commands. Lieutenant Robert B. Collins of Company B, 15th Texas Cavalry, had received a wound at the Battle of Peachtree Creek on July 19 and occupied himself "recovering" in a hospital by "laying up in day time and chewing sugar-cane, and running around courting at night," until "one day about the 11th of November, a red-headed, red-whiskered, red-eyed doctor by the name of Redwine, came into our room and remarked in a very authoritative manner, 'this outfit is about ready to go to the front.'" Collins received orders to gather all the men he could and report to his unit, "which was then at Florence, Alabama." Collins commented on the condition of the northern Mississippi countryside: "Corinth was a hard, dirty-looking town, the few people remaining seemed to be out of humor with themselves and all of their kind. The country around had the appearance of having been blasted by a curse of the gods."[23] Captain Foster also commented in his diary that the land the Confederates marched was "the richest country I have seen since I left Texas." Despite this richness, wrote Foster, "now it is a desert waste. . . . Fences burnt, large dwelling houses burnt, leaving two chimneys and their shade trees to mark the place, and sometimes as many as fifty negro cabins." In the midst of all this desolation he could not detect a single life form, "unless an occasional old negro came out of a hut." Foster also thought it strange to note that there remained "No cattle, horses, hogs chickens, nor people—nothing but desolation on every hand."[24]

With the beginning of November, Hood began to move his army across the Tennessee. On November 2 General Stephen D. Lee's I Corps crossed the river on massive pontoon bridges. Hood, however, frustrated by the lack of a railroad between Tuscumbia and Corinth, Mississippi, decided to remain in vicinity of Tuscumbia and Florence to gather supplies and await the arrival of Forrest. The army issued Granbury's Texans new clothing and shoes. On November 6, the Texans marched downriver in preparation for crossing.[25] A. L. Orr of the 18th Texas Dismounted Cavalry wrote his sister on November 9, "We are camped on the banks of the Tennessee River. We have been hear about ten days." The Confederates had "stoped to rest and wash our clothes." He related that "Stewart's Corps has already crossed the River," while the Texans had orders "to move this evening at four o'clock. I guess we will bee off for Tennessee in the morning. If so, we have a long and heavy march before ous." The Ellis County man ended his letter with a note of determination. "We have many hardships to endure, but I am willing to stand them all if it will doo any good. . . . Marchen is pretty hard, but I had rather march than fight."[26]

On November 13, Cheatham's Corps began to move across the pontoon bridge into Florence, and those who witnessed it thought it an imposing martial scene. The pontoon bridge became a feat of engineering in itself. After building it to an island in the middle of the Tennessee, the engineers had continued on to the north bank. In all, the bridge stretched for more than a mile. As Cheatham's Corps moved across, a brass band preceded each brigade, and marching by fours the Confederates crossed the Tennessee and marched into history.[27]

While Granbury's Brigade encamped along the river's banks on November 12 an unfortunate incident occurred. That night high winds toppled a tree, instantly killing a nineteen-year-old member of the 6th Texas. Lieutenant Stokes wrote to his sister that as the "rough, uncouth, yet tenderhearted soldiers" formed a semicircle around the boy's grave Stokes recited a few passages of Scripture from memory, including an extract from one of the Pauline epistles to the Corinthians: "For we must all appear before the judgment seat of Christ." Many Texans stayed up until dawn discussing the melancholy sight and the meaning of it all.[28] On November 16, Hood appointed a day of fasting and prayer and stipulated that every soldier in his army should attend a church service of some sort. Captain Foster attended a church service in Florence, about which he scribbled in his diary: "I went to church today in Florence, heard a good sermon, about 700 men present, and all seem quiet and attentive."[29]

Also on November 16, Hood set the final preparations for the Tennessee campaign in motion. General Nathan Bedford Forrest's tired cavalrymen arrived from western Tennessee and, with their arrival, Hood rushed to get Stewart's III Corps across the Tennessee River on the pontoons. Hood scheduled Stewart's crossing for sunrise of November 19, but drenching rains and overcrowding delayed the march until November 20.[30]

The anticipated northward advance into Tennessee lifted the spirits of the Army of Tennessee with hopes of victory, tempered by the harsh realizations of their prospects for success. On November 18 William Henderson of the 7th Texas wrote his parents: "Evry one thinks we are going into Tennessee. *God speed the day when we will start.* The army is in fine spirits and anxious for the journey into (as the Tennesseans calls it) God's country. The army is fast gaining confidence in Genl. Hood. and I think if he is successful on this campaign Hood will be THE man for this army." On November 17 Private William C. Young of the 15th Texas wrote his sister: "With this army we can tough it out four years longer. As for rations and clothing, we have done very well since here." Because of the decent weather while in northern Alabama, the youthful Texan estimated that the Army of Tennessee "will not go into winter quarters before the first of January." He also wrote of the hopes of many Texans of getting home at least temporarily in order to "recruit this winter." Despite this hope, he realistically concluded, "It is nothing to be relied on. I merely give you this hope so if such should be the case. At any rate there will be a trial made. This campaign is not ended yet. My opinion is we will have another fight, but where or when or if ever I can't say." According to Young, the 15th Texas was very badly under-strength. He stated that only he and two other men constituted his old Company A, 15th Texas. The following day, Young again wrote to his sister, after the receipt of a letter from her. He first related the position of Sherman, who "is now reported to have his army divided in three parts." Young confided that he did not care where the Federals went, "so they keep away from us." Though confident, he also wrote of his longing for the end of the war, "for I am worn out."[31] Young related one final piece of disheartening news to his sister on November 17: "Lincoln is elected we will have to fight him four years longer." The terrible truth of Lincoln's reelection victory had begun to circulate among the veterans of the Army of Tennessee. The Confederates knew all too well the implications of the election. Lincoln had committed himself to pursuing the war at all costs. This circumstance strengthened the resolve of the Texans to fight to the death in one last attempt for victory.[32]

Finally, on the morning of November 21, the Army of Tennessee started off in the long-awaited northward advance into Tennessee. That same day Captain Foster scribbled in his diary, "All the regimental commanders call their men out and say that Genl Hood says that we are going into Tenn. into the enemy's country, and we will leave our base of supplies here." Foster related that Hood promised his men "that we will have some hard marching and some fighting, but that he *is not going to risk a chance for defeat in Tenn. That he will not fight in Tenn. unless he has an equal number of men and choice of the ground.*" Hood also warned the Southerners that sometimes they "would be short of rations" but "that he would do his best" to keep them supplied. The Texans, including Foster, took faith in these promises, for "all felt confident" that they "could always whip an equal number of men with the choice of ground, and every man felt anxious to go under these promises from Genl Hood." No sooner had the Texans left their camp than it began snowing, and according to Captain Foster it became "very cold, with the wind from the north." The wintry conditions continued all day.[33] The hardships had just begun for the determined Army of Tennessee.

The optimism voiced by the Texans remains a clear indication that they felt they could still win the war, particularly with their leaders at their head. Although disheartening news continued to reach them from the rest of the Confederacy, their localized perspective and faith in their leaders kept their spirits intact. Moving north from Atlanta also boosted their morale because it gave them a chance, as they saw it, to retake ground that had been lost two years earlier. From the perspective of Granbury's Texans, with Cleburne, Granbury, and their regimental leaders at their head and with their high morale, who could stop them?

CHAPTER SEVENTEEN

SPRING HILL AND FRANKLIN

In Tennessee the Texans would soon experience disappointment and disaster at the battles of Spring Hill and Franklin. At the same time, they would also reach the zenith of their combat prowess despite the heavy losses at Franklin. As the Texans marched into Tennessee, they exhibited attachment to their leaders and the Confederate cause that defies explanation outside of the paradigm laid out in works like Gary Gallagher's *The Confederate War,* Jason Phillips's *Diehard Rebels,* and Larry Daniels's *Soldiering in the Army of Tennessee.* Despite the plight of the Confederacy as a whole, up until Spring Hill and Franklin the Texans believed they still had a chance to win the war, particularly at Spring Hill. Although the flanking maneuver at Spring Hill failed miserably for the Confederates, the Texans blamed the army commander, Hood, rather than Granbury, Cleburne, or their regimental commanders. At Franklin the Texans again blamed Hood for the disaster, and for the loss of Granbury, Cleburne, and all of their regimental commanders. This indicates how strongly the Texans felt about their regimental, brigade, and division commanders and how little they thought of their army commander following the debacle at Franklin. Although Franklin destroyed the effectiveness of Granbury's Brigade as a potent fighting force due to the death of their leaders, the fact that the Confederates stayed with the remnants of their brigade afterward is a testament to the idea that it was not just their leaders that held them with the colors, but a fidelity to the Confederate cause and their comrades as well.

For his line of advance from Florence, Hood sent his three corps on three parallel roads into central Tennessee. Hood assigned Cheatham's II Corps, which contained Granbury's Brigade, to the westernmost line of march, through Waynesboro. Hood instructed the three columns to unite again at Mount Pleasant, a little town just south of Columbia, Hood's first objective.[1]

Granbury's Texans led the advance of Cleburne's Division into Tennessee. On the night of November 22, Granbury sent the 24th & 25th Texas out as an advance guard during weather so miserable that William Young of the 15th Texas wrote that it was "freezing like the blue blazes."[2] The next day Granbury's Brigade passed through Waynesboro, which Captain Foster described as "a very nice little town, but nearly ruined by the war. Several houses burned down, some torn down, gardens destroyed." That night the Texans camped on a ridge north of town while the temperature reached zero. With dawn on November 24 the commissary issued Granbury's men scant rations and they marched fifteen miles, reaching Hervyville before dark. The wintry conditions continued to be miserable for the Texans, who endured icy winds from the north.[3]

The Texans did encounter some bright spots during their northward progress. On November 26 they marched through Mount Pleasant, passing by St. John's Episcopal Church and Ashwood, the home of General Leonidas Polk, who had perished in the Atlanta campaign. Captain Foster thought "it was the prettiest place I ever saw."[4] Patrick Cleburne, while passing St. John's Church, dismounted and walked through the chapel and the graveyard behind it. The cemetery reminded him of Athnowen churchyard in Ireland, where his father lay buried. Deeply moved, Cleburne remarked, "It would almost be worth dying to be buried in such a pretty place."[5]

Upon detecting the northward movement of the Army of Tennessee in mid-November, Union general John M. Schofield, whom Thomas had assigned to contest any advance by Hood, hurriedly gathered in his scattered units from Middle Tennessee. Schofield decided to concentrate his twenty thousand men in Columbia, the crossroads town which he divined as Hood's objective. On November 27 Hood's army arrived within three miles of Columbia, along the south banks of the Duck River, and there began a long-range skirmish with the Federals in the town. That night Schofield decided to abandon his position, cross the river to the north bank, and block the Confederate advance from a place of greater security. The weather had turned rainy and miserable, and Hood remained content to sit on the south bank of the river while he formulated his plan to get at and destroy Schofield.[6]

That night, Hood finished perfecting his strategy for getting rid of Schofield. The next morning, November 29, he would leave two divisions of S. D. Lee's I Corps and the army's artillery in place in front of Columbia to harass the Federals and make them believe that a general frontal assault was imminent. With these forces pinning down the Federals, Hood would march with the balance of his army, Cheatham's II Corps and Stewart's III Corps, along with Edward Johnson's division of Lee's Corps, and cross the Duck River at Davis Ford, east of Columbia. From here, Hood intended to get in the rear of the Federal army and cut them off by capturing the Columbia Pike in the little village of Spring Hill.

Early on the morning of November 29, Cleburne set his division in motion toward Davis Ford, the crossing point designated by Hood, five miles upriver from Columbia. Lowrey's Brigade led the column, followed by Govan's, and Granbury's Texans brought up the rear. Hood designated Cleburne's Division the vanguard of his flanking column, and Hood, along with Governor Isham Harris of Tennessee, accompanied Cleburne, who rode with Lowrey's Brigade.[7]

Though Hood's flanking maneuver remained sound in theory, in practice difficulties immediately arose. Lowrey's Alabamans crossed the river just after 7 A.M., and the rest of the column followed. Hood became impatient, and the shape of the road north of Davis Ford did not help matters. The narrow path wound and bent back on itself so many times that Hood in fact wondered if they had taken the right route. Stopping to consult a local scout, he confirmed that the road did indeed lead to the Franklin-Columbia Turnpike at the village of Spring Hill, but what he had originally anticipated as a twelve-mile march turned out to be closer to seventeen. Hood, who exhibited buoyant spirits initially, quickly fell into an ugly mood. At noon, with the column stopped for lunch, Hood, frustrated by the delays, exchanged heated words with General Granbury. Although the content of the argument between Hood and Granbury remains unknown, the intemperate exchange may explain the later conduct of the commander of the Texas Brigade.[8]

Meanwhile, on the north bank of the river Schofield soon discovered Hood's intention to trap him, and rapidly the Federal commander started his army north toward Spring Hill. Lowrey's Brigade crossed Rutherford Creek, south of Spring Hill, just after 3 P.M. Ahead, Forrest's Cavalry had already begun skirmishing with Federal infantry drawn up in a semicircle around the town. While Hood moved ahead to reconnoiter, he ordered Cleburne to form his division to the left of the road and attack toward Spring Hill. As Cleburne formed Lowrey's Brigade to the west of McCutcheon Creek, Hood returned from his reconnaissance and instructed Cleburne to form his division en echelon and then assault the Federals south of Spring Hill. This disposition would place Lowrey's Brigade in the most advanced position, Govan a little behind him and to the left, and Granbury a little behind that and to Govan's left.[9] While Cleburne formed his division, Hood remained at his newly designated headquarters, the Absalom Thompson home, located near where Cleburne's Division had crossed Rutherford Creek southeast of Spring Hill. Hood's withdrawal from the front left General Cheatham (the ranking officer present on the field) in the role of the battlefield commander.

As Hood established his headquarters, Cheatham, known as a ferocious fighter, pushed forward with the attack on Spring Hill. Forrest soon arrived on the scene and volunteered one of his brigades to cover Cleburne's right flank. Cleburne accepted, and at 4 P.M. he ordered his division to advance. The men moved due west, toward the Franklin-Columbia Turnpike. Because of the disposition of Cleburne's Division, they advanced toward the pike south of the Union troops around the town. As a consequence, a large body of Federals appeared on the right (or north) flank of Lowrey's Brigade, making considerable noise and waving their hats. Cleburne, believing they intended to charge, ordered Lowrey and Govan to swing north and charge, while Granbury's Texans continued west. Lowrey and Govan found themselves up against the inexperienced two-thousand-man Federal brigade of Luther Bradley, which fled in the face of the assault by the Arkansans and Alabamans. The two brigades chased the Federals across McCutcheon Creek and up the opposite bank.[10]

Just as everything seemed to fall into place, the advancing Confederates encountered difficulties in their attack on the Federals in Spring Hill. No sooner had Cleburne's men cleared the trees on the other side of the creek than eighteen Federal cannon, arrayed north of the pike, opened on them.

In addition, a two-gun section of Battery B, Pennsylvania Light Artillery, pounded Govan's left flank from west of the pike. The 36th Illinois, held in reserve to that point, rushed to the assistance of the two exposed cannons as Granbury's Texans, who had continued to advance west, quickly moved upon the small body of Federals, forcing the Pennsylvanians and Illinoisans to flee. Cleburne, realizing that he could not keep his division exposed, ordered his three brigades back to the line of McCutcheon's Creek. Meanwhile, Union brigadier general John Lane had moved his brigade out of its position facing east and advanced south toward Cleburne's men. Cleburne sent his aide, Lieutenant Leonard Mangum, to recall Granbury and place him in position to thwart Lane's advance.[11] Bate's Division, which Hood also counted on, had not yet arrived on the field.

Again, the Confederates seemed on the verge of victory, but Frank Cheatham developed tunnel vision. Hood originally intended to block Schofield's retreat along the Columbia Pike by having Bate's Division sweep west and then south along the pike while Cleburne captured Spring Hill itself. Cheatham, however, saw the Federals still in place around the village and decided that he should overwhelm them at any cost. Accordingly, Cheatham placed Major General John Brown's division on Cleburne's right flank with Jackson's Confederate cavalry division on the high ground north of Brown's right flank. In addition to placing Cleburne and Brown in position to attack, Cheatham also insisted that Bate realign his division with Cleburne's left flank in order to join in the assault. In a council of war just before 5 P.M. Cheatham arranged Brown's Division to initiate the assault on the Federals. Because of the gathering darkness, he ordered Cleburne not to attack until he heard the sound of Brown's guns to the north.[12] At 5 P.M., with the attack orders issued, Cheatham rode south with his staff to find Bate's Division, which had not yet arrived.

Though William Bate had difficulty bringing his men into position, by 5:30 P.M. he set his division in motion, advancing west according to Hood's original orders. The Confederates, after advancing west, struck the Columbia Pike, just north of the Nathaniel Cheirs residence, well south of the main action around Spring Hill. Now Bate and his full division were poised to sweep south along the pike toward Columbia, cutting off Schofield's retreat. Before he had a chance to block the pike, however, couriers arrived from Cheatham ordering him to align his troops with the left flank of Cleburne's Division. These confusing orders mystified Bate because they forced him to yield the wide-open turnpike; but adhering to Cheatham's directive, he withdrew his men from their position adjacent to the pike and marched north and east in search of Cleburne.[13]

Meanwhile to the north, Cleburne and his men waited and waited, but no sounds of assault from the direction of Brown's Division ever came. Brown had decided not to attack because of what he described as a large Federal force on his right flank. In order to counter this threat he at first looked to Forrest's cavalrymen positioned on his right flank, but to no avail. Half an hour earlier Forrest had withdrawn Jackson's tired troopers to the rear, leaving Brown's flank wide open. Though his flank now lay unprotected, the threat from the north remained minimal. The large Federal force that worried Brown in actuality consisted of a single regiment with two extra companies, about three hundred men in all, though the apprehensive Tennessean did not know this. Under these circumstances Brown, having entirely halted his advance, sent messages to Cheatham, and the corps commander rode back north, aborting his mission of finding Bate in order to consult with Brown. The sun had set at 4:26 P.M., and by 6:15 that evening it had become completely dark. Cheatham, not wanting to assume any undue risks, sought out Hood for orders concerning Brown's perceived predicament.[14]

John Bell Hood, in front of his headquarters at the Thompson home, fumed as the sun set on November 29. His commanders had obviously not carried out his orders to cut the pike and overwhelm the Federals in Spring Hill because he could not hear any sounds of battle from the front. During the night, while inaction and incompetence paralyzed the Army of Tennessee, the entire Federal army under Schofield quietly slipped by along the pike, north toward Franklin.[15]

That night Granbury had posted his men along an old farm fence within sixty yards of the Franklin-Columbia Turnpike. The Texans heard an occasional rustling, and many of them maintained that it was merely Bate's Division connecting with their right flank. Others insisted that it was the Yankees. In the midst of these conjectures Captain Richard English of Granbury's staff said, "I'll be d——d if I don't intend to find out." Some men of the brigade let down the fence for him, and English "went in on his mule."[16] He crept forward to investigate, and flankers of the 23rd Michigan captured him as they moved north.[17] The Texans remained along this fence line until 10 P.M., when Granbury moved them back about one hundred yards. Here, they built fires and ate their supper, which consisted of parched corn and "biled" pork. The Confederates remained so close to the pike that several Federal soldiers approached their campfires to light their pipes and the Texans captured them.[18]

This ended the Spring Hill fiasco. Hood and his subordinates had an excellent chance to destroy Schofield's army, but, just as had happened so many times in the past, the high command of the Army of Tennessee failed the fighting men in the ranks. Lieutenant Robert Collins of the 6th & 15th Texas wrote in later years that "the easiest and most charitable way to dispose of the whole matter is to say that the gods of battle were against us and injected confusion into the heads and tongues of our leaders."[19]

The morning of November 30, 1864, dawned "cold bright and frosty" for the soldiers of the Army of Tennessee. The men of Granbury's Texas Brigade awoke to find that the Federals had escaped. Oliver Bowser, a second lieutenant in the 18th Texas, remembered that the Columbia Pike "was literally strewn with broken-down and abandoned wagons, caissons, and dead mules, left by the retreating Federals the night before."[20] The Texans' officers issued them rations of three ears of corn apiece, the best they could procure under the circumstances.[21]

When Schofield reached the town of Franklin, some fifteen miles north of Spring Hill, he discovered, to his dismay, that the pontoon bridges he had requested from Thomas in Nashville had not yet arrived. Seeing that rains had swollen the Harpeth River, and that a narrow railroad bridge provided the most important passage across the river, he determined to place his men in the breastworks south and west of the town as a precaution while his engineers reconstructed the wagon bridge and replanked the railroad bridge across the river. Once his men completed these repairs, he would march his army north to Nashville to join Thomas.[22]

When Hood awoke on the morning of November 30 and learned what had happened, he became furious. His brilliantly planned flanking maneuver had gone awry, and he angrily sought the source of the failure. He immediately ordered a rapid pursuit of the Federals marching toward Franklin. At a conference of war that morning, Hood accused the men of the army of cowardice. When this stormy council of war broke up, Hood ordered his officers to rejoin their commands.[23]

As word of Hood's charges of cowardice began to permeate the ranks of the Army of Tennessee, the veterans took offense. The accusations bothered

Granbury, like his men, and he no doubt remained disturbed about his exchange with Hood the previous day. During the march toward Franklin, the lanky Texan rode the length of his brigade several times, as if agitated.[24] The reports of the meeting also deeply disturbed Cleburne. He confided his anger to General John Brown, whom Hood also held responsible. Cleburne stated to Brown, "Of course the responsibility rests with the Commander-in-Chief, as he was upon the field during the afternoon and was fully advised during the night." Cleburne was visibly upset, and informed Brown that he would resume his conversation with him at the "first convenient moment."[25]

When the Army of Tennessee arrived in front of Franklin, Hood had already made up his mind as to the course of action he would take against Schofield's Federals: he would order a direct, all-out frontal assault to overwhelm them in their fortifications. Because Cleburne's and Brown's divisions principally bore the blame for the debacle at Spring Hill, Hood reasoned, they would occupy the center of the Confederate line that would attack Franklin—so as to eradicate the evil of hesitancy to assault breastworks.

South of Franklin, Hood held one final council of war, this time in the parlor of the Harrison house, south of Winstead Hill. Here he outlined to his officers, including Cleburne, his plan to assault the Federals entrenched around Franklin. Hood expressed his insistence that the attacking force should "go over the main works at all hazards." The Irish general reportedly said, "I will take the enemy's works or fall in the attempt."[26]

Cleburne rode back to his division to give them the attack orders. He instructed Granbury, Lowrey, and Govan to move their men to the foot of Winstead Hill, on the east side of the pike. General Daniel Govan, seeing Cleburne's despondency, said: "Well, General, there will not be many of us that will get back to Arkansas." Cleburne replied, "Well, Govan, if we are to die, let us die like men."[27]

With this disheartening comment, Cleburne and his division began to make their preparations for the assault. As the men of the Texas Brigade moved through the saddle on Winstead Hill and began forming their line to the east of the pike, many of them did not like what they saw. A formal line of breastworks encircled the town of Franklin, built and strengthened during two years of occupation by Federal troops. In the center of this line, along the Franklin-Columbia Turnpike, the Federals had constructed a reserve line of breastworks around the Carter house, a fairly large brick home. To the east of the Carter house, across the Columbia Pike, stood the Carter cotton gin, which also served as a landmark. In addition, across the Harpeth River sat Fort Granger atop Figures Hill. This fort bristled with artillery and stood in position to sweep the southern approaches to the town. Into this formidable defense the Texans would soon march. Lieutenant Bowser recalled that at "three o'clock in the afternoon Hood's army halted about one mile south of Franklin, and he immediately formed his lines for a general assault on the enemy's works." He went on to write that from the position of Granbury's Brigade the fortifications "looked almost impregnable." To the left of the Texans "there was an open woodland," while "to the right and in front was an open field or valley." The left flank of the brigade rested on the Columbia Pike, while the right rested in the open farm field.[28] As Cleburne rode down to his command after one final futile consultation with Hood, the order drifted down the line to "fix bayonets." Upon reaching the base of Winstead Hill, Granbury halted the Texas Brigade to realign it, and here Granbury threw out the 7th Texas as skirmishers. He arranged the Texans with the 24th & 25th Texas on the extreme left of the brigade, their left flank resting on the Columbia Pike, while the 6th & 15th Texas occupied the extreme right of the brigade.[29] Captain Foster later wrote in his diary, "Our regiment [24th & 25th Texas] being on the left of the Brigd. put our Regt. Next the Pike," while Company H, which Foster commanded, "being on the left of the regiment—it puts us on the Pike."[30] On the right of Granbury's Brigade Cleburne placed Daniel Govan's brigade, and on the right of Govan he placed Mark Lowrey's Alabamans. To the left of Cleburne's Division, across the pike, lay John C. Brown's division. To the right of Cleburne and Brown, between Cleburne's right and the Harpeth River, Hood squeezed Stewart's entire III Corps into position to assault. To the left of Brown's Division, Hood aligned William Bate's division to attack up the Carters' Creek Pike.

Some of the advancing Texans had premonitions of death prior to Franklin. Second Corporal John W. Scott of Company H, 10th Texas, experiencing such a feeling, entrusted his watch and other effects to a comrade to give to his wife if he were killed.[31] As the soldiers of his brigade made their final preparations, Granbury also readied for battle, ordering his staff to dismount so as to make less inviting targets for Federal bullets. As the Texans formed their lines for the assault, Granbury stepped to the front of his brigade and said: "You have fought many hard battles but this will be the

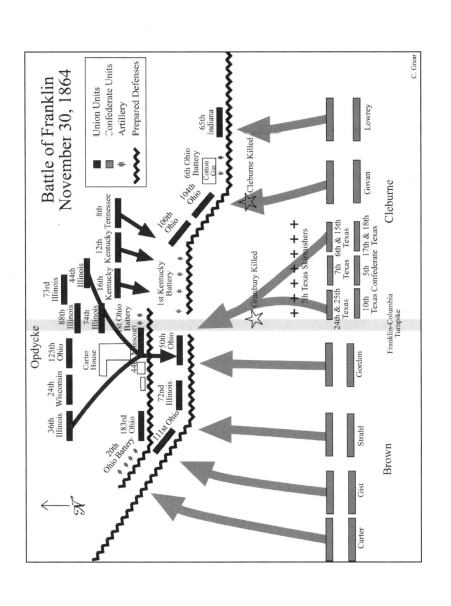

Battle of Franklin
November 30, 1864

Union Units
Confederate Units
Artillery
Prepared Defenses

Opdycke

36th Illinois
24th Wisconsin
125th Ohio
Carter House
44th
88th Illinois
73rd Illinois
74th Illinois
1st Ohio Battery
Missouri
16th Kentucky
12th Kentucky
44th Illinois
8th Tennessee
100th Ohio
104th Ohio
6th Ohio Battery
Cotton Gin
65th Indiana
1st Kentucky Battery
50th Ohio
72nd Illinois
111th Ohio
20th Ohio Battery
183rd Ohio

Cleburne Killed
Granbury Killed
7th Texas Skirmishers

24th & 25th Texas
10th Texas
7th Texas
6th & 15th Texas
5th 17th & 18th Texas Confederate Texas

Franklin-Columbia Turnpike

Lowrey
Govan
Cleburne

Gordon
Strahl
Gist
Carter
Brown

N

C. Grear

worst of all, the enemy being strongly entrenched and in plain view, now if I have a man not willing to go in this charge let him step to the rear." With this pronouncement, all of the Texans stepped forward with a wild yell.[32]

Nearby, Granbury's chief of staff, Lieutenant Colonel Robert Butler Young, also dismounted. After graduating from the Georgia Military Institute, Robert Young had been assigned to the command of the 338th Battalion of Georgia Militia. He married Josephine Florida Hill in Walton County, Georgia, in 1853. The couple had only one daughter, Ida, in 1853. In 1858, because of financial problems, Young moved his family to McLennan County, Texas, where he became involved in stock raising. He had strong Southern sentiments, and with the outbreak of hostilities he considered joining the Texas Rangers. Despite this early commitment, he later confided that he would rather "fight Yankees than Indians." The governor of Texas commissioned him a major of the 10th Texas Infantry, and he soon received promotion to lieutenant colonel. After his capture and imprisonment following Arkansas Post, Young's physical condition became so severe that he was forced to recuperate at his family's plantation home near Cartersville, Georgia. During the Atlanta campaign he rejoined the 10th Texas and received a slight wound at the Battle of Atlanta on July 22, 1864. Viewing the strong Federal fortifications, perhaps Young regretted his decision to fight Yankees rather than Indians, or perhaps his thoughts turned to his wife, Josephine, and eleven-year-old Ida in faraway Texas.[33]

The ranks of Granbury's Brigade marching into Franklin contained reminders of the Texas Revolution. Among the men of the 24th & 25th Texas on the left flank of the brigade, at least one veteran of that conflict marched into battle, Sergeant Jackson H. "Hawkeye" Griffin of Company I, 25th Texas, who had fought in the Battle of San Jacinto as a seventeen-year-old.[34]

At 3:30 P.M. the order to advance came, and the twenty thousand men of the Army of Tennessee stepped off as bands that accompanied the advancing Confederates began playing "Dixie." The Texans brought their arms with bayonets fixed to right shoulder shift and began to advance with their "lion-hearted Granbury" in the lead.[35] As they went forward, their blue Hardee-style flags waved overhead in the breeze of the Indian summer day. Colonel Ellison Capers, of the 24th South Carolina in Brigadier General States Rights Gist's brigade of Brown's Division, recorded the magnificent martial spectacle of the advance. "Just before the charge was ordered," he wrote, "the brigade passed over an elevation, from which I beheld the magnificent spectacle the battlefield presented." Bands "were playing and general and staff officers and gallant couriers were riding in front of and between the lines." Floating above the Army of Tennessee, "100 battle-flags" were "waving in the smoke of battle" while "bursting shells" wreathed the "air with great circles of smoke."[36]

The Texans' advance exposed them to artillery fire from Fort Granger across the river. A shell fragment struck Lieutenant Linson Keener of the 7th Texas in the chest, breaking a rib, whereupon he fell unconscious upon the field. "Keener's killed," yelled Gregg Pickett of Company D. The lieutenant revived, however, as litter bearers carried him from the field, and said, "Put me down, boys. I want to see how bad I am hurt. Help someone who needs it. I will take care of myself."[37]

As the Confederates had approached Winstead Hill in the early afternoon of November 30, another drama had occurred in the ranks of George Wagner's Federal division, posted as the rear guard of the Union army. In mid-morning Wagner had placed the brigade of Colonel Joseph Conrad (the brigade had been commanded by Brigadier General Luther Bradley until his wounding the day before at Spring Hill) about a half-mile in front of the main Federal line. Wagner placed John Lane's brigade farther south on the Columbia Pike, guarding the saddle on Winstead Hill. Wagner's third brigade, commanded by Colonel Emerson Opdycke, proved more of a problem. When Opdycke's men approached Conrad's brigade along the pike, Wagner ordered Opdycke into line with the other men. Opdycke refused, insisting that his men needed rest. In flat disobedience of his orders, Opdycke marched his men inside of the main Federal line, where they finally came to rest a few hundred yards north of the Carter house. The hapless Federals of Wagner's Division had little time to better their position.[38]

As the Confederates moved forward, the distance between Cleburne's and Brown's divisions and Wagner's two brigades decreased. Upon reaching within two hundred yards of the advance Federal line, the Confederate main line caught up with the skirmishers and the 7th Texas stepped back into formation with the Texas Brigade, neither force losing any time in the transition. The bugles sounded "double-quick," and the line of rapidly moving men with rifles at right shoulder shift began to gain momentum. As the Confederates reached within one hundred yards of the Federal position, Lane's and Conrad's bluecoats opened up and a sheet of flame exploded in the faces of the Southerners.

The Confederates, not halting to fire, rushed up and over the slight embankment. The Texans with Granbury at their head became the first to reach Wagner's line, and initially breached it.[39] The break then reminded Captain John Shellenberger of a powder train ignited, so fast did the panic spread among the Federals. Just as Wagner's men began to run, the Confederates delivered a point-blank volley into their backs. As the survivors of Lane's and Conrad's brigades sprinted back for the main Federal line, the Confederates, following on their heels, began to yell, "Go into the works with them."

The Southerners pursued, as Captain Foster wrote, "yelling like fury and shooting at them at the same time." The Texans killed some of the Federals before they reached the breastworks. Fortunately for the Confederates, the enemy "in the second line of works" were "not able to shoot" because their own men were in between them and the charging Confederates. "So here we go," wrote Foster, "Yanks running for life and we for the fun of it," but the difference in motivation for these "objects are so great that they out run us, but loose [lose] quite a number of their men before they get there."[40] When the Confederates reached within about eighty yards of the breastworks, the Federals opened a murderous fire on them. A soldier of the 64th Ohio wrote that "the long line of blue-coats within the trenches rose, and a flash of flame shot out in a sinuous line, and the white smoke rose like the foam on the crest of the breaker." The Ohioan remembered, "The few straggling blue-coats" from Wagner's Division "and the long line of gray went down like over-ripe grain before a blast of wind and hail. But the enemy," he lamented, "were legion."[41] As General Cleburne moved forward on horseback, he sent his aide Lieutenant Leonard Mangum to the left, instructing him, "go with Granbury," as Cleburne himself led Govan's Arkansans against the blazing entrenchments.

This murderous fire immediately had a terrible effect on the advancing Confederates. As Mangum moved among the Texans, he noted, "Generals Govan and Granbury on foot were in the midst of their men, cheering them on." Suddenly, within ten feet of Mangum, "General Granbury's voice rang out clear and commanding 'Forward men, forward! Never let it be said that Texans lag in the fight!'" At this instant a ball struck the Texan "in the lower part of the cheek and passed through his brain. Throwing both hands to his face as in the impulse of the instant to find where the pain was he sank forward on his knees, and there, half sitting, half crouching, with his hands over his face," he remained, "rigid in the attitude in which the bullet with its blow and its swift coming of death had left him."[42] Granbury had died squarely in the center of the Columbia-Franklin Turnpike, his last words obviously reflecting his desire to defend his honor and that of his men. About this time a ball also struck down Lieutenant Colonel Young, felling him not far from his commander. Meanwhile, Cleburne, who had his horse shot from under him, continued to lead Govan's Arkansans against the breastworks until a Minié ball found its mark. Struck squarely in the heart, the Irishman fell instantly dead.

The Texans continued to press forward into the face of triple-shotted canister from the Federal battery of Kentuckians in their front, and as they advanced farther the fire became hotter. The musketry became incredible, and about forty yards from the works Sergeant Jackson Griffin of the 25th Texas fell lifeless.[43] Thirty steps from the breastworks, Lieutenant Thomas Stokes of the 10th Texas also fell dead.[44] As the fire mowed the soldiers down in windrows, Private John T. Gillespie of Company B, 7th Texas, also died, pierced through both lungs by a Minié ball. Nearby, his twenty-two-year-old brother, William H. Gillespie, succumbed as well. Corporal Joseph Bookman of the 10th Texas became perhaps the youngest Texan to die that day when a ball struck him dead at the age of nineteen. Corporal John Scott of the 10th Texas, true in his premonition of death, also fell upon the field of Franklin, never to rise again. Nearby, the commander of Company G, 6th Texas, Lieutenant William Dunson, had several bullets pass through his clothes and one ball graze his cheek while shrapnel severed his accouterments.[45]

The fire hit the regimental commanders in Granbury's Brigade especially hard. Captain James W. Bron of the 7th Texas went down wounded, as did Captain Edward Broughton of the same regiment, struck in the thigh. Nearby, Captain Aaron Cox of the 5th Confederate also received a wound, and Major James Formwalt, commanding the 10th Texas, stumbled into the ditch in front of the Federal works after a Minié ball splintered his upper thigh. Major William A. Taylor of the 24th & 25th Texas also tumbled into the ditch and there took refuge with other Texans, too winded to scale the earthworks.[46] Granbury's Texans had drifted to the left during the advance, placing the left flank of the 24th & 25th Texas to the west of the Columbia Pike, while the center of the brigade struck near where the turnpike ran through the breastworks.

Despite their losses the Texans still possessed enough momentum to breach the Federal line, and once there all became chaos. The hard charging pressure of the Texas Brigade forced the green troops of the 100th and 104th Ohio on the east side of the pike, as well as the Kentucky gunners, to flee. The majority of the Texans crossed the Federal breastworks and began toward the reserve line of works. Inside the primary works, all became pandemonium; bullets whizzed demonically as men struggled for their lives amid the tumult of battle.

The confusion remained so great that men became widely separated from their regiments as the Texans fought tenaciously inside the breastworks. Though part of the 24th & 25th Texas fought west of the Columbia Pike, somewhere between the Columbia Pike and the cotton gin, east of the pike, Adjutant Phillip Curry of the 24th & 25th Texas went down wounded while cheering on his regiment. Nearby, Sergeant Miriam Sharp of Company G, 24th Texas, and Private R. G. Foster of Company F both received serious wounds inside the works and, along with Adjutant Curry, became prisoners.[47] The Texans, having captured the guns of the Kentucky battery east of the pike, tried in vain to turn the cannons on the enemy. Lacking primers for the guns, they attempted to find a way to discharge the cannons as the 12th and 16th Kentucky and 8th Tennessee countercharged them. Captain Asa Hutchison of the 16th Kentucky described how the three Federal regiments "at once opened fire upon the enemy and charged." The countercharge became brutal as "men clubbed with muskets and used the bayonet."[48]

In the melee some of the Texans penetrated deep into the Federal works, where Union soldiers captured most of them. Private Charles Leuschner crossed the "fourth line" of Federal works and forced several Yankees to surrender, only to be captured himself a short time later.[49] Private Valentine Hardt of Company K, 24th Texas, found himself inside the works, and after seizing a flag from a Union color-bearer he advanced all the way to the Wick home, "opposite the cotton gin." Like Leuschner, Hardt soon found himself a prisoner.[50]

Meanwhile, the Federal counterattack began to gain momentum as the fighting intensified around the gap in the breastworks at the Columbia Pike. In addition to the Kentuckians and Tennesseans, other Federal units joined in the counterattack to force the Confederates back out of the works.

The Texans who found themselves fighting west of the Columbia Pike had their own counterattack to deal with. Colonel Emerson Opdycke, who had earlier stubbornly refused to place his brigade in an advanced position, now swept forward with his western regiments, known as Opdycke's Tigers, in a vicious counterthrust against the men of Cleburne's and Brown's divisions swarming around the Carter house. With brutal Federal counterattacks on both sides of the pike, the Confederates reached their highwater mark at Franklin.

With the tide of battle turning against the Southerners, the Federals captured many of the Texans inside the fortifications, then forced the remnants of the brigade into the ditch outside of the works. The Federals advanced as darkness fell over the field of Franklin. Captain Foster recorded in his diary that the enemy came up and met the Confederates "on one side" of the breastworks while Foster and his comrades remained "on the other—with a bank of dirt between us." "By this time," recalled the Texan, "it was getting dark and the firing was stopping gradually." Despite the thick fog of dirt and smoke that enveloped the participants, Foster recognized that they were "just in the edge of town and the dead and wounded are all around us, Yank and Confed. Lie near each other." An hour after nightfall the firing had "nearly ceased, except when one man will hold his gun up as high as he can and shoot over the bank of dirt." The fighting remained so desperate that the Federals threw "clods of dirt over and sticks or anything they can get hold of." By this time the grim rumors had begun to circulate through the survivors of the Texas Brigade "that Gen. Pat. Cleburne and Gen. Granbury are both dead."[51]

Some of the Texans used the opportunity of night to slip back to their own lines, but most remained pinned down in the ditch in front of the Federal works. Many surrendered under the stress, while the Federals forcefully made others prisoners. Private Jim Turner of the 6th & 15th Texas remembered that as he and Major Rhoads Fisher (then commanding the regiment), along with Privates Frank Wilkes and James Baldwin, crouched near each other in the ditch the four Austinites "were dragged over the breastworks by the Federals and taken prisoners."[52] Captain Shellenberger of the 64th Ohio wrote that when some Confederates wanted to surrender, they "finally elevated their hats on the ends of their muskets . . . as a signal to us, and called over," saying that if the Federals "would stop shooting they would surrender." When the Federals granted this request, "many of them came over and surrendered, but many more," he wrote, "took the advantage of the darkness and confusion . . . to slip back to their own lines."[53] The Federals, who had only halted long enough to repair the bridges over the Harpeth River and let their wagon train cross, began withdrawing north toward Nashville around 1 A.M. The Confederates stayed in position, too decimated and exhausted to move.

The next morning the men of Granbury's Texas Brigade wearily regrouped for roll call, and the toll of the vicious fighting became readily apparent. Lieutenant Collins reported that prior to the battle eleven hundred men had reported for roll call in the brigade. Now only 460 remained—a casualty rate of nearly 60 percent. The actual loss in Granbury's Brigade amounted to a little over four hundred killed, wounded, or captured. Private Albert McKinney of the 24th Texas wrote that he believed the brigade loss to be close to 52 percent in killed and wounded.[54] Bullets killed General Granbury and Lieutenant Colonel Young, as well as nearly one hundred other Texans. A ball wounded Major James Formwalt, commanding the 10th Texas, and the Federals later captured him. The 10th Texas, which went into battle numbering 150 rifles, suffered nineteen killed, fourteen wounded, and thirteen captured, for a total of forty-six lost.[55] Captain John W. Brown, commanding the 7th Texas, was also wounded and captured; Brown's regiment suffered nineteen killed, twenty-nine wounded, and twenty-eight captured, for an aggregate of seventy-six casualties.[56] Major Rhoads Fisher, commanding the 6th & 15th Texas, also received a wound and suffered capture, and his regiment sustained fourteen killed, thirty-one wounded, nineteen captured, twelve missing, and three mortally wounded, for a sum of seventy-nine.[57] Major William A. Taylor, commanding the 24th & 25th Texas, also experienced capture, and according to Captain Foster the regiment suffered at least "eighteen dead on the ground."[58] Captain Edward T. Broughton of the 7th Texas, as the senior officer in the brigade, assumed command of what had been Granbury's Texas Brigade. Broughton had received a slight wound, and this prevented him from taking command for a few days.[59]

Litter bearers transported some of the wounded Texans to hospitals in Franklin, while they brought others to the McGavock residence, Carnton Plantation, south of Franklin. Mrs. McGavock had turned her large house into a hospital, and thousands of wounded Confederates lay in and around the mansion. The survivors conveyed still other members of Granbury's Brigade to local residences, such as Private Samuel W. Morris of the 6th & 15th Texas, who received transportation to a home near Franklin after having his leg amputated, only to die of his wounds.[60] In all, of the twenty thousand Confederates engaged in the Battle of Franklin, seven thousand were killed, wounded, or captured. These numbers included six generals killed or mortally wounded and six others wounded. The Federals, meanwhile, lost 2,326 total casualties.[61]

The morning after the battle, some Texans made efforts to locate the bodies of Generals Cleburne and Granbury. Albert McKinney of Company B, 24th & 25th Texas, and David Myers of Company G, 10th Texas, participated in the detail sent from Granbury's Brigade to recover the corpse of the fallen Texan. They discovered his body "within twenty steps of the breastworks and right in the edge of town." They found him in the same position in which he had fallen—on his knees with his hands to his face. The men also discovered the body of Lieutenant Colonel Robert Young nearby, and they placed them on litters and bore them to Carnton.[62] On the porch of Carnton, the Confederates laid the bodies of Generals Otho Strahl, Hiram Granbury, and Patrick Cleburne in state along with those of Lieutenant Colonel Young and Lieutenant John Marsh of Strahl's staff. Attesting to the relationship that existed between Cleburne and Granbury, Chaplain Robert F. Bunting of Terry's Texas Rangers wrote about Franklin and the death of Cleburne, and then concluded: "There, too, by his side is our own Granbury, the chivalric Texian General who was his counselor and bosom friend. In life they were united by the very perils through which, side by side, they passed, and in death upon the bloody field they were not divided."[63]

The men of Cleburne's Division were greatly demoralized by the death of their beloved commander, "old Pat." As one of the men of Granbury's Brigade made his way toward the rear the morning after the battle, he came across Hood sitting astride his horse smoking a cigar. Hood inquired what division the Texan belonged to. The man replied that he was a part of Cleburne's Division. When Hood asked about the location of his division, the Texan replied that they remained gathered around the body of Cleburne. Hood then took his cigar out of his mouth, lowered his head, and wept for half an hour.[64] Lieutenant Leonard Mangum, Cleburne's aide, recorded that on the morning of December 1, "Information came to our headquarters that General Cleburne's body had been found," and Mangum "procured coffins for Generals Cleburne and Granbury and Colonel Young of the Tenth Texas."[65]

That afternoon the Confederates loaded the five bodies into a wagon and took them to Columbia, where they again laid them in state. The next day, December 2, they interred the officers in Rose Hill Cemetery in a service presided over by the Reverend R. T. Quintard. Lucius Polk, a former brigade commander under Cleburne, made his appearance at the service as well. After the burial, neither Quintard nor Polk remained satisfied with the resting place of the five officers. Someone pointed out that the section in which they had buried the men was set aside for paupers. Hearing that Cleburne had made a remark about St. John's Episcopal Church, Quintard determined to have the five Confederates removed to that churchyard.[66] Colonel Robert F. Beckham, commander of artillery for Lee's I Corps, who had been mortally wounded in the fighting on November 29, also was buried at St. John's.

Elsewhere, concerned relatives laid other Texans to rest beneath the Tennessee soil. Ellen White, a small girl of Spring Hill, recorded the burial of Adjutant George Blaine of the 7th Texas. Blaine, on the eve of Franklin, "told his negro servant that he had a cousin, the wife of Dr. Aaron C. White, living at Spring Hill," twelve miles from Franklin. The Texan "wished to be taken to their home if killed or wounded in the battle." Blaine was killed and his servant took him to Spring Hill. Ellen "was one of the three small children of the home." There were, the girl remembered, "no military honors, no minister to conduct a religious service, and no crowd to follow him to his last resting place. Only three small children looked on in awed silence while their father helped the faithful servant lower the body into the grave and fill in the earth." Uncle Nick Blaine, the adjutant's servant, became very upset at the death of his master, and as Blaine's body was lowered into the ground Uncle Nick "shook with sobs and the tears rained down his face."[67]

Along the Franklin-Columbia Turnpike, where the majority of the fighting had taken place, the Confederates dug long trenches and laid their comrades to rest. Private Milton A. Ryan of the 14th Mississippi Infantry remembered that in some places, "the dead were piled upon each other three and four deep." "We dug trenches," wrote Ryan, "two and one half feet deep and wide enough for two to lay side by side. A piece of oil cloth was spread over their faces and covered up. Every one that could be identified, a small piece of plank was placed on their head with their names on it."[68]

Private William Stanton of the 6th & 15th Texas, assigned to such a burial detail, noted that the fighting had laid out many of the bodies in perfect rows as they had fallen on the field, obviously the victims of one massive volley. It also became apparent that the survivors had in many cases stacked the bodies in an effort to provide cover, and some bore the marks of being struck by hundreds of bullets. The detail threw some of the bodies in the ditch just outside the Federal breastworks and buried them by toppling the head logs and dirt on top of them.[69]

On the morning of December 1, Hood ordered his men to move north, up the Franklin-Columbia Pike, directly through the main area of the contest. This had, to say the least, a highly demoralizing effect on the twenty thousand remaining soldiers of the Army of Tennessee. Franklin broke the spirit of the Confederates in the Army of Tennessee. A Mississippian wrote in later years of the horror he experienced: "Franklin was the only battleground I ever saw where the faces of the majority of the dead expressed supreme fear and terror. . . . Their eyes were wide open and fear staring. Their very attitude," he remembered with abhorrence, "as they lay prone upon the ground, with extended, earth clutching fingers, their faces partially buried in the soil, told the tale of mental agony they had endured before death released them." This same Mississippian recalled that afterward the specter of Franklin "stalked among us."[70]

As the survivors of Cleburne's Division regrouped, the going became tough for Granbury's Texans. Captain Foster noted in his diary on December 1, "Our Brigd and the Ark. Brigd are so badly cut up that we can't move. Some officers have no men, and some men have no officers—so we have to reorganize and consolidate, a Captain has to command the Brigade." Many of the Texans harbored bitter feelings against Hood as they moved north toward Nashville. Captain Foster angrily wrote on December 1, "Gen. Hood has betrayed us (The Army of Tenn.). This is not the kind of fighting he promised us at Tuscumbia and Florence Ala. When we started into Tenn. This was not a 'fight with equal numbers and choice of the ground' by no means." Then Foster added bitterly, "The wails and cries of the widows and orphans made at Franklin Tenn Nov 30th 1864 will heat up the fires of the bottomless pit to burn the soul of Gen J.B. Hood for Murdering their husbands and fathers at that place that day."[71] The Battle of Franklin became the death of Cleburne's Division. Lieutenant General William J. Hardee, writing after the war, wrote of Cleburne and his men, "Where this division defended, no odds broke its lines; where it attacked, no numbers resisted its onslaught, save only once—there is the grave of Cleburne and his . . . division."[72]

The Battle of Franklin destroyed the morale of Granbury's Texans. Their leaders and many of their comrades lay dead on the field at Franklin. All of the motivation for the men in the ranks laid out by Larry Daniel in *Soldering in the Army of Tennessee* had disappeared in one day. With their leaders and many comrades gone, the primary motivation left for the Texans was a loyalty to the Confederacy that transcended all else. This clearly backs the thesis of Jason Philips in *Diehard Rebels* that Confederate soldiers never gave up and in essence became unconquered losers. The survivors of Franklin continued to go through the motions, but Granbury's Texas Brigade died on the night of November 30, 1864. Only the postmortem remained.

CHAPTER EIGHTEEN

NASHVILLE

Nashville and beyond began the final phase in the history of Granbury's Brigade. Amazingly, although their leaders had perished at Franklin, and the chances for the Confederacy looked bleaker than ever, an intrepid band of four hundred Texans stayed with the Confederate cause until the bitter end, proving once again their allegiance to the Confederacy, regardless of the odds or the costs.

In the wake of Franklin, Hood had a choice: either he could retreat and end the campaign, or he could follow the Federals to Nashville. Being a fighter and gambler, Hood chose the latter course, ordering an immediate pursuit of Schofield. On the morning of December 3, 1864, the battle-shocked soldiers of Granbury's Texas Brigade began the trek toward Nashville as part of the tail end of the army. That night the Texans took position on the hills south of the city. Captain Foster noted that it became "very clear and cold."[1]

Hood immediately made dispositions to besiege the Federals. He placed Cheatham's Corps on the right, Lee's in the center, and Stewart's to cover the left side of the line. He intended to force the Federals to come out of their entrenchments and attack him. However, the Confederates actually suffered much more from the "siege," with no shelter, scarce firewood, and no shoes in the cold December weather.

Hood's position, as finally established, stretched more than two miles from east to west. Cleburne's old division held the right flank of the army.

The right flank of Cleburne's Division rested on or near the Nolensville Pike as it ran southeast from Nashville. From this point the Confederate line ran southwest to just south of Montgomery Hill, and thence almost due west across the Granny White Pike to the Hillsboro Pike. Along this latter road the Confederates constructed five redoubts four hundred yards apart and numbered (from north to south) 1, 2, 3, 4, and 5. They manned these unconnected, partially constructed earthen fortifications with Stewart's III Corps. The line was too long to be adequately defended by the decimated survivors of Franklin. Also, because the position was concave toward Nashville, it deprived Hood of the advantage of interior lines. These weaknesses made it even more difficult for Hood's infantry to defend their overextended position.

As the cavalry skirmished with the Federals, the infantrymen continued to cope with the material privations and harsh weather as best they could. On December 4, Granbury's Texas Brigade moved toward the Murfreesboro Pike, and later in the day Hood ordered them toward the city, within reach of the Federal artillery. There, according to Captain Foster, the Texans constructed breastworks and "lay behind them all day." On December 5 Foster reported intermittent shelling of the Confederate position.[2] The weather rapidly deteriorated in the Tennessee winter, and soon the conditions became "bitterly cold" and included misting rain that froze as it fell. In this weather, the Texans soon erected "winter quarters," including huts constructed out of corn stalks, as well as shelters in the shape of an "old fashioned chicken-coop," which the men constructed "out of rails," then covered with dirt. Lieutenant Collins noted ruefully that "when the boys would bounce out early in the morning to answer to roll-call, their dens would be steaming like a bed where an old sow and a litter of pigs had roosted over night."[3] Because of a lack of shoes, many of the Texans tied blankets around their feet, but a new type of footwear soon appeared. As Captain Foster reported, "At Brigade Head Quarters there has been established a Shoe Shop, not to make shoes, for there is no leather." Rather, the Confederates would "take an old worn out pair of shoes and sew Moccasins over them of green cow hide with the hair side in. The shoe is put on and kept there, and as the hide dries it draws closer and closer to the old shoe. I am wearing just such foot coverings now," wrote Foster, "and they are about as pleasant to the foot and about as comfortable as any I ever had."[4]

While at Nashville, Hood also received the stragglers and slightly wounded from Franklin as well as those units that had guarded the wagon train during the campaign. This number included Brigadier General James A. Smith, former commander of Granbury's Brigade. As the senior officer present, he assumed command of Cleburne's old division.[5]

On December 9 the weather worsened, and it began sleeting as the Army of Tennessee took stock of its strength. Captain E. T. Broughton of the 7th Texas commanded the survivors of Granbury's Brigade. At this time, the brigade numbered 344 effectives. Captain O. P. Forrest commanded the 7th Texas, Captain R. D. Kennedy the 10th Texas, Captain B. R. Tyus commanded the 6th & 15th Texas, Captain F. L. McKnight took command of the 17th & 18th Texas, and Captain J. F. Matthews commanded the 24th & 25th Texas. Lieutenant W. E. Smith commanded the 5th Confederate, and the 35th Tennessee under Colonel Benjamin J. Hill remained on detached duty.[6] Captain George Williams of Govan's Brigade wrote Captain Irving Buck, Cleburne's former chief of staff, that the Arkansas brigade numbered 431 effectives, whereas "Granbury's is not so large and is commanded by a Captain."[7]

While the Texan infantrymen settled down for their siege, they continued to strengthen their position. On December 13, Smith ordered Granbury's Brigade to the north side of the Nashville & Chattanooga Railroad cut to construct a strong redoubt capable of holding three hundred men, which it promptly completed. The lunette the Texans created included a ditch around the perimeter and palisades of timber. The Texans now found themselves on the extreme right of the Confederate army.[8]

Meanwhile, Ulysses S. Grant had begun pressuring George Thomas, in communications from Washington, to attack Hood and break the siege. Thomas, despite his often-lethargic mood, prepared to strike. On December 15 he made his move. The Federal commander, seeing the weaknesses in Hood's position, ordered his troops to make a strong demonstration against the Confederate right flank while the main body of his army delivered a crushing blow to the vulnerable Confederate left. Accordingly, Thomas arranged for three corps to hit Stewart's men on the left. Meanwhile, he planned to distract Hood from the main assault by sending James Steedman's division to make a demonstration against the Confederate right. At 6 A.M. Steedman's Division moved southeast out of Nashville along the Murfresboro Pike until it reached the Rains house. From here,

Steedman positioned his men so as to advance southwest and take Cheatham's men in right-rear, rolling up their right flank.

At 8 A.M. Colonel Thomas J. Morgan's brigade of Steedman's Division, made up primarily of U.S. Colored Troops, began their advance on the Confederate right flank—the ground held by Cleburne's old division.[9] In his reconnaissance the night before, Colonel Morgan had failed to see the lunette occupied by Granbury's Brigade because of the heavily wooded nature of the hill the Texans occupied. He described it merely as a skirt of logs, and this miscalculation would cost his brigade. The 17th U.S. Colored Troops, commanded by Colonel William Shafter, led off Morgan's column. Shafter had orders to push southwest, through the Confederate skirmishers, and swing back north, thus surrounding the Southerners in their main line of works. After pushing back the skirmishers, Shafter and his men came upon the twenty-foot-deep railroad cut of the Nashville & Chattanooga Railroad. Here the colonel halted his force when suddenly, from atop the wooded hilltop to their right, Granbury's Texans, augmented by a four-gun battery of artillery, raked the front of the Federal regiment. In addition, across the railroad cut, to the southwest, another battery of artillery fired canister into the ranks of the Federals. Shafter's black troops, caught in this crossfire, rapidly fled. Colonel Morgan next rushed the 18th Ohio, under Colonel Charles Grosvenor, against the lunette, but the Texans slaughtered them as they attempted to make their way through the palisade. Grosvenor then attempted to push forward the 2nd Battalion, 14th U.S. Infantry, merely to have this regiment flee after only a few minutes of fighting.[10] Finally, around noon, Morgan withdrew his brigade. The small brigade of Texans suffered a loss of thirty killed and wounded, roughly 10 percent of their strength.[11] These casualties included Captain Edward Broughton, who suffered a wound. Captain James Selkirk of the 6th & 15th Texas succeeded Broughton in the command of the brigade.[12]

As the Federal demonstration on the right fizzled out, Thomas set into motion his crushing blow intended for the Confederate left, the position held by Stewart's III Corps. Redoubts 4, 3, and 5 fell in the face of the Federal advance. The situation looked critical, and Stewart begged Hood for reinforcements to shore up his sagging line. Hood, recognizing that the real Federal push lay on the left, ordered large portions of Lee's Corps as well as Cheatham's Corps, including Granbury's Brigade, to the rescue, but by early evening the Federals had put the left of the Confederate army to flight.

Fortunately for the Army of Tennessee, the fighting ended on December 15 as night closed in, before the Federals could push their advantage.[13]

That night the Texans of Granbury's Brigade, who had not reached the left flank before the Confederate line collapsed, slogged south with the rest of the army and bivouacked for the night near the Lea house on the Granny White Pike, in the rear of the new line. Just as the Texans bedded down for the night, orders arrived from Hood that they should march to the right. With Govan's Brigade in the lead, Cleburne's Division had not even reached its destination before Hood ordered them back to the far left. The hapless Texans spent the night of December 15 marching and countermarching in the freezing cold.[14]

As morning dawned on December 16, Thomas discovered that Hood remained, ready for a fight. Consequently, he decided to launch a strong demonstration against the Confederate right while delivering a hammer blow to the left, as he had done the day before. During the early morning, Steedman renewed his attacks on the Confederate right, this time against men of S. D. Lee's corps. While Steedman attacked the right, Thomas struck with the main body of his infantry at the left of the Confederate line. Because the Federals also experienced limited gains on the right, it looked for a time as if the Southerners would hold.

Elsewhere on the battlefield, Granbury's Brigade under Captain Selkirk spent much of the day marching and countermarching as Hood shifted units to meet new threats. With the coming of dawn on December 16, Granbury's Texans found themselves near the center rear of the Confederate line. Here Selkirk allowed them to rest on their arms for an hour before he awakened them with news that they must rush to the left to aid in the defense in that vicinity; quickly, Selkirk had his band of Texans up and moving. Before reaching their destination Hood ordered Cleburne's men back to the east again, backtracking yet another time. Upon reaching the right, Smith placed the men of Granbury's and Lowrey's old brigades in the Confederate battle line. Along with James Holtzclaw's Alabama brigade, they fought off attacks from Colonel Sidney Post's Federal brigade as well as some of the U.S. Colored Troops of Steedman's Division. These troops were some of the same men the Texans had fought the day before from their redoubt, and again they Federals suffered the same fate. The Union troops launched a determined attack against Granbury's Brigade, only to have the Texans mow them down. During this assault alone the 13th U.S.

Colored Troops suffered 220 casualties, nearly 40 percent of its strength, as the Texans and Alabamans soundly beat back the assault. At 2 P.M. Cleburne's Division reversed for the last time and marched back toward the vicinity of Compton's Hill.[15]

As Cleburne's men hurried toward the left, disaster struck the Confederates atop Compton's Hill. During one of the determined assaults against the Confederates on the hill, John McArthur's Federal division struck the Achilles heel of the Confederate position, the line of Smith's Tennessee brigade. Because of the poorly placed, inadequate breastworks, the Federals breached the center of Bate's thinly stretched division on the critical hill and the thin gray line completely collapsed.[16] Because of the prominence of Compton's Hill, the entire Army of Tennessee could see the disaster that had befallen their comrades, and panic spread like wildfire among the veteran troops. The men of Granbury's Brigade, marching to the rescue, soon realized the severity of the situation. Captain Selkirk nudged Lieutenant Collins, the acting assistant adjutant of the brigade, and admonished him to look to the right, saying, "we are whipped." Collins looked to his right, "up on the mountain field, and sure enough the Confederates were running like wild cattle, throwing everything away" that might slow them down. "About this time," recalled the lieutenant, "the enemy run a battery upon the pike and sent a shell about every two seconds down just to the left of our line, screaming like the damned in purgatory, plowing up the earth and spattering us with mud." Upon seeing this, the frightened Texans quickly joined the exodus of the Confederate army fleeing south.[17]

By 3:30 P.M. on December 16, 1864, the Army of Tennessee degenerated into chaos and panic, one of the few instances during the war in which a major Confederate army was completely routed and driven from the field. By the evening of December 17 the routed army reached Franklin, and all the wounded fit to travel joined the exodus for fear of capture. They left those unable to travel to the mercy of the Federals.

Granbury's Brigade recrossed the Tennessee River on December 26. As they marched over the pontoons, the Texans sang an altered version of a verse of the "Yellow Rose of Texas" that went like this:

> So now I'm marching southward;
> My heart is full of woe
> I'm going back to Georgia to find my Uncle Joe.

You may talk about your Beauregard
And sing of General Lee,
But the gallant Hood of Texas
Played Hell in Tennessee.[18]

After recrossing the river, Hood ordered his army to move toward Corinth, Mississippi. At Tuscumbia, Alabama, Granbury's Texans were detached as the provost guard, and after so much privation, according to William Stanton of the 6th Texas, the men, "feasted on fresh pork; washing it down with a gill of liquor." The men of Granbury's Brigade also took to looting and pillaging in the northern Alabaman countryside. Just before New Year's Day, the Texans marched to Iuka, Mississippi, many of them making this last march without any shoes.[19] By January 1, 1865, the remnants of the Army of Tennessee had reached Corinth, and the weather remained very cold. The Tennessee campaign had come to an end.

The Battle of Nashville finished what Franklin had started. Finally, the morale and dedication of the Texans began to fail at the bitter end of the war. Their dedication to the Confederate cause never wavered, although the idea of continuing to fight a now clearly losing war lost its appeal after Nashville. Despite these circumstances, and although they behaved badly in the last days of the war, the Texans stayed in the ranks until the final surrender. Those who slogged out the final months of the war proved to be some of the most dedicated of all.

CHAPTER NINETEEN

THE END OF THE WAR

The main thing that kept the Texans in the ranks in the last days of the conflict was their loyalty to the Confederacy. With their leaders dead, a deep emotional attachment to the cause they had fought so long to defend kept them going and kept their spirits up. Not until the actual surrender of the Army of Tennessee in April 1865 did these remaining Texans give up on the idea of an independent Confederacy. The last days of the war demonstrated not only the deep dedication to the Confederate cause as a prime motivating factor for Granbury's Texans, but also the primacy of a localized perspective when explaining the motivation of western Confederates.

The year 1865 dawned bleakly for the remnants of Granbury's Brigade. On New Year's morning the Texans awoke in their encampment three miles from Corinth, Mississippi, marched through the town, and went into camp two miles farther on. Here, the Texans viewed the discouraging evidence of the last several years of war. Captain Foster wrote in his diary of the old, abandoned forts and trenches stretching in every direction, and as he explored he noticed "the great many graves here . . . nearly all have a plain headboard with the name Co. Regiment &c. . . . This is one part of the war we have never seen before. The dead part. The graveyard."[1]

Despite these demoralizing sights, not all of the Texans had their spirits as completely crushed as Captain Foster. On January 17, William Stanton of the 6th Texas wrote his cousin Mary Moody in Victoria of the events that had transpired during the battles of Franklin and Nashville. He recorded, "It is given up that Texas has the best troops in the field, but a set of Rascalls. Our brigade is counted as the bigest set of theaves in the army." In this short statement Stanton revealed the frustrations felt by the Texans after the Tennessee campaign—frustrations they proceeded to take out on the local citizenry wherever they happened to be.[2]

On January 13, Hood requested that Davis remove him from command of the Army of Tennessee, and Davis readily complied. In his place, Davis instructed P. G. T. Beauregard, now commanding the Western Division of the Confederacy, to assign General Richard Taylor. The plans for the shattered Army of Tennessee then changed as Sherman began moving his Federal legions from Savannah, Georgia, into South Carolina on February 1. With this movement, Davis instructed Taylor to send the Army of Tennessee to aid General Joseph E. Johnston in stopping Sherman in the Carolinas.

On January 20, the Texas Brigade started out for Tupelo, Mississippi, the first leg of a journey to the Carolinas. Most of the Texans rode the railroad, while those with horses covered the distance in the saddle. Along the way Lieutenant Collins developed a severe infection, probably gangrenous, that almost cost him a limb, but after a brief respite at the house of a local farmer and his wife, he recovered enough to rejoin the brigade, which he found camped a mile west of Tupelo. Here, Collins began taking over the duties of brigade adjutant. At Tupelo, the weary Confederates approached their new commander, Dick Taylor, and asked him to grant them furloughs. Taylor acquiesced, and every fifth man received a furlough, never to return to the army.[3]

Collins reported that, like Corinth, Tupelo showed signs of the war. "Great farms gone to ruin," he wrote, "and fine mansions . . . were now the abode of owls, bats and hobgoblins." On January 26, the remnants of the Army of Tennessee boarded box and flat cars on their way to North Carolina. On the night of January 28 the brigade reached Mobile, Alabama.[4]

From Mobile, the Texans moved up the Tensas River to Tensas Landing, and then on to Montgomery via railroad cars, where they proceeded to take out their frustrations on the local population. Lieutenant Collins recalled that the reverses in battles and frustrations over the war put the Texans in an ugly mood and that Mobile was spared from their ravages only because they arrived there at night and boarded vessels early the next morning. Montgomery did not fare so well. The brigade arrived in the cradle of the

Confederacy just at dusk, and despite the fact that their officers had put an armed guard around the camp, after dinner many enterprising Texans slipped by the guards, intent on raising hell.[5]

Upon reaching town, the Texans and some Arkansas troops attacked the provost marshals and city police before turning their attention to a dance hall called "the Light House" in the middle of the city. Even though the Texans and Arkansans took over "management" of the place, everything went well until 10 P.M., when some of the troops discovered a grocery store across the street run by a "Dutch" proprietor. In an effort to stave off disaster, the store owner gave the Texans some whiskey—and all hell broke loose. The Texans next proceeded to "clerk" for the grocery store owner and then took over running the store, and commanded the store owner to go home to his wife and children, which he did without argument. The Texans rolled a barrel of whiskey from the store out into a defile behind the building, knocked the top off, and proceeded to indulge themselves. Private Lee Kinman of the 15th Texas approached Lieutenant Collins on the dance floor, blew his breath in Collins's face, and then led the lieutenant to the back of the store. When Collins reached the spot, he reported that "the boys were drinking out of the barrel like horses or thirsty chickens around a pan of water on a hot summer day." The Texans then went on a rampage. Some made it back to camp that night, some not until the next morning for roll call. "Some had one eye in a sling and some had two. Some didn't have as many ears nor as much hair as they took to town with them. The floor of that dance hall was a sight to look at."[6] Private William Stanton of the 6th Texas wrote his cousin Mary Moody, "Our Brig. behaved shamefully all the way around from Tupelo Miss to Raleigh, N.C. The boys had not been paid off in ten months they would not issue Tobacco and that made the Boys angry they would break open stores, get the Tobacco and Lichors. . . . I never seen men go do as our Brigade done after Maj Genl Cleburne and Granbury got killed there was not an officer who could do any thing with them."[7]

Early the next morning the Texans' commanders placed them aboard boxcars bound for Columbus, Georgia. Having gotten wind of what had happened in Montgomery, the citizens of Columbus turned out with tables of sumptuous food and banners, greeting the Confederates with messages like "Welcome, Army of Tennessee," "Welcome Heroes of Chickamauga." The soldiers proceeded to stuff themselves with the food, then took their rifles and went into town, where they ravaged the "gambling houses and saloons." They departed the next morning aboard trains, bound for Fort Valley, Georgia. Again at Fort Valley the citizenry turned out to welcome them. This time, instead of ravaging the town, the men merely behaved rudely in consuming the food. The brigade then passed through Macon, and according to Lieutenant Collins the Texans "had it in" for the city, but the train sped by rather than stopping.

The next stop along the way was Milledgeville, the Georgia state capital, where the Texans disembarked from the train a mile from town and began foraging for wood and food of any kind. It was at Milledgeville that the Texans encountered the results of Sherman's March to the Sea, and the desolation made a deep impression on the troops. Early in March, the Texans reached Augusta, Georgia, and crossed over the Savannah River into South Carolina, where they camped for the night. At Augusta, one Texan paid $75 for a cup of sweet milk and a little cornbread. That night, some of the brigade stayed in town to make trouble, but most of the troops behaved themselves on the South Carolina side of the river. The day after crossing the Savannah, the Texans marched to Chester, South Carolina, where they camped and continued to forage as best they could.[8]

With Sherman's forces moving through North Carolina, Joseph Johnston determined to try to stop the Federal advance. While most of the Army of Tennessee, including the Texas Brigade, moved north to reinforce him, Johnston decided to counterattack the left wing of Sherman's forces along the road to Goldsboro near the town of Bentonville, North Carolina. Johnston set a trap on March 19, and the Confederate cavalry served as a decoy, engaging the Federals along the road and then falling back through the ranks of the infantrymen. The Union troops marched into the trap, and Johnston launched his counterattack, initially driving back the Federal columns, but reinforcements soon arrived, driving back the Confederates. Johnston then withdrew his men into a defensive position to await developments.[9]

On the morning of March 20, Granbury's Texans debarked from their trains at Smithfield and immediately heard the booming of artillery to the south. Johnston detached the Texans from Cleburne's Division and moved them into position on the Confederate left, along with Cumming's Georgia brigade. Johnston placed Cumming's Brigade in reserve and moved the Texans back and forth to shore up weak points in the line. While Granbury's men remained on the line, some of the Texans went out to investigate the battlefield, and in particular the Federal dead, whose knapsacks still contained the contents they had plundered in Georgia and South Carolina.[10] Finally, on March 21, Sherman reached the battlefield with the rest of his men. Badly outnumbered, Johnston withdrew to the vicinity of Smithfield. Sherman advanced to Goldsboro. The last Confederate attempt to defeat Sherman had failed.

As Johnston waited in North Carolina, the Confederacy disintegrated. On April 2, Grant forced Lee to abandon Petersburg, and the Army of Northern Virginia began retreating west toward Appomattox Court House. At the same time President Davis and the rest of the Confederate government abandoned Richmond and fled southward.

On April 9, the day Lee surrendered to Grant at Appomattox, Johnston undertook a reorganization of the Army of Tennessee. Johnston consolidated the remnants of Granbury's Brigade into a single regiment, the 1st Texas Consolidated, under Lieutenant Colonel William A. Ryan, originally of the 18th Texas, the highest ranking officer left with the brigade. Major James A. Formwalt of the 10th Texas and Adjutant John A. Willingham of the 10th Texas served as the regimental field and staff. Ryan formed the old 6th Texas into Company A under Junior Second Lieutenant Mark A. Kelton. He formed the old 7th Texas into Company B under First Lieutenant James D. Miles and the old 15th Texas into Companies C and F under First Lieutenant James L. McCracken and Second Lieutenant Robert M. Collins. Ryan made the 10th Texas into Companies D and E under Captains Reuben D. Kennedy and John R. Kennard. He formed the old 17th Texas into Company G under Captain Louis Little and the original 18th Texas into Company H under Third Corporal Jesse Graham. The old 24th Texas comprised Company I under Captain Samuel T. Foster, and finally Third Lieutenant James Rotan commanded the old 25th Texas as Company K.[11] Johnston placed the 1st Texas Consolidated in Daniel Govan's brigade along with the 1st Arkansas (formerly the 19th & 24th Arkansas Infantry Regiment) and placed Govan's Brigade in Cleburne's Division, now under Major General John Brown.

In the first week of April some of the Texans sat down to write their loved ones of their circumstances and how to take care of business in their absence. William H. Henderson of the 7th Texas wrote to his parents, "It is thought this army is going to So. Ca. . . . I have a good Yankee overcoat wearing it, it was captured at Franklin. I gave a good blanket for it about two thirds of this army came out of Tenn without shoes I was barefooted myself. we drew shoes at Corinth Miss. . . . if I should be so unfortunate as to get killed or die in the army before the war is over, I want the negroes equally divided . . . I want them hired out to good men who will take good care of them, keep as many of them at home as you want."[12]

As what was left of Granbury's Brigade remained encamped around Smithfield, wild rumors and some facts circulated through the ranks. On April 10, Captain Foster remarked in his diary that the news had reached the Army of Tennessee that Lee had surrendered, and that it demoralized the Confederates a great deal. But he wrote, "I do hope and I believe that we will whip this fight yet." That same day, Johnston put the Army of Tennessee in motion toward Raleigh. Three days later Cleburne's old division marched from Raleigh to Chapel Hill and encamped near Salem. On April 16, rumors began circulating that Johnston had surrendered to Sherman, and the Texans remained very disheartened. On April 17 and 18 the Confederate commissary issued clothes to Granbury's Texans, and on the eighteenth Captain Foster wrote, "Had Battalion drill today just to see if the men would drill." Late that evening an order reached the Texans announcing that Johnston and Sherman had signed an armistice, but not a surrender, and this seemed to satisfy the veterans. On April 19 the Texans moved about a half mile, and word reached them that Lincoln had been assassinated and that Seward had been shot at the same time. "It is also reported," wrote Captain Foster, "that the United States has recognized the Confederacy and agrees to give us all our rights (and slavery) if we will help them fight all their enemies whatsoever." Soon after the Texans reached their camp on April 19 some Confederates discovered two barrels of apple brandy buried at the base of an old tree. The Texans received one of the barrels in their camp and immediately tapped it. While Foster reported that some of the men got "funny drunk" or "gentlemanly drunk," according to him all of the officers got "dog drunk." But he also wrote that no one got angry, and all remained in a good humor.[13]

On Sunday, April 23, Cleburne's old command marched ten miles or so west before encamping near Greensboro. The next day another wild rumor began circulating that a war was about to commence with the Confederacy, France, Austria, and Mexico on one side and England, Russia, and the United States on the other. In this case, Captain Foster reported the rumor that the Confederates would then take an oath of allegiance to France and fight under the French flag. Rumors like these kept up for the next three days.[14]

On April 26, word reached the Texans that hostilities would resume with the Federals if Johnston did not surrender within two days. That same day, word filtered down that Johnston had officially surrendered to Sherman, effective April 28. The night of April 27, Foster wrote in his diary that all the men stayed up talking about the situation despondently, and "if crying would have done any good, we could have cried all night." On the twenty-eighth, all of the Texans marched up, signed a document, received their paroles, and were issued one dollar in silver.[15] Later that day, the officers of the Texas Brigade sent a short but heart-filled message to General Johnston that stated, in part, "We . . . respectfully desire to assure Gen. Johnston of our undiminished confidence and esteem and fully sympathizing with him in the present unfortunate issue of our affairs, do most cordially tender him the hospitality of our State and our homes (such as the future may provide for us)." The Texans then requested that Johnston visit them before leaving. Eighteen officers signed the note. It is unclear whether Johnston ever visited Granbury's command.[16]

The muster rolls at the surrender revealed just how small Granbury's Brigade had become. Company A of the 1st Texas Consolidated, the old 6th Texas, surrendered with sixty-two members, the 7th Texas paroled forty-nine men, while the 10th Texas surrendered the most with seventy-six. The 15th Texas ended the war with only forty-four soldiers. The 17th Texas surrendered with thirty-seven men, and the 18th Texas paroled forty-eight. The 24th Texas surrendered with fifty-one men, and finally the 25th Texas retained the least number of any regiment in the brigade with only thirty-four, making a total of 401 Texans who surrendered—out of roughly 9,800 who were carried on the muster rolls of these regiments.[17]

By groups of two, three, and five, the Texans of Granbury's Brigade began making their way home from North Carolina. Lieutenant Collins traveled with various groups, going via New Orleans and finally Galveston. From Millican he took a buggy north to Decatur, where he arrived on June 25, 1865, after three years, three months, and twenty-five days away. Other members of the brigade made their way home from hospitals all over the South. Joseph McClure of Company A, 18th Texas, was wounded by several bullets in the fighting east of Atlanta on July 21, 1864. After he convalesced at Griffin hospital for a month, he was granted crutches and a sixty-day furlough. A kind woman named Mrs. John Garrick took McClure in and nursed him back to health from August 1864 until July 1865. On July 15 McClure started out for Texas on crutches, and after an arduous journey he arrived home in Alvarado, Johnson County, on August 15, 1865. After his capture at the Battle of Franklin, Charles Leuschner of the 6th Texas spent time in New Orleans and then Alexandria, Louisiana, until his release on May 26, 1865. From Alexandria, Leuschner made his way home to Victoria, arriving on June 16, 1865. At 9 A.M. on May 3, Captain Foster also began making his way home from Greensboro. Despite his earlier sadness at surrender, after turning in his weapons and signing his parole, he wrote that he felt relieved at the prospect of going home for the first time in four years. After traveling through Nashville, New Orleans, and Galveston, Foster reached his home at Hallettsville on June 16, 1865. As he contemplated the end of the war, Foster summed up the feelings of many former Confederates when he wrote, "Who is to blame for all this waste of human life? It is too bad to talk about. And what does it amount to? Has there been anything gained by all this sacrifice? What were we fighting for, the principles of slavery? And now the slaves are all freed and the Confederacy has to be dissolved. We have to go back into the Union."[18]

AFTERWORD

REMINISCENCES, REUNIONS, AND
THE LOST CAUSE

After the end of the war, the Texans of Granbury's Brigade returned home and tried to begin their lives again as best they could, but they never gave up on the ideals of the Confederacy. In 1871 survivors of the brigade began to gather annually to reminisce about the war, and to glory in their history as Confederate soldiers. In these gatherings and in their speeches, writings, and actions, Granbury's Texans fully embraced and pushed forward the Lost Cause myths of Civil War history.[1]

The myth of the Lost Cause contains several elements, all of which the Texans embraced after the end of the war. The first is the idea that slavery formed no part of the reason for Confederate secession or the motivations of Confederates in fighting the war. Despite the candid statement of Samuel Foster at the end of the war, and despite the declarations of many of the Texans at the beginning of the war that they wanted to fight to prevent Yankees from disturbing their "way of life," the postwar speeches they listened to and made themselves specifically repudiated slavery as a cause of the hostilities. In 1892 at a reunion of the United Confederate Veterans held at Weatherford, Texas, that included Granbury's Brigade, Congressman (later governor of Texas) S. W. T. Lanham, himself a Confederate veteran from South Carolina, addressed the gathering with the declaration: "So the non-slaveholding men of the South left their families at home to be protected by God. . . . they went and fought as ne'er men did before. It was the grand consummation of the purest patriotism. They had no slaves and fought only for principle." He went on to say that the "future of the United States lay in the hands of ex-Confederates" and that "the Anglo-Saxon of the South will control it and have charge of its affairs." In a particularly patronizing statement, Lanham concluded: "As to the black man I would say his freedom is absolutely assured, and the best friends you have are the people you lived with in the South." But, he continued, "it is the duty of the Confederate to repel every assault made upon our motive in fighting."[2]

Other claims of the Lost Cause myth include the idea that abolitionists came south, serving as provocateurs to stir up the "happy" slaves of the South, and that the Confederacy was not defeated but simply ran out of time. Recalling his life, Khleber M. Van Zandt, major of the 7th Texas, wrote about abolitionists: "Agitators from the North came to our part of the country and began doing all they could to incite the Negro slaves to rebellion." The Texans, in their reunions, also constantly stated that they had not lost the war outright, but, "seeing the inevitable," had simply returned home at the end of the war. A final element of the Lost Cause myth is the near canonization of Confederate leaders such as Robert E. Lee and, in the case of Granbury's Texans, Granbury and Cleburne. In addition to references to Robert E. Lee at their reunions, in 1866 survivors of Granbury's Brigade founded the towns of Granbury, Texas, in Hood County, and in 1867 Cleburne, Texas, in Johnson County, to honor their leaders.[3]

Although many former members of Granbury's Brigade played prominent roles in Texas in the postwar period, perhaps the two most prominent were Roger Q. Mills, colonel of the 10th Texas Infantry, and Khleber M. Van Zandt of the 7th Texas. Mills won election to Congress in 1872, spoke out against Reconstruction, fought against tariffs, and later fought prohibition as well. He became chairman of the House Ways and Means Committee and in 1891 narrowly lost an election for Speaker of the House. The other Democrats in the Texas legislature elected Mills to the U.S. Senate in 1892 and again in 1893. Oil wells on Mills's property in Corsicana, Texas, afforded him a comfortable retirement from the Senate in March 1899.[4]

Khleber Van Zandt moved to the area that is now Fort Worth in August 1865. Van Zandt ran a dry goods business and later built the Tarrant County

Construction Company, which laid down the railroad bed between Dallas and Fort Worth. In 1874 Van Zandt began to build up the Fort Worth National Bank, and served as its president for fifty-six years. Van Zandt also presided over the K. M. Van Zandt Land Company, the Fort Worth Life Insurance Company, the Fort Worth & Denver Railway, and the Fort Worth Street Railway Company. He helped to bring other railroads to Fort Worth, making it a transportation hub, served on the Fort Worth school board for twenty years, won election to the legislature in 1873–1874, and served as the president of the board of directors of the First Christian Church of Fort Worth from 1877 until his death in 1930.[5]

In 1893 the members of the Granbury Camp, United Confederate Veterans, appointed Dr. J. N. Doyle to travel to Tennessee to bring the remains of Hiram Granbury to the town of Granbury. Doyle reported that Granbury's uniform and the army blanket in which his men had buried him remained in a good state of preservation. The doctor escorted the body to Fort Worth, where Khleber Van Zandt agreed to store the casket in a bank vault until November 30, the twenty-ninth anniversary of the Battle of Franklin. On that day Granbury's remains traveled by rail to Granbury, his casket draped in a First National Confederate flag with the battle honors "Chickamauga, Ringgold Gap, Missionary Ridge, Dug Gap, Resaca" on one side and "New Hope Church, Kennesaw Mountain, Peach Tree Creek, Atlanta and Franklin" on the other. A huge procession accompanied Granbury to his final resting place in Granbury Cemetery, just off the town square. Major James A. Formwalt of the 10th Texas led the procession with Granbury's only remaining sibling, Nautie Granberry Moss. John Y. Rankin, John A. Willingham, William L. Moody, Khleber Van Zandt, and Albert McKinney were among the score of dignitaries present at the funeral procession. Granbury's funeral also became a forum for expressing Lost Cause sentiments. A poem read at the funeral included these lines:

> A monument of stone,
> shall mark our gallant Granbury's grave.
> For southern rights and honor's crown,
> He laid his grand life bravely down.
> Granbury and Pat Cleburne their names are immortal!
> The "Old South" still lives their memory to bless. . . .
> Brave spirits, though the cause you espoused was lost. . . .

In death you have conquered a host,
Won a victory heaven alone could confer.[6]

The veterans of Granbury's Brigade joined with the survivors of Ector's and Ross's Texas brigades to form the First Texas Division, United Confederate Veterans, and continued to hold reunions from 1871 until at least 1917. According to the sketchy records that exist, no members of the 6th Texas or 24th Texas ever attended any of the reunions, at least between 1885 and 1917. Of the recorded sixty-seven veterans who attended at one time or another, twenty-eight (41 percent) belonged to the 7th Texas, by far the largest contingent. It appears that Roger Q. Mills first helped to organize the reunions but rarely attended thereafter, probably due to the fact that he served in Congress during that time. Other presidents of the association included Captain Bryan Marsh of the 17th Texas (1885), Adjutant John A. Willingham of the 10th Texas (1892), Lieutenant Robert M. Collins of the 15th Texas (1893), Third Sergeant J. H. Mathias of the 18th Texas (1901, 1909), Lieutenant O. P. Bowser of the 18th Texas (1908), and Private W. H. Pearson of the 7th Texas (1906, 1907). Interestingly enough, thirty-three of the sixty-seven reunion participants (49 percent) were officers during the war, twenty noncommissioned and thirteen commissioned. In addition, only four of the sixty-seven men were not present with the brigade in 1864, and forty of them were wounded or captured at Atlanta or Franklin or surrendered at Greensboro in 1865. Clearly, the men celebrating the history of the brigade were the most committed of the diehard Confederates who survived the war.

Although the reunions often made overtures of loyalty to the United States, the lasting refrain of the "unreconstructed" Confederate continued to permeate the meetings, as evidenced by the poem "The Little Rebel," read by Miss Mary Guion Finney at a brigade reunion in 1916:

Oh, I'm a good old rebel,
Now that's just what I am,
For this "Fair Land of Freedom"
I do not care a damn.
I'm glad a fit agin it,
And I don't ask no pardon
For anything I done. . . .
I hates the "Freedman's Buro,"

In uniforms of blue;
I hates the nasty eagle,
With all his brags and fuss;
The lyin,' theivin' Yankees,
I hates them wuss and wuss.
I hates the Constitution,
I hates the Yankee Nation
And everything they do,
I hates the Declaration
Of Independence too. . . .
I can't take up my musket and fight 'em now any mo'.
But I ain't goin' to love 'em,
Now that is certain shore;
And I don't ask no pardon, fer what I was, I AM,
I won't be reconstructed,
and I don't care a damn.[7]

Granbury's Texas Brigade contributed immeasurably to the Confederate war effort in the West, and serves as a microcosm of the experience of the common Confederate soldier in that theater of war. Granbury's Texans stayed with the Confederate cause as long as they did due to a mixture of circumstances—some that were common to Confederate soldiers in the war, and some that remained unique to western Confederates. They stayed with the southern cause because of their devotion to the Confederacy and, just as important, because of their localized perspectives and the outstanding brigade, regimental, and division leaders who inspired them. From the perspective of Granbury's Brigade, it becomes clear that the efforts of the Confederate soldiers prolonged the Civil War far beyond the point where the Confederacy would have otherwise collapsed. It is also clear that these Texans did not lose heart (perhaps until after Franklin), and almost never questioned the righteousness of their cause or the idea that God remained on their side. They also never gave up on the ideals of the Confederacy, in essence becoming, as Jason Phillips in *Diehard Rebels: The Confederate Culture of Invincibility* put it, "unconquered losers." The tears of Captain Foster and other signs of frustration and despair at the surrender in 1865 bear ample witness to this fact.[8]

There is no evidence, in Granbury's Brigade, of a loss of faith, political dissent, class consciousness, or guilt over slavery playing any role whatsoever in the thought processes of these Confederates. This refutes the thesis of authors such as Richard Beringer et al. in *Why the South Lost the Civil War*. The arguments put forward in works like this appear to be an outgrowth of a presentist approach to history that obscures the thinking of the Confederates themselves at the time of the war. Likewise, desertion is often misunderstood in the context of Confederate history. Authors such as Mark Weitz in his study *More Damning Than Slaughter* point toward desertion as the primary reason the Confederacy failed from a military standpoint. What becomes readily apparent in a history of Granbury's Brigade is that desertion was not an absolute concept. Deserting one's original regiment typically indicated an urgent desire to fight closer to home. These men, such as the "deserters" from Arkansas Post, left to fight closer to home, but did not damage the Confederate cause through their absence. This does not mean, of course, that no deserters from Granbury's Brigade simply took themselves out of the war, but a majority did not.[9]

Instead, Granbury's Texans seem to fit the ideas laid out by Gary Gallagher and others regarding the Confederate soldier. Gallagher in *The Confederate War* puts forward the thesis that Confederates never really gave up on the war effort, and did not suffer from the internal schisms indicated by previous studies. Jason Phillips, as already mentioned, also indicates that the Confederates never gave up on their cause. A history of Granbury's Brigade bears these ideas out. It is apparent that even those who deserted their original units did not give up on the Confederate cause, and the majority who stayed in the ranks certainly did not. The question historians should focus on is, Why did the Confederacy last as long as it did? A study of Granbury's Brigade, as a microcosm of the war effort, certainly indicates that a loyalty to the Confederacy motivated Granbury's Texans.[10]

The other elements that galvanized Granbury's men remained largely unique to western Confederates, as indicated by Larry Daniel in his *Soldiering in the Army of Tennessee: A Portrait of Life in a Confederate Army*. These elements were their localized perspectives and effective brigade, division, and regimental leadership. Deprived of large battlefield victories and without inspiring army-level leadership such as Robert E. Lee, western Confederates looked to their lower-echelon commanders for inspiration, as Granbury's Texans did with Hiram Granbury and Patrick Cleburne. Furthermore, they developed localized perspectives. They did not focus on losses like Chattanooga and Vicksburg as the harbingers of defeat, as historians do, but rather on smaller victories like Pickett's Mill and Ringgold Gap that could win the war, or at least keep it going. This is demonstrated in the letters of Granbury's men. They spoke darkly of the defeats at Vicksburg, Gettysburg, and Chattanooga, but spoke more often of the battlefield victories they themselves had won. These two elements, leadership and a localized perspective, made the Army of Tennessee and Granbury's Brigade particularly effective fighting forces.[11]

In all four phases of the history of Granbury's Brigade, these Texans demonstrated a loyalty to the Confederacy and a faith in their line officers that refute the arguments of historians who claim the Confederacy collapsed from within. In the first phase the Texans joined up enthusiastically for field service and endured waves of disease, dismounting, and surrender while still demonstrating allegiance to the Confederacy and their regiments. Even though the dismounting and surrenders at Arkansas Post and Fort Donelson damaged their morale, it was not enough to stop the vast majority of the Texans from staying with their original regiments. Those who deserted most often did so to fight closer to home. Very few Texans abandoned the Confederate cause altogether. This first phase also made Granbury's Texans unique in their shared history of prison, which gave them a desire to prove themselves and began molding them into the hardest-fighting western Confederate brigade. In the second phase, the Texans demonstrated their fighting prowess from Raymond to Chickamauga, indicating that despite high battlefield casualties they would stay with the cause. In the third phase, from November 1863 to November 1864, Granbury's Brigade came together as a unit and became the hardest-fighting brigade in the hardest-fighting division in the Confederate Army of Tennessee. Finally, in the fourth phase, the Texans continued to exhibit a loyalty to the Confederacy that did not die with the surrender, but continued into the postwar years as Granbury's men strove to uphold the Lost Cause myths of Civil War history. These trends of behavior combined to earn Granbury's Texans the sobriquet of Diehard Western Confederates.

APPENDIX 1

THE DEMOGRAPHICS OF GRANBURY'S BRIGADE

SOCIOECONOMIC PROFILE OF GRANBURY'S BRIGADE

Company	Age (Median/Mean)	Married	% Reporting Personal Assets/Amount (Mean)	County(ies)	Majority Occupation	Slave Owners	Upper South/Lower South
Co. G, 6th Texas Infantry	21/18	6%	6%/$5,262	Travis	Farmer (68%)	4.4%	53%/22%
Co. A, 7th Texas Infantry	21/22	17%	17%/$3,156	McLennan	Farmer (64%)	7.5%	31%/39%
Co. H, 10th Texas Infantry	22/25	33%	50%/$1,600	Bosque, Coryell	Farmer (75%)	5.1%	35%/55%
Co. G, 15th Texas Cavalry	24/26	38%	50%/$2,600	Collin, Denton	Farmer (64%)	8.3%	38%/10%
Co. A, 17th Texas Cavalry	27/28	55%	72%/$5,234	Nacogdoches	Farmer (62%)	12.8%	35%/52%
Co. K, 18th Texas Cavalry	25/26	55%	64%/$2,506	Henderson, Anderson	Farmer (76%)	7.8%	31%/58%
Co. I, 24th Texas Cavalry	25/27	45%	55%/$6,531	Fayette, Karnes	Farmer (62%)	9.4%	34%/49%
Co. G, 25th Texas Cavalry	27/28	70%	75%/$1,256	Liberty, Tyler	Farmer (82%)	5%	23%/73%
Average:	25.5/25	38%	49%/$3,518		Farmer (69.1%)	7.5%	35%/45%

SOCIOECONOMIC PROFILE OF OTHER SIMILAR GROUPS

Group	Age (Mean)	Amount of Wealth (Mean)	Majority Occupation	Upper South/ Lower South
Texas Heads of Household (1860)[1]	NA	$6,393	Farmers (69.7%)	39%/45%
Confederate Soldiers[2]	NA	NA	Farmers (61.5%)	NA
The 13th Texas Cavalry[3]	27.4	NA	NA	NA
Walker's Texas Division[4]	26.9	$3,484	Farmers (78.1%)	NA
The 3rd Texas Cavalry[5]	NA	$12,812	NA	NA
The 28th Texas Cavalry[6]	26.3	$4,532	Farmers (75.3%)	29.7%/68.4%
Granbury's Brigade	25	$3,518	Farmers (69.1%)	35%/45%

1. Richard Lowe, *Walker's Texas Division, C.S.A.: Greyhounds of the Trans-Mississippi* (Baton Rouge: Louisiana State Univ. Press, 19–23).

2. James McPherson, *Battle Cry of Freedom: The Civil War Era* (Oxford: Oxford Univ. Press, 1988), 614.

3. Thomas Reid, *Spartan Band: Burnett's 13th Texas Cavalry in the Civil War* (Denton, Tex.: Univ. of North Texas Press, 2005), 29.

4. Lowe, *Walker's Texas Division*, 19–23.

5. Douglas Hale, *The Third Texas Cavalry in the Civil War* (Norman: Univ. of Oklahoma Press, 1993), 40.

6. M. Jane Johannson, *Peculiar Honor: A History of the 28th Texas Cavalry, 1862–1865* (Fayetteville: Univ. of Arkansas Press, 1998), 12–23.

APPENDIX 2

THE REGIMENTS OF GRANBURY'S BRIGADE

THE 6TH TEXAS INFANTRY

Company	Commander	County(ies)	Nickname
A	Capt. Alexander Hamilton Phillips Jr.	Calhoun	Lavaca Guards
B	Capt. James Rupley	Victoria	Lone Star Rifles
C	Capt. Alonzo Bass	Gonzales	
D	Capt. A. E. Pearson	Matagorda	Matagorda Coast Guards
E	Capt. John P. White	Guadalupe	
F	Capt. Henry Bradford	Bell	Bell County Invincibles
G	Capt. Rhoads Fisher	Travis	Travis Rifles
H	Capt. George P. Finley	Calhoun, Lavaca	
I	Capt. C. P. Nanuheim	Dewitt	
K	Capt. Samuel McCallister	Bexar	Alamo Rifles

THE 7TH TEXAS INFANTRY

Company	Commander	County	Nickname
A	Capt. Hiram Granbury	McLennan	Waco Guards
B	Capt. R. S. Camp	Upshur	
C	Capt. Edward T. Broughton	Kaufman	
D	Capt. Khleber Van Zandt	Harrison	Bass Greys
E	Capt. Jack Davis	Cherokee	
F	Capt. William H. Smith	Smith	Lone Star Rebels
G	Capt. William L. Moody	Freestone	Freestone Freemen
H	Capt. William B. Hill	Harrison	Texas Invincibles
I	Capt. John W. Brown	Rusk	Sabine Greys

THE 10TH TEXAS INFANTRY

Company	Commander	County(ies)	Nickname
A	Capt. John A. Kennard	Grimes	Grimes Boys
B	Capt. David Pendergast	Limestone	
C	Capt. William Shannon	Johnson	Rock Creek Guards
D	Capt. William Wilson	Freestone	
E	Capt. William McKamy	Parker	
F	Capt. Semore Brasher	Brazos	
G	Capt. John Lauderdale	Galveston, Washington	Labadie Rifles
H	Capt. Bruce Hartgraves	Coryell	
I	Capt. James Formwalt	Johnson	Stockton Cavalry
K	Capt. Byron Bassell	Bosque, Coryell	

THE 15TH TEXAS CAVALRY

Company	Commander	County(ies)	Nickname
A	Capt. William Bishop	Dallas, Bexar	
B	Capt. George Pickett	Wise	Wise Yankee Catchers
C	Capt. George Masten	Dallas	
D	Capt. A. J. Frizzell	Johnson	
E	Capt. M. D. Kennedy	Tarrant	
F	Capt. Benjamin Tyus	Limestone	
G	Capt. G. Harker	Red River	
H	Capt. William English	Hopkins	
I	Capt. James Moore	Van Zandt	
K	Capt. William Cathey	Johnson	

THE 17TH TEXAS CAVALRY

Company	Commander	County	Nickname
A	Capt. S. M. Noble	Nacogdoches	
B	Capt. O. C. Taylor	Cherokee	
C	Capt. William Thompson	Cherokee	
D	Capt. Bryan Marsh	Smith	Texas Mounted Volunteers
E	Capt. T. F. Tucker	Harrison	
F	Capt. J. G. McKnight	Harrison	
G	Capt. J. J. Wynn	Rusk	
H	Capt. William Simpson	Upshur	
I	Capt. I. J. Watkins	Red River	
K	Capt. Gil McKay	Harrison	Clough Rangers

THE 18TH TEXAS CAVALRY

Company	Commander	County(ies)	Nickname
A	Capt. Hiram Childress	Johnson	
B	Capt. Hiram Morgan	Bastrop	Morgan Rangers
C	Capt. Ed Crowder	Dallas	
D	Capt. William Damron	Bell	
E	Capt. John Coit	Dallas	
F	Capt. R. W. Calhoun	Williamson	Williamson County Blues
G	Capt. Felix McKittrick	Denton	Denton County Rebels
H	Capt. F. L. Farrar	Ellis	
I	Capt. Middleton Perry	Dallas	
K	Capt. George Manion	Henderson, Anderson	

THE 24TH TEXAS CAVALRY

Company	Commander	County(ies)	Nickname
A	Capt. Robert Poole	Austin, Brazos, Montgomery	
B	Capt. S. A. Woolridge	Montgomery	
C	Capt. William Taylor	Austin, Lampassas	
D	Capt. Patrick H. Swearingen	Tyler, Angelina	
E	Capt. John Morrison	Tyler, Angelina	
F	Capt. Thomas W. Mitchell	Fort Bend	
G	Capt. C. W. Bulloch	Smith, Jefferson	
H	Capt. John Connor	Tyler, Angelina	
I	Capt. Benjamin Fly	Fayette, Karnes	
K	Capt. Henry Woods	Lavaca	

THE 25TH TEXAS CAVALRY

Company	Commander	County(ies)	Nickname
A	Capt. B. F. Ross	Tyler, Galveston	
B	Capt. J. N. Dark	Liberty, Galveston	
C	Capt. Davis Stovall	Goliad, Refugio, Victoria	
D	Capt. J. P. Montgomery	Washington	
E	Capt. William Daniel	Brazos	
F	Capt. Enoch Pitts	Tyler	
G	Capt. W. D. Davis	Liberty	
H	Capt. Gilbert LaCour	Harris, Liberty	
I	Capt. E. B. Pickett	Liberty	
K	Capt. M. M. Singletary	Walker	

APPENDIX 3

THE BATTLE CASUALTIES OF GRANBURY'S BRIGADE

Regiment	No. (% of Total Reg.) Captured at Arkansas Post or Fort Donelson	No. (% of Those Captured) Who Died in P.O.W. Camps	Total No. (% of Total Reg.) Battle Casualties	No. Killed in Action	No. Wounded in Action	No. Wounded in Action (% of Total Wounded) Twice
6th Texas	589 (64%)	58 (9.8%)	259 (28%)	50 (19.3%)*	205 (79%)*	30 (14.6%)
7th Texas	379 (37%)	58 (15%)	420 (41%)	98 (23%)*	253 (60%)*	56 (22%)
10th Texas	715 (60%)	86 (12%)	267 (22.4%)	74 (27.7%)*	153 (57.3%)*	22 (14%)
15th Texas	478 (38%)	94 (19.6%)	119 (8.4%)	26 (21.8%)*	75 (63%)*	7 (9.3%)
17th Texas	390 (33%)	103 (26.4%)	86 (7.3%)	10 (11.6%)*	46 (53.4%)*	1 (2%)
18th Texas	533 (43%)	105 (19.7%)	221 (18%)	34 (15.3%)*	119 (53.8%)*	2 (1.7%)
24th Texas	652 (57.6%)	112 (17%)	193 (17%)	59 (30.5%)*	109 (56.4%)*	12 (11%)
25th Texas	555 (40%)	134 (24%)	158 (11.4%)	33 (20.8%)*	97 (61.3%)*	11 (11%)
Totals:	4,291 (46%)	750 (17.4%)	1,723 (18.5%)	384 (22.2%)	1,057 (61.3%)	141 (13.3%)

*Percentages are based on the total number of battle casualties within that regiment.

Regiment	No. Wounded in Action (% of Total Wounded) Three Times Plus	No. Captured (Excluding Arkansas Post and Fort Donelson)	No. Wounded or Captured (% of Total Wounded or Captured) Multiple Times	No. (% of Total Wounded or Captured) Who Died of Wounds or in a P.O.W. Camp	No. (% of Total Reg.) Who Died of Disease	No. (% of Total Who Surrendered) of Previously Wounded or Captured Who Surrerdered at Greensboro
6th Texas	3 (1.4%)	45 (17.3%)*	71 (27.3%)	8 (3%)	52 (5.6%)	34 (55%)
7th Texas	3 (1%)	87 (20.7%)*	120 (33.5%)	34 (9.4%)	233 (23%)	20 (41%)
10th Texas	0	43 (16%)*	52 (27.3%)	10 (5.2%)	190 (16%)	13 (17%)
15th Texas	0	24 (20%)*	15 (15%)	12 (12%)	87 (7%)	14 (32.5%)
17th Texas	1 (2%)	32 (37%)*	15 (18.7%)	5 (6.25%)	64 (5.45%)	9 (24%)
18th Texas	1 (0.8%)	74 (33.4%)*	53 (26.6%)	9 (4.5%)	64 (5.24%)	12 (25%)
24th Texas	2 (1.8%)	30 (15.5%)*	30 (20.6%)	11 (7.5%)	64 (5.6%)	14 (28%)
25th Texas	0	31 (19.6%)*	23 (17.5%)	4 (3%)	55 (3.9%)	9 (25.7%)
Totals:	10 (0.95%)	366 (21.2%)	379 (25%)	93 (6.1%)	809 (8.7%)	125 (31%)

*Percentages are based on the total number of battle casualties within that regiment.

NOTES

INTRODUCTION

1. Richard E. Beringer et al., *Why the South Lost the Civil War* (Athens: Univ. of Georgia Press, 1986); Mark A. Weitz, *More Damning Than Slaughter: Desertion in the Confederate Army* (Lincoln: Univ. of Nebraska Press, 2005); David Williams, *Rich Man's War: Class, Caste, and Confederate Defeat in the Lower Chattahoochee Valley* (Athens: Univ. of Georgia Press, 1998).

2. Gary Gallagher, *The Confederate War: How Popular Will, Nationalism and Military Strategy Could Not Stave off Defeat* (Cambridge: Harvard Univ. Press, 1997); Jason Phillips, *Diehard Rebels: The Confederate Culture of Invincibility* (Athens: Univ. of Georgia Press, 2007); Steven Woodworth, *While God Is Marching On: The Religious World of Civil War Soldiers* (Lawrence: Univ. Press of Kansas, 2001); James McPherson, *For Cause and Comrades: Why Men Fought in the Civil War* (Oxford: Oxford Univ. Press, 1997), and James McPherson, *What They Fought For, 1861–1865* (Baton Rouge: Louisiana State Univ. Press, 1994). See also Gary Gallagher, *Lee and His Army in Confederate History* (Chapel Hill: Univ. of North Carolina Press, 2001).

3. Norman Brown, ed., *One of Cleburne's Command: The Civil War Reminiscences and Diary of Capt. Samuel T. Foster, Granbury's Texas Brigade, CSA* (Austin: Univ. of Texas Press, 1980); James M. McCaffrey, *This Band of Heroes: Granbury's Texas Brigade, C.S.A.* (College Station: Texas A&M Univ. Press, 1996); Danny M. Sessums, "A Force to Be Reckoned With: Granbury's Texas Brigade, 1861–1865," Sessums Collection, Houston, Texas.

4. J. Tracy Power, *Lee's Miserables: Life in the Army of Northern Virginia from the Wilderness to Appomattox* (Chapel Hill: Univ. of North Carolina Press, 1998); Gallagher, *The Confederate War*; Larry J. Daniel, *Soldiering in the Army of Tennessee: Portrait of Life in a Confederate Army* (Chapel Hill: Univ. of North Carolina Press, 1991); Richard M. McMurry, *Two Great Rebel Armies: An Essay in Confederate Military History* (Chapel Hill: Univ. of North Carolina Press, 1989).

5. Charles Grear, "Texans to the Front: Why Texans Fought in the Civil War" (Ph.D. diss., Texas Christian University, 2005).

1. OFF TO WAR

1. Andrew F. Lang, "'Victory Is Our Only Road to Peace': Texas, Wartime Morale, and Confederate Nationalism, 1860–1865" (Master's thesis, University of North Texas, 2008); Richard Lowe, *Walker's Texas Division, C.S.A.: Greyhounds of the Trans-Mississippi* (Baton Rouge: Louisiana State Univ. Press, 2004).

2. Arthur James Lyon Fremantle, *Three Months in the Southern States: April–June, 1863*, ed. Walter Lord (Short Hills, N.J.: Burford Books, 2001), 75.

3. Lowe, *Walker's Texas Division*, 8–9.

4. 1860 Texas Census, www.heritagequest.com (accessed January 26, 2007). Of the ninety-three members of this company, the residency of forty-five (48.4 percent) could not be determined and were excluded from these numbers.

5. Robert M. Collins, *Chapters from the Unwritten History of the War Between the States: Or, The Incidents in the Life of a Confederate Soldier in Camp, On the March, In the Great Battles, And in Prison* (Dayton, Ohio: Morningside Press, 1988), 9–13.

6. Jim Turner, "Jim Turner, Co. G, 6th Texas Infantry, C.S.A. From 1861–1865," *Texana*, 12 no. 1 (1974): 150–151.

7. W. W. Heartsill, *Fourteen Hundred and Ninety-One Days in the Confederate Army: A Journal Kept by W.W. Heartsill For Four Years, One Month and One Day; or Camp Life; Day by Day, of the W.P. Lane Rangers From April 19, 1861 to May 20, 1865*, ed. Bell Wiley (Jackson, Tenn.: McCowat-Mercer Press, 1953), 2–3.

8. Ibid.

9. The slight difference in wealth between Granbury's Brigade and Walker's Division could merely be the result of sampling. There were also some companies in Granbury's Brigade where farming was not the majority occupation. For an example of this outlier, see Andrew F. Lang, "The Bass Grays: An Economic, Social and Demographic Profile of Company D, Seventh Texas Infantry," *East Texas Historical Journal* 48, no. 1 (winter 2010): 72–94.

10. Charles A. Leuschner, *The Civil War Diary of Charles A. Leuschner*, ed. Charles Spurlin (Austin, Tex.: Eakin Press, 1992), 1.

11. Ibid., 2.

12. Ibid., 2–3.

13. Compiled Service Records of the 6th Texas Infantry. Every company commander in a Confederate regiment was required to file bi-monthly reports on all the men under his command. These reports have been compiled for each man and organized alphabetically by regiment. These manuscripts were then microfilmed by the National Archives (microfilm series M323.) The Compiled Service Records for the 6th Texas Infantry are contained on microfilm rolls 308–314.

14. Leuschner, *The Civil War Diary of Charles A. Leuschner*, 3–4.

15. Ibid., 4.

16. Ibid., 4–5.

17. Ibid., 5.

18. Ibid., 6.

19. Ibid., 6.

20. Ibid., 7.

21. Khleber M. Van Zandt, *Force Without Fanfare: The Autobiography of K. M. Van Zandt* (Fort Worth: Texas Christian Univ. Press, 1968), 78–79.

22. Gregg to Mackall, "Hopkinsville, Kentucky November 7, 1861," in U.S. War Department, *The War of the Rebellion: A Compilation of the Official Records of the Union and Confederate Armies* (Washington, D.C.: Government Printing Office, 1883), series I, vol. 4, 524–525. (Hereafter referred to as *O.R.*)

23. *O.R.*, series I, vol. 4, 524–525; Van Zandt, *Force Without Fanfare*, 79.

24. *O.R.*, series I, vol. 4, 525.

25. *O.R.*, series I, vol. 4, 525.

26. Van Zandt, *Force Without Fanfare*, 80–81. Gregg's staff was as follows: Adjutant W. D. Douglas, Sergeant Major Thomas J. Beall, Commissary S. T. Bridges, Quartermaster William Bradford, and Surgeon John L. Alston.

27. Mike Polston, "Allison Nelson: Atlanta Mayor, Texas Hero, Confederate General," *Atlanta Historical Journal* 29, no. 3 (1985): 19–25.

28. Ibid., 24.

29. *Galveston Daily News*, October 17, 1861.

30. Compiled Service Records of the 10th Texas Infantry, National Archives microfilm series M323, rolls 337–343; Harold B. Simpson, ed., *The Bugle Softly Blows: The Confederate Diary of Benjamin M. Seaton* (Waco, Tex.: Texian Press, 1965), ix. (Seaton was a member of Company G, the Labadie Rifles.) Roger Q. Mills was an influential politician before and after the Civil War. For more on his prewar career, see C. Alwyn Barr, "The Making of a Secessionist: The Antebellum Career of Roger Q. Mills," *Southwestern Historical Quarterly* 79, no. 2 (1975): 129–144. Collections of Mills's papers are also housed at the Center for American History at the University of Texas at Austin and at the Dallas Historical Society Archives in Fair Park, Dallas, Texas.

31. Simpson, *The Bugle Softly Blows*, 71.

32. Ibid., 1–2.

33. Private Elijah Hull to his parents in Johnson County, Texas, February 23, 1862, http://www.armoryguards.org/10thTexas/letters/hull.htm; Simpson, *The Bugle Softly Blows*, 2.

34. Isaiah Harlan letters of November 10 and December 17, 1861, to his mother. Letters of Isaiah Harlan, vertical file of the 10th Texas Infantry, Simpson Confederate Research Center, Hill College, Hillsboro, Texas.

35. Simpson, *The Bugle Softly Blows*, 2–3.

36. Brown, *One of Cleburne's Command*, xxviii.

37. Marcus J. Wright, *Texas in the War 1861–1865*, ed. Harold B. Simpson (Hillsboro, Tex.: Hill Junior College Press, 1965), 26, 116.

38. Letter of William C. Young to his sister, March 22, 1862, in the "Letters and diary of Private William C. Young, 15th Texas Dismounted Cavalry," vertical file of the 15th Texas Cavalry, Simpson Confederate Research Center, Hill College, Hillsboro, Texas.

39. Collins, *Chapters*, 15–22.

40. Ibid., 22–23.

41. Compiled Service Records of the 17th Texas Cavalry, National Archives microfilm series M323, rolls 93–96.

42. L. W. Kemp, "Darnell, Nicholas H.," *Handbook of Texas Online*, http://www.tshaonline.org/handbook/online/articles/fda16 (accessed March 15, 2007).

43. Compiled Service Records of the 18th Texas Cavalry, National Archives microfilm series M323, rolls 99–103.

44. *Dallas Herald*, January 22, 1862. The other regiments besides the 15th, 17th, and 18th Texas Cavalries that were present at Camp McKnight were the 12th, 14th, and 16th Texas Cavalries. However, these regiments did not become a part of Granbury's Brigade. (Collins, *Chapters*, 22.)

45. Stephen Chicoine, *The Confederates of Chappell Hill, Texas: Prosperity, Civil War and Decline* (Jefferson, N.C.: McFarland, 2005), 58–61.

46. Ibid., 60.

47. These lancer regiments never actually used lances in battle. The only account of lances used in battle in the Civil War was at the Battle of Val Verde, New Mexico, in 1862. Dennis L. Potter, "Desperate Courage: An Account of the Texas Lancer Charge at the Battle of Val Verde, New Mexico," *Military History of the West*, 36 no. 1 (2006): 1–33.

48. Brown, *One of Cleburne's Command*, xxxviii–xl. General Twiggs is a reference to Major General David Twiggs, commander of the U.S. Military District of Texas before he surrendered his command and was commissioned by the Confederate government as a major general. It should be noted that perhaps the reason the call for lancers was so successful was the fact that the Confederate Conscription Act of 1862 was to go into effect in April 1862. Many of these men signed up to avoid the stigma of conscription.

49. *O.R.*, series IV, vol. 1, 1001–1002 and 1050–1051.

50. Brown, *One of Cleburne's Command*, xl.

51. Lieutenant Colonel Robert Reese Neyland was the grandfather of legendary University of Tennessee football coach General Robert Reese "Bob" Neyland.

52. Compiled Service Records of the 25th Texas Cavalry, National Archives microfilm series M323, rolls 126–130. William Neyland was the brother of Robert R. Neyland.

53. J. P. Blessington, *The Campaigns of Walker's Texas Division* (New York: Lang, Little and Co., 1875), 21–23.

2. FORT DONELSON

1. Daniel, *Soldiering in the Army of Tennessee*, 49.

2. For a good analysis of the reasoning of these historians, see Kendall D. Gott, *Where the South Lost the War: An Analysis of the Fort Henry–Fort Donelson Campaign, February 1862* (Mechanicsburg, Pa.: Stackpole, 2003).

3. Thomas L. Connelly, *Army of the Heartland: The Army of Tennessee, 1861–1862* (Baton Rouge: Louisiana State Univ. Press, 1967), 52.

4. Van Zandt, *Force Without Fanfare*, 81–82.

5. Ibid., 83–85. In actuality, 153 members of the 7th Texas died of disease from November to February. Apparently, Granbury also took a Mexican American man with him as a servant, and this Mexican died of disease in January 1862 along with the others. The manner in which Private Edward Estes of the 7th Texas refers to "the Mexican" gives credence to the idea that

African Americans and Mexican Americans were thought of as nonentities or somehow sub-human by the Anglo Texans. (Edward B. Estes to "My Brother," January 13, 1862, the Texas Collection, Baylor University.)

6. Connelly, *Army of the Heartland,* 106–108.

7. Ibid., 109–112.

8. Captain Van Zandt recounted the story of two privates in his company, Johnny Cave and Thomas Jennings, who were left behind at Clarksville due to illness. As soon as the 7th Texas reached their encampment the two reappeared, stating that they did not want to miss the fighting that was obviously imminent. During the battle for Donelson on February 15 both of them were killed in action. (Van Zandt, *Force Without Fanfare,* 86.) For an example of a member of the 7th Texas who was left behind sick before Fort Donelson, see Jennifer S. Mansfield, "Yours Fraternally Until Death: The Civil War Letters of the Brothers Love," *East Texas Historical Journal* 38, no. 1 (2000): 53–70. Cyrus Love enlisted as a member of Company G, 7th Texas, and was left behind before Donelson. He later joined Terry's Texas Rangers. The original collection of letters from the Love brothers is in the Special Collections of the Mary Couts Burnett Library at Texas Christian University, in Fort Worth, Texas.

9. *O.R.,* series I, vol. 7, 407.

10. Gideon Pillow's prior claim to fame was that during the Mexican War he at one time commanded his troops to build their breastworks backward, leaving them open to bayonet charges by the Mexican troops. John B. Floyd served as secretary of War under President James Buchanan and was accused of having misappropriated $870,000. The charges were later dropped for lack of evidence.

11. *O.R.,* series I, vol. 7, 376.

12. Connelly, *Army of the Heartland,* 120–121.

13. *O.R.,* series I, vol. 7, 376.

14. Van Zandt, *Force Without Fanfare,* 89; *O.R.,* series I, vol. 7, 376.

15. *O.R.,* series I, vol. 7, 376. According to the Compiled Service Records of the 7th Texas, nineteen were killed on the field, closely coinciding with the number given by Gregg. However, only twenty-one are listed as wounded. The remaining thirteen wounded were most likely only slightly wounded, not badly enough to permanently disable them. (Compiled Service Records of the 7th Texas Infantry, National Archives microfilm series M323, rolls 315–320.)

16. Pillow's odd decision to order his men back to their entrenchments has never been fully explained. However, considering his previous undistinguished military record, it is not all that surprising.

17. *O.R.,* series I, vol. 7, 407.

18. Van Zandt, *Force Without Fanfare,* 90–91.

19. Mark M. Boatner III, *The Civil War Dictionary* (New York: Vintage, 1959), 117; George Levy, *To Die in Chicago: Confederate Prisoners at Camp Douglas 1862–65* (Gretna, La.: Pelican Publishing, 1999), 31.

20. Van Zandt, *Force Without Fanfare,* 92.

21. John Gregg to William L. Moody, March 8, 1862, William L. Moody Papers, Moody Mansion and Museum, Galveston, Texas.

22. John Gregg to William L. Moody, April 22, 1862, William L. Moody Papers, Moody Mansion and Museum, Galveston, Texas.

23. Van Zandt, *Force Without Fanfare*, 93–94.

24. Hiram Granbury to William L. Moody, June 23, 1862, William L. Moody Papers, Moody Mansion and Museum, Galveston, Texas; Lonnie Speer, *Portals to Hell: Military Prisons of the Civil War* (Mechanicsburg, Pa.: Stackpole, 1997).

25. Compiled Service Records of the 7th Texas Infantry, National Archives microfilm series M323, rolls 315–320.

26. *O.R.*, series II, vol. 4, 265–268.

3. SOJOURN IN ARKANSAS

1. Weitz, *More Damning Than Slaughter*, 5; Lang, "'Victory Is Our Only Road to Peace,'" 3.

2. *O.R.*, series I, vol. 9, 700.

3. Leuschner, *The Civil War Diary of Charles A. Leuschner*, 7.

4. Ibid.

5. Ibid., 8.

6. Ibid.

7. Ibid.

8. Simpson, *The Bugle Softly Blows*, 3–10.

9. McCaffrey, *This Band of Heroes*, 11.

10. Compiled Service Records of the 10th Texas Infantry, National Archives microfilm series M323, rolls 337–343.

11. Ibid.

12. Simpson, *The Bugle Softly Blows*, 18; Isaiah Harlan to his brother, dated "Little Rock July 18, 1862," vertical file of the 10th Texas Infantry, Simpson Confederate Research Center, Hill College, Hillsboro, Texas.

13. Simpson, *The Bugle Softly Blows*, 19.

14. Compiled Service Records of the 15th, 17th, and 18th Texas Cavalry Regiments, National Archives microfilm series M323, rolls 85–89, 93–96, and 99–103.

15. Joe R. Wise, ed. "The Letters of Flavius W. Perry, 17th Texas Cavalry 1862–1863," *Military History of Texas and the Southwest* 12, no. 3 (April 1976): 12.

16. Collins, *Chapters*, 30.

17. Ibid., 60.

18. Compiled Service Records of the 15th, 17th, and 18th Texas Cavalry Regiments, National Archives microfilm series M323, rolls 85–89, 93–96, and 99–103.

19. Collins, *Chapters*, 62.

20. Brown, *One of Cleburne's Command*, xlii.

21. Ibid., xliv.

22. *O.R.*, series I, vol. 15, 822–825.

23. Thomas Elliott to his wife, Emma (Felder) Elliott, July 3, 1862, as quoted in Chicoine, *The Confederates of Chappell Hill*, 61. Elliott was a member of Company D, 24th Texas.

24. Brown, *One of Cleburne's Command*, xlvi; Chicoine, *The Confederates of Chappell Hill*, 62.

25. Compiled Service Records of the 24th and 25th Texas Cavalry Regiments, National Archives microfilm series M323, rolls 119–123 and 126–130.

26. Brown, *One of Cleburne's Command*, xlvii.

27. McCaffrey, *This Band of Heroes,* 25–26.

28. Ezra J. Warner, *Generals in Gray* (Baton Rouge: Louisiana State Univ. Press, 1959), 223–224.

29. Ibid., 71–72; Richard C. Sheridan, "Brigadier-General James Deshler: Professional Soldier," *Alabama Historical Quarterly* 26, no. 2 (1964): 203–216.

30. McCaffrey, *This Band of Heroes,* 33.

4. ARKANSAS POST

1. Grear, "Texans to the Front"; Compiled Service Records of the 17th Texas Dismounted (Consolidated) Cavalry, National Archives microfilm series M323, rolls 97–98.

2. Edwin C. Bearss, "The Battle of Arkansas Post," *Arkansas Historical Quarterly* 18, no. 3 (1959): 237.

3. Ibid., 239. The Confederates named the position the Post of Arkansas, while the Federals referred to it as Fort Hindman.

4. *O.R.,* series I, vol. 17, pt. 1, 705.

5. Bearss, "The Battle of Arkansas Post," 247.

6. Ibid.; Heartsill, *Fourteen Hundred and Ninety-One Days,* 88. The Confederates captured quite a bit of Federal mail aboard the *Blue Wing* and distributed it among themselves for amusement (Turner, "Jim Turner," 155.)

7. *O.R.,* series I, vol. 17, pt. 1, 780, 783, and 790. McClernand had approximately thirty-two thousand men.

8. Bearss, "The Battle of Arkansas Post," 257–258.

9. *O.R.,* series I, vol. 17, pt. 1, 781.

10. Edwin Bearss, *The Vicksburg Campaign,* vol. 1, *Vicksburg Is the Key* (Dayton, Ohio: Morningside Press, 1985), 381.

11. Ibid.

12. Ibid., 382.

13. Ibid., 383.

14. Ibid., 401.

15. Ibid., 402.

16. At this point Garland had posted himself on the left flank of the 6th Texas, also the right of the 24th Texas. *O.R.,* series I, vol. 17, pt. 1, 781–785.

17. Bearss, *Vicksburg Is the Key,* 404–405.

18. Brown, *One of Cleburne's Command,* 23.

19. Compiled Service Records of the 6th, 24th, and 25th Texas Regiments, National Archives microfilm series M323, rolls 308–314, 119–123, and 126–130; Bearss, *Vicksburg Is the Key,* 418–419. In Garland's Brigade, Hart's Arkansas Battery had three killed, thirteen wounded, and twenty-two missing, while Denson's Louisiana Cavalry Company had two wounded.

20. Compiled Service Records of the 10th, 15th, 17th, and 18th Texas Regiments, National Archives microfilm series M323, rolls 337–343, 85–89, 93–96, and 99–103. Included in the number who escaped are those left behind sick in various hospitals at the time of the surrender (Bearss, *Vicksburg Is the Key,* 418–419). For an example of a Texan who escaped, see Norman C. Delaney, ed. "Diary and Memoirs of Marshall Samuel Pierson, Company C, 17th Regt., Texas Cavalry, 1862–1865," *Military History of Texas and the Southwest* 13, no. 3 (1977):

23–38. In the spring of 1863 Confederate authorities ordered that the Arkansas Post refugees from all seven regiments gather at Elysian Fields, where they formed them into a regiment designated the 17th Texas Dismounted (Consolidated) Cavalry. A total of 777 refugees from Arkansas Post signed up for service in the regiment, organized on July 1, 1863, under Colonel James R. Taylor, who had been displaced from command. The regiment subsequently saw action at the Battle of Mansfield in April 1864 in Polignac's Brigade, where Taylor and Lieutenant Colonel Sebron M. Noble were killed and the regiment suffered a total of twenty-one killed and forty-five wounded. Major (later colonel) Thomas Tucker took command and the regiment disbanded in the summer of 1865. Compiled Service Records of the 17th Texas Dismounted (Consolidated) Cavalry, National Archives microfilm series M323, rolls 97–98.

21. Brown, *One of Cleburne's Command*, 23.

22. Ibid., 49. The documents relevant to Garland's petition can be found in the *O.R.*, series I, vol. 17, pt. 1, 780–796.

23. Bearss, *Vicksburg Is the Key*, 402–403.

5. FIGHTING FOR VICKSBURG

1. Gallagher, *The Confederate War*; Phillips, *Diehard Rebels*.

2. Alexander, commander of Company A, apparently never returned to the regiment from Texas. He was listed as "absent on recruiting mission" and dropped from the rolls on December 22, 1863.

3. For the formation of the 7th Texas companies, see chapter 1. Company B gained twenty-three recruits; Company C, ten; Company D, twenty-four; Company E, ten; Company F, one; Company G, four; Company H, thirty-eight; Company I, twenty; and Company K, eighty-seven. Compiled Service Records of the 7th Texas Infantry, National Archives microfilm series M323, rolls 315–320.

4. Rebecca Blackwell Drake and Thomas D. Holder, *Lone Star General: Hiram B. Granbury* (Raymond, Miss.: Drake Publishing, 2004), 35.

5. Ibid., 38.

6. Ibid., 40.

7. Ibid., 39–40.

8. Minerva Van Zandt to Khleber Van Zandt, March 26, 1863, letter in the possession of E. P. Cranz of Fort Worth, Texas.

9. Van Zandt, *Force Without Fanfare*, 98.

10. Ibid., 99.

11. Bearss, *The Vicksburg Campaign*, vol. 2, *Grant Strikes a Fatal Blow* (Dayton, Ohio: Morningside Press, 1987), 485.

12. Ibid.

13. Ibid., 486.

14. Ibid., 487.

15. At this time Gregg still believed that he was facing only a single brigade, or at most a division.

16. *O.R.*, series I, vol. 24, pt. 1, 747.

17. Bearss, *Grant Strikes a Fatal Blow*, 495.

18. *O.R.*, series I, vol. 24, pt. 1, 747.

19. Bearss, *Grant Strikes a Fatal Blow*, 495–498; *O.R.*, series I, vol. 24, pt. 1, 747–748; Steven Woodworth, *Nothing But Victory: The Army of the Tennessee, 1861–1865* (New York: Knopf, 2005), 358–359. Later, when this same Union soldier advanced, he saw the meerschaum pipe lying on the ground. It is unclear who the officer in question was.

20. Bearss, *Grant Strikes a Fatal Blow*, 498.

21. Ibid., 500–501; *O.R.*, series I, vol. 24, pt. 1, 748.

22. *O.R.*, series I, vol. 24, pt. 1, 501.

23. Colonel McGavock was killed in the fighting. Ironically, many casualties of the 7th Texas and the rest of Granbury's Brigade, along with the body of Hiram Granbury, were taken to McGavock's plantation house near Franklin, Tennessee, in the aftermath of the battle there on November 30, 1864.

24. Bearss, *Grant Strikes a Fatal Blow*, 515–517; *O.R.*, series I, vol. 24, pt. 1, 748; Compiled Service Records of the 7th Texas Infantry, National Archives microfilm series M323, rolls 315–320.

25. Hiram Granbury was born Hiram Granberry, but decided to change the spelling of his name upon reaching adulthood. His father continued to spell his name Granberry, hence the discrepancy in spelling. Granbury's parents and sister had passed away before the war and were buried on their farm in Hinds County. (Drake, *Lone Star General*, 51, 54.)

26. Ibid.

27. Ibid.

28. Ibid., 55.

29. Daniel, *Soldiering in the Army of Tennessee*, 8; McMurry, *Two Great Rebel Armies*, 12.

6. PRISON

1. Power, *Lee's Miserables*, 12; Daniel, *Soldiering in the Army of Tennessee*, 5.

2. Heartsill, *Fourteen Hundred and Ninety-One Days*, 98–99.

3. Brown, *One of Cleburne's Command*, 22–23. Of course, this was a false hope. See chapter 4.

4. The ships apparently were segregated by brigade. Heartsill notes that except for his company, all of the troops aboard the *Sam Gatey* were Arkansans, with Dunnington's Brigade being the only command that fits that description. This is further corroborated by the fact that Lieutenant Robert Collins of the 15th Texas in Deshler's Brigade boarded the *Nebraska* and Captain Samuel Foster of the 24th Texas in Garland's Brigade boarded the *John J. Roe*. Heartsill, *Fourteen Hundred and Ninety-One Days*, 98; Collins, *Chapters*, 72; Brown, *One of Cleburne's Command*, 22.

5. Collins, *Chapters*, 72–73.

6. Heartsill, *Fourteen Hundred and Ninety-One Days*, 101; Brown, *One of Cleburne's Command*, 23.

7. Ibid.; William Oliphant, "Arkansas Post," *Southern Bivouac* 1 (1886): 738–739.

8. McCaffrey, *This Band of Heroes*, 46–47.

9. Compiled Service Records of the 6th, 10th, 15th, 17th, 18th, 24th, and 25th Texas Regiments, National Archives microfilm series M323, rolls 308–314, 337–343, 85–89, 93–96, 99–103, 119–123, and 126–130.

10. McCaffrey, *This Band of Heroes*, 46–47.

11. Joseph Hinkle, "The Odyssey of Private Hinkle," *Civil War Times Illustrated* 8, no. 8 (1969): 27.

12. Collier and Oliphant, as quoted in Leuschner, *The Civil War Diary of Charles A. Leuschner*, 14–15.

13. William J. Oliphant, "Memoirs of William J. Oliphant," hand-written manuscript in the Austin History Center, Austin Public Library, Austin, Texas.

14. For other places in which the Union forces used the oath of allegiance, see Weitz, *More Damning Than Slaughter*, 58–59.

15. Compiled Service Records of the 6th, 24th, and 25th Texas, National Archives microfilm series M323, rolls 308–314, 119–123, and 126–130. The number of 1,693 enlisted men excludes the approximately 103 officers from these regiments who were imprisoned at Camp Chase. It is impossible to determine how many men escaped from the *John J. Roe* or Camp Chase during the incarceration. These escapees added to the total number of casualties, doubtlessly pushing the percentage over 25 percent.

16. McCaffrey, *This Band of Heroes*, 51; *Confederate Soldiers, Sailors and Civilians Who Died as Prisoners of War at Camp Douglas, Chicago, Ill., 1862–1865* (Kalamazoo, Mich.: Edgar Gray Publications, 1912). There is some confusion as to the exact location of Camp Douglas. James McCaffrey in *This Band of Heroes* states that the site of Camp Douglas is now bounded by Cottage Grove Avenue, South Parkway, Thirty-First Street, and Thirty-Sixth Street. However, George Levy, in his book *To Die in Chicago*, states that Camp Douglas ran four blocks west from Cottage Grove Avenue to MLK Boulevard and was bounded on the south by East Thirty-Third Place and on the north by East Thirty-First Street (31). This description agrees with the author of *Confederate Soldiers, Sailors and Civilians*, who states that a monument over the tomb of Stephen A. Douglas, just west of the Illinois Central Railroad at Thirty-Fourth Street, marked the camp's location. (This would have been near the southeast corner.) But Levy contradicts himself by stating that Camp Douglas lay "just across the street" from the University of Chicago. The present-day University of Chicago is located approximately 2.7 miles south of the above-described location.

17. The 10th Texas Infantry surrendered 656 members at Arkansas Post, who departed for Camp Douglas, as did 439 members of the 15th Texas, 351 of the 17th Texas, and 493 of the 18th Texas. Approximately 177 officers from these regiments were sent to Camp Chase. (Compiled Service Records of the 10th, 15th, 17th, and 18th Texas Regiments, National Archives microfilm series M323, rolls 337–343, 85–89, 93–96, and 99–103.)

18. McCaffrey, *This Band of Heroes*, 52–53.

19. Compiled Service Records of the 10th, 15th, 17th, and 18th Texas Regiments, National Archives microfilm series M323, rolls 337–343, 85–89, 93–96, and 99–103. These totals do not include those who escaped, or whose death went unrecorded. Those numbers would undoubtedly push the total much closer to a 25 percent death rate.

20. Collins, *Chapters*, 83–86; Compiled Service Records of the 15th Texas Cavalry, National Archives microfilm series M323, rolls 85–89.

21. Collins, *Chapters*, 85–89.

22. Brown, *One of Cleburne's Command*, 29; Collins, *Chapters*, 90.

23. Collins, *Chapters*, 91–92. Captain Foster also recorded the sermon preached by Colonel Wilkes. It occurred on March 27, 1863, the day that Jefferson Davis had set aside for prayer and fasting. (Brown, *One of Cleburne's Command*, 32.)

24. Woodworth, *While God Is Marching On*, 25.

25. Brown, *One of Cleburne's Command*, 32–33.

26. Collins, *Chapters*, 94.

27. Ibid.

28. Only six Texan officers are recorded as having died at Camp Chase. Lieutenant Rogers of Company F, 15th Texas (1-27-63), First Lieutenant E. R. Allen, Company E, 10th Texas (2-11-63), Second Lieutenant James Weatherly of Company H, 17th Texas (2-11-63), Second Lieutenant William Malone, Company E, 6th Texas (3-11-63), Captain Joseph L. Lindsey, Company C, 24th Texas (2-6-63) and Junior Second Lieutenant John Thomas, Company K, 25th Texas (2-7-63). Compiled Service Records of the 6th, 10th, 15th, 17th, 18th, 24th, and 25th Texas Regiments, National Archives microfilm series M323, rolls 308–314, 337–343, 85–89, 93–96, 99–103, 119–123, and 126–130.

7. A NEW START

1. Daniel, *Soldiering in the Army of Tennessee*, 8; Grear, "Texans to the Front," 7.

2. Sessums, "A Force to Be Reckoned With," 349–353.

3. Mamie Yeary, *Reminiscences of the Boys in Gray* (Dayton, Ohio: Morning House, 1986), 746.

4. Ibid., 552.

5. Thomas L. Connelly, *Autumn of Glory: The Army of Tennessee, 1862–1865* (Baton Rouge: Louisiana State Univ. Press, 1971), 110. For more on Braxton Bragg, see Grady McWhiney, *Braxton Bragg and Confederate Defeat*, vol. 1 (Tuscaloosa: Univ. of Alabama Press, 1969), and vol. 2 (Tuscaloosa: Univ. of Alabama Press, 1991).

6. Brown, *One of Cleburne's Command*, 43.

7. Ibid.

8. R. Q. Mills to his wife, June 13, 1863, Roger Q. Mills Papers, box 2F42, Briscoe Center for American History, University of Texas at Austin. When the 6th, 10th, and 15th Texas Regiments were consolidated, the three original Company A's became Company A in the new regiment, etc. The company consolidations for the 17th, 18th, 24th & 25th Texas are given below:

COMPANY CONSOLIDATIONS IN THE
17TH, 18TH, 24TH, & 25TH TEXAS INFANTRY

	Co. A	*Co. B*	*Co. C*	*Co. D*	*Co. E*	*Co. F*	*Co. G*	*Co. H*	*Co. I*	*Co. K*
17th	Cos. A, E, F, G		Co. D			Co. B	Co. H	Cos. C, I	Co. K	
18th	Co. A	Co. B	Co. C	Co. D	Co. E	Co. F	Co. G	Co. H	Co. I	Co. K
24th	Co. A	Co. B	Cos. I, K	Co. D	Co. E	Co. F	Co. G	Co. H	Co. C	
25th	Co. A	Co. B		Co. D	Co. E	Co. F	Co. G	Cos. C, H	Co. I	Co. K

9. Bryan Marsh, "The Confederate Letters of Bryan Marsh," *Chronicles of Smith County* 14, no. 2 (1975): 24.

10. John Q. Anderson, ed. *Campaigning with Parsons' Texas Cavalry Brigade, C.S.A.: The War Journal and Letters of the Four Orr Brothers, 12th Texas Cavalry Regiment* (Hillsboro, Tex.: Hill Junior College Press, 1967), 108.

11. Marsh, "The Confederate Letters of Bryan Marsh," 24.

12. Ibid., 25.

13. Anderson, ed., *Campaigning with Parsons' Texas Cavalry Brigade*, 108.

14. Heartsill, *Fourteen Hundred and Ninety-One Days*, 131. Sergeant William W. Heartsill was a member of Company F, 2nd Texas Cavalry Regiment, under Colonel John S. Ford. This company titled themselves the W. P. Lane Rangers, under Captain Samuel J. Richardson. Richardson and his company were initially stationed on the Texas frontier guarding the settlers against Indian attacks. However, Heartsill and his comrades wanted to fight Yankees and at length were ordered to Arkansas, arriving in November 1862. They were immediately ordered to the Arkansas Post, where they were captured with the rest of the garrison on January 11, 1863. After their exchange the officers and many of the enlisted men were reassigned west of the Mississippi, while Heartsill and a little less than twenty of his comrades were folded in with Captain L. M. Nutt's company of Louisiana cavalry, which was designated Company L, 10th Texas Infantry. Heartsill and his comrades thus became a part of Mills's 6th, 10th & 15th Texas.

15. Peter Cozzens, *This Terrible Sound: The Battle of Chickamauga* (Urbana: Univ. of Illinois Press, 1992), 14–17.

16. Ibid., 18–19.

17. Lucia R. Douglas, ed., *Douglas's Texas Battery, CSA* (Tyler, Tex.: Smith County Historical Society, 1966), 69.

18. *O.R.*, series I, vol. 23, pt. 1, 587.

19. Collins, *Chapters*, 135.

20. Cozzens, *This Terrible Sound*, 19–20.

21. Heartsill, *Fourteen Hundred and Ninety-One Days*, 134.

22. Collins, *Chapters*, 136.

23. Heartsill, *Fourteen Hundred and Ninety-One Days*, 136–37.

24. Collins, *Chapters*, 140.

25. Brown, *One of Cleburne's Command*, 48–49.

26. *O.R.*, series I, vol. 17, pt. 1, 780–796. The surrender of the garrison at Arkansas Post was indeed very suspicious. Secretary of War James A. Seddon himself wrote on May 9, 1863, "The strange circumstances causing the capture of Arkansas Post demand investigation. I recommend a court of inquiry" (*O.R.*, series I, vol. 17, pt. 1, 782).

27. Brown, *One of Cleburne's Command*, 49.

28. Daniel Harvey Hill, "Chickamauga—The Great Battle of the West," in *Battles and Leaders of the Civil War*, vol. 3, ed. Robert U. Johnson and Clarence C. Buell, 638 (New York: Thomas Yuseloff, 1956).

29. Turner, "Jim Turner," 162.

30. Ibid.

31. Heartsill, *Fourteen Hundred and Ninety-One Days*, 139.

32. Ibid.

33. Roger Q. Mills to his wife, August 16, 1863, Roger Q. Mills Papers, Dallas Historical Society Archives, Fair Park, Dallas, Texas; Heartsill, *Fourteen Hundred and Ninety-One Days*, 141. Heartsill's comments in this case must be taken with a grain of salt. It must be remembered that this disaffected Confederate sergeant was separated from the rest of his company, forced to serve under unfamiliar officers, and disgruntled from having to serve as an infantryman instead of his usual role in the cavalry.

34. Heartsill, *Fourteen Hundred and Ninety-One Days*, 37.

35. Ibid., 37–38.

36. Ibid., 38–48.

37. Cozzens, *This Terrible Sound*, 55–57.

38. Collins, *Chapters*, 145.

39. Heartsill, *Fourteen Hundred and Ninety-One Days*, 147.

40. Cozzens, *This Terrible Sound*, 63.

41. Ibid., 65.

42. Ibid., 71.

43. Ibid., 72.

44. Ibid., 72–74; Steven E. Woodworth, *A Deep Steady Thunder: The Battle of Chickamauga* (Abilene, Tex.: McWhiney Foundation Press, 1998), 26.

45. Woodworth, *A Deep Steady Thunder*, 26–27.

46. Cozzens, *This Terrible Sound*, 89.

47. Ibid., 97.

48. Ibid.; Heartsill, *Fourteen Hundred and Ninety-One Days*, 150.

49. Daniel, *Soldiering in the Army of Tennessee*, 8; Grear, "Texans to the Front," 5.

8. CHICKAMAUGA

1. Harold B. Simpson, *Hood's Texas Brigade: Lee's Grenadier Guard* (Waco, Tex.: Texian Press, 1970), 308; Cozzens, *This Terrible Sound*, 104–108.

2. Cozzens, *This Terrible Sound*, 196–200.

3. Ibid., 200.

4. Ibid., 201–202.

5. *O.R.*, series I, vol. 30, pt. 2, 455; Van Zandt to his wife, September 28, 1863, vertical file of the 7th Texas Infantry, Simpson Confederate Research Center, Hill College, Hillsboro, Texas.

6. Cozzens, *This Terrible Sound*, 259–260; Simpson, *Hood's Texas Brigade*, 320. Ironically, the man that Robertson's Texans saved at Chickamauga would become their commander when he replaced Jerome Robertson in late 1863. Gregg would also die at the head of the Texas Brigade, at the Battle of Darbytown Road during the siege of Petersburg, on October 7, 1864 (Warner, *Generals in Gray*, 118–119).

7. Craig L. Symonds, *Stonewall of the West: Patrick Cleburne and the Civil War* (Lawrence: Univ. Press of Kansas, 1997), 143–144. William Heartsill wrote in his diary that some of the men recognized "Captain Charlie Talley" of the 7th Texas on their way to the front that night (Heartsill, *Fourteen Hundred and Ninety-One Days*, 152; Cozzens, *This Terrible Sound*, 263).

8. Symonds, *Stonewall of the West*, 144–145.

9. Ibid., 145–146.

10. Colonel Frank C. Wilkes, commanding the 17th, 18th, 24th & 25th Texas, reported that the honors for capturing the colors of the 77th Pennsylvania should go to Private Lewis Montgomery of Company B, 18th Texas, and that the honors for capturing the banner of the 79th Illinois should go to Privates C. C. Martin and Benjamin G. Pippin of Company K, 18th Texas. *O.R.*, I, vol. 30, pt. 2, 194.

11. *O.R.*, I, vol. 30, pt. 2, 194.

12. Collins, *Chapters*, 151–152.

13. Ibid.

14. Heartsill, *Fourteen Hundred and Ninety-One Days*, 153.

15. Cozzens, *This Terrible Sound*, 305–309.

16. The Confederates could have no way of knowing just how costly the delays had been. On the front of Hazen's Brigade, where Deshler's men attacked, the Federals did not begin constructing earthworks until dawn, and the fortifications played a large role in allowing Thomas's men to hold their position. For further details see *O.R.*, series I, vol. 30, pt. 1, 763.

17. Collins, *Unwritten Chapters*, 154.

18. Cozzens, *This Terrible Sound*, 339, 348–349.

19. Ibid., 348–349.

20. Heartsill, *Fourteen Hundred and Ninety-One Days*, 159.

21. Collins, *Chapters*, 158–159.

22. *O.R.*, series I, vol. 30, pt. 2, 188–189. After several of Hazen's officers were felled by these snipers, he ordered concentrated volleys aimed at them. This measure put a stop to the sniping, as the Confederates began to tumble out of the trees (*O.R.*, series I, vol. 30, pt. 1, 763).

23. *O.R.*, series I, vol. 30, pt. 2, 190–191.

24. Ibid., 457–458.

25. Ibid., 495–496; John T. Goodrich, "Gregg's Brigade in the Battle of Chickamauga," *Confederate Veteran* 22 (1914): 264–265.

26. The twenty-one casualty discrepancy between Anderson's report and my casualty list resulted from those who were deemed "missing" at the roll call returning to the regiment in the aftermath of the battle.

27. The casualties for the Texas regiments come from newspaper reports and the compiled service records of the regiments. The casualties of the 6th, 10th & 15th Texas can be found in the *Galveston Daily News*, November 11, 1863. Those of the 17th, 18th, 24th & 25th Texas are reported in the *Galveston Daily News* of November 25, 1863, and those of the 7th Texas appear in the *Memphis Daily Appeal* of October 10, 1863. The strengths of the regiments before the battle come from *O.R.*, series I, vol. 30, pt. 2, 193–194.

28. Yeary, *Reminiscences of the Boys in Gray*, 575, 251.

29. Collins, *Chapters*, 160–161.

9. CHATTANOOGA

1. Daniel, *Soldiering in the Army of Tennessee*, 53.

2. Collins, *Chapters*, 163; Brown, *One of Cleburne's Command*, 56; Simpson, *The Bugle Softly Blows*, 41.

3. Symonds, *Stonewall of the West*, 153.

4. Anderson, ed., *Campaigning with Parsons' Texas Cavalry Brigade*, 122; H. T. Curl to his parents, October 8, 1863, Henry T. Curl Papers, Dallas Historical Society Archives, Fair Park, Dallas, Texas; Irving A. Buck, *Cleburne and His Command* (Jackson, Tenn.: McCowat-Mercer Press, 1959), 328.

5. Warner, *Generals in Gray*, 281–282; Brown, *One of Cleburne's Command*, 57.

6. Marsh to his wife, Mittie, dated "Chattanooga Tenn Oct. 15/63," in Marsh, "The Confederate Letters of Bryan Marsh," 29.

7. Henry V. Smith to his mother and father, dated "In the field near Chattanooga Tenn Oct. 12, 1863," vertical file of the 25th Texas Cavalry, Simpson Confederate Research Center, Hill College, Hillsboro, Texas. Private Thomas Richards of Company H, 24th Texas Dismounted Cavalry, deserted on October 8, 1863 (Compiled Service Records of the 24th Texas Cavalry, National Archives microfilm series M323, rolls 119–123).

8. Collins, *Chapters*, 169–172.

9. Brown, *One of Cleburne's Command*, 58–59.

10. Hiram Granbury to G. M. Sorrell, dated "Look Out Mountain, November 13, 1863," John Gregg Papers, U.S. Army Military History Institute, Carlisle Barracks, Pennsylvania; Davis Blake Carter, *Two Stars in the Southern Sky: General John Gregg, C.S.A. and Mollie* (Spartanburg, S.C.: Reprint Company, 2001), 199–200. After the war, C. W. Trice of Company A, 7th Texas, expressed the same disgust that Granbury felt at the Texans not receiving their due credit while in Gregg's Brigade. See C. W. Trice, "Seventh Texas Regiment in Gregg's Brigade," *Confederate Veteran* 22 (1915): 77.

11. Peter Cozzens, *The Shipwreck of Their Hopes: The Battles for Chattanooga* (Urbana: Univ. of Illinois Press, 1994), 411.

12. Brown, *One of Cleburne's Command*, 59.

13. Symonds, *Stonewall of the West*, 163.

14. Cozzens, *The Shipwreck of Their Hopes*, 151–152.

15. Symonds, *Stonewall of the West*, 164.

16. Ibid., 166.

17. Brown, *One of Cleburne's Command*, 59–60; Collins, *Chapters*, 176; Albert Jernigan to his Parents, dated "Austin, Texas May 18, 1872," Albert Jernigan Papers, Briscoe Center for American History, University of Texas at Austin.

18. Cozzens, *The Shipwreck of Their Hopes*, 208; Brown, *One of Cleburne's Command*, 61–62.

19. Cozzens, *The Shipwreck of Their Hopes*, 208; Albert Jernigan to his Parents, dated "Austin, Texas May 18, 1872," Albert Jernigan Papers, Briscoe Center for American History, University of Texas at Austin.

20. Albert Jernigan to his Parents, dated "Austin, Texas May 18, 1872," Albert Jernigan Papers, Briscoe Center for American History, University of Texas at Austin.

21. Ibid.; Collins, *Chapters*, 180.

22. Jernigan survived his wound but lost his right arm to amputation on November 29, 1863.

23. Brown, *One of Cleburne's Command*, 62–63.

24. Symonds, *Stonewall of the West*, 168–169.

25. *O.R.*, series I, vol. 30, pt. 2, 753.

26. Albert Jernigan to his Parents, dated "Austin, Texas May 18, 1872," Albert Jernigan Papers, Briscoe Center for American History, University of Texas at Austin.

27. *Galveston Tri-Weekly News,* February 3, 1864; *O.R.,* series I, vol. 31, pt. 2, 752.

28. Collins, *Chapters,* 186.

29. Ibid., 188–189; Symonds, *Stonewall of the West,* 171.

30. *O.R.,* series I, vol. 30, pt. 2, 776; Symonds, *Stonewall of the West,* 172–173.

31. Cozzens, *The Shipwreck of Their Hopes,* 370–384.

32. Ibid.

33. Ibid.

34. *O.R.,* series I, vol. 31, pt. 2, 773–778. The resolution of thanks to Cleburne and his men can be found in the same volume, page 758.

35. Simpson, *The Bugle Softly Blows,* 46.

36. Grear, "Texans to the Front," 5.

10. CAMP LIFE

1. Simpson, *The Bugle Blows Softly,* 46.

2. Symonds, *Stonewall of the West,* 182.

3. There are two good sources for the relationship between Davis and Johnston. The first is Craig L. Symonds, *Joseph E. Johnston: A Civil War Biography* (New York: Norton, 1992). However, Symonds's treatment of Johnston is often too kind. For a more objective perspective, see Steven Woodworth, *Jefferson Davis and His Generals: The Failure of Confederate Command in the West* (Lawrence: Univ. Press of Kansas, 1990).

4. Stephen Davis, *Atlanta Will Fall: Sherman, Joe Johnston and the Yankee Heavy Battalions* (Wilmington, N.C.: Scholarly Resources, 2001), 28. One must also take into account Johnston's perfectionism and micromanagement in his decision not to advance.

5. McCaffrey, *This Band of Heroes,* 98.

6. Collins, *Chapters,* 192.

7. Sessums, "A Force to Be Reckoned With," 512–513.

8. McCaffrey, *This Band of Heroes,* 98.

9. Erasmus E. Marr, "Letters of E. E. Marr, 10th Texas Infantry," unpublished letters in the vertical file of the 10th Texas Infantry, Simpson Confederate Research Center, Hill College, Hillsboro, Texas.

10. Anderson, ed., *Campaigning with Parsons' Texas Cavalry Brigade,* 127. When the regiments were consolidated, many of their officers found themselves without commands and were reassigned to the Trans-Mississippi (Scott McKay, "The History of the 10th Texas Infantry," http://www.armoryguards.org/10thTexas/letters/hull.htm.

11. Collins, *Chapters,* 193–194.

12. Ibid., 49–50.

13. *O.R.,* series I, vol. 32, pt. 2, 414.

14. Symonds, *Stonewall of the West,* 196–197.

15. Lieutenant Robert Collins of the 15th Texas Dismounted Cavalry had two such correspondents "on his string, Miss Rebecca Savage, of Savage Station, Ga., and Miss Mollie E. Harris, of Auburn Alabama" (Collins, *Chapters,* 198–199).

16. Turner, "Jim Turner," 167–168; Symonds, *Stonewall of the West,* 197.

17. Carter, *Two Stars in the Southern Sky,* 209–211.

18. Turner, "Jim Turner," 168; McCaffrey, *This Band of Heroes,* 99. The strength of the brigade as of March 1 was reported to be 530 men present in the 6th, 10th & 15th Texas, 117 men present in the 7th Texas, and 584 in the 17th, 18th, 24th & 25th Texas—for a total of 1,231 (*O.R.,* series I, vol. 31, pt. 3, 824).

19. Buck, *Cleburne and His Command,* 203. Granbury also did other things to try and improve the situation of his men. On March 16, he wrote a letter to Samuel H. Stout, medical director of the Army of Tennessee, requesting that Stout establish a Texas hospital for the Army of Tennessee. It is unknown whether Stout ever complied with Granbury's request. (H. B. Granbury to Samuel Hollingsworth Stout, March 16, 1864, "Camp Near Dalton Georgia," in the Samuel H. Stout Papers, microfilm reel 782, box 1, folder 1, Tennessee State Archives, Nashville, Tennessee.)

20. Mary A. H. Gay, *Life in Dixie During the War* (Atlanta, Ga.: DeKalb Historical Society, 1979), 78–79.

21. Ibid., 80–81.

22. For more on the religious life of Civil War soldiers, see Woodworth, *While God Is Marching On.*

23. Buck, *Cleburne and His Command,* 203. This deserter's sentence was the only such execution to occur in Cleburne's Division during the war.

24. Turner, "Jim Turner," 169.

25. Collins, *Chapters,* 201.

26. Turner, "Jim Turner," 169–170.

27. Sam Watkins, "Snowball Battle at Dalton," *Confederate Veteran* 12 (1904): 261; Buck, *Cleburne and His Command,* 203.

28. Turner, "Jim Turner," 170.

29. Collins, *Chapters,* 200–201.

30. Turner, "Jim Turner," 170.

31. Letter of Lieutenant Overton Davenport to his father, April 9, 1864, http://www.armoryguards.org/10thTexas/letters/hull.htm.

32. Albert Castel, *Decision in the West: The Atlanta Campaign of 1864* (Lawrence: Univ. Press of Kansas, 1992), 105–106.

33. Gay, *Life in Dixie During the War,* 85.

11. FROM DALTON TO PICKETT'S MILL

1. Gallagher, *The Confederate War,* 55; Phillips, *Diehard Rebels,* 8; Daniel, *Soldiering in the Army of Tennessee,* 23.

2. Daniel, *Soldiering in the Army of Tennessee,* 130.

3. Davis, *Atlanta Will Fall,* 38.

4. Bennet H. Young, *Confederate Wizards of the Saddle: Being Reminiscences of One Who Rode with Morgan* (Kennesaw, Ga.: Continental Book, 1958), 79–80.

5. Nathaniel C. Hughes Jr., *General William J. Hardee: Old Reliable* (Baton Rouge: Louisiana State Univ. Press, 1965), 199–200.

6. Sessums, "A Force to Be Reckoned With," 549.

7. Castel, *Decision in the West,* 136.

8. Symonds, *Stonewall of the West*, 204.

9. Castel, *Decision in the West*, 140.

10. Brown, *One of Cleburne's Command*, 73.

11. Castel, *Decision in the West*, 145.

12. Brown, *One of Cleburne's Command*, 73.

13. Castel, *Decision in the West*, 144.

14. Ibid., 150.

15. Ibid., 150–151.

16. Brown, *One of Cleburne's Command*, 74.

17. Sessums, "A Force to Be Reckoned With," 553–554.

18. Castel, *Decision in the West*, 153.

19. Gay, *Life in Dixie During the War*, 87. This phenomenon, which Charles Grear has labeled "multiple local attachments," the idea that Texans fighting for the Confederacy held a loyalty both to their adopted state, Texas, and their original home states, in this case Georgia, provided a strong motivation to fight for the Confederacy (Grear, "Texans to the Front," 5).

20. Davis, *Atlanta Will Fall*, 47.

21. Brown, *One of Cleburne's Command*, 77.

22. Ibid., 179–180.

23. Davis, *Atlanta Will Fall*, 53.

24. Ibid.

25. Sessums, "A Force to Be Recknoned With," 559.

26. Davis, *Atlanta Will Fall*, 203.

27. Castel, *Decision in the West*, 206.

28. Samuel G. French, *Two Wars: The Autobiography of Major General Samuel G. French* (Nashville, Tenn.: Confederate Veteran, 1901), 198.

29. Brown, *One of Cleburne's Command*, 79.

30. Castel, *Decision in the West*, 209.

31. Brown, *One of Cleburne's Command*, 79.

32. Ibid., 80.

33. Davis, *Atlanta Will Fall*, 63.

34. Ibid.

35. Buck, *Cleburne and His Command*, 218.

36. Collins, *Chapters*, 210–211.

37. Lucius Polk is not to be confused with his uncle, the bishop general Leonidas Polk.

38. Buck, *Cleburne and His Command*, 218.

39. The Texans of Granbury's Brigade referred to the Arkansans as Joshes, while the Texans were known as Chubs. Each state, during the course of the war, developed nicknames for themselves by which they were known to troops of other states. Brown, *One of Cleburne's Command*, 81–82.

40. Sessums, "A Force to Be Reckoned With," 567.

41. Castel, *Decision in the West*, 229–230.

42. Ibid., 230.

43. Ibid., 235.

44. *Voices of the Civil War: Atlanta* (Alexandria, Va.: Time Life Books, 1996), 60.

45. Collins, *Chapters*, 211–212.

46. Sessums, "A Force to Be Reckoned With," 572.

47. *Voices of the Civil War: Atlanta*, 60.

48. Castel, *Decision in the West*, 237.

49. Gay, *Life in Dixie During the War*, 89.

50. Sessums, "A Force to Be Reckoned With," 578.

51. *Voices of the Civil War: Atlanta*, 61.

52. Scott Cantwell, "The 15th Wisconsin Volunteer Infantry: The Scandinavian Regiment," www.15thwisconsin.net/15story6.htm (accessed July 16, 2003).

53. Collins, *Chapters*, 214.

54. Brown, *One of Cleburne's Command*, 85.

55. Ibid.

56. Leuschner, *The Civil War Diary of Charles A. Leuschner*, 35.

57. Brown, *One of Cleburne's Command*, 86.

58. Buck, *Cleburne and His Command*, 355.

59. Oliver P. Bowser, "Notes on Granbury's Brigade," in *A Comprehensive History of Texas 1685–1897*, ed. Dudley G. Wooten, 746 (Dallas, Tex.: W. G. Scariff, 1898).

60. Sessums, "A Force to Be Reckoned With," 585, 576; *Galveston Daily News*, August 3, 1864.

61. Castel, *Decision in the West*, 245–246.

12. STUCK IN THE THICKETS OF NORTH GEORGIA

1. Buck, *Cleburne and His Command*, 222.

2. Brown, *One of Cleburne's Command*, 91.

3. Mary Lee Anderson Barnes, comp., "Letters to Mollie: The Letters of Colonel Edward T. Broughton to his wife, Mary Elizabeth Douglas Broughton and other letters," 39, typescript, vertical file of the 7th Texas Infantry, Simpson Confederate Research Center, Hill College, Hillsboro, Texas.

4. Castel, *Decision in the West*, 258.

5. Sessums, "A Force to Be Reckoned With," 593.

6. Ibid., 259.

7. Brown, *One of Cleburne's Command*, 93.

8. Ibid., 91.

9. Ibid.

10. Castel, *Decision in the West*, 267–268.

11. Buck, *Cleburne and His Command*, 223.

12. Brown, *One of Cleburne's Command*, 95.

13. Ibid.

14. Castel, *Decision in the West*, 281.

15. Sessums, "A Force to Be Reckoned With," 598.

16. Collins, *Chapters*, 219. Graybacks are the derisive term given to the large body lice that tortured Civil War armies in camp and on the march.

17. Ibid., 220–221.

18. Brown, *One of Cleburne's Command*, 97.

19. Davis, *Atlanta Will Fall*, 86.

20. Ibid., 87.

21. Sessums, "A Force to Be Reckoned With," 594.

22. Collins, *Chapters*, 223.

23. This letter of F. E. Blossman of Company A, 6th Texas, came to light in a rather unusual way. Blossman wrote the letter to his mother, and it was captured by the U.S.S. *Curlew* at Rodney, Mississippi, on July 19, 1864. Blossman was killed on July 21 at the Battle of Bald Hill, and in 1897 the letter was discovered among the effects of an A. Beal in South Bend, Indiana. Mrs. H. S. Stanfield, the vice president of the Northern Indiana Historical Society in South Bend, contacted R. G. Blossman, F. E. Blossman's brother, then living in Corpus Christi, Texas, and delivered the letter. (F. E. Blossman, "Long-Delayed Letter," *Confederate Veteran* 7 [1899]: 221–222.)

24. Castel, *Decision in the West*, 340–344.

25. Ibid., 353. For a good discussion of this matter, see Woodworth, *Jefferson Davis and His Generals*, 354–356.

13. HOOD TAKES COMMAND

1. Brown, *One of Cleburne's Command*, 106–107.

2. Collins, *Chapters*, 226.

3. Oliphant, "Memoirs of William J. Oliphant," 38–39.

4. Gallagher, *The Confederate War*, 42.

5. Ibid., 68.

6. Castel, *Decision in the West*, 378.

7. Collins, *Chapters*, 227–230.

8. Ibid.

9. Leuschner, *The Civil War Diary of Charles A. Leuschner*, 43, 61–99; *Confederate State Roster: Texas Name Roster*, vol. 1 (Wilmington, N.C.: Broadfoot, 1998). According to the *Galveston Daily News*, March 3, 1865, the casualties incurred by this direct shell hit included:

Captain Benjamin R. Tyus, Company F, 15th Texas, severely wounded in the ankle;
Second Lieutenant Robert M. Collins, Company B, 15th Texas, severely wounded in the thigh;
Private Michael Schweitz, Company B, 6th Texas, wounded;
Private Joseph A. Pace, Company F, 6th Texas, killed;
Private Fritz Shugart, Company E, 6th Texas, severely wounded in the leg, "since amputated";
Sergeant Alonzo Steele, Company F, 6th Texas, wounded severely in both thighs;
Sergeant Alfred Alexander, Company E, 6th Texas, mortally wounded in the body, "since dead";
Private James Herod, Company F, 15th Texas, wounded slightly in the thigh;
Private L. R. Pearsons, Company F, 15th Texas, wounded severely in the arm;

Musician John A. Bates, Company F, 15th Texas, killed;

Private Ambrose Hawkins, Company K, 6th Texas, wounded slightly;

Private George Horl, Company K, 6th Texas, wounded slightly in the arm.

Total: two killed, two mortally wounded, eight wounded.

10. Collins, *Chapters*, 229–230.

11. Leuschner, *The Civil War Diary of Charles A. Leuschner*, 43.

12. Buck, *Cleburne and His Command*, 232.

13. The 6th & 15th Texas lost two killed and fifteen wounded, the 7th Texas had one wounded, and the 17th & 18th Texas suffered two wounded (*O.R.*, series I, vol. 38, pt. 3, 748 749, 751).

14. Robert U. Johnson and Clarence C. Buell, eds., *Battles and Leaders of the Civil War* (New York: Yoseloff, 1956), 4:337.

15. Buck, *Cleburne and His Command*, 233.

16. Sessums, "A Force to Be Reckoned With," 615–616. Bald Hill stood at approximately 1,050 feet in elevation, compared to 1,000 feet for the surrounding ridgeline and 980 feet in the low-lying areas around the ridge.

17. Ibid., 618.

18. Ibid., 616–617.

19. Ibid., 618–619.

20. Ibid.

21. Brown, *One of Cleburne's Command*, 108–109; Sessums, "A Force to Be Reckoned With," 619.

22. Yeary, *Reminiscences of the Boys in Gray*, 656. The man who was killed was Private William Simms, Company K, 18th Texas.

23. Brown, *One of Cleburne's Command*, 109.

24. Sessums, "A Force to Be Reckoned With," 620.

25. Ibid., 621–623.

26. Brown, *One of Cleburne's Command*, 109.

27. Sessums, "A Force to Be Reckoned With," 623–625; Woodworth, *Nothing But Victory*, 535–537.

28. *O.R.*, series I, vol. 38, pt. 3, 749–754.

29. Castel, *Decision in the West*, 389–393.

30. Ibid., 393–394.

31. Castel, *Decision in the West*, 400.

32. Sessums, "A Force to Be Reckoned With," 635.

33. Castel, *Decision in the West*, 402.

34. Ibid. Because the left flank of the Texas Brigade struck the Union line with Govan's Brigade, the left-most regiment, the 6th & 15th Texas, found itself separated from the rest of the brigade. As such, they fought alongside the Arkansans for the majority of the battle.

35. Errol MacGregor Clauss, "The Atlanta Campaign 18 July–2 September 1864" (Ph.D. diss., Emory University, 1965), 132.

36. There are several accounts as to who killed James McPherson on the afternoon of July 22. Captain Beard's account seems to be the most compelling, as the 5th Confederate on the

right flank of Smith's Texans would have been in the right place at the right time, so to speak, to encounter McPherson. Beard claims that it was Corporal Robert Coleman of his regiment who fired the fatal shot. Captain Samuel Foster of the 24th & 25th Texas claims that a man named "Cowan" of the 24th Texas fired the shot that killed McPherson. While there is no Cowan listed on the regiment's muster rolls, there is a Sergeant Robert D. Compton of Company I, 24th Texas, whom Captain Irving Buck of Cleburne's staff also credits with having killed McPherson. After the war, Private H. S. Halbert of Company I, 24th Texas, also claimed that Compton was the one who killed McPherson, and he was seconded by a letter written by Lieutenant P. K. Smith of the same company. Conversely, Sergeant Major James Mathias of the 17th & 18th Texas claims that several men from his regiment fired simultaneously and killed the Federal commander. Private W. W. Royall of the 17th & 18th Texas credited McPherson's demise to yet another man in his regiment. An interesting parallel is the names of the men who claimed to have killed McPherson: Robert Coleman (5th Confederate) and Robert Compton (24th & 25th Texas). Clauss, "The Atlanta Campaign," 132; Sessums, "A Force to Be Reckoned With," 645–647.

37. McCaffrey, *This Band of Heroes*, 119.

38. *O.R.*, series I, vol. 38, pt. 3, 753–754. From all available sources it appears that the 24th & 25th Texas had by this time captured the battle flags of the 3rd and 16th Iowa Regiments as well as eight pieces of artillery encountered during their advance.

39. Letter of Private W. E. Smith, Company B, 7th Texas, to his mother, dated "Bivouac Near Atlanta July 31, 1864," vertical file of the 7th Texas Infantry, Simpson Confederate Research Center, Hill College, Hillsboro, Texas.

40. Castel, *Decision in the West*, 402.

41. Lieutenant Colonel Frederick Hutchinson of the 15th Michigan reported that when his regiment came upon the flank of the Texas Brigade and forced the surrender of the 17th & 18th Texas and 5th Confederate, his regiment captured seventeen officers, 165 men, and the battle flags of both regiments. Out of ninety-two members of the 5th Confederate who started the day, only twenty-one remained at the end of the battle. Similarly, the 17th & 18th Texas began with 160 rifles and suffered roughly 119 casualties. Men who were captured accounted for the majority of the casualties in both regiments. *O.R.*, series I, vol. 38, pt. 3, 353.

42. Castel, *Decision in the West*, 402. Apparently a rivalry existed between these two Union regiments, stemming from the efforts of brigade commander Colonel John Oliver to obtain a commission as a brigadier general. Oliver had been the commander of the 15th Michigan, and the Indianans at one point refused to sign a petition recommending him for promotion. In any event, when the 5th Confederate and 17th & 18th Texas were cut off and captured, uncertainty existed as to which regiment actually captured the battle flag of the 17th & 18th Texas. It may well have been the Indianans, but because of the favoritism shown to the Michiganders the flag bears to this day an inscription in ink indicating that it was captured by the 15th Michigan. (McCaffrey, *This Band of Heroes*, 120.)

43. Castel, *Decision in the West*, 404–405.

44. Ibid., 405–409.

45. By this time the 6th and 15th Texas had rejoined the Texas Brigade after fighting with the Arkansans for the balance of the day.

46. Letter of Ensign Hosea Garrett, Company G, 10th Texas Infantry, to his uncle Hosea Garrett Sr. at Chapel Hill, Texas, dated "Atlanta, Ga. August 1, 1864," http://www.armoryguards .org/10thTexas/letters/hull.htm.

47. Lieutenant Colonel Young, who commanded the brigade after the battle, reported these figures. Smith estimated in his report that the casualties were twenty-three killed, one hundred wounded, and seventy-five captured. Because Smith was not with the command, Young's figures are likely to be more accurate. *O.R.*, series I, vol. 38, pt. 3, 747–748.

48. *O.R.*, series I, vol. 38, pt. 3, 730–31, 748–754.

49. Sessums, "A Force to Be Reckoned With," 635–642.

50. The two men who returned were Privates Alf Neil and Ogle Love (Brown, *One of Cleburne's Command*, 115).

51. Leuschner, *The Civil War Diary of Charles A. Leuschner*, 44.

52. Brown, *One of Cleburne's Command*, 116.

53. Ibid.

14. THE FALL OF ATLANTA

1. Phillips, *Diehard Rebels*, 7.

2. Brown, *One of Cleburne's Command*, 118.

3. Symonds, *Stonewall of the West*, 233–234. Symonds identifies Private Moore as being a member of the 6th Texas. However, he actually belonged to Company F, 7th Texas. This evidence is further corroborated by the fact that Captain Samuel Foster stated that the 7th Texas was posted on the picket line with the 24th and 25th Texas in the first week of August (Brown, *One of Cleburne's Command*, 119).

4. Brown, *One of Cleburne's Command*, 118–121.

5. Ibid., 123.

6. Ibid., 125.

7. Castel, *Decision in the West*, 495–496.

8. Brown, *One of Cleburne's Command*, 125.

9. Castel, *Decision in the West*, 499–500.

10. Ibid., 501.

11. Brown, *One of Cleburne's Command*, 126.

12. Castel, *Decision in the West*, 509.

13. Symonds, *Stonewall of the West*, 240.

14. Clauss, "The Atlanta Campaign," 331.

15. Ibid., 337.

16. Brown, *One of Cleburne's Command*, 126.

17. Castel, *Decision in the West*, 515–516.

18. Ibid., 516–518.

19. T. B. Roy, "General Hardee and the Military Operations Around Atlanta," *Southern Historical Society Papers* 8 (1880): 374–375.

20. *O.R.*, series I, vol. 38, pt. 3, 745.

21. Ibid.

22. Bowser, "Notes on Granbury's Brigade," 750.

23. Brown, *One of Cleburne's Command*, 129–130; Buck, *Cleburne and His Command*, 258–259.

24. Letter from Lieutenant Sebron G. Sneed to Mrs. Susan Piper, Barnesville, Ga., September 17, 1864, Piper Papers, Briscoe Center for American History, University of Texas at Austin.

25. Phillips, *Diehard Rebels*, 7.

15. THE INTERLUDE

1. Weitz, *More Damning Than Slaughter*.

2. Brown, *One of Cleburne's Command*, 135; William H. Henderson to his parents, dated "Camp near Jonesboro Ga Sept 4th 1864," William Henry Henderson Papers, Pearce Collection, Navarro College, Corsicana, Texas.

3. Brown, *One of Cleburne's Command*, 130.

4. Leuschner, *The Civil War Diary of Charles A. Leuschner*, 47.

5. McCaffrey, *This Band of Heroes*, 126.

6. Symonds, *Stonewall of the West*, 243.

7. Gay, *Life in Dixie During the War*, 85, 273; 1860 Census for Johnson County, Texas, www.heritagequest.com (accessed January 26, 2007).

8. Gay, *Life in Dixie During the War*, 185–188; McCaffrey, *This Band of Heroes*, 127; Sessums, "A Force to Be Reckoned With," 688.

9. Symonds, *Stonewall of the West*, 243; Sessums, "A Force to Be Reckoned With," 683.

10. Warner, *Generals in Gray*, 195; Symonds, *Stonewall of the West*, 243–244.

11. Brown, *One of Cleburne's Command*, 131–132.

12. Connelly, *Autumn of Glory*, 477–478.

13. Brown, *One of Cleburne's Command*, 133. Lubbock had stopped in front of the 5th Confederate Regiment, primarily made up of Irishmen from Memphis, Tennessee. Though a part of Granbury's Texas Brigade, the Irishmen apparently had no appreciation for Texan politicians. Sessums, "A Force to Be Reckoned With," 694.

14. Brown, *One of Cleburne's Command*, 135–136.

15. Ibid., 136–137; Sessums "A Force to Be Reckoned With," 696.

16. T. O. Moore, "Anecdotes of General Cleburne," *Southern Historical Society Papers* 21 (1893): 299–300.

17. Clayton Rand, *Sons of the South* (New York: Fairfax Press, 1978), 138.

16. FLANKING SHERMAN

1. Wiley Sword, *Embrace an Angry Wind: The Confederacy's Last Hurrah* (New York: General's Books, 1994), 54.

2. Anderson, ed., *Campaigning with Parsons' Texas Cavalry Brigade*, 146.

3. Brown, *One of Cleburne's Command*, 138.

4. Ibid., 139.

5. Sword, *Embrace an Angry Wind*, 56.

6. Brown, *One of Cleburne's Command*, 139; Sessums, "A Force to Be Reckoned With," 700.

7. Sword, *Embrace an Angry Wind,* 56.

8. Brown, *One of Cleburne's Command,* 139.

9. Patrick Cleburne Diary, September 28–October 16, 1864 (transcribed by and in the possession of Lee White, Chickamauga and Chattanooga National Battlefield Park). It is easy to see how a six-foot, five-inch Granbury would easily beat Cleburne at a standing jump, but how he might be a little too gangly to win at a running jump with the agile Irishman.

10. Sword, *Embrace an Angry Wind,* 56.

11. Ibid., 57.

12. Symonds, *Stonewall of the West,* 247.

13. Ibid.; Sessums, "A Force to Be Reckoned With," 701.

14. Brown, *One of Cleburne's Command,* 140.

15. Ibid.

16. Sword, *Embrace an Angry Wind,* 59, 62.

17. Brown, *One of Cleburne's Command,* 141.

18. Gay, *Life in Dixie During the War,* 246.

19. Ralph A. Wooster and Robert Wooster, "Rarin' For a Fight: Texans in the Confederate Army," in *Lone Star Blue and Gray: Essays on Texas in the Civil War,* ed. Ralph A. Wooster, 77 (Austin, Tex.: Eakin Press, 1995).

20. Brown, *One of Cleburne's Command,* 141–142; Sessums, "A Force to Be Reckoned With," 704.

21. Brown, *One of Cleburne's Command,* 142.

22. Ibid., 143–144.

23. Collins, *Chapters,* 237–238.

24. Brown, *One of Cleburne's Command,* 142–143.

25. McCaffrey, *This Band of Heroes,* 131; Sessums, "A Force to Be Reckoned With," 706.

26. Anderson, ed., *Campaigning with Parsons' Texas Cavalry Brigade,* 148.

27. Brown, *One of Cleburne's Command,* 144.

28. Gay, *Life in Dixie During the War,* 248–249; Sessums, "A Force to Be Reckoned With," 707.

29. Brown, *One of Cleburne's Command,* 145.

30. Sword, *Embrace an Angry Wind,* 74.

31. William Henry Henderson to his parents, dated "Camp Near Florence Ala. Nov 18th 1864," William Henry Henderson Papers, Pearce Collection, Navarro College, Corsicana Texas; letters from Private William Young to his sister, November 16–17, 1864, vertical file of the 15th Texas Dismounted Cavalry, Simpson Confederate Research Center, Hill College, Hillsboro, Texas.

32. Sessums, "A Force to Be Reckoned With," 707.

33. Brown, *One of Cleburne's Command,* 145.

17. SPRING HILL AND FRANKLIN

1. Symonds, *Stonewall of the West,* 248.

2. Sessums, "A Force to Be Reckoned With," 711–712.

3. Brown, *One of Cleburne's Command,* 146.

4. Ibid.

5. Symonds, *Stonewall of the West,* 249.

6. Ibid.

7. Ibid.

8. Sword, *Embrace an Angry Wind*, 117.

9. Ibid., 126.

10. Symonds, *Stonewall of the West*, 250–252.

11. Ibid., 251–252; Sword, *Embrace an Angry Wind*, 130.

12. Sword, *Embrace an Angry Wind*, 133.

13. Ibid., 136–137.

14. Ibid., 135; Symonds, *Stonewall of the West*, 252.

15. For a full explanation of Spring Hill, see Sword, *Embrace an Angry Wind*, 135–136, 138–139, 147.

16. Collins, *Chapters*, 243–244.

17. McCaffrey, *This Band of Heroes*, 135. Captain English was the only Confederate captured at Spring Hill on November 29.

18. Collins, *Chapters*, 244.

19. Ibid., 245.

20. Bowser, "Notes on Granbury's Brigade," 751.

21. Sessums, "A Force to Be Reckoned With," 730.

22. Sword, *Embrace an Angry Wind*, 159–160.

23. Symonds, *Stonewall of the West*, 254–255.

24. Sessums, "A Force to Be Reckoned With," 732.

25. Symonds, *Stonewall of the West*, 255.

26. Ibid., 254–255.

27. David R. Logsdon, *Eyewitnesses at the Battle of Franklin* (Nashville, Tenn.: Kettle Mills Press, 1991), 7.

28. Bowser, "Notes on Granbury's Brigade," 751–752.

29. Sessums, "A Force to Be Reckoned With," 748.

30. Brown, *One of Cleburne's Command*, 147.

31. Scott McKay, "Casualty Rolls for the 10th Texas Infantry at Franklin," http://www.armoryguards.org/10thTexas/letters/hull.htm.

32. Letters and diary of William Young, unpublished manuscript, vertical file of the 15th Texas Cavalry, Simpson Confederate Research Center, Hill College, Hillsboro, Texas; Orderly Sergeant Tillman Fowler, 7th Texas Infantry, to Colonel Thomas O. Moore, dated "Paso Robles California August 15, 1904," in an article titled "Resume of War Experiences," *Comanche (Texas) Chief*, September 3, 1904.

33. Biographical file of Lieutenant Colonel R. B. Young in the possession of the Carter House Museum Archives, Franklin, Tennessee.

34. Biographical sketch of Sergeant Jackson H. Griffin in the possession of the Carnton Cemetery Archives, Franklin, Tennessee.

35. Collins, *Chapters*, 248.

36. *O.R.*, series I, vol. 45, pt. 1, 737.

37. "Lieutenant Linson Montgomery Keener: His Four Years With the Seventh Texas Infantry C.S.A. as told by him to Mrs. W.U. Carre," unpublished manuscript, vertical file of the 7th Texas Infantry, Simpson Confederate Research Center, Hill College, Hillsboro, Texas.

38. Logsdon, *Eyewitnesses at the Battle of Franklin*, 23. It was Conrad's Brigade, and particularly the 79th and 51st Illinois Regiments, that Granbury's Texans were directly facing in this advance line.

39. Sword, *Embrace an Angry Wind*, 191.

40. Brown, *One of Cleburne's Command*, 147–148.

41. Logsdon, *Eyewitnesses at the Battle of Franklin*, 23.

42. Leonard H. Mangum, "General P. R. Cleburne," *Kennesaw State Gazette*, June 15, 1887.

43. Biographical sketch of Sergeant Jackson H. Griffin in the possession of the Carnton Cemetery Archives, Franklin, Tennessee.

44. Gay, *Life in Dixie During the War*, 272.

45. Scott McKay, "Casualty Rolls for the 10th Texas Infantry at Franklin," http://www.armoryguards.org/10thTexas/letters/hull.htm.

46. Sessums, "A Force to Be Reckoned With," 758.

47. Sessums, "A Force to Be Reckoned With," 758, 760, 772–773.

48. Logsdon, *Eyewitnesses at the Battle of Franklin*, 28.

49. Leuschner, *The Civil War Diary of Charles A. Leuschner*, 50–51.

50. Sessums, "A Force to Be Reckoned With," 773.

51. Brown, *One of Cleburne's Command*, 150.

52. Turner, "Jim Turner," 177.

53. Logsdon, *Eyewitnesses at the Battle of Franklin*, 56–57.

54. There are several conflicting sources for the numbers and casualties of Granbury's Brigade at Franklin. Major J. A. Formwalt of the 10th Texas stated in an interview with Dr. J. N. Doyle in the *Confederate Veteran* that Granbury's Brigade went into Franklin 450 strong, and only 175 answered the roll call the next morning. However, Lieutenant Robert M. Collins of the 15th Texas Dismounted Cavalry, in his book *Chapters from the Unwritten History of the War Between the States*, said that Granbury's Brigade went into Franklin 1,100 strong and only 450 answered the roll the next morning. Formwalt was eighty-three years old when Doyle interviewed him, and Doyle may have even misunderstood the old soldier. Furthermore, 1,100 would coincide with the numbers that Cleburne's Division possessed at Franklin: approximately 3,000 men in three brigades. In addition, Collins was present with the brigade after the battle, while Formwalt was wounded and captured and thus would have obtained his information secondhand. However, the figures of Major Formwalt are corroborated by the letter of Private James McCord of the 30th Georgia, who wrote to his brother on December 3, 1864, that "Granbury's celebrated brigade left this place yesterday morning with 137 guns all told." Most sources seem to agree that Granbury's Brigade lost somewhere over 400 men killed, wounded, and captured at Franklin. This added to the 344 effectives at Nashville on December 10 would give them a strength of 750–800 going into Franklin. It is quite possible that only 150–200 men answered the roll call on the morning of December 1 and the rest—stragglers from the campaign, unarmed or slightly wounded—merely rejoined the brigade in front of Nashville. Collins, *Chapters*, 249; J. N. Doyle, "Gen. H. B. Granbury of Texas," *Confederate Veteran* 12 (1904): 175; Anderson, ed., *Campaigning with Parsons' Texas Cavalry Brigade*, 154; Sessums, "A Force to Be Reckoned With," 775; letter of Private James A. McCord to his brother, December 3, 1864, from the Special Collections of the Woodruff Library of Emory University, Atlanta, Georgia, http://civilwargazette.wordpress.com/2006/12/04/soldier-letter-30th-georgia-details-battle/.

55. Compiled Service Records of the 10th Texas Infantry, National Archives microfilm series M323, rolls 337–343; Scott McKay, "Casualty Rolls for the 10th Texas Infantry at Franklin," http://www.armoryguards.org/10thTexas/letters/hull.htm.

56. Compiled Service Records of the 7th Texas Infantry, National Archives microfilm series M323, rolls 315–320.

57. Compiled Service Records of the 6th Texas Infantry and 15th Texas Cavalry, National Archives microfilm series M323, rolls 308–314 and 85–89; casualty rolls for the 6th & 15th Texas in the *Galveston Daily News*, March 6, 1865.

58. Brown, *One of Cleburne's Command*, 150.

59. Douglas, ed., *Douglas's Texas Battery*, 149–150.

60. Letter from James B. Morris to Mrs. S. F. Glass, January 20, 1866, Carter House Museum Archives, Franklin, Tennessee (ac #90.471); *McGavock Confederate Cemetery*, (Franklin, Tenn.: United Daughters of the Confederacy, 1987), 40.

61. Symonds, *Stonewall of the West*, 261.

62. Sessums, "A Force to Be Reckoned With," 766.

63. Thomas W. Curter, ed., *Our Trust Is in the God of Battles: The Civil War Letters of Robert Franklin Bunting, Chaplain, Terry's Texas Rangers, C.S.A.* (Knoxville: Univ. of Tennessee Press, 2006), 294.

64. Letter from Private William Stanton, Company A, 6th Texas, to his cousin Mary L. Moody, of Victoria, Texas, January 17, 1865, William Stanton Papers, Briscoe Center for American History, University of Texas at Austin.

65. Logsdon, *Eyewitnesses at the Battle of Franklin*, 80.

66. Symonds, *Stonewall of the West*, 261.

67. Logsdon, *Eyewitnesses at the Battle of Franklin*, 69.

68. Ibid., 79.

69. Letters of Private William E. Stanton, Company A, 6th Texas, to his cousin Mary L. Moody, of Victoria, Texas, William Stanton Papers, Briscoe Center for American History, University of Texas at Austin.

70. Sword, *Embrace an Angry Wind*, 267–268. S. D. Lee's I Corps had arrived during the night, bringing the force back up to twenty thousand effectives.

71. Brown, *One of Cleburne's Command*, 150–151.

72. Ibid., title page.

18. NASHVILLE

1. Brown, *One of Cleburne's Command*, 152.

2. Ibid.

3. Collins, *Chapters*, 251.

4. Brown, *One of Cleburne's Command*, 153.

5. *O.R.*, series I, vol. 45, pt. 1, 739.

6. Ibid.

7. Sessums, "A Force to Be Reckoned With," 784.

8. *O.R.*, series I, vol. 45, pt. 1, 739–740.

9. Sword, *Embrace an Angry Wind*, 324.

10. After the war, Colonel William Shafter would become known in the American West as "Pecos Bill" (ibid., 324–326).

11. *O.R.*, series I, vol. 45, pt. 1, 739–740.

12. Collins, *Chapters*, 253.

13. Stanley F. Horn, *The Army of Tennessee* (Wilmington, N.C.: Broadfoot, 1987), 413–414.

14. Sessums, "A Force to Be Reckoned With," 789–790.

15. Ibid., 793; Anne J. Bailey, *The Chessboard of War: Sherman and Hood in the Autumn Campaigns of 1864* (Lincoln: Univ. of Nebraska Press, 2000), 160.

16. Sword, *Embrace an Angry Wind,* 373. During the struggle Lieutenant Colonel William Shy of the 20th Tennessee was killed after a .58 caliber rifle was discharged at point-blank range into his skull. After the war the hill upon which Shy fell would be renamed in his honor.

17. Collins, *Chapters*, 254–255.

18. Brown, *One of Cleburne's Command,* 156.

19. Sessums, "A Force to Be Reckoned With," 796–799.

19. THE END OF THE WAR

1. Brown, *One of Cleburne's Command,* 160.

2. William E. Stanton to Mary Moody, January 17, 1865, William Stanton Papers, Briscoe Center for American History, University of Texas at Austin.

3. Collins, *Chapters*, 272.

4. Ibid., 272–273.

5. Ibid., 273–274.

6. Ibid., 275–276.

7. William E. Stanton to Mary Moody, March 30, 1865, William Stanton Papers, Briscoe Center for American History, University of Texas at Austin.

8. Collins, *Chapters*, 283–285.

9. McCaffrey, *This Band of Heroes,* 151–152.

10. Mark L. Bradley, *The Battle of Bentonville: Last Stand in the Carolinas* (Mason City, Iowa: Savas Publishing, 1996), 345; Collins, *Chapters*, 286–287.

11. *O.R.*, series I, vol. 47, pt. 3, 848–849.

12. William Henry Henderson to his parents, undated, William Henry Henderson Papers, Pearce Collection, Navarro College, Corsicana Texas.

13. Brown, *One of Cleburne's Command,* 166–171.

14. Ibid., 167.

15. Ibid., 169; Collins, *Chapters*, 300–301.

16. The note was signed by Captain R. D. Kennedy, Company E, 10th Texas; Captain A. L. Steele, Company G, 10th Texas; Captain Jim D. Miles, Company B; Captain L. W. Little, Company G; Lieutenant J. Graham, Company H; Adjutant J. A. Willingham, 10th Texas; Captain S. T. Foster, Company H, 24th Texas; Lieutenant P. M. Curry, Company D, 24th Texas; Lieutenant J. M. Rotan, Company F, 25th Texas; Captain M. A. Kelton, Company F, 6th Texas; Lieutenant B. D. Foscue, Company C, 7th Texas; Lieutenant L. F. Moody, Company B, 7th Texas; Second Lieutenant A. H. Hardin, Company G, 17th Texas; Second Lieutenant M. V. Tate, Company F,

15th Texas; Second Lieutenant James D. Shaw, 10th Texas; Second Lieutenant J. H. Logan, 10th Texas; Major J. A. Formwalt, Granbury's Brigade; and Lieutenant Colonel W. A. Ryan, Granbury's Brigade. *O.R.*, series I, vol. 47, pt. 3, 848–849.

17. Compiled Service Records of the 6th, 7th, and 10th Texas Infantry Regiments and the 15th, 17th, 18th, 24th, and 25th Texas Cavalry Regiments, National Archives microfilm series M323, rolls 308–314, 315–320, 337–343, 85–89, 93–96, 99–103, 119–123, and 126–130.

18. Collins, *Chapters*, 333; Joseph McClure, "A Wounded Texan's Trip Home on Crutches," *Confederate Veteran* 8 (1909): 162–163; Leuschner, *The Civil War Diary of Charles A. Leuschner*, 52–54; Brown, *One of Cleburne's Command*, 170.

AFTERWORD: REMINISCENCES, REUNIONS, AND THE LOST CAUSE

1. For more on the Lost Cause, see Gary W. Gallagher and Alan T. Nolan, eds., *The Myth of the Lost Cause and Civil War History* (Bloomington: Indiana Univ. Press, 2000).

2. *Proceedings of the Reunion of the First Division of Texas Veterans, C.S.A., Composed of Ross', Ector's and Granbury's Brigades Held at Weatherford, Texas August 9, 1892*, Briscoe Center for American History, University of Texas at Austin, 51–52.

3. Van Zandt, *Force Without Fanfare*, 77.

4. Alwyn Barr, "Mills, Roger Quarles," *Handbook of Texas Online*, http://www.tshaonline.org/handbook/online/articles/fmi40 (accessed March 17, 2010).

5. Patricia P. Kinkade, "Van Zandt, Khleber Miller," *Handbook of Texas Online*, http://www.tshaonline.org/handbook/online/articles/fva13 (accessed March 17, 2010).

6. Doyle, "Gen. H. B. Granbury of Texas," 175; *Dallas Morning News*, December 1, 1893.

7. *Minutes of the Annual Reunion of the First Texas Division of Confederate Veterans, Composed of Ross', Ector's and Granbury's Brigades and Douglas' Battery 1880–1917*, Briscoe Center for American History, University of Texas at Austin; *Minutes of the Forty-First Annual Reunion of the First Division of Confederate Veterans Composed of Ross', Ector's and Granbury's Brigades and Douglas' Battery Held at Wills Point, Texas August 9 and 10 1916*, Briscoe Center for American History, University of Texas at Austin.

8. Phillips, *Diehard Rebels*.

9. Beringer et al., *Why the South Lost the Civil War*; Weitz, *More Damning Than Slaughter*.

10. Gallagher, *The Confederate War*, 12.

11. Daniel, *Soldiering in the Army of Tennessee*, 5.

BIBLIOGRAPHY

PRIMARY SOURCES

MANUSCRIPTS

Austin History Center, Austin Public Library, Austin, Texas
  Oliphant, William J. "Memoirs of William J. Oliphant."
Briscoe Center for American History, University of Texas at Austin
  Jernigan, Albert. Papers.
  Mills, Roger Q. Papers.
  Minutes of the Annual Reunion of the First Texas Division of Confederate Veter-ans, Composed of Ross', Ector's and Granbury's Brigades and Douglas' Battery 1880–1917.
  Proceedings of the Reunion of the First Division of Texas Veterans, C.S.A., Composed of Ross', Ector's and Granbury's Brigades Held at Weatherford, Texas August 9, 1892.
  Robertson, Benjamin C. Papers.
  Sneed, Sebron G. Letters (Piper Papers).
  Stanton, William. Papers.
Carnton Cemetery Archives, Franklin, Tennessee
  Griffin, Jackson H. Biographical sketch.
Carter House Museum Archives, Franklin, Tennessee
  Morris, James B. Letter to Mrs. S. F. Glass, January 20, 1866 (acc. no. 90.471)
  Young, Robert B. Biographical file.

Dallas Historical Society Archives, Fair Park, Dallas, Texas
    Coit, John T. Papers.
    Curl, Henry T. Papers.
    Mills, Roger Q. Papers.
East Texas Research Center, Stephen F. Austin State University, Nacogdoches, Texas
    Birdwell, John C. Papers (Box A-116).
    Curl, Henry T. Papers (Box A-13).
Layland Museum, Cleburne, Texas
    Allen, Newton. Letters.
    Bransome, James. Autobiography.
Moody Mansion and Museum, Galveston, Texas
    Gregg, John. Papers.
    Moody, William L. Papers.
Pearce Collection, Navarro College, Corsicana, Texas
    Henderson, William Henry. Papers.
    Smith, Fred. Papers.
Simpson Confederate Research Center, Hill College, Hillsboro, Texas
    Barnes, Mary Lee Anderson, comp. "Letters to Mollie: The Letters of Colonel Edward T. Broughton to his wife, Mary Elizabeth Douglas Broughton and other letters." Typescript.
    Betts, Vicki ed. "The Civil War Letters of Elbridge Littlejohn, Part 2."
    Carre, Mrs. W.U. "Lieutenant Linson Montgomery Keener: His Four Years with the 7th Texas Infantry, C.S.A. as Told by Him to Mrs. W.U. Carre."
    Harlan, Isaiah. Letters.
    Hurst, James M. Diary.
    Snider, Noah T. Letters.
    Van Zandt, Khleber M. "Civil War Letters of Khleber Miller Van Zandt Major, 7th Texas Infantry, C.S.A."
    Young, William C. "Letters and diary of Private William C. Young, 15th Texas Dismounted Cavalry."
Tennessee State Archives, Nashville, Tennessee
    Stout, Samuel H. Papers.
Texas Collection, Baylor University, Waco, Texas
    Estes, Edward. Letters.
    Jones Family. Papers.
U.S. Army Military History Institute, Carlisle Barracks, Pennsylvania
    Gregg, John, Papers.
Victoria College Library, Victoria, Texas
    Phillips, A. H., Jr. Letters (Lucille Pool Collection).
    Phillips, William W. Letters (Lucille Pool Collection).

ONLINE SOURCES

1860 Census. http://www.heritagequest.com.

The Battle of Franklin. http://www.franklin-stfb.org/letters1.html.

Cantwell, Scott. "The 15th Wisconsin Volunteer Infantry: The Scandinavian Regiment." www.15thwisconsin.net/15story6.htm.

Handbook of Texas Online. http://www.tshaonline.org/handbook/online.

McKay, Scott. "The History of the 10th Texas Infantry." http://www.armoryguards.org/10thTexas/letters/hull.htm.

PRIVATE COLLECTIONS

Cleburne, Patrick. Diary, September 28–October 16, 1864. Transcribed by and in the possession of Lee White, Chickamauga and Chattanooga National Battlefield Park.

Sessums, Danny M. "A Force to Be Reckoned With: Granbury's Texas Brigade 1861–1865." Sessums Collection, Houston, Texas.

Van Zandt, Minerva, and Khleber Van Zandt. Letters. E. P. Cranz Collection, Fort Worth, Texas.

GOVERNMENT DOCUMENTS (UNPUBLISHED)

National Archives, Washington, D.C.

    Compiled Service Records of:

    6th Texas Infantry, National Archives Microfilm Series M323, Rolls 308–314.

    7th Texas Infantry, Series M323, Rolls 315–320.

    10th Texas Infantry, Series M323, Rolls 337–343.

    15th Texas Cavalry, Series M323, Rolls 85–89.

    17th Texas Cavalry, Series M323, Rolls 93–96.

    17th Texas Dismounted (Consolidated) Cavalry, Series M323, Rolls 97–98.

    18th Texas Cavalry, Series M323, Rolls 99–103.

    24th Texas Cavalry, Series M323, Rolls 119–123.

    25th Texas Cavalry, Series M323, Rolls 126–130.

NEWSPAPERS

Comanche (Texas) *Chief*

Dallas Herald

Dallas Morning News

Galveston Daily News

Galveston Tri-Weekly News
Houston Telegraph
Kennesaw State Gazette
Memphis Daily Appeal

BOOKS

Anderson, John Q., ed. *Campaigning with Parsons' Texas Cavalry Brigade, C.S.A.: The War Journal and Letters of the Four Orr Brothers, 12th Texas Cavalry Regiment.* Hillsboro, Tex.: Hill Junior College Press, 1967.

Blessington, J. P. *The Campaigns of Walker's Texas Division.* New York: Lang, Little and Co., 1875.

Brown, Norman, ed. *One of Cleburne's Command: The Civil War Reminiscences and Diary of Capt. Samuel T. Foster, Granbury's Texas Brigade, CSA.* Austin: Univ. of Texas Press, 1980.

Buck, Irving A. *Cleburne and His Command.* Jackson, Tenn.: McCowat-Mercer Press, 1959.

Collins, Robert M. *Chapters from the Unwritten History of the War Between the States: Or, The Incidents in the Life of a Confederate Soldier in Camp, On the March, In the Great Battles, And in Prison.* Dayton, Ohio: Morningside Press, 1988.

Confederate Soldiers, Sailors and Civilians Who Died as Prisoners of War at Camp Douglas, Chicago, Ill., 1862–1865. Kalamazoo, Mich.: Edgar Gray Publications, 1912.

Confederate State Roster: Texas Name Roster, vol. 1. Wilmington, N.C.: Broadfoot, 1998.

Curter, Thomas W., ed. *Our Trust Is in the God of Battles: The Civil War Letters of Robert Franklin Bunting, Chaplain, Terry's Texas Rangers, C.S.A.* Knoxville: Univ. of Tennessee Press, 2006.

Douglas, Lucia R., ed. *Douglas's Texas Battery, CSA.* Tyler, Tex.: Smith County Historical Society, 1966.

Fremantle, Arthur James Lyon. *Three Months in the Southern States: April–June, 1863.* Edited by Walter Lord. Short Hills, N.J.: Burford Books, 2001.

French, Samuel G. *Two Wars: The Autobiography of Major General Samuel G. French.* Nashville, Tenn.: Confederate Veteran, 1901.

Gay, Mary A. H. *Life in Dixie During the War.* Atlanta, Ga.: DeKalb Historical Society, 1979.

Gilbert, R. R. *High Private's Confederate Letters: Written for the Houston Telegraph, During the War of 1861-2-3-4-5, With a Short Autobiographical Sketch of the Author.* Austin, Tex.: Eugene Von Boeckman, 1890.

Heartsill, W. W. *Fourteen Hundred and Ninety-One Days in the Confederate Army: A Journal Kept by W.W. Heartsill For Four Years, One Month and One Day; or Camp*

Life; Day by Day, of the W.P. Lane Rangers From April 19, 1861 to May 20, 1865. Edited by Bell Wiley. Jackson, Tenn: McCowat-Mercer Press, 1953.

Hood, John Bell. *Advance and Retreat: Personal Experience in the United States and Confederate States Armies.* 1880. Reprint, Bloomington, Ind.: N.p., 1959.

Johnson, Robert U., and Clarence C. Buell, eds. *Battles and Leaders of the Civil War,* vols. 1–4. New York: Yoseloff, 1956.

Jordan, Weymouth T., Jr. *North Carolina Troops, 1861–1865, A Roster,* vols. 8 and 10. Raleigh: North Carolina Division of Archives and History, 1981.

Kight, L. L. *Their Last Full Measure: Texas Confederate Casualty Lists, 1864–1865.* Arlington, Tex: G. T. T. Publishing, 1997.

Leuschner, Charles A. *The Civil War Diary of Charles A. Leuschner.* Edited by Charles Spurlin. Austin, Tex: Eakin Press, 1992.

Logsdon, David R. *Eyewitnesses at the Battle of Franklin.* Nashville, Tenn.: Kettle Mills Press, 1991.

McCaffrey, James M., ed. *Only a Private, a Texan Remembers the Civil War: The Memoirs of William J. Oliphant.* Houston: Halcyon Press, 2004.

McGavock, Randal. *Pen and Sword: The Life and Journals of Randall W. McGavock, Colonel, C.S.A.* Edited by Herschel Gower and Jack Allen. Nashville: Tennessee Historical Commission, 1959.

McGavock Confederate Cemetery. Franklin, Tenn.: United Daughters of the Confederacy, 1987.

Peebles, Ruth. *There Never Were Such Men Before: The Civil War Soldiers and Veterans of Polk County, Texas, 1861–1865.* Livingston, Tex: Polk County Historical Commission, 1987.

Praus, Alexis A., comp. *Confederate Soldiers and Sailors Who Died as Prisoners of War at Camp Butler, Illinois 1862–1865.* Kalamazoo, Mich.: Edgar Gray Publications, 1976.

Scaife, William R. *Order of Battle: The Campaign for Atlanta.* Saline, Ga.: McNaughton and Gun, 1992.

Simpson, Harold B., ed. *The Bugle Softly Blows: The Confederate Diary of Benjamin M. Seaton.* Waco, Tex.: Texian Press, 1965.

U.S. War Department, *The War of the Rebellion: A Compilation of the Official Records of the Union and Confederate Armies.* Washington, D.C.: Government Printing Office, 1883.

Van Zandt, Khleber M. *Force Without Fanfare: The Autobiography of K. M. Van Zandt.* Fort Worth, Tex.: Texas Christian Univ. Press, 1968.

Voices of the Civil War: Atlanta. Alexandria, Va.: Time Life Books, 1996.

Watkins, Sam R. *"Co Aytch": A Side Show of the Big Show.* New York: Collier Books, 1962.

Yeary, Mamie. *Reminiscences of the Boys in Gray.* Dayton, Ohio: Morning House, 1986.

Young, Bennet H. *Confederate Wizards of the Saddle: Being Reminiscences of One Who Rode with Morgan.* Kennesaw, Ga.: Continental Book, 1958.

ARTICLES AND BOOK CHAPTERS

Blossman, F. E. "Long-Delayed Letter." *Confederate Veteran* 7 (1899): 221–222.

Bowser, Oliver P. "Notes on Granbury's Brigade." In *A Comprehensive History of Texas 1685–1897,* edited by Dudley G. Wooten, 744–754. Dallas, Tex.: W. G. Scarff, 1898.

Cuthbertson, Gilbert. "Coller of the 6th Texas." *Military History of Texas and the Southwest* 9 no. 1 (1971): 129–136.

Delaney, Norman C., ed. "Diary and Memoirs of Marshall Samuel Pierson, Company C, 17th Regt., Texas Cavalry, 1862–1865." *Military History of Texas and the Southwest* 13, no. 3 (1977): 23–29.

Doyle, J. N. "Gen. H. B. Granbury of Texas." *Confederate Veteran* 12 (1904): 175–176.

Goodrich, John T. "Gregg's Brigade in the Battle of Chickamauga." *Confederate Veteran* 22 (1914): 264–265.

Hill, Daniel Harvey. "Chickamauga—The Great Battle of the West." In *Battles and Leaders of the Civil War,* vol. 3, edited by Robert U. Johnson and Clarence C. Buell, 638–662. New York: Yuseloff, 1956.

Hinkle, Joseph. "The Odyssey of Private Hinkle." *Civil War Times Illustrated* 8, no. 8 (1969): 24–31.

Mangum, Leonard H. "General P. R. Cleburne." *Kennesaw State Gazette,* June 15, 1887, 2–6.

Mansfield, Jennifer S. "Yours Fraternally Until Death: The Civil War Letters of the Brothers Love." *East Texas Historical Journal* 38, no. 1 (2000): 53–70.

Marsh, Bryan. "The Confederate Letters of Bryan Marsh." *Chronicles of Smith County* 14, no. 2 (1975): 9–55.

McClure, Joseph. "A Wounded Texan's Trip Home on Crutches." *Confederate Veteran* 8 (1909): 161–162.

Moore, T. O. "Anecdotes of General Cleburne." *Southern Historical Society Papers* 21 (1893): 299–301.

"Obituary of Stephen E. Trice." *Confederate Veteran* 12 (1904): 298–299.

Oliphant, William. "Arkansas Post." *Southern Bivouac* 1 (1886): 736–739.

O'Neal, Bill, ed. "The Civil War Memoirs of Samuel Alonzo Cooke." *Southwestern Historical Quarterly* 74, no. 4 (1971): 535–548.

Roy, T. B. "General Hardee and the Military Operations Around Atlanta." *Southern Historical Society Papers* 8 (1880): 337–387.

Trice, C. W. "Seventh Texas Regiment in Gregg's Brigade." *Confederate Veteran* 22 (1915): 77.

Turner, Jim. "Jim Turner, Co. G, 6th Texas Infantry, C.S.A. From 1861–1865," *Texana* 12, no. 1 (1974): 149–178.

Watkins, Sam. "Snowball Battle at Dalton." *Confederate Veteran* 12 (1904): 261–262.

Wise, Joe R., ed. "The Letters of Flavius W. Perry, 17th Texas Cavalry 1862–1863." *Military History of Texas and the Southwest* 12, no. 3 (1976): 11–37.

SECONDARY SOURCES

BOOKS

Bailey, Anne J. *The Chessboard of War: Sherman and Hood in the Autumn Campaigns of 1864*. Lincoln: Univ. of Nebraska Press, 2000.

Bearss, Edwin. *The Vicksburg Campaign*. Vol. 1, *Vicksburg Is the Key*. Dayton, Ohio: Morningside Press, 1985.

———. *The Vicksburg Campaign*. Vol. 2, *Grant Strikes a Fatal Blow*. Dayton, Ohio: Morningside Press, 1987.

Beringer, Richard E., et al. *Why the South Lost the Civil War*. Athens: Univ. of Georgia Press, 1986.

Boatner, Mark M., III. *The Civil War Dictionary*. New York: Vintage, 1959.

Bradley, Mark L. *The Battle of Bentonville: Last Stand in the Carolinas*. Mason City, Iowa: Savas Publishing, 1996.

Carlock, Chuck. *History of the 10th Texas Cavalry (Dismounted) Regiment, 1861–1865*. North Richland Hills, Tex.: Smithfield Press, 2001.

Carter, Davis Blake. *Two Stars in the Southern Sky: General John Gregg, C.S.A. and Mollie*. Spartanburg, S.C.: Reprint Company, 2001.

Castel, Albert. *Decision in the West: The Atlanta Campaign of 1864*. Lawrence: Univ. Press of Kansas, 1992.

Chicoine, Stephen. *The Confederates of Chappell Hill, Texas: Prosperity, Civil War and Decline*. Jefferson, N.C.: McFarland, 2005.

Connelly, Thomas L. *Army of the Heartland: The Army of Tennessee, 1861–1862*. Baton Rouge: Louisiana State Univ. Press, 1967.

———. *Autumn of Glory: The Army of Tennessee, 1862–1865*. Baton Rouge: Louisiana State Univ. Press, 1971.

Connelly, Thomas L., and James Lee McDonough. *Five Tragic Hours: The Battle of Franklin*. Knoxville: Univ. of Tennessee Press, 1983.

Cozzens, Peter. *The Shipwreck of Their Hopes: The Battles for Chattanooga*. Urbana: Univ. of Illinois Press, 1994.

———. *This Terrible Sound: The Battle of Chickamauga*. Urbana: Univ. of Illinois Press, 1992.

Crute, Joseph H. *Units of the Confederate States Army*. Gaithersburg, Pa.: Old Soldier Books, 1987.

Daniel, Larry J. *Soldiering in the Army of Tennessee: Portrait of Life in a Confederate Army.* Chapel Hill: Univ. of North Carolina Press, 1991.

Davis, Stephen. *Atlanta Will Fall: Sherman, Joe Johnston and the Yankee Heavy Battalions.* Wilmington, N.C.: Scholarly Resources, 2001.

Drake, Rebecca Blackwell, and Thomas D. Holder. *Lone Star General: Hiram B. Granbury.* Raymond, Miss.: Drake Publishing, 2004.

Gallagher, Gary *The Confederate War: How Popular Will, Nationalism and Military Strategy Could Not Stave off Defeat.* Cambridge: Harvard Univ. Press, 1997.

———. *Lee and His Army in Confederate History.* Chapel Hill: Univ. of North Carolina Press, 2001.

Gallagher, Gary W., and Alan T. Nolan, eds. *The Myth of the Lost Cause and Civil War History.* Bloomington: Indiana Univ. Press, 2000.

Gott, Kendall D. *Where the South Lost the War: An Analysis of the Fort Henry-Fort Donelson Campaign, February 1862.* Mechanicsburg, Pa.: Stackpole, 2003.

Grear, Charles. *Why Texans Fought in the Civil War.* College Station, Tex.: Texas A&M Univ. Press, 2010.

Hale, Douglas. *The Third Texas Cavalry in the Civil War.* Norman: Univ. of Oklahoma Press, 1993.

Haughton, Andrew. *Training, Tactics and Leadership in the Confederate Army of Tennessee.* London: Frank Cass, 2000.

Horn, Stanley F. *The Army of Tennessee.* Wilmington, N.C.: Broadfoot, 1987.

Hughes, Nathaniel C., Jr. *General William J. Hardee: Old Reliable.* Baton Rouge: Louisiana State Univ. Press, 1965.

Johannson, M. Jane. *Peculiar Honor: A History of the 28th Texas Cavalry, 1862–1865.* Fayetteville: Univ. of Arkansas Press, 1998.

Levy, George. *To Die in Chicago: Confederate Prisoners at Camp Douglas 1862–65.* Gretna, La.: Pelican Publishing, 1999.

Lowe, Richard. *Walker's Texas Division, C.S.A.: Greyhounds of the Trans-Mississippi.* Baton Rouge: Louisiana State Univ. Press, 2004.

Lundberg, John R. *The Finishing Stroke: Texans in the 1864 Tennessee Campaign.* Abilene, Tex.: McWhiney Foundation Press, 2003.

McCaffrey, James M. *This Band of Heroes: Granbury's Texas Brigade, C.S.A.* College Station: Texas A&M Univ. Press, 1996.

McMurry, Richard M. *Atlanta 1864: Last Chance for the Confederacy.* Lincoln: Univ. of Nebraska Press, 2000.

———. *Two Great Rebel Armies: An Essay in Confederate Military History.* Chapel Hill: Univ. of North Carolina Press, 1989.

McPherson, James. *Battle Cry of Freedom: The Civil War Era.* Oxford: Oxford Univ. Press, 1988.

———. *For Cause and Comrades: Why Men Fought in the Civil War.* Oxford: Oxford Univ. Press, 1997.

———. *What They Fought For, 1861–1865.* Baton Rouge: Louisiana State Univ. Press, 1994.

McWhiney, Grady. *Braxton Bragg and Confederate Defeat,* vol. 1. Tuscaloosa. Univ. of Alabama Press, 1969.

———. *Braxton Bragg and Confederate Defeat,* vol. 2. Tuscaloosa: Univ. of Alabama Press, 1991.

McWhiney, Grady, and Perry Jamieson. *Attack and Die: Civil War Military Tactics and the Southern Heritage.* Tuscaloosa: Univ. of Alabama Press, 1982.

The New Handbook of Texas, vol. 3. Austin: Texas State Historical Association, 1996.

Phillips, Jason. *Diehard Rebels: The Confederate Culture of Invincibility.* Athens: Univ. of Georgia Press, 2007.

Power, J. Tracy. *Lee's Miserables: Life in the Army of Northern Virginia from the Wilderness to Appomattox.* Chapel Hill: Univ. of North Carolina Press, 1998.

Rand, Clayton. *Sons of the South.* New York: Fairfax Press, 1978.

Reid, Thomas. *Spartan Band: Burnett's 13th Texas Cavalry in the Civil War.* Denton, Tex.: Univ. of North Texas Press, 2005.

Ridley, B. L. *Battles and Sketches of the Army of Tennessee.* Mexico, Mo.: Missouri Printing Co., 1906.

Simpson, Harold B. *Hood's Texas Brigade: Lee's Grenadier Guard.* Waco, Tex.: Texian Press, 1970.

Smith, Frank H. *History of Maury County, Tennessee.* Columbia, Tenn.: Maury County Historical Society, 1969.

Speer, Lonnie. *Portals to Hell: Military Prisons of the Civil War.* Mechanicsburg, Pa.: Stackpole, 1997.

Sword, Wiley. *Embrace an Angry Wind: The Confederacy's Last Hurrah.* New York: General's Books, 1994.

Symonds, Craig L. *Joseph E. Johnston: A Civil War Biography.* New York: Norton, 1992.

———. *Stonewall of the West: Patrick Cleburne and the Civil War.* Lawrence: Univ. Press of Kansas, 1997.

Warner, Ezra J. *Generals in Gray.* Baton Rouge: Louisiana State Univ. Press, 1959.

Weitz, Mark A. *More Damning Than Slaughter: Desertion in the Confederate Army.* Lincoln: Univ. of Nebraska Press, 2005.

Welsh, Jack D. *Medical Histories of Confederate Generals.* Kent, Ohio: Kent State Univ. Press, 1995.

Williams, David. *Rich Man's War: Class, Caste, and Confederate Defeat in the Lower Chattahoochee Valley.* Athens: Univ. of Georgia Press, 1998.

Woodworth, Steven E. *A Deep Steady Thunder: The Battle of Chickamauga*. Abilene, Tex: McWhiney Foundation Press, 1998.

———. *Jefferson Davis and His Generals: The Failure of Confederate Command in the West*. Lawrence: Univ. Press of Kansas, 1990.

———. *Nothing But Victory: The Army of the Tennessee, 1861–1865*. New York: Knopf, 2005.

———. *While God Is Marching On: The Religious World of Civil War Soldiers*. Lawrence: Univ. Press of Kansas, 2001.

Wooster, Ralph A. *Lone Star Generals in Gray*. Austin, Tex.: Eakin Press, 2000.

———. *Lone Star Regiments in Gray*. Austin, Tex.: Eakin Press, 2002.

Wright, Marcus J. *Texas in the War, 1861–1865*. Edited by Harold B. Simpson. Hillsboro, Tex.: Hill Junior College Press, 1965.

ARTICLES AND BOOK CHAPTERS

Barr, C. Alwyn. "The Making of a Secessionist: The Antebellum Career of Roger Q. Mills." *Southwestern Historical Quarterly* 79, no. 2 (1975): 129–144.

Bearss, Edwin C. "The Battle of Arkansas Post." *Arkansas Historical Quarterly* 18, no. 3 (1959): 237–279.

Lang, Andrew F. "The Bass Grays: An Economic, Social and Demographic Profile of Company D, Seventh Texas Infantry." *East Texas Historical Journal* 48, no. 1 (winter 2010): 72–94.

Polston, Mike. "Allison Nelson: Atlanta Mayor, Texas Hero, Confederate General." *Atlanta Historical Journal* 29, no. 3 (1985): 19–25.

Potter, Dennis L. "Desperate Courage: An Account of the Texas Lancer Charge at the Battle of Val Verde, New Mexico." *Military History of the West* 36, no. 1 (2006): 1–33.

Pruitt, Francelle. "We've Got to Fight or Die: Early Texas Reaction to the Confederate Draft, 1862." *East Texas Historical Journal* 36, no. 1 (1998): 3–17.

Sheridan, Richard C. "Brigadier-General James Deshler, Professional Soldier." *Alabama Historical Quarterly* 26, no. 2 (1964): 203–216.

Wooster, Ralph A., and Robert Wooster. "Rarin' for a Fight: Texans in the Confederate Army." In *Lone Star Blue and Gray: Essays on Texas in the Civil War*, edited by Ralph A. Wooster, 47–78. Austin, Tex.: Eakin Press, 1995.

DISSERTATIONS AND THESES

Clauss, Errol MacGregor. "The Atlanta Campaign 18 July–2 September 1864." Ph.D. diss., Emory University, 1965.

Grear, Charles. "Texans to the Front: Why Texans Fought in the Civil War." Ph.D. diss., Texas Christian University, 2005.

Lang, Andrew F. "'Victory Is Our Only Road to Peace': Texas, Wartime Morale, and Confederate Nationalism, 1860–1865." Master's thesis, University of North Texas, 2008.

Newsom, James Lynn. "Intrepid Gray Warriors: The 7th Texas Infantry 1861–1865." Ph.D. diss., Texas Christian University, 1995.

INDEX